ELEMENTARY ASPECTS OF PEASANT INSURGENCY IN COLONIAL INDIA

ELEMENTARY ASPECTS OF PEASANT INSURGENCY IN COLONIAL INDIA

RANAJIT GUHA

FOREWORD BY JAMES SCOTT

DUKE UNIVERSITY PRESS

Durham and London, 1999

© 1999 Duke University Press
All rights reserved
Printed in the United States of America on acid-free paper ∞
Library of Congress Cataloging-in-Publication Data
appear on the last printed page of this book.

This edition is published for North America, New Zealand, Australia,
and Japan by arrangement with Oxford University Press, New Delhi.

To
Mechthild Guha

CONTENTS

FOREWORD TO THE DUKE EDITION

A book of great originality and large ambition might usefully be thought of as a shipyard. A sure mark of its influence would be how many ships were launched from its dock. By this standard alone, Ranajit Guha's *Elementary Aspects of Peasant Insurgency in Colonial India* has had an enormous impact. Thousands of ships have since sailed forth flying his pennant. Given the fact that the shipwright in this case had more of a philosophy of boat building than a rigid design, it is not surprising that the shipyard could launch vessels of greatly varying designs, sailing to unknown ports, and carrying new and exotic cargoes. The shipwright, I imagine, would not even recognize some of these vessels as having been inspired by him and, in fact, would probably want to disown any association with quite a few. That, however, is the unavoidable fate of a master-builder: his ideas are simply incorporated into the routines of shipbuilding, often without acknowledgment. Though he may often feel misrepresented and pirated, it is surely a better fate than being ignored.

Published originally by Oxford University Press, Delhi, in 1983, but much discussed by Indian scholars well before publication, *Elementary Aspects* became, in effect, the founding document of what is now known as the Subaltern Studies School. The term *school* conveys far too much in the way of a rigid orthodoxy for what is a loose and collegial assemblage of scholars inspired by the democratic spirit of Guha's work and pursuing its promise in their own creative and idiosyncratic ways. By now, many of the fine scholars from this circle have, in addition to collaborating on eight volumes of collected essays (*Subaltern Studies,* volumes I–VIII), come to occupy major chairs of history throughout South Asia. More important, they have changed the landscape of historiography permanently. A selection from these volumes with American readers in mind was edited by Gayatri Chakravorty Spivak and Ranajit Guha, *Selected Subaltern Studies* (New York: Oxford University Press, 1988). A more recent selection may be found in Ranajit Guha, ed., *A Subaltern*

Studies Reader: 1986–1995 (Minneapolis: University of Minnesota Press, 1998).

Outside the field of Indian historiography Guha's volume quickly became something of an "underground classic." I say "underground classic" in the sense that the few copies that arrived early in North America, Africa, and Latin America were passed from hand to hand as valuable ritual objects. Brief status advantages were gained by those who were the first to read *Elementary Aspects* and work out its implications for their own work. A great many scholars heard of Guha's ideas by word of mouth before they managed to get hold of a copy. I think it is fair to say that along with "dependency theory," emanating from Latin America, "subaltern studies" has been the "southern" intellectual import that has had the greatest influence on the conduct of the history and social science of popular movements.

In the brief space remaining to me, I hope to recapture the reasons for the intellectual excitement occasioned by Guha's book and why it amply repays reading today.

Guha is concerned with the mentality, values, ideas, and structure behind peasant movements in colonial India between 1783 and 1900. Above all, he wants to understand them *in their own terms.* This is already a signal step forward, because the great mass of histories of peasant uprisings were devoted not to understanding them in their own terms but, rather, as a prologue or pre-history of the central "social movement events" of modern histories: nationalist and/or revolutionary movements. In this respect, it had been common to see rural uprisings throughout India in the nineteenth century as assemblages of "primitive rebels" unwittingly laying the groundwork for the development of the Indian National Congress, Gandhi's noncooperation movement, and the Marxist parties of modern India. For all its originality, Eric Hobsbawm's influential book *Primitive Rebels* was clear about the normative and developmental sequence popular movements did and should follow. Banditry, millenarian outbreaks, jacqueries were the admirable but futile gropings of popular classes for an end to their oppressions. They lacked either the size or the secular view of history that would make them capable of anything more than spasms of rage and revenge. Their interest, and hence their place in history, was determined by the contribution that they might make, ultimately, to modern political movements (most particularly in Hobsbawm's case, Marxist-Leninist revolutionary parties) that aspire realistically to state power. Guha, to his great credit, abandons this teleology and asks: who were these people, what did they want, how did they express themselves, how did they act collectively?

This focus in Guha's hands provides the reader with a wholly new view and new landscape of resistance. But the novelty of Guha's approach hardly stops there. As he is writing with a comprehensive grasp of contemporary work on popular movements in France, Germany, England, he is able to carve out a unique and self-conscious analytical path of his own. Critical of the foundational work of Gustave Le Bon on *The Crowd in History*, many historians had been at pains to stress the finely targeted, rational, and strategic qualities of rural and urban uprisings. The result in the case of Georges Rudé's work, for example, was a rather attenuated, cold-blooded crowd whose actions were all but indistinguishable from the daily calculations of the petite bourgeoisie. What Guha does is to restore the passion, anger, and indignation to popular movements while, at the same time, showing the tactical and political logic in their action. The result is a fully rounded portrait with reason and the passions effectively joined, as they must be in any plausible history of consciousness and political action.

Two key terms in Guha's scheme of analysis are *subaltern* and *elementary*. The former derives, of course, from Antonio Gramsci's *Prison Notebooks* and the latter from Emile Durkheim's *The Elementary Forms of the Religious Life*. Each points to something distinctive in Guha's new optic. The presumed cultural, economic, and social inferiority of the tribal, the peasant, the outcast(e) in a complex indigenous and colonial order—their subaltern status—is precisely the relationship that forms the basis for all acts of insubordination, resistance, refusal, and self-assertion. Peasant insurgency is in a dialectical relationship, in the literal sense of the term, with the forms of domination (in Guha's case, the triad of landlord, moneylender, and official). Neither the forms of domination nor resistance to them can be conceived of, let alone understood, without its dialectical twin. On

Guha's reading, insurgency and domination are the two voices in an adversarial conversation composed of gestures, violence, symbolic claims, negations, etc.

The term *elementary forms* signals the reader that Guha is not interested in the narrow and particular historiography of one or a few insurgencies. Instead, he aims to sketch the broad schematic pattern of a century's worth of uprisings on the subcontinent. Hence the prominence of certain nouns that capture both the dialectical as well as the schematic structure of the analysis: negation, desecration, inversion, solidarity, territoriality, transmission. In Guha's hands, what might have been rather crude functionalist headings are imaginatively used to link the case material to the overall analysis. The particular idiom and vernacular of an individual revolt will be distinctive, but they will follow a logic of a grammar that his analysis has outlined. Guha's capacity to tease out the larger dialectical logic of insurgency is what makes his analysis so valuable to scholars of popular movements elsewhere; he offers a novel perspective and something of a new road map to orient "histories from below." Guha has read and thoroughly assimilated the Western European works on "history from below"; one hopes, for a refreshing change, that Western historians and social scientists will, in turn, take advantage of the intellectual riches Guha has to offer them here.

For historians of popular movements in epochs where most of the lower-class actors are silent owing to their illiteracy and where the only written sources are those of officials and elites, Guha offers an ingenious way forward. It is perhaps for his capacity to read the official sources "against the grain" or, to use his words, to "read from a distorting mirror" that he will be most remembered. Thus, in a hierarchical social order where status and power are coded by body language, dress, deferential speech, and a certain ritual order, breaches of physical decorum, dress, insults, or ritual desecration are sure signs of a contest for power. Every political and cultural order is, in effect, a daily ritual performance that serves to both illustrate and reinforce power relations; each performance may potentially be spoiled or desacralized by the insubordination of those whose inferiority is being acted out. By reading the official accounts, the court records, the interrogations of insurgency in the light of the juxtaposition of two mutually antagonistic cognitions, Guha can artfully read subordinate intentions through the veil of official rhetoric. The semiotic, dialectical turn of *Elementary Aspects* turns the bias of the sources and what appeared to be an "archival stalemate" for those who desired to practice history from below into an opportunity to read those sources with a wholly new eye. The results are surely not definitive and I, for one, think more can be squeezed out of folklore than does Guha, but no one can come away from Guha's reading of the sources without a new confidence in what can be achieved.

At every turn *Elementary Aspects* emphasizes the dangers of reading the process of insurgency with a political grammar based on mid-twentieth century nation-state political forms. In place of formal organization with office-bearers, manifestos, and tables of organization Guha finds informal networks based on kinship, coresidence, ethnicity, ritual links, or a common subordination; in place of formal messages and public conflict, Guha finds the world of rumor, anonymous threat, arson, and surreptitious attacks; in place of radical public movements, he finds banditry, low-level resistance, and symbolic attacks on elite property and status. These patterns are not "pre-political," much as it is in the interest of official elites to characterize them so. They are, on the contrary, the variety of political action that defined nineteenth-century peasant insurgency in India and which can be found, even today, as a substrate within many otherwise "modern-looking" social movements. The world of open, formal, and public organizations, however radical, is, by contrast, largely the world of middle-class, educated elites—a world in which Guha's subalterns have far fewer political resources at their disposal.

Readers for whom this volume is their first exposure to the original and foundational work of Ranajit Guha may well want to read his fine earlier work: *A Rule of Property for Bengal: An Essay on the Idea of Permanent Settlement* (Duke University Press, 1996; Paris: Mouton, 1963), the finest analysis of the logic of liberal and physiocratic property-regimes as they encounter Indian colonial realities. Those wishing to follow the evolution of Guha's thought on the issues raised in this book are advised to read "The Prose of Counter-Insurgency," *Subaltern Studies* 2

(Delhi, 1983) and his contributions to each of the subsequent volumes of *Subaltern Studies.* By now there is also a large critical literature assessing the subaltern studies "intellectual movement." A valuable and balanced introduction to that literature is available in K. Sivaramakrishnan, "Situating the Subaltern: History and Anthropology in the Subaltern Studies Project," *Journal of Historical Sociology* 8 (December 1990): 395–429.

James C. Scott
Yale University

PREFACE

This book owes much to two groups of scholars of the younger generation. Some of them were undergraduates at the University of Sussex and studied a number of courses in South Asian history with me. Many of the ideas in this essay were tried out at tutorials and seminars and during extra-mural conversations with them. I want them—and particularly Roger Coote, Anna Fairtlough, Gabriel Irwin and Gillian Scott—to know how encouraged I felt in my work because of the interest they took in it.

My work on this book developed over the years concurrently with and as integral to the collective project designated now as *Subaltern Studies*. Indeed it constitutes the initial moment of my own participation in that project. As such, it has had the benefit of interacting at many levels with the work and ideas of my colleagues Shahid Amin, David Arnold, Gautam Bhadra, Dipesh Chakrabarty, Partha Chatterjee, David Hardiman, Gyan Pandey and Sumit Sarkar. All have been kind enough to go through the final draft and offer their comments on it. I am immeasurably in debt to them for their help. Working with them has been a privilege and a genuine education for me.

This book would have taken much longer to write and publish but for the excellent working conditions provided by the Research School of Pacific Studies, Australian National University. I wish to thank my colleagues and especially Anthony Low for their support.

My thanks are also due to Ellice Begbie for typing an earlier version, to Gouri Chatterjee for help in reading the proofs and to Margaret Hall for typing, proof-reading and generally for bearing with the tantrums of a fastidious colleague always in a hurry to meet deadlines.

I am most grateful to Oxford University Press, New Delhi, and Eastend Printers, Calcutta, for the trouble they have taken to go carefully through my manuscript and save me from many errors.

In an infinite number of ways this essay is the outcome of my collaboration with Mechthild Guha. It is not only that she helped me to overcome many of the practical problems which made research and writing desperately difficult at times. In all the nine years it has taken to write this book she was always the first and often the only person to listen to a new thought as it was put in words or to share the excitement of a new discovery of fact. Above all, it was her intelligence and critical response which enabled me objectively to assess my own ideas and struggle against the conceptual and stylistic weaknesses of this work at every stage of its tortuous progress. I dedicate this book to her as a token of my appreciation of all that she has done to make it possible.

Canberra,
January 1983

ABBREVIATIONS

(For details of the entries in the right-hand column see BIBLIOGRAPHY at the end of this work.)

BC	*Board's Collections*: India Office Library.
BDR	*Birbhum, 1786–1797 and 1855.*
BJD	*Bombay Judicial Department Proceedings*: India Office Library.
BSM	Bombay, Government of: *Source Material etc.*
CR	Anon., 'The Sonthal Rebellion'.
DRCR	*Report of the Commission etc.* (Cmd. 2071).
DRCR(B)	Ibid., Appendix B.
DRCR(C)	Ibid., Appendix C.
FSUP	Rizvi (ed.), *Freedom Struggle in Uttar Pradesh.*
GOB	Government of Bengal.
GOI	Government of India.
H & R	Hobsbawm and Rudé, *Captain Swing.*
JC	*Fort William Judicial Consultations* in BC 1361 (54222).
JP	*Judicial Proceedings*: West Bengal State Archives.
JP(P)	File no. 448: 'Pubna Riots' in *Judicial Proceedings* (*Police Department*): West Bengal State Archives.
K & M	Kaye and Malleson, *History of the Indian Mutiny.*
MDS	*Maharaja Deby Sinha.*
MECW	Marx and Engels, Collected Works.
MHKRK	*Mare Hapram Ko Reak Katha.*
NNQ	*North Indian Notes and Queries.*
Reak Katha	*Mare Hapram Ko Reak Katha.*
RIC	*Report of the Indigo Commission etc.*
TTP	JP, 4 October 1855: 'The Thacoor's Perwannah'.

Taṁ kim maññasi, Assalāyana? Sutan te: Yona-Kambojesu aññesu ca paccantimesu janapadesu dveva vaṇṇā, ayyo c'eva dāso ca; ayyo hutvā dāso hoti, dāso hutvā ayyo hotīti?

Majjhima-Nikāya: Assalāyanasuttaṁ (93)

[Buddha to Assalāyana:] "What do you think about this, Assalāyana? Have you heard that in Yona and Kamboja and other neighbouring *janapadas* there are only two varnas, the master and the slave? And that having been a master one becomes a slave; having been a slave one becomes a master?" This is a slightly modified version of the translation of the passage as given in *The Middle-Length Sayings*, vol. II, pp. 341–2 (Pali Text Book Society, London, 1957).

CHAPTER 1

INTRODUCTION

Colonialism and the historiography of peasant insurgency—the character of the latter as a discourse of power—insurgency: the name of a consciousness—a critique of the notion of pure spontaneity and pre-political peasant rebellion—political character of peasant's relationship with sarkar, sahukar *and* zamindar *—leadership, aim, programme of insurgency—a naive theoretical consciousness —its 'common forms' or 'general ideas' and their 'first elements'—some questions of evidence.*

The historiography of peasant insurgency in colonial India is as old as colonialism itself. It originated at the intersection of the East India Company's political concerns and a characteristically eighteenth-century view of history—a view of history as politics and of the past as a guide to the future—which they brought with them. They were concerned to stop their newly acquired dominions from disintegrating like the moribund empire of the Mughals under the impact of peasant insurrections. For agrarian disturbances in many forms and on scales ranging from local riots to war-like campaigns spread over many districts were endemic throughout the first three quarters of British rule until the very end of the nineteenth century. At a simple count[1] there are no fewer than 110 known instances

N.B. References to manuscripts and printed works have been indicated by abbreviations (see ABBREVIATIONS) or by authors (see BIBLIOGRAPHY), and *not* by titles.

A Roman numeral after a colon specifies the volume(s) and an Arabic numeral the page(s) of a publication.

An Arabic numeral before an oblique indicates chapter or section and that after it verse or paragraph in a Sanskrit text or its translation.

A date enclosed in brackets after an author's name distinguishes that publication from his other writings. Of any two books published by an author in the same year one has been marked by an asterisk.

[1] The estimate is based on events catalogued in three standard works, viz. S. B. Chaudhuri (1955) and Ray (1966, 1970). A complete list, yet to be put together by

of these even for the somewhat shorter period of 117 years—from the Rangpur *dhing* to the Birsaite *ulgulan*—spanned by the present work. The formative layers of the developing state were ruptured again and again by these seismic upheavals until it was to learn to adjust to its unfamiliar site by trial and error and consolidate itself by the increasing sophistication of legislative, administrative and cultural controls.

Insurgency was thus the necessary antithesis of colonialism during the entire phase between its incipience and coming of age. The tension of this relationship required a record for the regime to refer to so that it could understand the nature and motivation of any considerable outbreak of violence in the light of previous experience and by understanding suppress it. Historiography stepped in here to provide that vital discourse for the state. This is how the very first accounts of peasant uprisings in the period of British rule came to be written up as administrative documents of one kind or another—despatches on counter-insurgency operations, departmental minutes on measures to deal with a still active insurrection and reports of investigation into some of the more important cases of unrest. In all this literature, known to the profession as 'primary sources', one can see the official mind struggling to comprehend these apparently unanticipated phenomena by means of analogy, that is, to say it after Saussure, by an 'awareness and understanding of a relation between forms'.[2] Just as one learns the use of a new language by feeling one's way from the known elements to the unknown, comparing and contrasting unfamiliar sounds and meanings with familiar ones, so did the early administrators try to make sense of a peasant revolt in terms of what made it similar to or different from other incidents of the same kind. Thus the Chota Nagpur uprisings of 1801 and 1817 and the Barasat *bidroha* of 1831 served as points of reference in some of the most authoritative policy statements on the Kol insurrection of 1831–2, the latter in its turn figured in official thinking at the highest level on the occasion of the Santal *hool* of 1855,

---

historians as a serious project for research, will of course show a much higher total, for it should be obvious to scholars working on particular regions that these compilations, based on published sources and secondary works, do not include numerous local instances still to be retrieved from the archives and oral literature.

[2] Saussure: 165.

and that last event was cited by the Deccan Riots Commission as a historic parallel to the subject of its investigation—the Kunbi uprising of 1875 in Poona and Ahmadnagar districts.[3]

The discourse on peasant insurgency thus made its debut quite clearly as a discourse of power. Rational in its representation of the past as linear and secular rather than cyclical and mythic, it had nothing but reasons of state as its *raison d'être*. Drafted into the service of the regime as a direct instrument of its will it did not even bother to conceal its partisan character. Indeed, it often merged, both in its narrative and analytic forms, into what was explicitly official writing. For administrative practice turned it almost into a convention that a magistrate or a judge should construct his report on a local uprising as a historical narrative, as witness the classic series, 'Narrative of Events', produced by the heads of the districts caught up in the disturbances of the Mutiny years. And again, causal explanation used in the West to arrive at what its practitioners believed to be the historical truth, served in colonialist historiography merely as an apology for law and order—the truth of the force by which the British had annexed the subcontinent. As the judicial authorities in Calcutta put it in a statement soon after the insurrection led by Titu Mir, it was 'an object of paramount importance' for the government 'that the cause which gave rise to [those disturbances] should be fully investigated in order that the motives which activated the insurgents [might] be rightly understood and such measures adopted as [were] deemed expedient to prevent a recurrence of similar disorders'.[4] Causality was harnessed thus to counter-insurgency and the sense of history converted into an element of administrative concern.

The importance of such representation can hardly be overestimated. By making the security of the state into the central problematic of peasant insurgency, it assimilated the latter as merely an element in the career of colonialism. In other words, the peasant was denied recognition as a subject of history in his own right even for a project that was all his own. This

[3] BC 1363 (54227): Vice-President's Minute (30 Mar. 1832); Blunt's Minutes (24 Mar. and 4 Apr. 1832). BC 1363 (54228): Neave to Government (29 Mar. 1832). JP, 19 July 1855: Elliott to Grey (15 July 1855). JP, 8 Nov. 1855: Lieutenant-Governor's Minute (19 Oct. 1855).

[4] JC, 22 Nov. 1831 (no. 91).

denial came eventually to be codified into the dominant, indeed, the only mode of historiography on this subject. Even when a writer was apparently under no obligation to think like a bureaucrat affected by the trauma of a recent jacquerie, he was conditioned to write the history of a peasant revolt as if it were some other history—that of the Raj, or of Indian nationalism, or of socialism, depending on his particular ideological bent. The result, for which the responsibility must be shared equally by all schools and tendencies, has been to exclude the insurgent as the subject of his own history.[5]

To acknowledge the peasant as the maker of his own rebellion is to attribute, as we have done in this work, a consciousness to him. Hence, the word 'insurgency' has been used in the title and the text as the name of that consciousness which informs the activity of the rural masses known as jacquerie, revolt, uprising, etc. or to use their Indian designations—dhing, bidroha, ulgulan, hool, *fituri* and so on. This amounts, of course, to a rejection of the idea of such activity as purely spontaneous—an idea that is elitist as well as erroneous. It is elitist because it makes the mobilization of the peasantry altogether contingent on the intervention of charismatic leaders, advanced political organizations or upper classes. Consequently, bourgeois-nationalist historiography has to wait until the rise of Mahatma Gandhi and the Congress Party to explain the peasant movements of the colonial period so that all major events of this genre up to the end of the First World War may then be treated as the pre-history of the 'Freedom Movement'. An equally elitist view inclined to the left discerns in the same events a pre-history of the socialist and communist movements in the subcontinent. What both of these assimilative interpretations share is a 'scholastic and academic historico-political outlook which sees as real and worthwhile only such movements of revolt as are one hundred per cent conscious, i.e. movements that are governed by plans worked out in advance to the last detail or in line with abstract theory (which comes to the same thing)'.[6]

[5] For a more elaborate presentation of the argument stated so far see Guha (1983).

[6] This and other observations attributed to Gramsci on the question of spon-

But as Antonio Gramsci whose words are quoted above has said, there is no room for pure spontaneity in history. This is precisely where they err who fail to recognize the trace of consciousness in the apparently unstructured movements of the masses. The error derives more often than not from two nearly interchangeable notions of organization and politics. What is conscious is presumed in this view to be identical with what is organized in the sense that it has, first, a 'conscious leadership', secondly, some well-defined aim, and thirdly, a programme specifying the components of the latter as particular objectives and the means of achieving them. (The second and the third conditions are often collapsed in some versions.) The same equation is often written with politics as a substitute for organization. To those who prefer this device it offers the special advantage of identifying consciousness with their own political ideals and norms so that the activity of the masses found wanting in these terms may then be characterized as unconscious, hence pre-political.

The image of the pre-political peasant rebel in societies still to be fully industrialized owes a great deal to E. J. Hobsbawm's pioneering work published over two decades ago.[7] He has written there of 'pre-political people' and 'pre-political populations'. He uses this term again and again to describe a state of supposedly absolute or near absence of political consciousness or organization which he believes to have been characteristic of such people. Thus, 'the social brigand appears', according to him, 'only before the poor have reached *political consciousness* or acquired *more effective methods of social agitation*', and what he means by such expressions (emphasized by us) is made clear in the next sentence when he says: 'The bandit is a *pre-political phenomenon* and his strength is in *inverse* proportion to that of *organized revolutionism* and *Socialism* or *Communism*.' He finds the 'traditional forms of peasant discontent' to have been 'virtually devoid of any explicit ideology, *organization* or *programme*'. In general, '*pre-political* people' are defined as those 'who have not

taneity are taken from 'Spontaneity and Conscious Leadership' in Gramsci: 196–200.

[7] For the citations and attributions in this and the next paragraph see Hobsbawm: 2, 5, 13, 23, 96, 118 and H & R: 19, 205.

yet found, or only begun to find, a specific language in which to express their aspirations about the world'.

Hobsbawm's material is of course derived almost entirely from the European experience and his generalizations are perhaps in accord with it, although one detects a certain contradiction when he says at the same time that 'social banditry has next to *no organization or ideology*', and that 'in one sense banditry is a rather primitive form of *organized social protest*'. Again his characterization, in *Captain Swing*, of the English agricultural labourers' movement of 1830 as 'spontaneous and unorganized' does not match fully the observation of his co-author George Rudé to the effect that many of its militant 'undertakings' such as wage-riots, machine-breaking and the 'mobbing' of overseers and parsons 'even if erupting spontaneously, quickly developed the nucleus of a local organisation'.

Whatever its validity for other countries the notion of pre-political peasant insurgency helps little in understanding the experience of colonial India. For there was nothing in the militant movements of its rural masses that was not political. This could hardly have been otherwise under the conditions in which they worked, lived and conceptualized the world. Taking the subcontinent as a whole capitalist development in agriculture remained merely incipient and weak throughout the period of a century and a half until 1900. Rents constituted the most substantial part of income yielded by property in land. Its incumbents related to the vast majority of agricultural producers as landlords to tenant-cultivators, sharecroppers, agricultural labourers and many intermediate types with features derived from each of these categories. The element that was constant in this relationship with all its variety was the extraction of the peasant's surplus by means determined rather less by the free play of the forces of a market economy than by the extra-economic force of the landlord's standing in local society and in the colonial polity. In other words, it was a relationship of dominance and subordination—a political relationship of the feudal type, or as it has been appropriately described, a semi-feudal relationship which derived its material sustenance from pre-capitalist conditions of production and its legitimacy from a traditional culture still paramount in the superstructure.

The authority of the colonial state, far from being neutral to this relationship, was indeed one of its constitutive elements. For under the Raj the state assisted directly in the reproduction of landlordism. Just as Murshid Quli Khan had reorganized the fiscal system of Bengal in such a way as to substitute a solvent and relatively vigorous set of landlords for a bankrupt and effete landed aristocracy,[8] so did the British infuse new blood for old in the proprietary body by the Permanent Settlement in the east, ryotwari in the south and some permutations of the two in most other parts of the country. The outcome of all this was to revitalize a quasi-feudal structure by transferring resources from the older and less effective members of the landlord class to younger and, for the regime politically and financially, more dependable ones. For the peasant this meant not less but in many cases more intensive and systematic exploitation: the crude medieval type of oppression in the countryside emanating from the arbitrary will of local despots under the previous system was replaced now by the more regulated will of a foreign power which for a long time to come was to leave the landlords free to collect *abwab* and *mathot* from their tenants and rack-rent and evict them. Obliged under pressure eventually to legislate against such abuses, it was unable to eliminate them altogether because its law-enforcing agencies at the local level served as instruments of landlord authority, and the law, so right on paper, allowed itself to be manipulated by court officials and lawyers in favour of landlordism. The Raj even left the power of punishment, that ultimate power of the state, to be shared to some extent by the rural elite in the name of respect for indigenous tradition, which meant in effect turning a blind eye to the gentry dispensing criminal justice either as members of the dominant class operating from *kachari* and *gadi* or as those of dominant castes entrenched in village panchayats. The collusion between *sarkar* and zamindar was indeed a part of the common experience of the poor and the subaltern at the local level nearly everywhere.

One important consequence of this revitalization of landlordism under British rule was a phenomenal growth of peasant indebtedness. For with a land market flourishing under the triple impact of agrarian legislation, demographic increase and a progressively larger money supply, many *mahajans* and *banias*

[8] J. Sarkar: 409–10.

bought up estates by the dozen at auctions from impoverished landlords and evicted tenants. Set up as rural proprietors they brought to bear all their usurious skill on their function as rentiers. They were encouraged to do so by a whole set of factors specific to colonial rule—the near or total absence of rent laws to protect tenant-cultivators until towards the last quarter of the nineteenth century, the lack of any effective and enforceable ceilings on local interest rates, the want of co-ordination between a harvest calendar geared to traditional agricultural practices and a fiscal calendar geared to the routine of imperial management, and the development of a market economy luring the peasant with little or no capital to turn his field into a frontier of commercial agriculture and consequently himself into a perpetual debtor. A cumulative result of all this was to make landlords into moneylenders—as much as 46 per cent of all peasant debt in the then United Provinces was owed to landlords in 1934[9]—and give rise to yet another of those historic paradoxes characteristic of the Raj—that is, to assign to the most advanced capitalist power in the world the task of fusing landlordism and usury in India so well as to impede the development of capitalism both in agriculture and in industry.

It was thus that the hitherto discrete powers of the landlord, the moneylender and the official came to form, under colonial rule, a composite apparatus of dominance over the peasant. His subjection to this triumvirate—*sarkari*, *sahukari* and zamindari—was primarily political in character, economic exploitation being only one, albeit the most obvious, of its several instances. For the appropriation of his surplus was brought about by the authority wielded over local societies and markets by the landlord-moneylenders and a secondary capitalism working closely with them and by the encapsulation of that authority in the power of the colonial state. Indeed, the element of coercion was so explicit and so ubiquitous in all their dealings with the peasant that he could hardly look upon his relationship with them as anything but political. By the same token too in undertaking to destroy this relationship he engaged himself in what was essentially a political task, a task in which the existing power nexus had to be turned on its head as a necessary condition for the redress of any particular grievance.

[9] Bengal: I 98.

There was no way for the peasant to launch into such a project in a fit of absent-mindedness. For this relationship was so fortified by the power of those who had the most to benefit from it and their determination, backed by the resources of a ruling culture, to punish the least infringement, that he risked all by trying to subvert or destroy it by rebellion. This risk involved not merely the loss of his land and chattels but also that of his moral standing derived from an unquestioning subordination to his superiors, which tradition had made into his dharma. No wonder, therefore, that the preparation of an uprising was almost invariably marked by much temporization and weighing of pros and cons on the part of its protagonists. In many instances they tried at first to obtain justice from the authorities by deputation (e.g. Titu's bidroha, 1831), petition (e.g. Khandesh riots, 1852), and peaceful demonstration (e.g. Indigo rebellion, 1860) and took up arms only as a last resort when all other means had failed. Again, an *émeute* was preceded in most cases by consultation among the peasants in various forms, depending on the organization of the local society where it originated. There were meetings of clan elders and caste panchayats, neighbourhood conventions, larger mass gatherings, and so on. These consultative processes were often fairly protracted and could take weeks or even months to build up the necessary consensus at various levels until most of an entire community was mobilized for action by the systematic use of primordial networks and many different means of verbal and non-verbal communication.

There was nothing spontaneous about all this in the sense of being unthinking and wanting in deliberation. The peasant obviously knew what he was doing when he rose in revolt. The fact that this was designed primarily to destroy the authority of the superordinate elite and carried no elaborate blueprint for its replacement, does not put it outside the realm of politics. On the contrary, insurgency affirmed its political character precisely by its negative and inversive procedure. By trying to force a mutual substitution of the dominant and the dominated in the power structure it left nothing to doubt about its own identity as a project of power. As such it was perhaps less primitive than it is often presumed to be. More often than not it lacked neither in leadership nor in aim nor even in some rudiments of a programme, although none of these attributes could compare in maturity or sophistication with those of the historically more advanced movements of the twentieth century. The evidence is ample and unambiguous on this point. Of the many cases discussed in this work there is none that could be said to have been altogether leaderless. Almost each had indeed some sort of a central leadership to give it a name and some cohesion, although in no instance was it fully in control of the many local initiatives originating with grassroot leaders whose authority was as fragmented as their standing short in duration. Quite clearly one is dealing here with a phenomenon that was nothing like a modern party leadership but could perhaps be best described, in Gramsci's words, as 'multiple elements of "conscious leadership" but no one of them . . . predominant'. Which is of course a very different thing from stigmatizing these loosely oriented struggles as 'sub-political' outbreaks of mass impetuosity without any direction and form.

Again, if aim and programme are a measure of politics, the militant mobilizations of our period must be regarded as more or less political. Not one of them was quite aimless, although the aim was more elaborately and precisely defined in some events than in others. The Barasat peasantry led by Titu Mir, the Santals under the *Subah* brothers and the Mundas under Birsa all stated their objectives to be power in one form or another. Peasant kings were a characteristic product of rural revolt throughout the subcontinent, and an anticipation of power was indexed on some occasions by the rebels designating themselves as a formally constituted army (*fauj*), their commanders as law-enforcing personnel (e.g. *daroga*, *subahdar*, *nazir*, etc.), and other leaders as ranked civilian officials (e.g. *dewan*, *naib*, etc.)—all by way of simulating the functions of a state apparatus. That the raj they wanted to substitute for the one they were out to destroy did not quite conform to the model of a secular and national state and their concept of power failed to rise above localism, sectarianism and ethnicity, does not take away from the essentially political character of their activity but defines the quality of that politics by specifying its limitations.

It would be wrong of course to overestimate the maturity of this politics and read into it the qualities of a subsequent phase of more intensified class conflict, widespread anti-imperialist struggle and generally a higher level of militancy among the masses. Compared to these, the peasant movements of the first three-quarters of British rule represented a somewhat inchoate and naive state of consciousness. Yet we propose to focus on this consciousness as our central theme, because it is not possible to make sense of the experience of insurgency merely as a history of events without a subject. It is in order to rehabilitate that subject that we must take the peasant-rebel's awareness of his own world and his will to change it as our point of departure.

For however feeble and tragically ineffective this awareness and will might have been, they were still nothing less than the elements of a consciousness which was learning to compile and classify the individual and disparate moments of experience and organize these into some sort of generalizations. These were, in other words, the very beginnings of a theoretical consciousness. Insurgency was indeed the site where the two mutually contradictory tendencies within this still imperfect, almost embryonic, theoretical consciousness—that is, a conservative tendency made up of the inherited and uncritically absorbed material of the ruling culture and a radical one oriented towards a practical transformation of the rebel's conditions of existence[10]—met for a decisive trial of strength.

The object of this work is to try and depict this struggle not as a series of specific encounters but in its general form. The elements of this form derive from the very long history of the peasant's subalternity and his striving to end it. Of these the former is of course more fully documented and represented in elite discourse because of the interest it has always had for its beneficiaries. However, subordination can hardly be justified as an ideal and a norm without acknowledging the fact and possibility of insubordination, so that the affirmation of dominance in the ruling culture speaks eloquently too of its Other, that is, resistance. They run on parallel tracks over the same stretches of history as mutually implied but opposed aspects of a pair of antagonistic consciousnesses.

It is thus that the oppression of the peasantry and the latter's revolt against it figure again and again in our past not only as intermingled matters of fact but also as hostile but concomitant

[10] Gramsci: 333.

traditions. Just as the time-honoured practice of holding the rural masses in thraldom has helped to develop codes of deference and loyalty, so has the recursive practice of insurgency helped to develop fairly well-established structures of defiance over the centuries. These are operative in a weak and fragmentary manner even in everyday life and in individual and small-group resistance, but come into their own in the most emphatic and comprehensive fashion when those masses set about turning things upside down and the moderating rituals, cults and ideologies help no longer to maintain the contradiction between subaltern and superordinate at a non-antagonistic level. In their detail of course these larger structures of resistance vary according to differences between regional cultures as well as between styles of dominance and the relative weights of the dominant groups in any given situation. But since insurgency with all its local variations relates antagonistically to this dominance everywhere throughout the historical period under study, there is much to it that combines into patterns cutting across its particular expressions. For, as it has been said,

> The history of all past society has consisted in the development of class antagonisms, antagonisms that assumed different forms at different epochs. But whatever form they may have taken, one fact is common to all past ages, viz. the exploitation of one part of society by the other. No wonder, then, that the social consciousness of past ages, despite all the multiplicity and variety it displays, moves within certain common forms, or general ideas, which cannot completely vanish except with the total disappearance of class antagonisms.[11]

It will be our aim in this work to try and identify some of these 'common forms or general ideas' in rebel consciousness during the colonial period. However, within that category we have chosen to concentrate on 'the first elements' which make it possible for the general ideas to combine in complex formations and constitute what Gramsci has described as 'the pillars of politics and of any collective action whatsoever'.[12] These *elementary aspects*, as we propose to call them, are subject to a high degree of redundancy: precisely because they recur again and again and almost everywhere in our agrarian movements, they

[11] MECW: VI 504. [12] Gramsci: 144.

are the ones which are the most overlooked. The result has been not merely to exclude politics from the historiography of Indian peasant insurgency but to reduce the latter to a mere embellishment, a sort of decorative and folklorist detail serving primarily to enliven the *curricula vitae* of the indigenous and foreign elites. By contrast, it is rebel consciousness which will be allowed to dominate the present exercise. We want to emphasize its sovereignty, its consistency and its logic in order to compensate for its absence from the literature on the subject and to act, if possible, as a corrective to the eclecticism common to much writing on this theme.

Our choice of historical evidence within the colonial period has been more or less restricted to a span of 117 years between the revolt against Deby Sinha in 1783 and the end of the Birsaite rising in 1900. Although some instances from other times (as well as other countries) have been mentioned for purposes of comparison, the substantive experience used as the basis of the argument falls between these dates. The first twenty-five years of British rule have not been taken into account simply because of the paucity of information about the rural disturbances of that period. Thus, the activities of the sannyasis and the fakirs in the 1770s have been left out because not enough is known at the present state of research about the volume and character of actual peasant involvement in them. And we have taken the end of the last great wave of the Munda ulgulan and the death of its celebrated leader as our terminal point primarily in order to study the elementary aspects of rebel consciousness in a relatively 'pure' state before the politics of nationalism and socialism begin to penetrate the countryside on a significant scale.

No attempt has been made in this work to achieve an exhaustive coverage of events between 1783 and 1900. The information on some of these is not accessible to us either because it has not been recovered from the primary sources or because it is available only in a language not known to the author. Yet there are other peasant movements of the period which though not unfamiliar have found no mention here because they have little to add to the argument. However, with all such omissions, deliberate or otherwise, we trust this essay to stand its ground, for the evidence on which it draws is sufficient for its purpose.

Most, though not all, of this evidence is elitist in origin. This has come down to us in the form of official records of one kind or another—police reports, army despatches, administrative accounts, minutes and resolutions of governmental departments, and so on. Non-official sources of our information on the subject, such as newspapers or the private correspondence between persons in authority, too, speak in the same elitist voice, even if it is that of the indigenous elite or of non-Indians outside officialdom. Staple of most historical writing on colonial themes, evidence of this type has a way of stamping the interests and outlook of the rebels' enemies on every account of our peasant rebellions.

One obvious way of combating such bias could perhaps be to summon folklore, oral as well as written, to the historian's aid. Unfortunately however there is not enough to serve for this purpose either in quantity or quality in spite of populist beliefs to the contrary. For one thing, the actual volume of evidence yielded by songs, rhymes, ballads, anecdotes, etc. is indeed very meagre, to the point of being insignificant, compared to the size of documentation available from elitist sources on almost any agrarian movement of our period. This is a measure not only of the monopoly which the peasant's enemies had of literacy under the Raj, but of their concern to watch and record every hostile gesture among the rural masses. They simply had too much to lose, and fear which haunts all authority based on force, made careful archivists of them. Take, for instance, the Santal hool of 1855 which is richer than many others in this respect. Yet what we know about it from the *Judicial Proceedings* series of the West Bengal State Archives alone, that is, not counting the district records, far outweighs the information to be had from Jugia Harom's and Chotrae Desmanjhi's reminiscences taken together with the folklore collected by Sen, Baskay, and Archer and Culshaw.[13] For most other events the proportion is perhaps even higher in favour of the elitist sources. Indeed, for one of the most important of these, namely, the

[13] For these see MHKRK: *passim*, but especially pp. *clxxvi–viii*; Culshaw & Archer: 218–39; D. C. Sen (1926): 265–71; Baskay: *passim*.

Barasat revolt of 1832, it would be hard to find anything at all that does not derive from a quarter identified with opinions hostile to Titu and his followers.

An equally disappointing aspect of the folklore relating to peasant militancy is that it can be elitist too. Not all singers and balladeers took a sympathetic view of it. Some of them belonged to upper-caste families fallen on hard times or to other impoverished groups within the middle strata of rural society. Cut off from the tillers of the soil by status if not by wealth, they hung on to the rural gentry for patronage and expressed the latter's anxieties and prejudices in their compositions on the theme of agrarian disturbances. Thus, the insurgent voice which comes through the Mundari poetry and homiletics published by Singh, or the anti-survey song in Sandip dialect published by Grierson, is more than balanced out in folk literature by the representation of an obviously landlord point of view in some of the verses cited in Saha's account of the Pabna bidroha, Ray's of the Pagalpanthi insurrection, and so on.[14]

How then are we to get in touch with the consciousness of insurgency when our access to it is barred thus by the discourse of counter-insurgency? The difficulty is perhaps less insurmountable than it seems to be at first sight. For counter-insurgency, which derives directly from insurgency and is determined by the latter in all that is essential to its form and articulation, can hardly afford a discourse that is not fully and compulsively involved with the rebel and his activities. It is of course true that the reports, despatches, minutes, judgments, laws, letters, etc. in which policemen, soldiers, bureaucrats, landlords, usurers and others hostile to insurgency register their sentiments, amount to a representation of their will. But these documents do not get their content from that will alone, for the latter is predicated on another will—that of the insurgent. It should be possible therefore to read the presence of a rebel consciousness as a necessary and pervasive element within that body of evidence.

There are two ways in which this presence makes itself felt. In the first place, it comes as a direct reporting of such rebel utterances as are intercepted by the authorities from time to

[14] Singh: Appendices H, I, K; Grierson: 257; Saha: III 97–100; Ray (1966): 235.

time and used for pacification campaigns, legal enactments, judicial proceedings and other interventions of the regime against its adversaries. Witness to a sort of official eavesdropping, this discourse enters into the records of counter-insurgency variously as messages and rumours circulating within a rural community, snatches of conversation overheard by spies, statements made by captives under police interrogation or before courts, and so on. Meant to assist the Raj in suppressing rebellion and incriminating rebels, its usefulness in that particular respect was a measure of its authenticity as a documentation of the insurgent's will. In other words, intercepted discourse of this type testifies no less to the consciousness of the rebel peasantry than to the intentions of their enemies, and may quite legitimately serve as evidence for a historiography not compromised by the latter's point of view.

The presence of this consciousness is also affirmed by a set of indices within elite discourse. These have the function of expressing the hostility of the British authorities and their native protégés towards the unruly troublemakers in the countryside. The words, phrases and, indeed, whole chunks of prose addressed to this purpose are designed primarily to indicate the immorality, illegality, undesirability, barbarity, etc. of insurgent practice and to announce by contrast the superiority of the elite on each count. A measure of the difference between two mutually contradictory perceptions, they have much to tell us not only about elite mentality but also about that to which it is opposed—namely, subaltern mentality. The antagonism is indeed so complete and so firmly structured that from the terms stated for one it should be possible, by reversing their values, to derive the implicit terms of the other. When, therefore, an official document speaks of badmashes as participants in rural disturbances, this does not mean (going by the normal sense of that Urdu word) any ordinary collection of rascals but peasants involved in a militant agrarian struggle. In the same context, a reference to any 'dacoit village' (as one comes across so often in the Mutiny narratives) would indicate the entire population of a village united in resistance to the armed forces of the state; 'contagion'—the enthusiasm and solidarity generated by an uprising among various rural groups within a region; 'fanatics'—rebels inspired by some kinds of revivalist or puritanical doctrines; 'lawlessness'—the defiance by the people of what they had come to regard as bad laws, and so on. Indeed, the pressures exercised by insurgency on elite discourse force it to reduce the semantic range of many words and expressions, and assign to them specialized meanings in order to identify peasants as rebels and their attempt to turn the world upside down as crime. Thanks to such a process of narrowing down it is possible for the historian to use this impoverished and almost technical language as a clue to the antonymies which speak for a rival consciousness—that of the rebel. Some of that consciousness which is so firmly inscribed in elite discourse will, we hope, be made visible in our reading of it in this work.

CHAPTER 2

NEGATION

'Negative consciousness': the concept explained—discrimination—some instances—extension of insurgency by atideśa*—the term discussed—logic of* atideśa*—caution against overestimating this type of consciousness—inversion: the principal modality of negation—'world turned upside down': universality and antiquity of this notion—inversion: prescriptive versus real—insurgency as a semiotic break—how codes of dominance and subordination are formed—revolt against 'official language'—spoken and written utterances—kinesic and proxemic codes of authority—how these are defied in rebellion—other conspicuous symbols of power—physical appearance, dress, transport, residence, etc.—how these are appropriated or destroyed in the process of inversion—undermining spiritual dominance—desecration: its meaning—inversion as a struggle for prestige.*

It is not by insurgency alone that the peasant comes to know himself. In colonial India a sense of identity was imposed on him by those who had power over him by virtue of their class, caste and official standing. It was they who made him aware of his place in society as a measure of his distance from themselves—a distance expressed in differentials of wealth, status and culture. His identity amounted to the sum of his subalternity. In other words, he learnt to recognize himself not by the properties and attributes of his own social being but by a diminution, if not negation, of those of his superiors.

All the force of the ruling ideologies, especially that of religion, imbued the peasant with this negative consciousness and pandered to it by extolling the virtues of loyalty and devotion, so that he could be induced to look upon his subservience not only as tolerable but almost covetable. There were ancient cults which fostered *bhakti*—'the basic need in feudal ideology', according to Kosambi[1]—to make total dedication to one's superiors. divine as well as human, a matter of spiritual com-

[1] Kosambi (1962): 32.

mitment. There were the consecrated memories of legendary low-born servants who had died for their high-caste masters. In Bengal, Kalu the Dom was immortalized in a cycle of late medieval ballads composed in honour of the deity, Dharma. Born to one of the most 'unclean' of Hindu castes, he was slain in battle while trying to help his lord recover some lands usurped by a rival magnate.[2] Then there was the Poleya who, according to a legend of the Coorgs, was so grieved at his master's death that he committed suicide by throwing himself into the latter's funeral pyre and earned his reward posthumously in the form of an offering of food and drink in a ritual of ancestor worship.[3] And in many of the Nayar *taravads* of Malabar propitiatory rites of the same kind were addressed to the spirit of faithful serfs who had died similarly broken-hearted at the loss of their patrons or in the course of heroic ventures to defend the prestige and properties of their owners—as did the Tiyyar servant in Kottayam who, so goes the story, first killed his master at his bidding and then courted death fighting rather than be captured and converted to Islam by raiders who had come with Tipu Sultan's army in the 1780s.[4]

Thus the power of ideas and the circumstances corresponding to them made the peasant sensitive to the distance which separated him from the pillars of that society, a distance regarded by him as almost the natural condition of his existence. Indeed, the authority of all superordinate classes and groups was secure only so far and as long as he was reconciled to that condition. However, paradoxically enough, his revolt against that authority, when the hour struck, derived much of its strength from the same awareness. Taken by itself this did not of course constitute a mature and fully evolved class consciousness. Yet it would be wrong not to regard this as the very beginning of that consciousness. Gramsci helps us to grasp its precise moment in characterizing this 'merely as the first *glimmer* of such consciousness, in other words, merely as the basic negative, polemical attitude'. Indeed, with all his warning against overestimating it, he acknowledges its importance as a necessary beginning. 'The lower classes, historically on the defensive,' he writes, '*can only achieve self-awareness via a series of*

[2] D. C. Sen (1914): 421–36. [3] Srinivas (1952): 172.
[4] Gough: 464–5.

negations, via their consciousness of the identity and class limits of their enemy.'[5]

This consciousness has a historical tendency to 'come to the surface' locally among some of the more radical sections of the rural masses long before being generalized on a national scale in any country. This can be seen from Hilton's study of the peasant movements in late medieval Europe. In spite of all dissimilarities in other respects, 'there was one prominent feature which they had in common', he says: 'the emergence, among some of the participants, of a consciousness of class. It was, however, a *negative class consciousness* in that the definition of class which was involved was that of their enemies rather than of themselves: in other words, the nobility.'[6]

Our study of peasant insurgency in colonial India too must take such negation as its point of departure. This is not only because of the precedence due to it as that form of rebel consciousness which anticipated others but also because it provides us with an insight into some of the more important principles governing the practice of rebellion. These principles have not always received the attention they merit. The bustle and panic caused by agrarian violence has often been responsible for highlighting its drama rather than its logic and consistency. However, once the glare of burning mansions died down and the eye got used to the facts of an uprising, one could see how far from haphazard it had been.

The negations characteristic of insurgency in our period were worked out in terms of two sets of principles. The first, which we shall call *discrimination*, was realized in its most explicit form in the violence selectively directed by the peasants at particular targets. The frequency and regularity with which this occurred make no sense except as symptoms of wilful commission. The pattern shows up most obviously of course in those cases where the rebels had only one or two clearly specified foes to deal with, such as the notorious Deby Sinha of Rangpur or the indigo planters of lower Bengal, so that the uprisings of 1783 and 1860 could be clearly seen as having their edge turned respectively against the kacharis and the factories. However, even in the course of violence that was more comprehensive in

[5] Gramsci: 273. Emphasis added. [6] Hilton: 130. Emphasis added.

scope, its protagonists often made their emphasis speak for itself. It was this which enabled some of the local administrators in Uttar Pradesh to discern an element common to all the many-sided disturbances in that province in 1857. 'Here as in other parts of the country', wrote the magistrate of Muzaffarnagar, 'the Buneahs and Mahajuns were in the majority of cases the victims',[7] an observation echoed by his opposite number in Hamirpur for his own district when he said that 'the great feature' of the *émeute* there had been 'the universal ousting of all bankers, Buniyas, Marwarees, etc. from landed property . . . by whatever means they acquired it, whether at auction, by private sale or otherwise'.[8]

Concentration such as this was all the more remarkable for the care with which it chose its object and demonstrated how clearly the peasants distinguished between enemies and allies. The definition of friend and foe could of course vary from one insurrection to another and occasionally between groups of protagonists within the same event depending on the conditions in which they operated and the levels of their consciousness. However, the fact that a discrimination of this order entered into insurgent practice at all, must be understood as indicative of its rationale. Hilton brings out this element of 'conscious hostility' in his observations on the Jacquerie of 1358. 'Without any declaration of aims', he says, 'its existence could be concluded from the fact that the objects of the peasants' attacks were *exclusively* knights, squires and ladies along with the castles in which they lived.'[9] The Peasant War in Germany, too, witnessed much selective violence of this kind. During the sack of Weinsberg in April 1525 Metzler and Hipler made their men limit plunder strictly and exclusively to the properties of the clergy and to those of the Keeper of the Wine-cellar, the Bailiff, the City Clerk and the Mayor among the burghers. All others of the latter category were spared on the condition that they provided the victors with food and drink and looked after their wounded so long as they were there.[10] To Engels this phenomenon was important enough to be picked out of the tangled history of that great revolt. The insurgents, he observed, had won over the burghers of Heilbronn to their side, so that when

[7] FSUP: V 82. [8] Ibid.: III 121. [9] Hilton: 131. Emphasis added.
[10] Zimmermann: I 389; Bax: 125.

the town capitulated to them, it was '*only* the possessions of the clergy and the Teutonic Order' which were singled out for the customary pillage.[11] 'They *only* wanted the clergy, their *enemies*', according to Zimmermann[12] on whose documentation Engels based his account. Lefebvre, too, made it a point to emphasize how in the course of the jacqueries of the French Revolution the peasants used all possible means to wreck the properties of those opposed to the Third Estate, but often stopped short of arson, although that would have been simpler and more effective. They were 'reluctant to use it [i.e. fire] because they naturally feared that it might get out of control and spread to the village'. He cites an occasion when a crowd proceeded to destroy and burn a seigneur's farms and residence 'in a very methodical way . . . carefully evacuating anything belonging to the farmers and the servants'. According to him, 'all the peasant revolts followed this pattern'.[13]

The Indian experience agrees with this pattern to some extent. In the course of the popular disturbances following the Mutiny in Aligarh, for instance, the crowds plundered European properties with much thoroughness but did relatively less damage to those of the natives.[14] Again, nothing illuminates more the character of the Kol and Santal uprisings of 1832 and 1855 respectively than the well-known fact that in both instances the peasants spared the tribal population and concentrated their attack on the non-tribal 'outsiders'—*suds* and *dikus*, as they called them. 'Throughout the whole of this devastation', wrote one administrator to another about the first of these events, 'not a single Cole's life was sacrificed nor a home belonging to them destroyed except by accident, and self-interested motives induced the Insurgents to exempt Blacksmiths Gwalas and occasionally the manufacturers of earthen vessels (who were not Coles) from their indiscriminate slaughter.'[15] Indeed, as grudgingly acknowledged in these words, the limits of solidarity and antagonism were specified by the distinctions made between those elements of the non-tribal population to whom the rebels were positively hostile, e.g. landlords

[11] MECW: X 453–4. Emphasis added. Also see Bax: 136.

[12] Zimmermann: II 20. [13] Lefebvre (1973): 119. [14] FSUP: V 657.

[15] BC 1502 (58893): Master to Thomason (17 Jan. 1833). For further evidence and detailed discussion on this point see Chapter 5 below.

and moneylenders, and those subaltern classes and castes who lived and worked with them in the same rural communities and were treated as loyal allies. Such discrimination about which official notice was taken to the effect that 'in many villages the houses of Mahajuns were burnt & those of ryots spared' by the Santals,[16] showed where ethnicity stopped and an incipient form of class consciousness began. Conversely, the selective violence of the Kunbi peasantry in Poona and Ahmadnagar districts in 1875 testified to a modification of class consciousness by localism. 'The Marwari and Gujur sowkars were almost *exclusively* the victims of the riots', wrote the Commissioners appointed to inquire into those disturbances, 'and in villages where sowkars of the Brahmin and other castes shared the money lending business with Marwaris it was usual to find that *the latter only* were molested.'[17]

Negative consciousness of this type had a tendency to extend its domain by a process of analogy and transference, which we shall call its *atideśa* function (following the usage in Sanskrit grammar and linguistics).[18] A detail of the Swing movement in England may help to illustrate this. The violence of the rural proletariat on this occasion had only threshing machines as its initial object. However, this was soon generalized in two ways—first, as an attack on all farming implements including iron

[16] JP, 4 Oct. 1855: Money to Bidwell (6 Sept. 1855).

[17] DRCR: 3. Emphasis added.

[18] The meaning of the term *atideśa*, as used in Sanskrit grammar, is given thus in Apte's dictionary: 'Extended applications, application by analogy, transference of one attribute to another, attraction of one case or rule to another'. (Apte: 29). Such transference is prescribed by Pāṇini, for instance, in *sthānivad ādeśo 'nalvidhau* (I.1.56) indicating 'that the operations to be performed on or by the original may be similarly performed on or by the substitute, but with certain restrictions', i.e. except in cases covered by what is technically known as *al-vidhi* (Pāṇini: 42–3). The general and particular aspects of the concept of *atideśa* are discussed respectively in Chapters VII and VIII of Jaiminī's *Pūrva-Mīmāmsā*, especially in connection with the transference of the details of a model sacrifice (*prakṛti-yāga*) such as the Darśapūrṇamāsa to any other sacrifice (*iṣṭi*) modelled on it (*vikṛti-yāga*). (For text and commentaries see Jaiminī: 417–503.) Since Vedic rituals are governed by *mantras*, such transference requires the latter to be modified (*ūha*) in certain cases, and 'the modification usually consists in picking out one word of a *mantra* and substituting another for it' (Iyer: 190). Bhartṛhari justified such uses of *atideśa* in his great work on linguistics, *Vākyapadīyam* (II. 78), and one of his commentators has pointed out that 'in everyday life also such transference often takes place, as, for instance, when one says: 'Behave towards this Kṣattriya as towards a Brāhmaṇa' (Bhartṛhari: 38).

ploughs, harvesters, chaff-cutters, hay-makers and seed and winnowing machines, and then, as an attack on industrial machines of all kinds such as those used in foundries, sawmills, woollen manufactories and so on.[19] The rioters themselves made the point quite clearly when in order to justify the destruction of a winnowing machine 'they said it must go, as it was a machine, and it was broke to pieces',[20] or as one of their leaders declared, after his men had wrecked all the machinery in two neighbouring mills—one that made threshing-machines and the other sacking—'they had come from 20 miles above London and were going as far down the country as there was any machinery, to destroy it'.[21] Violence extended thus by *atideśa* from one particular implement to all other implements in the same class and from one class of machinery to another.

The logic of this extension applies to people as much as to things. It is indeed usual for a rebellion to broaden its thrust as it develops and include among its targets groups and individuals who may have no part at all in causing the outbreak. This implies, first, that under such circumstances peasant violence may tend to direct itself against all members of a given class of enemies without pausing to sort out the 'good' individuals among them from the 'bad', and secondly, that it may tend to hit out against all classes and sections of the population hostile to the peasantry, irrespective of whichever of these might have been the rebels' initial object of attack. This is why in 1830 the incendiary's torch did not spare the barns and outhouses of a Surrey farmer although (as *The Times* ruefully observed after the event) he 'neither used a thrashing machine nor even employed strangers to work in his employment'—two practices the labourers were known most to hate.[22] For, by the time this act of arson was committed in the autumn of that year the battle lines had been drawn far too clearly to induce any leniency among the village poor towards even the least oppressive of their enemies in south-eastern England. The same tendency, the negative character of which was emphasized by Trotsky when he described it as a 'wave of class hatred', was conspicuous in the peasant riots of the Russian Revolution of 1905 too. 'Estates were sacked almost regardless of the existing

[19] H & R: 116, 118, 119, 121, 124, 125, 198.
[20] Ibid.: 118. [21] Ibid.: 121. [22] Ibid.: 101.

relations between peasants and individual landowners', he wrote: 'if the estates of reactionary landlords were wrecked, so were those of liberals.'[23] The jacqueries triggered off by the revolt of the sepoys in 1857 provided a good many Indian parallels of this phenomenon. When, for instance, the villagers in Allahabad district responded to the mutiny at the *sadar* station by their own uprising, they made little distinction in their attack between official and non-official institutions. 'The very asylums built from charitable funds provided by the Christian population for the relief of the people were burnt down and demolished with as much ill-will as our public offices', wrote a bewildered and somewhat pained British magistrate reporting the holocaust to his superior.[24]

The same official report also testified to the other and even more significant, because radical, aspect of the *atideśa* function, that is, to the manner in which rebel violence tended to spread analogically developing its initial attack on any particular element among the peasants' enemies into a general attack on all or most of them, a process by which insurgency came to permeate an entire domain constituted by such authorities, institutions and groups as were hostile to the subaltern population. Thus the rebellion of 1857 in Allahabad extended soon beyond the barracks where it had originated and hurtled against everything which, like the army, represented the authority of the Raj. A prison, a *chowkidar*'s post, a factory, a railway station, 'every house or factory belonging to Europeans and every building however large or however insignificant', in fact everything '*with which we are connected*', became, according to the local magistrate, an object of pillage, destruction and arson in the city and the surrounding countryside.[25] The pattern occurs again and again in the course of all the major uprisings during our period. Whatever might have been the immediate cause of any particular outbreak, the rebels almost invariably enlarged the scope of their operations to include all British 'connections' —all white military and civilian officials as well as non-official whites such as planters, missionaries, railwaymen, etc.; all seats of official power such as courts, jails, police stations, treasuries and so on as well as non-official buildings (e.g. factories, bungalows, churches, etc.) symbolizing British presence. The

[23] Trotsky: 204–5. [24] FSUP: I 476. [25] Ibid.: Emphasis added.

evidence on this point is far too abundant and accessible to require citing here in detail. One has only to recall the threat to the East India Company's headquarters at Rangpur and its granaries at Bhowaniganj during the dhing of 1783, the attacks on churches and clergymen during the Birsaite ulgulan, the Santal hostilities towards railway engineers and planters during the hool, and the numerous raids on *thanas*, jails and public offices in all these instances and at the time of the Mutiny—to realize the almost universal tendency of the more militant peasant uprisings to take on the entire range of British authority in both its official and non-official sectors.

Generalized violence of this kind was not necessarily delimited by ethnicity. The whites were not alone in being subjected to it. On the contrary, it was not unusual for attacks on government property and personnel and Europeans directly associated with these to develop into attacks on the principal native collaborators of the Raj as well. For, no matter which one of their three main oppressors—sarkar, sahukar or zamindar—was the first to bear the initial brunt of a jacquerie in any particular instance, the peasants often showed a remarkable propensity to extend their operations widely enough to include among their targets the local representatives of one or both of the other groups too. Many of the more powerful events of our period testify to this. Titu Mir's bidroha in Barasat and the series of Moplah rebellions in nineteenth-century Malabar started off as anti-landlord struggles but culminated as campaigns against the Raj itself. Conversely, the movements of the Farazis and the indigo ryots against European planters often developed into resistance to rack-renting and other forms of zamindari despotism. The Kol insurrection of 1832 in Chota Nagpur had landlords and moneylenders among the suds as its initial objects of hostility but ended up as a war against the Company's government itself. And, conversely again, the Birsaite ulgulan launched with the declared aim of liberating the Mundas from British rule made no secret of its hatred for banias and mahajans as it progressed.

Transference of this kind was most conspicuous in the course of the peasant uprisings of the period of the Mutiny. Inspired by and foil to a revolt in the armed forces threatening the very foundation of the regime, these jacqueries were directed as much against the government as against moneylenders. Indeed, the expression of anti-bania hatred was widespread enough to be regarded by many contemporaries as the principal aspect of these disturbances. Yet as Stokes has shown by a careful investigation of this phenomenon in Uttar Pradesh, there was little in the incidence of usurious transactions to justify the extent and intensity of the aggression against their protagonists in the regions where this occurred most in 1857–8. The attacks on mahajans and auction-purchasers, he concludes, were motivated less by economic than political considerations.[26] The importance of this finding can hardly be exaggerated. For the symbiosis of sarkar, sahukar and zamindar was a political fact rooted in the very nature of British power in the subcontinent. By directing his violence against all three members of this trinity irrespective of which one of them provoked him to revolt in the first place, the peasant displayed a certain understanding of the mutuality of their interests and the power on which this was predicated. However feeble and incipient, this represented the emergence of a political consciousness, even if no more than its very 'first glimmer'.

An *atideśa* function of the Santal rebellion of 1855 may be recalled here to illuminate further this particular type of rebel perception. As is well known, violence spread in this case with the utmost speed from targets identified with the colonial administration and the whites to those representing the authority of landlords and moneylenders, though by no means in the same sequence in all regions. The Santals made it obvious that they intended to spare no person or property associated with sarkar, sahukar or zamindar, and thus established within a matter of days a well-defined domain of insurgency in which their operations had a free play between all three categories of their foes and were permuted in all possible ways. That this was not just the work of some kind of 'instinct' characteristic of 'primitive rebels' but followed from the logic of a certain understanding and will, is easily documented. For it conforms fully to the view that Sido and Kanhu, the leaders of the insurrection, had of their enemies and which they had recorded in their historic parwana sent out long before the outbreak of the insurrection. 'The Mahajuns have committed a great sin', it

[26] Stokes: 138, 179.

declared. 'The Sahibs and the amlah have made everything bad, in this the Sahibs have sinned greatly. Those who tell things to the Magistrate and those who investigate cases for him, take 70 or 80 Rs. with great oppression in this the Sahibs have sinned. On this account the Thacoor has ordered me saying that the country is not the Sahibs.'[27] There is some evidence here of a grasp, however weak and crudely stated, of the linkage between the indigenous exploiters and the colonial authorities with the emphasis weighted slightly—albeit very slightly—in favour of the suggestion that the transactions of the former were contingent on the power of the latter.

It will be wrong not to see in all this the imprint of a consciousness trying to identify some of the basic elements of economic exploitation and the political superstructure which legitimized these. However, to overestimate its lucidity or depth will be equally ill-advised. For it is still a rather hesitant, inchoate and disjointed perception, not unlike the discourse which registered it. It describes empirically some aspects of the peasant's conditions of existence, but falls far short of conceptualizing the structure of authority which made such conditions possible. 'The only form in which the State is perceived', one could say after Gramsci,[28] is in terms of officialdom—of the sahibs. This characteristic expression of a negative consciousness on the insurgent's part matched its other symptom, that is, his self-alienation. He was still committed to envisaging the coming war on the Raj as the project of a will independent of himself and his own role in it as no more than instrumental. 'Kanoo and Seedu Manjee are not fighting. The Thacoor himself will fight', stated the parwana in which the authors did not recognize even their own voice, but heard only that of God: 'This is the order of the Thacoor.'[29]

The other modality of negation characteristic of insurgency consists of the peasants' attempt to destroy or appropriate for themselves the signs of the authority of those who dominate them. The inversion which is necessarily brought about by such a process has been frequent and widespread enough to constitute a stereotyped figure of speech in many languages. 'Those who used to rank lowest now rank above everybody else; and

[27] TTP. [28] Gramsci: 272. [29] TTP.

so this is called "turning things upside down".'[30] When Mao Tse-tung wrote this in his *Hunan Report* as a summing up of the achievements of the peasant uprising of 1927 in his home province, he used a phrase almost identical to one in *The Acts of the Apostles XVII, 1–6,* describing the impact of Paul and the early Christians on Thessalonica when they arrived there with their revolutionary message: 'These that have turned the world upside down are come hither also', cried their enemies.

In the course of the centuries which intervened between these two texts the same imagery phrased in much the same way in many languages has been used to uphold, denounce or simply describe rebellion. Zimmermann tells us of the order issued by a leader of the German peasant army to a town taken by them in 1525 asking it to treat his troops well 'or else they would want to turn the lowliest into the highest' (*oder sie wollten das Unterste zuoberst kehren*).[31] And Lefebvre mentions how during the French Revolution the peasants came to a small town in the Maconnais on one occasion, wrecked the offices of the 'crues', fined the curé and the local gentry, smashed the weathercocks, and generally, *ils en profitèrent pour tout mettre sens dessus dessous,* that is, 'put upright what was below'.[32] In colonial India the British described the Kol rebels as 'endeavouring to excite the lower orders against the higher', while the seditious posters which appeared in the bazaar at Lucknow on the eve of the Mutiny were seen by a local correspondent of the *Bengal Hurkaru and India Gazette* as the work of 'the scum of the populace who like the Scottish robber would like to see the world turned upside down'.[33] All such expressions, in German, French and English, come close to echoing Manu's ancient fear of the consequences which could follow from any lapse in the violence of the state. For if the king did not exercise his power of punishment (*daṇḍa*) relentlessly enough, 'the crow would eat the sacrificial cake, the dog lick up the food put out for ritual oblation and no right of ownership (*svāmyam*) would be there for anyone to retain'—in short, we are warned, 'the lower would become the higher' (*pravarteta adharottaram*).[34] This brahmanical

[30] Mao: I 30. See also I 28. [31] Zimmermann: II 20.

[32] Lefebvre (1970): 139.

[33] BC 1362 (54224): Neave to Lambert (4 Feb. 1832); Lambert to Government (6 Feb. 1832). FSUP: II 8. [34] Shiromani: 7/20–1.

dread of the inversive process was to be systematized later into a chiliastic image of total cataclysm in the *Vāyupurāṇam*. It envisaged a great upheaval (*samkshovah*) with the advent of Kali at the epoch's end (*yugānta*). Among the many reversals characteristic of that topsy-turvy age, Brahmans, it was predicted, would behave like Sudras and Sudras like Brahmans, kings would take to the vocation of thieves and thieves to that of kings, women would be faithless to their husbands and servants to their masters.[35]

It is precisely in order to prevent such inversions from occurring in real life that the dominant culture in all traditional societies allows these to be simulated at regular calendric intervals, and in so far as such a culture is almost invariably mediated by religion, the reversals condoned, in fact enjoined, by it, are acted out as sacred rituals. Hence the religiosity associated with such prescriptive inversions everywhere no matter whether the protagonists are Europeans involved in Shrove Tuesday carnivals or Zulu women in ceremonies meant to propitiate the goddess Nomkubulwana. The vast literature on the subject[36] shows how on such privileged occasions the 'structural inferiors' in the given societies enjoy the licence to indulge in rites of status reversal with respect to their superordinates. Servants act like masters, women like men, children like grown-ups, juniors like seniors, and so on. 'Degree, priority and place' are not observed so long as these festivals of contraries continue and most of the visual and verbal signs of authority and obedience which represent social morality are mutually substituted for the time being. Yet, as all observers agree, the outcome of such prescriptive inversion is not to destroy or even weaken a social order, but to buttress it. It is of course possible that on some of these occasions the liminality of the participants and their particular circumstances might bring about a sudden switching of codes turning what is intended as a mock rebellion into a real one, a festival into an insurrection.

[35] Tarkaratna: 58/38, 41–3. For other inversions characteristic of Kali, see ibid., 58/31–70 *passim*.

[36] For some outstanding samples of this literature see Gluckman's pioneering works, Gluckman (1963): 110–36 and (1966): 109–36. V. W. Turner: 166–203, contains some important theoretical considerations on this phenomenon and Burke: 182–204 a rich collection of European instances relating to carnival and the carnivalesque.

For the liminal, as Turner has emphasized, is 'necessarily ambiguous' and tends to 'elude or slip through the network of classifications that normally locate states and positions in cultural space'.[37] Hence the not too rare correspondence between sacred days and insurgency as witnessed, for instance, by the incursion of Wat Tyler's men into London on the morning of Corpus Christi, 13 June 1381, the beginning of the great series of peasant revolts in Germany during Fastnacht 1525, the conversion of a carnival featuring Mère Folle and her Infanterie into a riot in masquerade against the royal tax officials in Dijon in 1630, the coincidence of some of the jacqueries of 1789 in France with Sundays, feast days, etc. as mentioned by Lefebvre and the threat of a massive uprising in Bombay during Muharram and Diwali in the year of the Mutiny.[38] However, it is important to remember that such cases, numerous as they are, occur in spite of prescriptive inversion and represent the failure of what is meant and indeed has generally proved to be a safety-valve device. For the purpose of such rituals is clearly to empty rebellion of its content and reduce it into a routine of gestures in order to reinforce authority by feigning defiance. Gluckman's observation about the Zulu ceremony mentioned above could indeed apply to the entire genre. 'This particular ritual', he wrote, 'by allowing people to behave in normally prohibited ways, gave expression, in a reversed form, to the normal rightness of a particular kind of social order.'[39] Some of the more permissive Hindu festivals may be said fully to bear this out.

Take, for instance, the Teyyam festival as celebrated in parts of Malabar. This centres around the shrines of the female deity Bhagavadi, which are attached to the landowning and politically as well as economically dominant Nayar taravads. The propitiatory rituals are, for each taravad, officiated by one of its lower-caste servants who puts on a mask at a particular point of the ceremonial process and is possessed by a malevolent ghost of the *teyyam* (derived from the Sanskrit word *deva*, 'god') type. While in this state, the servant can and often does adopt an

[37] V. W. Turner: 95.

[38] Hilton: 138–9; Franz: 137, 139, 143, 165, 174; Davis: 178; Lefebvre (1973): 43; Holmes: 467–70; Burke: 203–4.

[39] Gluckman (1966): 116.

aggressive or authoritative attitude towards his superiors, demands gifts and voices threats and blessings—all as an instrument of the spirit of the dead working through him. And when at the end of the ceremony the oracle takes off his mask and reverts to his menial status, he receives a fee for the ritual service rendered and gets on with his other customary duties. Kathleen Gough, to whom we owe this account, has stated the importance of such prescriptive reversal in emphasizing the traditional authority of the Nayar landed gentry over the subaltern groups in their villages. 'For the low caste officiant', she writes, 'these festivals permit a limited, stylized expression of aggression and a temporary assumption of authority towards their high caste masters. At the same time, the festivals underline both the interdependence between the castes, and ultimately, the lower castes' permanent, secular role as submissive servants.'[40]

A very similar dialectic of ritual inversion and reinforcement of authority has been observed by Srinivas in his study of the Coorgs. Among them the Banna constitute an inferior caste whose traditional duty has been to serve aristocratic *okkas* as priests and oracles on certain ritual occasions. They are a polluting caste, so polluting indeed that at the annual festival of the deity Kakkot Achchayya a Brahman priest carrying the idol risks defiling it as well as himself even by catching a glimpse of the Banna oracle. Normally the latter is regarded as too unclean to have access to the central hall of any upper-caste Coorg ancestral house, which must be kept in the highest state of ritual purity. Yet it is precisely in that central hall that he is made to preside over the prestigious ceremony of ancestor worship as its chief officiant. And when in the course of performing the propitiatory rites he is possessed by each of the ancestral spirits in turn, he feels free not merely to press sumptuous demands for food and drink on his landlord hosts but even to admonish the head of the okka for neglecting the paddy, for not looking after his inheritance assiduously enough and generally for failing in his duties. 'As the temporary vehicle of the spirit of an ancestor he is entitled to say and do things which he normally would not dream of saying or doing.' But the licence is short-lived. Srinivas insists on the purely temporary character of such role reversal which does little to

[40] Gough: 472–3.

diminish, far less end, the structural cleavages in Coorg society. The same could be said also of the ritual elevation of the Poleya, one of the most impure and exploited of all castes in this region —traditionally a caste of agrestic slaves—who are required 'to exercise power over people belonging to the higher castes' during certain festivals, thereby 'compensating them for the low position they normally occupy in the caste structure'. In the event, however, it is not their inclusion in some festivals and its 'compensation-aspect' but their exclusion from most of these as indicative of their real, ineradicable state of degradation which emerges as the central fact of their existence. As at the end of the splendid oracular drama the Banna returns to his role as the musty repository of landlord family tradition, so after his exposure to a modicum of simulated authority in short sacred seasons the Poleya sinks back to his place at the bottom of Coorg society as its most disenfranchised member. The only purpose which the process of ritual inversion may be said to serve in either case is to affirm and make explicit at regular intervals the distance separating each of these subaltern groups from those who rule the villages.[41]

What emerges clearly from these instances is the part played by religion in sacralizing the authority of the rural elites. But more than in any other festival this is made explicit in the celebration of Holi in the course of which these reversals are acted out with a vigour and on a scale as at no other occasion of the same kind. One of the most ancient of popular ceremonies in this ancient land, its origins go back to prehistoric times—to the late Stone Age according to some scholars[42]—long before the beginnings of feudalism. Yet when the latter came to be established in the subcontinent, brahmanical Hinduism, often so hostile to vestiges of the autochthonous culture, bent backwards to confer on it full shastric status. Having made a début in some of the later medieval Puranas it was already enfranchised as a sacred event in the sixteenth-century law-books of Raghunandana and Govindananda.[43] And by the time British officials and American anthropologists had come to write about it, spanning roughly a century and a half between Buchanan-Hamilton and McKim Marriott, it had settled down com-

[41] Srinivas (1952): 19, 40, 42, 75, 102, 107 n., 162–3, 164, 191, 199 *et passim*.
[42] Kosambi (1975): 199. [43] Chakravarti: 131.

fortably in its role as a *vrata* complete with fasting, bathing, puja and other concomitants of the Hindu ritual process. Hence nothing happens at this festival to upset society in spite of the seemingly radical *bouleversement* of the Holi schedule. The saturnalia, the systematic violation of structural distances between castes and classes, the defiance of rules governing interpersonal relationships between members of the family and community, the blatant undermining of private and public morality—all of which feature in this ceremony,[44] add up not to a disruption of the political and social order in the village but to its reinforcement. A great deal of verbal and physical violence, inflicted respectively by abusive speech and actual belabouring by cudgels, takes place on this occasion as all observers agree. But there is no punishment for it and yet the world is not turned upside down in spite of Manu's fear to the contrary. The impunity is, of course, deceptive. If the exercise of *daṇḍa* is suspended, it is only because none of these stylized reversals constitutes a real transgression. Just as in Sanskrit grammar the injunction against any breach of rules is emphasized by the licence allowed to deviant usage in the holiest of all texts. the Vedas—*chandasi*, as Panini would put it ever so often turning aside from the rigour of his own great discourse[45]—so too does the ritual of inversion at Holi affirm the general legitimacy of spiritual and social sanctions against nonconformity by condoning the latter on one prescribed occasion. Its overall effect is 'the stressing, not the overthrowing of the principle of hierarchy . . . through reversal, a process whereby it *remains* the structural vertebra of village life'.[46]

But it is not the collusion between religion and authority which alone makes Holi, like other ceremonies of this type, so innocuous. Predictability which goes with tradition, has also a part to play in this. For all such festivals based on prescriptive inversion are necessarily *anticipated* by their protagonists and the local communities where they belong. They are a part of the

[44] For two of the best modern accounts of Holi see Lewis: 229–33 and Marriott in Singer: 200–31. Some of the nineteenth-century observations are summarized in Crooke (1968): II 313–22.

[45] As is well known to students of Sanskrit grammar all such exceptions are compiled from Pāṇini's *Ashṭādhyāyī* by Bhaṭṭoji Dīkshita in his great work, the *Siddhānta Kaumudī* in the chapter, 'Vaidikī Prakriyā'. See Dīkshita: II.

[46] V. W. Turner: 188.

cyclical rhythm of life in any society based on a stagnant economy, primitive technology and pre-capitalist culture. Such 'calendrical rites', as Turner calls this genre, 'are performed at well-delineated points in the annual productive cycle, and attest to the passage from scarcity to plenty (as at first fruits or harvest festivals) or from plenty to scarcity (as when the hardships of winter are anticipated and magically warded against)'.[47] The Indian villager recognizes them as a fixture in the annual schedule of public celebrations. Co-ordinated closely with the farm calendar and the seasons they make up an established and irrevocable sequence. They are indeed almost as 'natural' to him as, for instance, is the order of transplanting in monsoon and harvesting in winter to the rice-growing peasant of Bengal. Religion helps to promote this 'natural' look of most folk festivals and intercalate them with the seasonal routines of work on the land. It does so by, among other devices, inserting in their ritual procedure such markers as refer directly to agricultural products, many of them grown in the festival seasons. Hence the association that is there between the popular rituals of this type in each region and some of its principal crops of grain and fruit—rice and coconut in the south and the east, wheat and barley in western Uttar Pradesh (UP) and Punjab, sugarcane in Bihar and eastern UP, mangoes in UP again, and so forth. It is this mediation by religion of the natural conditions of the peasant's labour and its products which makes the villager look upon these festivals as pre-ordained as the coming of the rains and the hoar-frost and agricultural operations dependent on them. This is why he is not taken by surprise at Holi or any other 'calendrical ritual' of prescriptive inversion. On the contrary, he anticipates it in every detail, if only because its conventions are all too familiar to him. Marriott's dramatic account of the beginning of the 'Feast of Love' as he witnessed it in a north Indian village should lead no one to believe that the natives, too, shared his sense of alarm and astonishment on that fateful night. For they had been coolly preparing for this sacred rumpus for some time, as the author himself indicates.[48] As a matter of fact, organization for this particular event begins at least a month in advance, as another anthropologist reports from the same cultural region.[49] In

[47] Ibid.: 168–9. [48] Marriott in Singer: 200. [49] Lewis: 229.

other words, ritual inversion stands for a continuity turned into sacred tradition by long recursive use under the aegis and inspiration of religion. As such, it represents the very antithesis of peasant insurgency.

For if the function of prescriptive reversal is to ensure the *continuity* of the political and moral order of society and *sacralize* it, that of peasant insurgency is to *disrupt* and *desecrate* it. In conditions governed by the norm of unquestioning obedience to authority, a revolt of the subaltern shocks by its relative entropy. Hence the suddenness so often attributed to peasant uprisings and the verbal imageries of eruption, explosion and conflagration used to describe it. What is intended by such usage in many languages and cultures is to communicate the sense of an unforeseen break, a sharp discontinuity. For while ritual inversions help to ensure the continuity of village society by allowing its upper and nether elements to change places at regular intervals and for strictly limited periods, the aim of peasant insurgency is to take it by surprise, put the existing power relation on its head and do so for good. As Christopher Hill has pointed out, the traditional foolery of Shrove Tuesday and the Feast of Fools used to serve as a safety-valve for medieval European society releasing tension and making the social order 'perhaps that much more tolerable', but 'what was new in the seventeenth century was the idea that the world might be *permanently* turned upside down'.[50] It is this threat, real or imaginary, that it carries of a permanent subversion of the local hierarchies of power which distinguishes a peasant rebellion from the simulated upheavals discussed above.

Such radical subversion, this *real* turning of things upside down, which is only another name for rebellion, constitutes a semiotic break: it violates that basic code by which the relations of dominance and subordination are historically governed in any particular society. Indeed, there is no society where politics, like every other department of the superstructure, is not regulated by such a code. For, to paraphrase Barthes, man is busy everywhere all the time charging reality with meaning and setting up semiological systems by converting things into

[50] Hill (1972): 14.

signs and attributing signification to what is perceived by the senses.[51] However, the degree of semioticity varies according to whether the dominant culture of a society is more or less feudal in character. Juri Lotman's comments on the 'medieval type' (as against the 'enlightenment type') of Russian culture can help us to grasp this distinction:

> The 'medieval' type is distinguished by its high semioticity. It not only tends to impart the character of a cultural sign to everything that has meaning in natural language, but proceeds from the assumption that everything is significant. For this type of code, meaning is the index of existence: nothing is culturally meaningless.[52]

This could be said of the medieval type of culture in all other countries too. Huizinga has shown how the authority of the sign permeated every aspect of Western thought during the Middle Ages. It is not only that icons and images figured prominently in religious expression, but politics, too, was highly semioticized. Liveries, colours, badges and party cries were conspicuously displayed in the course of public disputes, and notions of power and subalternity worked out in elaborate sets of symbols: for, 'feudal or hierarchic thought expresses the idea of grandeur by visible signs, lending to it a symbolic shape, of homage paid kneeling, of ceremonial reverence'.[53]

Feudal culture in the Indian subcontinent also waxed fat on signs systematized into codes of authority and deferential response. Two contrasting and yet complementary processes, one popular and the other elitist, went into the making of such codes. First, it was through centuries of recursive practice at the grassroot level that these signs congealed into a naive tradition. Secondly, the literati, especially the sacerdotal class, conceptualized and formalized these into a set of influential, indeed decisive, prescriptions constituting the vast shastric literature of the Smṛtis. This priestly intervention went a long way to add a touch of sanctity to these codes. Even more importantly, perhaps, this helped to perpetuate and generalize them. For as Indian feudalism came of age, some of the more important sets of power relations, e.g. those between parents and sibling, guru and *śishya* (spiritual disciple), god and man,

[51] Barthes (1967*): 285. [52] Lotman: 216–17.

[53] Huizinga: 21–2, 26, and Chs 12 & 15 *passim*.

etc., emerged as paradigmatic in the sense that others were derived from or modelled on them, and it was the function of the Smṛtis to record and confirm this development.

The first of two devices generally employed for this purpose was grammatical, that is, to insert the Sanskrit equivalent of a sign of predication between a derivative and its paradigm. The copulae italicized in the following selection of sentences from the *Laws of Manu* offer a fair sample of such use:

> ... between [a ten-year old Brāhmaṇa and a hundred-year-old Kshatriya] the Brāhmaṇa *is* the father. (II 135)
>
> ... he [an infant king] *is* a great deity in human form. (VII 8)
>
> ... the wife of an elder brother *is* for his young (brother) the wife of a Guru. (IX 57)
>
> A maternal aunt, the wife of a maternal uncle, a mother-in-law, and a paternal aunt ... *are equal* to the wife of one's teacher. (II 131)
>
> ... the (pupil) *shall consider* [his Vedic instructor] as his father and mother. (II 144)
>
> Towards a sister of one's father and of one's mother, and towards one's own elder sister, one *must behave as towards* one's mother ... (II 133)
>
> ... a husband *must* be constantly *worshipped* as a god by a faithful wife. (V 154)

The other device was structural and this operated in two ways. For one thing, it was as a matter of convention that each of these sacred texts reproduced the more important hierarchical prescriptions already laid down by its predecessors. This was true even of the most celebrated of all such compilations—the one quoted above, and it is clear from Bühler's edition of this work that large chunks from it had found their way into the later Smṛtis.[54]

Intertextuality helped thus to sustain tradition. However, the law-givers did not stop at that: they innovated too and went on adding to the range of some of the older paradigms with almost each recension. Thus, the paradigm guru/śishya which, according to Manu, subsumed no more than two other dyads represented by the guru's wife (if of the same caste) as the first term in one pair and by his son (if also a teacher) as that in the other, came to serve, some centuries later, for as many as sixty

[54] For Manu's borrowings see Bühler: 'Introduction', *passim*, and for quotations from it and parallel passages as found in other law books, see ibid.: 515–82.

other relations in the *Viṣṇusmṛti*.[55] The outcome of such accretion was, in the long run, vastly to extend the scope of feudal authority by distributing its signs among the constituent paradigms. For as the latter had more and more relations stacked into them, their boundaries overlapped and they tended to merge into a generalized system signifying dominance and subordination in the society as a whole. By the time that colonialism came to establish itself firmly in the subcontinent, it had already at its disposal a well-developed semiotic apparatus which was partly inherited and partly its own invention. This was comprehensive enough to express its authority and that of the collaborating native elites. The subaltern masses too were familiar with this apparatus if only as those whose deference it was primarily designed to enforce and it is by throwing a spanner or two into the works from time to time that they learnt the rudiments of rebellion. Indeed, it would be quite in order to say that insurgency was a massive and systematic violation of those words, gestures and symbols which had the relations of power in colonial society as their significata.

This was perceived as such both by its protagonists and their foes. The latter were often quick to register their premonition of an uprising as a noise in the transmission of some of the more familiar signals of deference. A resident at Saharanpur on the eve of the Mutiny wrote thus of the anxieties of the white community there in those days: 'Early in the month of May, it became a subject of general remark with us, that the sepoys on duty at this station had thrown off their customary quiet and respectful behaviour, and had become forward, if not insolent; they paraded the public roads in parties, scarcely deigning to move to one side for a passing carriage, and singing at the highest pitch of their unmelodious voices, heedless of who heard them.'[56] Later on, when the violence of that 'Red Year' had already reached its height, an army doctor on the run through the Gwalior countryside was to notice how 'every villager was uncivil, and the smile of respectful submission with which the European officer was to be greeted, was displaced by an angry

[55] Ibid.: 2/208, 210. For the date of *Viṣṇusmṛti* see Jolly: 'Introduction', especially p. *xxxii*. The relations subsumed under the guru/śishya paradigm have been worked out on the basis of Jolly: 28/29, 31; 32/1–3.

[56] FSUP: V 93.

scowl and haughty air towards the despicable Feringhee whose raj was at an end'.[57] Quite clearly the British expected Indians to show their subservience to the governing race by a series of abject gestures and self-imposed restraints in their public behaviour. To make room for a sahib's landau on the road, to refrain from raising one's voice within his earshot, to smile submissively in his presence had all come to be regarded as 'customary', that is, as part of an established code signifying the power of the rulers over the ruled. Crowded streets, noisy singing, 'angry scowls and haughty air' were therefore suspect in the eyes of those who had the most to benefit from deference. They saw in these reversals not only an absence of the highly cherished collaboration between master and servant but, indeed, its replacement by hostility on the latter's part. There was no room for neutrality in this binary relationship: non-antagonism could turn only into antagonism.

Evidence of this kind is by no means rare, although it has not often been read as an index of a clash between rival consciousnesses. The signs of elite authority were so ubiquitous, so completely did they pervade the whole of our life under the Raj and so common indeed was their violation in the course of any popular disturbance that the historian's sensitivity to his *matériel* has been numbed with redundancy. Yet the character of the subaltern movements in India can hardly be grasped without specifying how dominance and subordination were represented in the ruling culture and their subjects forced to change places by the activity of the masses.

The class of signs most often and most instinctively reversed by insurgents and hence the least noticed in studies of insurgency is what constitutes, according to Bourdieu, an 'official language'. One of its functions, he writes, is to service 'the system of concepts by means of which the members of a given group provide themselves with a representation of their social relations (e.g. the lineage model or the vocabulary of honour)' and in this way it 'sanctions and imposes what it states, tacitly laying down the dividing line between the thinkable and the unthinkable, thereby contributing towards the maintenance of the symbolic order from which it draws its authority'.[58] This was

[57] Carey: 196. [58] Bourdieu: 21.

precisely how verbal deference functioned in colonial India, upholding semi-feudal relationships between old and young, male and female, high caste and low caste. For as Durkheim has observed, 'the word is [a] way of entering into relations with persons'.[59] It was therefore essential that in a society which enjoined formal respect for senior kin on the part of their juniors there should be some rules of speech strictly to govern such behaviour. The latter are forbidden from mentioning any of the elders by their proper names in many communities. 'This is because calling a person by name', says Srinivas with reference to the Coorgs, 'is not consistent with putting him in a position of respect.'[60] With the Kamar of Chhatisgarh the range of interdiction included a man's father, mother, grandparents, uncles, aunts, father-in-law and elder brothers. The ban was even more severe when applied to a woman. Particularly excluded were the names of her husband and some of his relatives. Transgression in the former respect could lead her to being put out of caste at least for some time, as was the custom among the Dhanwar of Madhya Pradesh even until a few decades ago.[61]

If deference in speech mattered so much in demarcating kinship and sexual status, it did so to a still greater extent in the domain of caste and class relationship where feudal authority prevailed in its most explicit and effective form. Here again one can go far back into the past and find the elements of a linguistic discrimination between castes entrenched in some of the most ancient Sanskrit texts. Thus, a well-known Paninian rule was interpreted in such a way as to make the words standing for the four varnas replicate the varna hierarchy itself in a compound of the *dvandvasamāsa* class and put them together in their ascriptive order descending from Brahman to Sudra.[62]

[59] Durkheim: 543.

[60] Srinivas (1952): 48. Cf. Durkheim: 343–4: 'Every proper name is considered an essential element of the person who bears it . . . So if the one is sacred, the other is. Therefore, it may not be pronounced in the course of the profane life.'

[61] For the Kamar, see Dube: 77. For similar customs among the Santals see Bompas: 356–7; the Chamars—Russel & Lal: II 12; the Bhatra—ibid.: II 277; the Halba—ibid.: III 198; the Dhanwar—ibid.: II 501.

[62] The compound would then read: *brāhmaṇakshattriyabiṭśudrāh.* The sutra, '*alpāchtaram*' (II.2.34), has a *vārtika* laying down that 'the castes are placed according to their order' (*varṇānām ānupūrvyeṇa pūrvanipātah*) so that the rule governing

Again, Manu (II 49) prescribed a series of syntactic variations on a string of words to make beggars identify themselves by their respective castes while calling for alms:

An initiated Brāhmaṇa should beg, beginning (his request with the word) lady (bhavati); a Kshatriya, placing (the word) lady in the middle, but a Vaiśya, placing it at the end (of the formula).

This meant in effect that if ABC could be said to represent the sequence of the three words in the sentence '*Bhabati bhikshām dehi*' as uttered by a Brahman beggar, a Kshatriya's call was to be construed as BAC and a Vaisya's BCA.[63] Vocabulary, too, could serve for caste markers. Among acquaintances, for instance, phatic statements about each other's health had to include the word *kuśala* if addressed to a Brahman, *anāmaya* to a Kshatriya, *kshema* to a Vaisya and *anārogya* to a Sudra (*Manu* II 127).

This tradition of using language as a register of caste status was still very much alive when Logan came across it in late nineteenth-century Malabar. A man's deference towards those ranked higher than himself was demonstrated in explicit verbal acknowledgements of his own inferiority. In any conversation he had to debase himself by stigmatizing whatever he had. Convention required him to refer to his own food not simply as rice, but as 'stony or gritty rice', his money as nothing more than 'copper cash', his house as a 'dungheap'.[64] The indigenous perception of the structural cleavages in Malabar society of a century ago was recorded in a list of words for houses, as given by Logan. He wrote:

The *house* itself is called by different *names* according to the occupant's caste. The house of a Pariah is a *cheri*, while the agrestic slave—the Cheraman—lives in a *chala*. The blacksmith, the goldsmith, the carpenter, the weaver, etc., and the toddy-drawer (*Tiyan*) inhabit houses styled *pura* or *kudi*; the temple servant resides in a *variyan* or *pisharam* or *pumatham*, the ordinary Nayar in a *vidu* or *bhavanam*, while the man in authority of this caste dwells in an *idam*; the Raja lives in a *kovilakam*

---

combination in a *dvandvasamāsa* according to the relative weight of syllables would not apply in this particular instance—a clear case of ideology moulding grammar in its own image (Pāṇini: 273–4).

[63] Bühler: 2/49. The beggars' calls are taken from Kullūka's commentary as given in Shiromani. [64] Logan: 85, 127.

or *kottaram*, the indigenous Brahman (Nambutiri) in an *illam*, while his fellow of higher rank calls his house a *mana* or *manakkal*.[65]

This imprint of hierarchical divisions within a speech community is perhaps most clearly witnessed in diglossia. Ferguson (to whom we owe the initial use of this term in English) had noticed this phenomenon in the coexistence of 'high' and 'low' varieties of dialects in Arabic, Modern Greek, Swiss German and Haitian Creole. The first and more prestigious of the two was used for religious sermons, academic or political lectures, personal correspondence, newspaper editorials, etc., and the second for instructions to servants, waiters, workmen and clerks, for conversation among friends, colleagues and members of one's family, for use in folk literature, and so on.[66] The same could be said of the native speakers of Java where, as Geertz has observed, 'the entire etiquette system is perhaps best summed up and symbolized in the way [they] used their language'. He goes so far as to say that 'in Javanese it is nearly impossible to say anything without indicating the social relationship between the speaker and the listener in terms of status and familiarity'.[67]

Diglossia of this kind, if not quite on the same scale, has been a traditional feature of many of the linguistic communities in India. For instance, the well-entrenched caste division between Brahman and non-Brahman in parts of southern India has been found to correspond to dialectal differences between Brahman and non-Brahman speech in Tamil and Kannada both with regard to vocabulary and to salient aspects of phonology and morphology.[68] Class characteristics, too, are often branded on speech. Thus, in a Hindi-speaking village of northern India, Gumperz noticed how the distinction between *moti boli* (coarse speech) and *saf boli* (refined speech) stood for the social distance separating the 'poorer Rajputs and members of the lower castes who spend their days in physical labour' from the 'wealthier Rajputs, merchants and artisans, those who held clerical positions, and especially political leaders'. The speech of the untouchable sweeper, ranked lowest both in class and caste, diverged significantly from that of his high-caste

[65] Ibid.: 85. [66] Ferguson: 233–7 *et passim*. [67] Geertz: 167.
[68] Bright & Ramanujan: 158–61 *et passim*.

master although he spent much of his time every day on chores around the latter's household.[69]

There is yet another aspect to differences of this kind. The same speaker would often vary his speech between the 'high' and the 'low' dialectal modes depending on the solemnity of an occasion or the importance of the person addressed. Even a person of high status could use the moti boli in speaking to his servants or his junior kin, while he would almost invariably adopt the saf boli as a vehicle of discourse on elevated political or religious topics.[70] Such switching between a formal and an informal style, corresponding by and large to a literary and a colloquial style, is common to speakers of many Indian languages including the two Dravidian varieties mentioned above. However, the freedom of switching from one to the other, especially from low to high, is far from absolute. Whether this is permitted at all, and if so to what extent, depends on the speaker's standing relative to the addressee's: this is all right when a person is speaking to his subordinates or equals, but anathema if the addressee happens to be of superior status. For the formal or high style is often closely associated with education, and in a land where most people are illiterate and far too poor to pay for schooling of any kind, this appears, by contrast, as an unmistakable sign of elite culture and authority. To adopt that mode of speech is therefore to claim an elite standing which is, of course, denied to the subaltern. This is why in a UP village the Chamar may not imitate Rajput speech 'for fear of incurring the displeasure of the higher castes'[71] nor a Bengali peasant utter *sadhubhasha*, the characteristic speech of the bhadralok elite, as an indigo planter's dewan drives it home to an erring ryot in Dinabandhu Mitra's *Neel-Darpan*.[72]

Nothing demonstrates the involvement of language with authority more forcefully than the fact that usages such as these should be regarded as deviant, hence reprehensible. And it is precisely in order to prevent transgressions of this kind from

[69] Gumperz: 170–1, 194. [70] Ibid.: 168–9. [71] Ibid.: 41.

[72] In an obvious reference to this type of Bengali speech a writer in *Sadhana*, a periodical closely associated with Rabindranath Tagore, wrote in 1891 of *bhadratar bhasha*—speech appropriate to the status of one belonging to any of the three highest Hindu castes in Bengal. *Vide* Anon. (1891): 78. For a discussion of this particular passage in Dinabandhu Mitra's play see Guha (1974): 7.

occurring in real life that societies allow a degree of licensed violation of linguistic etiquette to be ritually acted out at calendrical intervals just as they provide for prescriptive rebellions as an insurance against real ones. This is why verbal aggression figured so prominently in carnivals which, as we have noticed above, functioned as a safety-valve for popular discontent in early modern Europe.[73] Similarly, the ritual exchange of 'cathartic abuse' (*les insultes cathartiques*) by means of 'shameless ditties' (*chants qui point pas la honte*) sung by rival groups of men and women in the course of harvesting and mowing was regarded as a positively 'liberating' influence on the Dogon of western Africa.[74] To the south of that continent the chanting of lewd songs was a customary part of certain Zulu agricultural operations as well as of the ceremonial shifting of a Tsonga village site. 'The village is broken to pieces', it was said in justification of the latter, 'so are the ordinary laws. The insults which are taboo are now allowed.'[75] In southern India much the same kind of indulgence was shown towards low-caste officiants at Nayar and Coorg propitiatory festivals: they could, on such occasions, utter the unspeakable in voicing pent-up grievances against their high-caste masters or even reprimanding them.[76] And in the northern parts of the country the profusion of verbal abuse has always been a well-established feature of that most radical of all mock rebellions—Holi.

However, indulgence such as this stopped as soon as a breach of verbal etiquette strayed beyond the privileged domain of ritual inversion. It amounted then to what Narada, an ancient Hindu law-giver, had defined as a form of *sāhasa*, that is, a crime of violence.[77] Indeed, the chapter dealing with this type of 'crime' in Kautilya's *Arthaśāstra* finds its place, appropriately enough, between the chapters on robbery and assault.[78] 'Calumny, contemptuous talk or intimidation' are mentioned there as the constituents of such crime and it is a measure of the sensitivity of the elite to unauthorized speech that an expression such as 'a bad Brahman' was to be regarded as 'contemptuous'

[73] Burke: 183–4, 187. [74] Calame-Griaule: 301–6.

[75] Gluckman (1966): 110–11, 116–17.

[76] Gough: 464; Srinivas (1962): 42, 164. [77] G. Jha: 375.

[78] In Shamasastry's translation of Kauṭilya's *Arthaśāstra*, these constitute Chapters 17–19 of Book III.

and punishable.[79] The scale of penalties is revealing too. Though the precise amount of fines imposed on the offender is not quite the same in all the texts, they concur on one basic principle: that is, the lower the status of the speaker relative to that of the object of his insult the higher the penalty, which, as readers familiar with the Smṛtis will recognize, is the very reverse of what was prescribed in the case of 'crimes' of pollution. One could hardly improve on that as an instance of the correspondence between language and social hierarchy. Thus, as Manu says (VIII 267), the penalty for speaking ill of a Brahman increased with the hierarchical distance between him and the speaker: 100 *paṇas* for a Kshatriya offender, 150–200 for a Vaisya, and corporal punishment (*vadham*) for a Sudra. The latter could be imposed in one of three ways depending on the precise character of the Sudra's crime; he could 'have his tongue cut out', or get 'an iron nail, ten fingers long . . . thrust red-hot into his mouth', or have 'hot oil . . . poured into his mouth and into his ears' (*Manu* VIII 270–2).

This ancient recipe (by no means uniquely Indian[80]) for dealing with verbal delinquency by destroying the organs of speech offers some idea of linguistic control in an authoritarian society. And what was sought to be controlled was not the spoken word alone, but also the zero sign of utterance[81]—that

[79] Kauṭilya: 220–1.

[80] For an English and relatively recent parallel see the case of the seventeenth-century author of a blasphemous publication who was punished by having a hole bored through his tongue. Hill (1972): 176.

[81] This conceptualization of prescriptive silence as the zero degree of utterance is based on Saussure's dictum that 'language is satisfied with the opposition between something and nothing' (Saussure: 86). As Barthes has observed, 'the zero degree is . . . not a total absence (this is a common mistake), *it is a significant absence.* We have here a pure differential state; the zero degree testifies to the power held by any system of signs of creating meaning "out of nothing" ' (Barthes (1967): 77). For a detailed discussion of the zero sign, see '*Signe Zéro*' in Jakobson (1971): 211–19. Here again, as in the case of some other concepts, Pāṇini anticipated modern linguistic theory by many centuries. The notion figures in his sutra, '*adarśanam lopaḥ*' (I.1.60) and some of the subsequent rules, such as VI.1.66, VI.4.118, etc. As Vasu has explained it in his edition of the *Ashṭādhyāyī*: 'This *lopa* is considered as a substitute or *ādeśa*, and as such this grammatical *zero* has all the rights and liabilities of the thing which it replaces. This blank or *lopa* is in several places treated as having a real existence and rules are made applicable to it in the same way as to any ordinary substitute that has an apparent form. The Grammarians do not content themselves with one sort of blank but have invented several others . . . which

is, silence used formally and yet eloquently enough as 'a significant absence' of speech. It was as if language was made to operate in a state of Paninian *lopa* and was known only by virtue of its elision so that the ban imposed by custom on various kinds of discourse could announce and display the subordination of junior kin to senior, of wife to husband, of low caste to high caste and generally of the underdog to the elite. In Gujarat a Patidar youth was not to initiate conversation in the company of his elders,[82] and as Beals found out in an Andhra village a young man would be sharply rebuked if he tried to put in a word edgeways 'when big people are talking'. In the same village nuptial songs would insist that to 'keep silent in your husband's house' was a part of a young bride's novitiate.[83] And silence was a sign of subordination to authority in other spheres too. In Orissa, a Bauri untouchable was not to speak to a high caste person until spoken to,[84] while in a UP village 'one frequently finds a lower-caste individual sitting or standing at a slight distance from a higher group engaged in discussion, listening to what is said, but not participating'.[85] In parts of southern India a servant would cover his mouth while receiving his master's command in a sort of metalinguistic acknowledgement of the latter's power over himself.[86] In Bengal a landlord would feel it an affront if a peasant were to speak up to him. When Abu Molla, the hapless tenant-cultivator in Mir Mosharraf Hosein's play, *Jamidar-Darpan*, pleads his inability to pay a fine arbitrarily imposed by the wicked zamindar, the latter has a fit of temper not so much because of what is said but because it is a subordinate talking back. 'Shut up, you son of a pig', he shouts; 'How dare you open your mouth and utter anything in my presence! Take him away at once. Take him away.'[87]

In that play the poor ryot's verbal protest is not followed up by any militant act of resistance to his oppressor. But when a real uprising takes place and turns things upside down, the norms of verbal deference too are demolished together with the authority structures corresponding to them. There has never been an occasion of this kind when the peasant did not desecrate

---

like different sorts of zeroes of a Mathematician have different functions' (Pāṇini: 56).

[82] Pocock: 95. [83] Beals: 46, 73. [84] Freeman: 85.
[85] Gumperz: 194. [86] NNQ: 80. [87] Hosein: 50.

language either by direct abuse addressed to his superiors or by adopting the latter's mode of speech and thereby breaking into the hallowed precincts of elite culture. 'Violent, even ferocious, language used by rioting groups' was a prominent feature of the agricultural labourers' revolt in England in 1830.[88] And it was all a part of the rebellious self-assertion of the Hunan peasantry in 1927 that, as Mao Tse-tung reported at the time, 'not a day passes but they drum some harsh, pitiless words of denunciation into these [evil] gentry's ears'.[89]

There is hardly an instance of open and violent conflict between Indian villagers of different castes or classes that does not lower and often cross the threshold of verbal etiquette. The terms of an altercation as recorded by Freeman in an Oriya village bring this out. The exchange of insults here between an untouchable farm hand of the Bauri caste and his landowning, Brahman master reaches a climax making the latter scream, 'This wife's-brother Bauri boy speaks like a king. Has your face gone up, as if proud, or what?'[90] Clearly, the unspeakable has been spoken and a social distance measured out in words or denoted by their absence, violated. This however was merely a quarrel between two individuals involving no physical assault at all. A great deal more can and does happen when violent disputes involving large masses of the local population break out in any particular village or region. The abuses, insults and, generally speaking, breaches in the norm of social discourse are often far too numerous and figure far too integrally in such cases to be noticed and reported on their own. Indulgence in 'bad' language is taken for granted on these occasions. Indeed the violence against person and property dominates events of this kind to such an extent as to make verbal violence relatively unimportant for purposes of administrative or judicial intervention. Since official records constitute the principal source of our information about such conflicts, it is easily understood why the Kautilyan category of *vākpārushyam* (verbal violence) had so

[88] H & R: 211–12. Breaches of verbal deference in times of acute class conflict were not an exclusively rural phenomenon in England. During the uneasy times preceding the outbreak of the civil war the 'hatred of the citizens' of London 'unto gentlemen, especially courtiers' was such that very few of the latter 'durst come into the City, or if they did, they were sure to receive affronts and be abused' (Hill (1972): 18).

[89] Mao: I 30.

[90] Freeman: 363.

little to do with the historical evidence on rural crimes under the Raj. Yet one can perhaps make up for this lacuna to some extent by recalling some of the idealized accounts of peasant violence in nineteenth-century literature. Take, for instance, Act III, Scene 3 of *Neel-Darpan* where Torap, the rebel peasant, confronts the white planter and beats him up to the accompaniment of a shower of abuse describing the latter variously as wife's-brother, as a dog and a thief—insults which under conditions other than insurgency would be addressed, the other way round, by planter to peasant. This linguistic inversion was homologous to the reversal brought about by the 'blue mutiny' in the relationship which had existed until then between the indigo factories and the rural masses in the Bengal districts dominated by them.

A conspicuous aspect of this verbal inversion, as anyone familiar with the text of this play would notice, is Torap's use of the intimate, hence in this case derogatory, pronoun *tui* and its derivatives rather than the reverential *apni*, in addressing his superordinate foe. These Bengali words correspond respectively to the French *tu* (*T*) and *vous* (*V*), and stand for what has been described as the 'nonreciprocal power semantic'. According to this notion the more powerful of any two interlocutors says *T* and receives *V*, all relations such as 'older than', 'parent of', 'employer of', 'stronger than', 'nobler than' and other hierarchical expressions which can be assimilated to these being subsumed for the purpose of this generalization under the term 'more powerful than'. Brown and Gilman who have done much to investigate the *T–V* index of authority in many cultures, past and present, have observed that it is 'associated with a relatively static society in which power is distributed by birthright and is not subject to much redistribution'.[91] They have situated it historically in the feudal and manorial systems of medieval Europe and identified it as a marker of 'caste difference' between the black native and the white colonialist in French Africa. In post-colonial India they found 'this truly feudal pronominal pattern', part of a long-standing tradition,[92] still largely

[91] Brown & Gilman: 265. Much of the argument and information in this paragraph and the one which follows, is based on this excellent article, and all direct quotations are taken from it, unless otherwise stated.

[92] To address one's superior by *T* was an offence according to Manu: *tvamkāraṃ-*

operative in the *T–V* expressions used in the Gujarati and Hindi languages nonreciprocally between elder brother and younger brother as well as between husband and wife. The series could of course be extended to the entire range of power relations including those of caste and class in many of the other Indian speech communities too.

When the feudal or semi-feudal authority structure of a society like any of these is overturned or seriously challenged by insurgency, the conventional use of *T–V* as a particularly sensitive register of existing power relations comes under attack at the same time. The French Revolution has provided us with a classic instance of such verbal *bouleversement*. A speaker at a session of the new parliament in 1793 condemned the asymmetric deployment of these pronouns as an expression of 'l'esprit de fanatisme, d'orgueil et de féodalité' and the Committee for the Public Safety 'ordered a universal reciprocal *T*'. For some time the mutual *tu* became a sort of linguistic badge of revolutionary citizenship and when Robespierre addressed the president of l'Assemblée Nationale by this pronoun, it was clear that the old order had indeed come to an end. But here, as in some other respects, the innovations of a victorious bourgeois democracy were anticipated by its uncouth and naive precursor—peasant insurgency. The substitution, albeit spontaneous, of *V* by *T* was a well established feature of the German Peasant War of 1525 and we have it on Zimmermann's authority that the rebels often used the more familiar *du* instead of the honorific *Sie* in denouncing and mocking the nobility overpowered by them.[93] In colonial India the Bengali ryot's violation of the rules of pronominal deference in the course of disturbances like those of 1860 had its parallel in Malayali usage during the Moplah risings of the 1850s. It was a sign of these Malabar peasants' subalternity that the powerful Nayar landlords addressed them

---

cha gariasah (XI. 205) and required a penitential bath, fasting and a conciliatory bow before the offended person as a corrective.

[93] See, for instance, Zimmermann: I 393, 394. 'Das hast *du* nun lange genug gehabt, ich will auch einmal ein Graf sein', says a piper of the peasant army to a Count as he grabs the latter's hat and puts it on (ibid.: 393); and the rebels mock a Countess thus as they put her in a dung cart: 'in einem goldenen Wagen bist *du* nach Weinsberg eingefahren; in einem Mistwagen fährst *du* hinaus' (ibid.: 394) Emphasis added. For some other instances of such use of *T* in 1525, see Bax: 127.

in terms of *T* while they responded by *V*. In 1852, however, in a series of instructions aimed at stimulating Moplah resistance the Thangal of Thirurangadi called upon his followers to drop the customary *V* and return *T* for *T* in verbal exchanges with the *jenmi* as an open demonstration of their will to challenge the latter's overlordship.[94]

The inversion of verbal authority brought about by rebellion was not limited to spoken utterance alone but extended to its graphic form as well. There was hardly a peasant uprising on any significant scale in colonial India that did not cause the destruction of large quantities of written or printed material including rent rolls, deeds and bonds, and public records of all kinds. When in the course of the dhing against Deby Sinha the ryots of Dinajpur attacked his kachari at Dihi Jumtah, they made it a point to take away the papers they found there,[95] and this was the fate common to landlords' estate offices wherever these lay in the path of a jacquerie. Again, popular violence was often astutely selective about all written evidence of peasant debts. Even the semi-official *Calcutta Gazette* noticed how during the Barasat insurrection led by Titu Mir a raid on an indigo factory in the neighbourhood did not lead to 'mere wanton destruction', for apart from a little damage done to some furniture only its 'papers were destroyed [and done so] most probably by the villagers for the purpose of destroying the record of their own debts'.[96] In much the same way, the revolt of the Kunbi peasantry in Poona and Ahmadnagar districts in 1875 was distinguished by its singular concentration on the instruments of usury. 'The object of the rioters was in every case to obtain and destroy the bonds, decrees etc in their creditors' possession', according to the Commission set up to inquire into these disturbances. Indeed it was led to believe that this 'was not so much [a] rebellion against the oppressor as an attempt to accomplish a definite and practical object, namely, the disarming of the enemy by taking his weapons (bonds and accounts)'.[97] Large deposits of official documentation too were often wrecked by insurgent crowds. The *levée en masse* triggered off by the Mutiny ended up by destroying 'all records of every kind' in Hamirpur district of Uttar Pradesh, as its magistrate

[94] Dhanagare: 124. [95] MDS: 582.
[96] Das Gupta: 686. [97] DRCR: 3, 4.

was ruefully to observe soon after the event. In Muzaffarnagar, again, the records of the Civil, Criminal and Collectorate Duftars were burnt by the local population on the night of 14 May 1857, an incident regarded by the irate local officer as by no means 'a solitary instance' but as part of a pattern seen 'throughout this rebellion' of the burning of government offices by 'budmashes'.[98]

Regarded from a less hostile perspective, however, one could see in all this a rather different pattern—that of the objectification of the peasants' hatred for the written word. He had learnt, at his own cost, that the rent roll could deceive; that the bond could keep him and his family in almost perpetual servitude; that official papers could be used by clerks, judges, lawyers and landlords to rob him of his land and livelihood. Writing was thus, to him, the sign of his enemy, and 'favoured the exploitation of human beings rather than their enlightenment'.[99] The sense of these words was dyed into his soul by his everyday experience. On Lévi-Strauss, to whom we owe this formulation, its truth dawned in a flash as he witnessed the very first attempts at a crude mimicry of writing (inspired unintentionally by the anthropologist himself) and the uses made of it by a Nambikwara chief fraudulently to retain his authority over his illiterate people living in conditions of a Stone Age culture in the Brazilian jungles.

The reaction of the Nambikwara to writing was as forthright as it was negative. Having 'felt in some obscure way that writing and deceit had penetrated simultaneously into their midst' they deserted their chief and their village and retreated to a remote area of the bush.[100] In an equally negative gesture the Indian peasant who had nowhere to hide when driven to desperation, burnt down the graphic instruments of zamindari, sahukari and sarkari dominance—the deeds, bonds, *khatas* and files, and their repositories—the kachari, the gadi and the government office. This by itself contributed significantly enough to turning things upside down in the countryside and conformed, as such, to a

[98] FSUP: III 113; V 80–1.

[99] Lévi-Strauss (1976): 392. For a full account of the episode which inspired this observation and other reflections on writing, see ibid.: 385–99. The author returns to this subject in his conversations with Charbonnier: see Lévi-Strauss (1969): 29–31.

[100] Lévi-Strauss (1976): 394.

tradition of insurgency as old as Jack Cade.[101] But the process was taken a step further in some instances by the rebel trying, positively, to appropriate the sign of writing for himself.

Ideally such appropriation should have been no problem at all. The peasant could avail himself of the institutional means which were there precisely for this purpose. He could go to school, at least to its lowest denomination, at the village *pathsala* and acquire the three Rs. Unfortunately, however, he lived in no ideal world. The colonial government, keen on educating the middle classes in order to ensure manpower for its administration, was hardly interested in bringing literacy to the tillers of the soil. Primary education for the latter was left to the mercy and munificence of local landlords who took pride in setting up schools on their estates but were careful not to encourage too much literacy among the ryots. When Govinda Samanta, the hero of Lal Behari Day's well-known story about rural Bengal, pleads his inability to pay an arbitrary feudal levy (mathot), this is immediately seen as insolence bred by primary education. For he had indeed attended the village pathsala for some years when he was a child. 'So you have become a *pandita* [man of learning]', shouts the zamindar at him, 'and your eyes have got opened, therefore you refuse to pay the mathot. I must forbid Rama Rupa [the schoolmaster] to teach any peasants' sons.'[102] This was fairly representative of the attitude of the rural elite towards education for the peasantry under the Raj. Teach the *chasha* the three Rs and he will 'have his eyes opened' and learn to resist!

In no way therefore was the peasant in a position to appropriate writing as it really was, that is, as the graphic re-

[101] Jack Cade, the leader of the peasant rising in Kent in 1450, 'proposed to burn all legal records, and "henceforward all things shall be in common".' Hill (1974): 185.

[102] Day: 198. To some extent the attitude seems to have continued into the present century. As a nationalist organizer active among the peasantry in a northern Bengal region in the late 1920s found out, a white man in charge of a local office of the Midnapore Zamindari Company's estates in these parts was extremely upset to learn that the peasants had started a *pathshala* (indigenous primary school) in a certain village. He ordered it to be burnt down at once (S. Chowdhury: 43). Even in post-colonial India Beals was to find the landlord of an Andhra village and his assistant, the Police Headman, unenthusiastic about promoting education for the village children (Beals: 62–3).

presentation of a natural language. Want of literacy barred him access to it as a secular, intellectual aid to remembering, learning, understanding. In order therefore to use it for insurgency, for purposes of reversing the world, he appropriated it symbolically. He had been conditioned by his own subalternity and the elite monopoly of culture to look upon writing as a symbol of dominance. Lévi-Strauss noticed how in some of the villages of what is now Bangladesh the moneylender also functioned as the local scribe and this combination gave him a 'hold over others'.[103] Indeed all who had a hold over the peasant, whether as rentiers, usurers or officials, used writing as a direct instrument of authority in one form or another. He regarded this, as he did many other expressions of power in a semi-feudal society, not as a social, empirical phenomenon, but as something that was quasi-religious and magical: to write was not a matter of skill but of inspiration. The written word was endowed with the same sort of mediatory, occult quality as he customarily attributed to the spoken utterances of an oracle possessed by the spirit of the dead during a propitiatory ceremony. The popular Hindu association of writing with priesthood on the one hand and with deities like Ganesa and Saraswati on the other enhanced this sense of sanctity about it. It was this sacred and magical power of writing which Sido and Kanhu appropriated for themselves as they declared war on the sahib and the diku.

Writing figures so prominently indeed in the Santal leaders' own perception of the hool that it is not possible for the historian to ignore it. The uses made of it for the transmission of insurgency will be discussed in Chapter 5 below. What concerns us here is the authority they derived from it in the conduct of the hostilities. Both the Subahs acknowledged, in retrospect, that their decision to launch the insurrection had been directly prompted by writing. But this was writing seen as divine intervention. As Sido explained at the interrogation following his arrest,

> half a piece of paper fell on my head before the Thacoor came & half fell afterwards. I could not read but Chand & Seheree & a Dhome read it, they said 'The Thacoor has *written* to you to fight the Mahajens & then you will have justice'.[104]

[103] Lévi-Strauss (1976): 391.

[104] JP, 8 Nov. 1855: 'Examination of Sedoo Sonthal late Thacoor'. Emphasis added.

This, he said, was 'the Thacoor's order'—an order given in *writing*. Kanhu was to confirm this later on when he, in his turn, was captured and related the circumstances leading to the revolt. Asked, 'What was the Thacoor like?' he replied:

Ishwar [God] was a white man with only a dootee & chudder he sat on the ground like a Sahib he wrote on this bit of paper. He gave me 4 papers but afterwards presented 16 more.[105]

Thus the authority of the graphic form was further reinforced by fusing together the images of a supernatural being, a white official and a native scribe sitting cross-legged on the floor and scribbling away. In what was clearly a case of overdetermination, the power of the colonialist sahib and that of the pen-pushing dhoti-clad babu were telescoped here in a composite vision and raised to divine power. The apotheosis of writing could not be more explicit nor indeed its use by the insurgents to justify turning the world upside down in the Thakur's name.

Of the non-verbal expressions of authority which come under attack in all uprisings, there are those which are paralinguistic in character and operate as kinesic and proxemic systems under the sign respectively of gestures and body movements and that of distances in space and time.[106] Every society treats the body as a memory in which to store the basic principles of its culture 'in abbreviated and practical, i.e. mnemonic form', as Bourdieu has observed. This is particularly true of pre-literate societies 'which lack any other recording and objectifying instrument' so that 'inherited knowledge can survive only in its embodied state'.[107] It is quite in order therefore that gestures of obeisance should figure so prominently in the Hindu Dharmaśāstras as the key to a better life. Why, for instance, must a youth leave his seat and greet an older man? 'For', says Manu, 'the vital airs of a young man mount upwards to leave his body when an elder approaches; but by rising to meet him and saluting he recovers them.' (II 120) There are many other verses in that text devoted to the virtues of rising, prostrating, clasping of feet, etc. as indicative of subordinate status. And the authority of this

[105] JP, 20 Dec. 1855: 'Examination of Kanoo Sonthal'.

[106] Our use of the terms 'paralinguistic', 'kinesic' and 'proxemic' follows the sense in which these have been defined in Lyons: I 63–7.

[107] Bourdieu: 170, 218 n. 44.

language of the body derived not only from sacerdotal prescriptions but also from the power of the state. Thus according to Abū-l Fazl, kings 'made regulations for the manner in which people are to show their obedience'. This was meant to promote 'true humility'. For instance, *kornish*, an approved mode of salutation at the Mughal court, signified that the saluter 'placed his head . . . (the seat of the senses and the mind) into the hand of humility, giving it to the royal assembly as a present', and another, known as *taslim*, that he was 'ready to give himself as an offering'.[108]

The substitution of Mughal royalty by the British made little difference to such feudal kinesics. They continued to operate as status markers in colonial India too. 'When a Coorg meets an elder on a ritual occasion', wrote Srinivas, 'he has to salute the latter by bending the upper half of his body and touching the elder's feet thrice with both hands. After each touch the younger man takes his hands to his forehead, where he folds them together.' This, he remarked, was not very different from the form of salutation one adopted towards a deity.[109] In fact, variations of 'bodily automatism' of this kind featured in all homologous relations—between father and son, husband and wife, landlord and tenant, high caste and low caste. In Madhya Pradesh, for instance, it was customary for the wife to demonstrate her fidelity by bending down before her husband at a distance and touching the earth with her fingers. A Balahi, ranked as one of the lowliest in rural society in this region, would replicate this movement on meeting a Brahman, bending forward to touch the ground and lifting his hands, palms folded to his forehead. Elsewhere, in Orissa, a Bauri untouchable had to adopt much the same self-debasing posture under similar circumstances. 'When we passed by higher-caste people', said Muli to the visiting anthropologist, 'we crouched so that one hand touched the ground; we walked by in that position, so that our faces were toward the ground.'[110]

It was not the rise and fall of empires but the violence of the masses which alone interrupted from time to time this age-old avowal of subservience by gestures. Yet another index of the world turned upside down, this might have been the reversal

[108] Abū-l Fazl: 166–7. [109] Srinivas (1952): 47, 96.
[110] Dube: 77; Fuchs: 80; Freeman: 85.

feared by the dominant brahmanical culture when among the many topsy-turvy features of the mythical 'epoch's end' (*yugānta*) it counted Sudras who were 'controlled in the movement of their eyes' (*jitākshah*), not unlike, presumably, their superiors in the varna hierarchy![111] Less fantastically, however, and indeed in our own epoch there have been occasions in the course of agrarian disturbances when insulting gestures appeared to have hurt the peasants' enemies no less than acts of physical assault. A detail of the Birsaite ulgulan should make this clear. On 16 August 1895 the villagers of Chalkad drove out a police party which had camped out there for about a week in an attempt to seize the Munda chief but had failed to do so. As the posse began to withdraw in the face of superior insurgent forces, this was how it felt to the Head Constable of Tamar to be, for once, at the receiving end:

> We then moved off by the Birbanki road towards Tamar followed by some 800 to 900 men who were having [sic] winnowing fans, beating toms and waving bows as insults to us. They were also carrying the three bedsteads (*khatia*) on which we had lain. These latter they flung into the river which we reached about one mile from Chalkad . . . In throwing the *khatias* in the river the crowd exclaimed, 'The Sarkar's Raj is at an end and their servants are dead, hence we throw their beds into the river.' They were beating the toms and the fans not only as insulting signs but as a very inauspicious thing, as they consider Birsa was preaching to the people not to attend to the *bhooth* or make sacrifice but to obey him.[112]

There are references in this account to physical violence, too—to the guardians of the law being pushed and hustled and pricked with spears by the pursuing Mundas. What however sticks out in the Head Constable's memory of this ordeal is the rebels' use of the 'insulting signs'. Far from being treated as the august representatives of the sarkar to the accompaniment of obsequious body movements they were treated as *bhut*, dead souls fit only to be exorcised by the whiff of winnowing fans and the noise of drums. Far from being regarded as distinguished guests who brought prestige to a village by visiting it, they were unceremoniously rejected as polluting agents so that even the beds they had slept in had to be thrown away in a simulation of funerary rites. Far from being feared as the strong arm of the

[111] Tarkaratna (1910): 58/59. [112] Singh: 56–7.

state they were mocked and defied by the Mundas flaunting their bows at them. In other words, what shocked the Head Constable was that these downtrodden and docile people had 'now audaciously *lifted up their heads*' (as Mao was to say of the Hunan peasantry)—a figure of speech signifying the very opposite of what bending and prostrating stood for.

There is yet another class of paralinguistic signs which represents social rank and grade in terms of distances. Thus temporal distances indicating degrees of authority were often expressed as rights of precedence. In nineteenth-century Calcutta clan leaders used to fight over precedence during the ceremonial distribution of sandal paste and flowers at sacred recitals and funeral banquets.[113] Again in Malwa, according to Mayer, a wife's standing in her husband's family varied according to whether she was allowed to have her meal at the same time as the other women of the household or afterwards.[114] Among the Coorgs the headman was traditionally called the *mūpayanda*, which means 'having precedence', and as Srinivas observes, 'the sense of precedence is ubiquitous'. It was the headman who took the first shot at target-shooting contests on ritual occasions, it was he who led the village dance at harvest festivals, and it was his pack-bullocks which had the right to lead a caravan.[115] Precedence such as this governed relations between castes as well. In Nimar district a high-caste villager's bullock-cart had the right of way over a Balahi's, and in agricultural operations high-caste farmers had the right to help themselves first to the local supplies of labour: 'Only after they are satisfied will field servants go to work on the fields of their Balahi creditors.'[116]

Foil to these were distances in space used both laterally and vertically as status markers. 'The regulation of the difference among men in rank' at Akbar's court was quite clearly a matter of seating and standing arrangements: the nearer a royal prince or nobleman was to the throne, the more important he was supposed to be.[117] Centuries later distance was still very much in evidence as an index of seniority in age and caste in rural society. It was a part of Coorg etiquette that a youth did not

[113] Bandyopadhyay: 28. [114] Mayer: 220.
[115] Srinivas (1952): 63, 205.
[116] Fuchs: 81, 93. [117] Abū-l Fazl: 168–9.

walk with an elder side by side but a few respectful paces behind him.[118] Informal gatherings around a cot in a UP village often conformed to the same pattern. 'If all are members of one caste, the oldest person sits at the head of the cot . . . others sit next in order of prestige ranking. If a Brahman is present he will be offered the head seat. Lower caste persons and sometimes also poor Rajputs will sit on the floor and untouchables at a slight distance from the group.'[119] Notice how the inferiority of the poorer Rajputs and untouchables is indicated by the fact of their having to squat on the floor while the Brahman has his seat on the cot. This constitutes yet another aspect of proxemics, that is, the expression of hierarchical differences in terms of levels of seating. The subordinate must not be seated above the superordinate. An unmistakably feudal notion, this too has an ancestry stretching back to the Smṛtis. 'When his teacher is nigh', said Manu (II 198), a pupil must 'let his bed or seat be low'. The principle worked with the followers of Islam as well. When the Pir Pagaro was taken out in a ceremonial procession, a devout Hur, we are told, left her perch on the roof of a nearby house so that she would not be situated higher than her spiritual leader when the latter passed along that road.[120] Secular authority also operated by the same sign. Beals observed that in Gopalpur even the more important men of the village would, when they called on the landlord, sit on the ground beneath the platform occupied by the latter.[121]

Distance thus was a measure of prestige. No wonder that the followers of Birsa remembered this when in explaining to their people how they 'had lost their honour and were biting dust', they mentioned that the Mundas were, among other humiliations, barred by the Raja and the zamindars from using chairs and high seats.[122] Indeed their revolt, like all others of its kind, was made up of the peasant's urge to recover his self-respect by eliminating or turning against his oppressors the apparently innocuous, because traditionally tolerated, signs of subalternity, such as those of prescribed distances, which had been imposed on them. Inversions of this order occur frequently and on a large scale in the course of all such massive explosions of violence. The rule of differential heights is broken whenever the

[118] Srinivas (1952): 48. [119] Gumperz: 159. [120] Lambrick: 31.
[121] Beals: 61. [122] Singh: 77.

peasants ride past a landlord's or an upper-caste man's house on horseback during a riot in defiance of customary prohibitions. The calculated and otherwise inviolable margins of avoidance in a caste-ridden society sensitive to pollution are necessarily infringed whenever they raid a zamindar's or a bania's residence, or lay their hands on the person of anyone in authority.[123] Violations of this kind are indeed so numerous that these are almost taken for granted in reporting or commenting on rural disturbances, so that what catches the observer's eye and survives the levelling influence of redundancy in his narrative is the destruction by the rebel of the more obvious symbols of his enemy's power.

Such symbols constitute the staple of peasant grievances. The rural masses everywhere use these both as a measure of their own deprivation and as objectives worth fighting for when roused to do so. These figure therefore conspicuously in all rebel discourse—in that ancestral voice of insurgency, John Ball's Sunday exhortations, as well as in the Birsaite propaganda on the eve of the ulgulan. 'They are clad in velvet and camlet lined with squirrel and ermine, while we go dressed in coarse cloth', said the 'crack-brained priest of Kent', contrasting the lords' way of life with the serfs': 'They have the wines, the spices and the good bread: we have the rye, the husks and the straw, and we drink water. They have shelter and ease in their fine manors, and we have hardship and toil, the wind and the rain in the fields. And from us must come, from our labour, the things which keep them in luxury.'[124] Dress, food, mansions—these and other 'things which keep them in luxury', crowd into all *cahiers de doléances* wherever they originate. Adapted to Indian

[123] Anthropological literature is packed with details of prohibitions imposed on low-caste villagers with regard to riding, access to upper-caste houses, etc. Thus, in Nimar district of Madhya Pradesh, 'a Balahi riding a horse must dismount when he meets a high-caste man or when he passes through a village. Rajputs often force a Balahi rider to dismount if he forgets to do so' (Fuchs: 81). Again, in Malabar a high-caste Hindu's main house used to be located, according to Logan, at the very centre of a rectangular residential space surrounded by a garden. 'The reason for the selection of this spot is explained to be that a Malayali tries to be as far as possible away from the polluting caste people who may approach the house as far as the fence, but may not enter the garden' (Logan: 84).

[124] Froissart: 212.

conditions, hence with some variation of detail, the same sort of contrast is implied in the Munda *pracharaks*' enumeration of the wrongs (some elements of which have been noticed above) suffered by their tribe.

The Raja and zamindars exploited them and reduced them to a position of carriers (forced and unpaid labourers) and dependants, deprived them 'of their clothes, their *dhoti* and garments, turban and footwear'; they could not use even an umbrella. They were not allowed to sit on chairs and high seat, to enter a temple or to eat from golden or silver or brass plates . . .[125]

The list of course could be longer. For the authority the elite had over the peasantry was nearly all-pervasive and symbolized by many objects and attitudes. Indeed the struggle for any significant change in existing power relations in the countryside often appears as a contest between those who are determined to retain their traditional monopoly of such status symbols and others who are keen on appropriating them—that is, as a cultural conflict. This is why all dominant cultures are particularly sensitive to anything which even remotely looks like usurpation and quick to discipline offenders.

Take, for instance, the set of symbols which related directly to the body either as its parts or as ornament and garment. Physical characteristics were often regarded as indicative of rank both by peasants and their enemies. The leaders of the rebel Tuchin movement of central France in the fourteenth century suspected courtliness or elegance in all who had smooth uncalloused hands, and rather than recruiting them to their bands, marked them out for killing.[126] Conversely, the brahmanical nightmare of a cataclysmic upheaval, as evoked by the *Vāyupurāṇam* (58:59), had in it the image of Sudras with teeth as white as those of members of the higher varnas. Even under less mythical circumstances the rural elite have been known for their aversion to sharing any of their own distinctive physical styles with their social inferiors. The curled, up-turned moustache represents one such style for upper-caste upper-class males in many parts of India. When a member of the traditionally labouring community of Bareias was found sporting such a moustache in a Gujarat village dominated by rich and

[125] Singh: 77. [126] Hilton: 132.

politically powerful Patidars, he was forcibly shaved, beaten up and driven out beyond its boundaries. This anecdote was recorded by an anthropologist as evidence of 'greater concern with caste order in the past',[127] presumably in colonial times and before. However, in the light of the facts published by the Elayaperumal Committee's report, it seems that the ban on the up-turned moustache continues to be a feature of the outcaste's subalternity even in India today.[128]

Objects of wear too were seen as status markers. It was 'out of respect to the higher castes' that no woman of the Bharia caste of farm-servants and agricultural labourers in Madhya Pradesh would wear a nose-ring, as Russell and Lal had noticed.[129] Many decades later social inferiority still continued to be denoted in much the same way in Uttar Pradesh by means of sanctions against the use of jewellery by outcastes: 'Shoemaker women, for example, report having been prevented by Rajputs from wearing ornaments and clothes similar to those of the Rajput women.'[130] Umbrellas and shoes too have been jealously guarded symbols. A part of the insignia of feudal monarchies the umbrella retained some of its importance as an exclusive 'sign of noble rank . . . not permitted to the commonalty', even after it had ceased to be an appanage of kings.[131] Throughout the colonial period it continued to operate as a general index of dominance and subordination, sorting out, especially in the rural areas, the rulers and the ruled, high caste and low caste, and so on: in Champaran no Indian 'whatever his status' could hold an umbrella on his head in the presence of a white planter, nor could a Bania do so while passing by a Bundela Rajput's house in Saugor.[132] Shoes, too, could offend if worn in the presence of one's superiors. Members of the lower castes, particularly if they were women, had to take these off on meeting a high-caste man and in some villages even while going past an upper-caste residence or through caste Hindu wards.[133] Indeed, umbrellas or shoes could be so suggestive of power that often

[127] Pocock: 28. [128] Hiro: 9. [129] Russell & Lal: II 249–50.

[130] Gumperz: 41.

[131] Russell & Lal: II 451. Abū-l Fazl: 52 mentions the *Chatr* and the *Saya-ban* among the 'ensigns of royalty'.

[132] Kripalani: 66; Russell & Lal: II 453, IV 439.

[133] Fuchs: 81; Russell & Lal: II 249, IV 439; Hiro: 9.

under conditions of growing antagonism between the peasant and his enemies both sides regarded these as symbolic sites of conflict. The ban imposed on their use by the diku landlords was felt to be an unbearable tyranny by the Mundas as they became increasingly politicized. Conversely, the Tamil Nadu landlord who identified shod feet as the symptom of rebelliousness among agricultural labourers at the time of the Kilvenmani massacre, spoke up against what was, to his class, a real affront: 'Things used to be very peaceful here some years ago. The labourers were very hard-working and respectful. But now . . . the fellow who used to stand in the backyard of my house to talk to me comes straight to the verandah wearing slippers and all. . . . These fellows have become lazy and arrogant, thanks to the Communists. They have no fear in them any more.'[134]

However, of all things worn on the person it is clothes which are the most semioticized. For the body 'as purely sensuous, is without significance',[135] and it is clothing, writes Barthes following this Hegelian dictum, which 'ensures the passage from the sensuous to the meaningful: it is, one could say, the signified par excellence'.[136] Nowhere is this more explicit than in the countryside where the distinction between peasants and others—townsmen, officials, gentry, etc.—is often perceived as one of dress in the first instance. 'Dress is a fundamental element of distinction', said Gramsci about Italy.[137] Indeed, this was true of most societies, especially of those vegetating for long under colonial and semi-feudal conditions. It is known, for instance, that in Bolivia under Spanish rule dress was 'a means of publicly manifesting the status of the *persona*' and of 'social control in favour of the estamental order'.[138] In India too castes, classes and ethnic groups were often differentiated by the clothes their members wore and the manner of wearing them. The Bengali bhadralok was utterly self-conscious about his dress, for 'no self-respecting person could go about his business in society wrapping himself up in a dirty knee-length *gamcha*', wrote the *Sadhana* in a clear reference to typically lower-class garment.[139]

134 Anon. (1973): 926–7. 135 Hegel (1975): 745.
136 Barthes (1967*): 261. 137 Gramsci: 272. 138 Pearse: 138.
139 Anon. (1891): 78. A *gamchha* is a short, hand-woven cotton fabric used mostly to dry the body after a bath, but also worn sometimes as a loin-cloth by those too poor to afford a dhoti.

In south India it was obligatory for a low-caste man to approach anyone of the upper castes or indeed for a servant his master by first stripping himself to the waist as a mark of respect.[140] In Gujarat, the so-called impure Mahars 'were not allowed to tuck up their loin-cloth but had to trail it along the ground', while in central India among the Kurmi the difference in length between the peasant's jacket, *bandi*, covering the trunk only up to the hips and the landlord's long coat, *angrakha*, reaching down to the knees, was indicative of the difference in their social standing.[141] And among the Santals the word *deko* referred not only to alien Hindu landlords, but also, according to Bödding, 'any Indian in good clothing'.[142]

It is not surprising therefore that in societies so sensitive to dress differentials any serious crisis of authority should be expressed in sartorial terms as well. Dress has indeed a way of insinuating itself into the history of all of the more widespread and militant agrarian movements. It is at such times that distinctions of this order tend to generate the utmost animosity and many of the reversals characteristic of these conflicts are acted out symbolically by the reallocation of garments and styles of wear between peasants and their enemies. Zimmermann recorded a number of such incidents in his account of the German Peasant War of 1525—an insurgent snatching away a nobleman's hat and putting it on himself, some of the counts forced to take off their gloves by the peasants while the latter keep theirs on in defiance of all rules of etiquette, and so on.[143] During the Bolivian peasants' revolt of 1899 all who wore trousers (*pantalones*) or rather were not clad in coarse rustic homespuns, were marked out by the rebels as their enemies. Willka, their leader, had it as one of his aims to try and abolish distinctions of dress between the estaments by introducing the use of homespun for all; and following a tradition of insurgency going back to the eighteenth century they forced homespun peasant clothes on townsfolk in some instances.[144] And in Tanzania during the Maji Maji rebellion the Christian missionaries feared that the Ngoni would kill all who wore European clothes.[145]

In rural India, too, dress which discriminated so clearly

[140] Logan: 127–8; NNQ: 80. [141] Russell & Lal: IV 91, 143.
[142] Sinha *et al.*: 122. [143] Zimmermann: I 377, 393.
[144] Pearse: 136–9. [145] Gwassa & Iliffe: 20.

between the elite and the subaltern as a matter of course, acquired an added significance in the eyes of both the parties in periods of serious confrontation between them. The Rangpur dhing of 1783, for instance, broke out at a time when widespread disturbances were not uncommon in that part of Bengal, thanks to gang robberies and incursions of fakirs, sannyasis and predatory soldiers of the East India Company's army. When, therefore, a large gathering was reported from Kadagaon and Magurrah, its character as a mass of rebel peasantry was identified, among other things, by the dress worn by the members of the crowd. 'Each of these peasants has a stick or bamboo in his hand', reported an official witness, 'their dress is like that of the ryots or villagers, they are neither sepahis, fakirs or night robbers.'[146] In yet another historic struggle, that of the tenant cultivators of Pabna in 1873, the manner of dress was recognized by all concerned—landlords, their *proja* and the administration—as an index of class divisions made explicit by antagonism over the rent question. The officer in charge of the sub-division most affected by the bidroha put it in unmistakable terms in a report to the higher authorities:

> This class feeling was so universal that the opinion of any native on the agrarian question may be told to a certainty by looking at his dress. If he wore a light chadar on his shoulder, used shoes on his feet and carried an umbrella, one could make sure that he was a zamindar's man. If merely clad in the dhoti and gamcha he was at heart an unionist.[147]

Dress had a place in the Santal hool, too, as an element of the idiom of that revolt. At the battle of Maheshpur, said Sido after his capture, 'many of the Manjees were dressed in red clothes'. Neither he nor his brothers had taken to wearing red until then. However, it appears that after his death, when the insurrection was at its peak, Kanhu, Chand and Bhairab adopted this rather conspicuous garment as an assertion of authority,[148] as indeed a

[146] Kaviraj: 37. [147] Quoted in Saha. III 108.

[148] JP, 8 Nov. 1855: 'Examination of Sedoo Sonthal late Thacoor'. About three months after Sido's capture, his brothers had set up camp at a village where in an obvious exercise of insurgent authority they had taken a number of hostages in reprisal against what they considered as an act of betrayal by the local community. A raid led by a Major Breuere on that village on 22 October 1855 sur-

gesture of turning things upside down, just as 'Giuliano's solitaire ring, the bunches of chains and decorations with which the anti-French bandits of the 1790s festooned themselves in Southern Italy, would be regarded by the peasants', according to Hobsbawm, 'as symbols of triumph over the rich and powerful'.[149] There was yet another striking instance of the use of dress—the turban (*pagri*), to be precise—as a means of reversal during this rebellion. This form of headgear carries much weight in many regions of rural India. With some local communities, such as the Balahi, it is only the headmen who have the right to wear this. In Gujarat this used to be an exclusive privilege of the dominant caste of Patidars, so that anyone of a lower caste risked being severely punished if he was tempted publicly to try it on. The Mundas, as noticed above, held it against the dikus that the latter denied them the right to put on a turban.[150] And if it was a matter of prestige to wear a pagri, to confer it was all the more so. This is precisely what Kanhu, the supreme commander of the Santals, did at the very height of the insurrection. As stated in a report from Major-General Lloyd on 19 November 1855, 'Kanoo Manjhee with his Brothers and Followers had visited on Bechoo Raout a gwallah the head of the village of Sooria Haut . . . Kanoo had created him a Soobah and as a Symbol of the rank conferred, had bound a turban on his head.'[151] The turban came thus to stand for a historic inversion, for nothing turns the world upside down more radically than when the subaltern feel bold enough to delegate power seized in an act of rebellion.

There were of course other objects, apart from those worn on one's person, which also acted as status symbols and had a part to play in the negative articulation of rebel consciousness. Some of these were means of transport identified with rank in many feudal societies and subject, like the latter, to the shocks and tremors of agrarian disturbances. In a well-known incident of the Peasant War in Germany the rebels used this symbolism

---

prised them and they narrowly escaped falling into enemy hands. 'The three leaders were conspicuous in red garment amonst the fugitives', wrote Major-General Lloyd reporting the incident to GOI in his letter of 1 November 1855 (JP, 22 Nov. 1855).

[149] Hobsbawm: 22. [150] Fuchs: 31; Pocock: 28; Singh: 77.

[151] JP, 6 Dec. 1855: Lloyd to GOB, 19 Nov. 1855.

for a particularly dramatic act of reversal: forcing a wicked countess to sit in a dungcart they mocked her, 'In a golden carriage camest thou to Weinsberg, in a dungcart must thou depart!'[152] The Hunan movement, reported by Mao Tse-tung, saw a good deal of smashing of sedan-chairs.[153] And in the period of the civil war in England fraught with so many threats to the status quo, 'the wisest of men saw it to be a great evil that servants should ride on horses: an evil now both seen and felt in this unhappy kingdom'.[154]

The use of horses by low-born villagers was unacceptable to the Indian elite as well. No Balahi was to ride on his horse past an upper-caste person or village, no Bania past a Bundela Rajput's house, no subordinate past his superior officer.[155] The equestrian figure was embedded in the traditions of the meek and much harassed Santals as an image of pure force. 'Kings and rich people move about on horseback as conquerors', according to the *Mare Hapram Ko Reak Katha*.[156] The other privileged form of transport in India was the palanquin. Some of the foreign powers who had acquired territorial bases in the subcontinent used this to indicate their superior standing as rulers: in Bombay under Portuguese occupation no native was ever allowed to ride in a palanquin except with the Viceroy's permission, a practice which the British kept in force in their turn at least until 1788.[157] In rural India the native elite, especially the big landlords, continued for a long time to treat the palanquin as a part of the insignia of their authority and no one of inferior standing was allowed to ride in it through their residential villages. If a zamindar was really powerful, even some junior white officials could risk being thrown out of his village for violating this code.[158] It was therefore symptomatic of a radical inversion in rural society that the peasants should publicly appropriate such vehicles. They did so when during the Rangpur insurrection they carried around their leader, Dirjenarain, in a palanquin. Nothing could have been more topsy-turvy than that. For as we know from Ratiram's ballad on this event, no one could pass through the hated Deby Sinha's estate

[152] Zimmermann: I 394. [153] Mao: I 28. [154] Hill (1974): 200.
[155] Fuchs: 35; Russell & Lal: II 453, III 293, IV 439.
[156] MHKRK: *cxxxii*. [157] Russell & Lal: III 293.
[158] C. Datta: I 4–5.

in that district in any form of transport whatsoever without being beaten up by his *paiks* and that too in the most defiling manner—that is, with shoes.[159] And palanquins as well as horses were used by the leaders of the Santal forces during the hool. 'There were five or six Palkees [palanquins] with us', said a rebel taken captive soon after the outbreak. 'Sidoo and Kanoo ride in them. Whatever horses we found at Putgutteeah were mounted by the Sonthal Darogahs (Sirdars).' Kanhu himself was to state later on that he 'was on horseback' leading his men in some of the more dramatic actions such as the sack of the Pakur Raj—a neat inversion by which a symbol of the authority of rajas and the rich was transformed into an instrument of their destruction by the poor.[160]

The power of the rural elite in all pre-industrial societies is perhaps most conspicuously displayed by the size and elegance of their residence. In periods of sharpening antagonism in the countryside this can provoke much hostility among the peasant masses. John Ball's bitter contrast between the living conditions of lords and serfs was to be echoed five centuries later in the complaint of a peasant woman of Palermo during the uprising of 1893: 'I have five small children and only one little room, where we have to eat and sleep and do everything, while so many lords (*signori*) have ten to twelve rooms, entire palaces.'[161] It is not to be wondered therefore that stately homes have often been the object of violence in many of the major peasant revolts in Europe—manor houses during the Jacquerie, castles and abbeys in the German Peasant War, chateaux in the French Revolution.

All over the Indian subcontinent difference in types of residence was—and still continues to be[162]—a fairly accurate indication of difference in status. In colonial times this was true of distinctions between the rulers and the ruled as well as of those between the indigenous castes and classes themselves. As Anthony D. King has demonstrated so well by his researches,

[159] MDS: 580. 'Sowarit choria jay paike mare juta', reads the relevant line in that ballad. D. C. Sen (1914): 1415.

[160] JP, 19 July 1855: Statement of Balai Majhi recorded on 14 July 1855; JP, 20 Dec. 1855: 'Examination of Kanoo Sonthal'.

[161] Hobsbawm: 183.

[162] For some light on the situation in post-colonial India in this respect, see Bopegamage & Veeraraghavan: 142–3 *et passim*.

what he calls 'the bungalow-compound complex' functioned throughout this period as 'the basic residential unit of the colonial community'.[163] Originating from a traditional house-type known in Bengal the bungalow was adapted to the urge of the governing elite to use residence as a space to demarcate itself politically and culturally from the natives without involving the actual loss of that direct physical contact so essential for purposes of administration. The result was of course that by the middle of the nineteenth century the bungalow, 'the most usual class of house occupied by Europeans in India', came to be regarded as a symbol of the authority of the whites and the Raj. In all hostile demonstrations against the government or its European associates such as planters and railway officials, it featured almost inevitably as a target of popular wrath. The Santal rebellion, for instance, was only eight days old when the Magistrate of Murshidabad arrived at Pulsa, a principal station, to find the bungalows built by the railroad engineers there 'entirely destroyed'. His was by no means a unique experience. For as one of his fellow officers was to report three days later, 'the whole of the Bungalows along the line from Rajmehal to Pulsa have been burnt down and sacked'.[164]

The size and character of the residence were also regarded as a clear indication of status differences among the Indians themselves. As noticed above, this was integral enough to the culture of Malabar to show up in the regional language by way of a direct correspondence between caste names and hierarchically ordered names for caste dwellings. In general, a brick-built house was a decisive sign of affluence and high standing in the rural areas, as James Forlong, the planter, said about Bengal in his evidence before the Indigo Commission in 1860.[165] This seems to have been the case in the Madhya Pradesh region too where by the end of the century a *pucca* building had come to be recognized as evidence of the malguzars' prosperity and power raising them distinctively above the level of the mass of the tenantry: 'They have almost without exception good *pucca*

[163] King: 32. This illuminating and highly original work has many important things to say about the bungalow-compound complex: *vide* King: 89, 91, 123, 146–50 *et passim*.

[164] JP, 23 Aug. 1855: Toogood to Grey (15 July 1855); Rose to Elliott (18 July 1855).

[165] RIC: para. 3509.

houses built with an elaborate main entrance (*darwaza*) which is easily distinguishable from the houses of the tenants, and around which cluster their cattle sheds and granaries.'[166] Further up the scale, a big landlord's house was often very conspicuous indeed both in size and in elegance. Day wrote of one of these in his *Bengal Peasant Life* as 'the largest and best building in the village', with its solid masonry outer gate, imposing wooden door, the complex of inner compounds, halls and suites of rooms constituting the *kachari-badi*, the *dalan-badi* and the *andar-mahal*.[167] Fairly true to life, such structures testified to the disparity between the bigger zamindars and the rest of the rural population both in terms of material resources and of power. The idealized description of landlords' houses (often seen as the earthly replica of Indra's celestial palace) in some of the traditional Bengali narrative verse reflects not only the admiration but also the envy for their occupants on the part of its talented but impoverished authors.

The chagrin felt by the peasant on this score would also occasionally find its way into the otherwise placid prose of our primary sources to accuse his oppressors.

> The Wani uses the large house now. We can't get houses for hire. I would be willing to give up everything and be free, but I should like a bit of a hut somewhere in the village.[168]

In testifying thus before the Deccan Riots Commission a potter, Tatya Saloo, convicted of rioting against a Wani in his own village Supa, gave voice to that bitterness and desperation which drove the rural poor so often to vent their anger on such conspicuous symbols of the power of local landlords and moneylenders. Far too numerous and well documented to need recounting here, the attacks on the kacharis at Boda, Saal Ullah, Allanchurry, Dhee Hat, Baragang, Jamta and Dimla as well as on Deby Sinha's palace during the dhing of 1783, on the mansion of Krishnadeb Ray, zamindar of Punrah by Titu Mir's men during the Barasat rebellion of 1830, on 'all the respectable looking houses in the villages' within the area of the Kol insurrection of 1832, on the kachari of the zamindar of

[166] *Hoshangabad Settlement Report 1891–96* quoted in Stokes: 258. Also see Russell & Lal: IV 87.

[167] Day: 195–6.

[168] DRCR (B): 3.

Ambar pargana at Jhikarhati and the house of the Raja of Maheshpur by the Santals in 1855, on the kacharis at Mirpur, Pasuria Bari, Chitturlia and Woodhunia and the house of the Majumdars of Gopalnagar during the Pabna bidroha of 1873, and on the residence and gadis of banias and mahajans throughout Uttar Pradesh in 1857–8 and in the Poona and Ahmadnagar districts of Maharashtra in 1875 are among some of the instances which come readily to one's mind.[169]

It was not only by attacking the material symbols of governmental and landlord authority that the insurgents upset the established order. They did so by undermining its dominant semi-feudal culture as well. In so far as religion constituted the most expressive sign of this culture in many of its essential aspects, the peasants' defiance of the rural elite often involved an attempt to appropriate the dominant religion or to destroy it. To those who were high up in society the emulation of their culture by the lower strata seemed always fraught with danger. There have been occasions when, thanks to the stimulus given to casteism by British colonial policy, sanskritizing movements among the lower castes to upgrade themselves by adopting the rituals and religious idioms of their superiors were resisted by the latter and generated much social tension and even some actual violence. If this could happen in conditions of social peace, the subaltern's urge to assert his identity not in terms of his own culture but his enemy's—a characteristic index of negative consciousness—was boosted, understandably enough, when the existing structure of authority in rural areas began to crumble under the impact of a mass uprising.

The Santal hool of 1855 was a clear demonstration of this phenomenon. Involved in a bitter and bloody war against Hindu landlords and moneylenders, the rebels took to Hindu religious practice with a vengeance. Certain forms of ritual worship (*puja*) regarded as conducive to spiritual merit by the Hindus were adopted by the insurgents too. Indeed the very first intelligence report about their movements which we have on record, speaks of their 'intention' to march to Baniagram

[169] For these instances see Kaviraj: 24, 27; Ray (1966): 273; J. C. Jha: 183; K. K. Datta: 74–5; FSUP: II–IV, *passim*; DRCR, *passim*; JP(P): 'Pubna Riot Case'.

'where they are to do Poojah and bathe in the Ganges' before proceeding to Rajmahal.[170] This Hindu idiom showed up emphatically and with a certain amount of consistency in the conduct of their leaders whom the crisis had invested with a degree of spiritual authority too. Thus, a headman called Ram, a local leader, was taken prisoner while 'engaged in performing Poojah', for he 'could not . . . be disturbed or warned by his followers' as the counter-insurgency forces closed in on his village and surrounded it.[171] Kanhu himself is on record as having said that he 'made poojah' at a difficult moment during the battle of Maheshpur in an attempt, presumably, to influence its outcome in favour of his fauj.[172] His brother Sido, the co-leader of the hool, had, we are told, his own plans to celebrate Durga Puja in the grand manner of the Hindu gentry of Bengal for whom the pomp and scale of this autumn festival served as a customary affirmation of religiosity as well as of social authority. And to leave no one in doubt about the genuinely Hindu character of this ceremony the insurgents abducted two Brahmans to make them perform the prescribed rituals correctly and in accordance with the highest standards of purity. As the Magistrate of Birbhum wrote to his superior officer: 'The gang of from 5 to 7,000 Sonthals under Seeroo Manghee whom they term Soobha Thacoor at Telabonee have strengthened their position by earthen works and dug Tanks there they have also made preparations for celebrating the Doorgapooja, for which purpose they have carried off and detained two Brahmins from one of the villages plundered by them in Thanna Nagoolea.'[173] Such an open and energetic avowal of Hinduism on the part of a lowly, 'unclean' tribal peasantry could not have been regarded by the Hindu elite as anything but subversive. For it was indeed an integral aspect of their dominance that they should consider it threatened by any unauthorized affiliation to the ruling culture. This is why the prospect of Sudras practising dharma in the manner of the

[170] JP, 19 July 1855: Eden to Grey (9 July 1855).

[171] JP, 8 Nov. 1855: Ward to GOB (19 Oct. 1855).

[172] JP, 20 Dec. 1855: 'Examination of Kanoo Sonthal'.

[173] JP, 4 Oct. 1855: Rose to Elliott (24 Sept. 1855). Ward, the Officer on Special Duty, also wrote to the Government of Bengal to the same effect on 21 September 1855. (Ibid.) For the Santals' belief in the magical powers of brahmans, see a folk-tale in Bompas: 356.

upper varnas was envisaged in Puranic literature as a sign of the cataclysmic advent of Kali, and the slaying of Śambūka was instigated by the Brahmans and applauded by the gods as a great deed on the part of its eponymous hero in the Ramayana.[174]

The insurgents undermined the dominant culture in its most important, that is, religious aspect not only by emulating it, but more directly and dramatically by acts of desecration. The Peasant War in Germany has provided us with some classic instances of this particular form of reversal. There in the first quarter of the sixteenth century the Catholic church was still a major feudal power in its own right and commanded wealth and political authority on a vast scale through its abbeys and monasteries. To the peasants it was as much of an enemy as any of the secular lords of the land, and consequently when they rose up in arms in the spring of 1525 there was little to restrain them from defying conventions and defiling objects sanctified by the church. It was Lent and time for fasting, yet they behaved as if they were Protestants and fasting did not concern them. They ate and drank freely. At Roggenburg drunken peasants broke up the church organ, battered the tabernacle with a rod, took away the chalices and other sacred vessels and shredded the vestments and flags for use as trouser belts. At Kempten armed contingents of them paraded past the church during the hour of high mass laughing and mocking. They brought down the pictures of the saints, sawed off the head of a beautiful statue of the Virgin Mary and smashed up the figure of the child in her arms. Indeed they made a mess of 'everything considered holy' (*übten den grössten Unfug an allem aus, was man für heilig hielt*).[175]

In India the temple was an outstanding symbol of Hindu religion and often of the prestige of a local Hindu landlord if it happened to be patronized by his family or situated within his residential precincts. As such it often figured as a focus of conflict between Hindu landlords and non-Hindu peasantry. Being denied the right to enter a temple was among the grievances the

[174] As the *Vāyupurāṇam* has it: 'Śūdrā dharmam charishyanti yugānte paryupasthite'. Tarkaratna (1910): 58/59. For the Śambūka episode see Rāmāyaṇam, Uttarakāṇḍa, *lxxxvi-ix* in Tarkaratna (1908).

[175] Zimmermann: I 269, 283, 365.

Birsaite pracharaks made much of in their propaganda against zamindars, and it was as a decisive step towards the ulgulan that the Munda chief led his men into the forbidden Chutia temple, held a nautch there, threw down and defiled the images, and altogether desecrated this place of worship held sacred by the dikus. The violence of this sacrilege was not lost on the authorities who promptly issued a warrant for Birsa's arrest and put up a reward for his capture.[176]

Attacks of this kind acquired a very special significance when the peasantry concerned happened to be Muslims. For apart from affecting power relations in the countryside even to the point of reversing them in some cases, these often led to the overdetermination of class struggle by sectarian conflict in a manner which was a commonplace of Indian politics under the Raj. Instances abound. In Malabar where the authority of the jenmi landlords derived not merely from their near monopoly of landed property but also, as Logan observed, from their function as trustees of village temples, attacks on and defilement of the latter featured in almost each of the numerous Moplah risings throughout the nineteenth century.[177] Again in some parts of eastern Bengal where the Farazi movement launched by Shariatullah converged with militant resistance to Hindu zamindars' tyranny on the part of predominantly Muslim tenant populations, the latter were accused of defiling private shrines in landlords' houses by slaughtering cows, by forcing their entry there in clothes fastened by strips of cow-hide and at least in one case, by demolishing a set of lingas, a traditional surrogate for the image of the deity Siva.[178] The correspondent who reported these outrages in a mufassil periodical in 1837 voicing the alarm that spread among the Hindu gentry of Dacca and Faridpur districts at the time, recalled the not very dissimilar pattern of violence witnessed during the Barasat insurrection only a few years ago. Places of worship sacred to both the faiths had come under attack during that historic struggle. In order to terrorize the mass of the peasantry inspired by Titu's

[176] Singh: 77, 79.

[177] Logan: 554, 555, 559, 560, 565, 582, 588 *et passim.*

[178] Khan (1965): 17–19. The incidents which occurred in 1837 were reported in a contemporary periodical, *Darpan*, published from Dacca, and quoted in Brajendranath Bandyopadhyay, *Sambad Patre Sekaler Katha,* III 311–12.

Islamic revivalism and roused and organized by him to resist zamindari oppressions, Krishnadeb Ray, a powerful Hindu landlord, had raided a Muslim hamlet and burnt down some houses and a mosque. The insurgents returned the compliment by invading Ray's own residential village, Punrah. 'The Zemindars had put a slight on their religious feeling', reads the official report on this event, 'and they retaliated [by] seizing a cow which they killed in the public market place of the village, scattered the blood over the walls of a Hindu temple and hung up the four quarters of the animal in derision before it.' And as if to emphasize the purely symbolic character of this act 'on this occasion they committed no plunder beyond carrying of[f] what articles they found lying immediately exposed in the shops in the market place'.[179] Desecration was used thus by both the parties to undermine each other's prestige—by the Hindu zamindar the prestige of the rebellion and the new faith which fuelled it; by the Muslim peasantry the prestige of the landlords and its emblem, the old established religion.

It was this fight for prestige which was at the very heart of insurgency. Inversion was its principal modality. It was a political struggle in which the rebel appropriated and/or destroyed the insignia of his enemy's power and hoped thus to abolish the marks of his own subalternity. Inevitably, therefore, by rising in revolt the peasant involved himself in a project which was, by its very nature, negatively constituted. The 'names, battle-cries and costumes' he assumed in order to carry this out were all taken over from his adversaries. It was no doubt a project predicated on power, but its terms were derived from the very structure of authority against which he had been driven to revolt. He spoke thus in a 'borrowed language'—that of his enemy, for he knew none other. 'In like manner', wrote Marx as he framed the paradoxes of the first bourgeois-democratic revolutions of modern Europe in a linguistic analogy, 'a beginner who has learnt a new language always

[179] BC 54222: Metcalfe & Blunt to Court of Directors (10 Apr. 1832), paras 13, 15. For some other allegations of cow killing, physical assaults on brahmans and forcible conversion to Islam, see ibid., para. 17, as well as JC, 6 Dec. 1831: Money to Thomason (28 Nov. 1831) and JC, 3 Apr. 1832: Alexander to Barwell (28 Nov. 1831).

translated it back into his mother tongue.'[180] The peasant rebel of colonial India, the infantile, blundering and alas, invariably frustrated, precursor of a democratic revolution in the subcontinent had set out to learn his very first lesson in power, but in this earlier period prior to the emergence of a modern bourgeoisie, an industrial proletariat and advanced ideas of democracy he could do so only by translating it backwards into the semi-feudal language of politics to which he was born. A historically necessary exercise in negative consciousness, this was demonstrated in its general form as a process of inversion turning, as Manu had warned, the lower (*adhara*) into the higher (*uttara*).

[180] MECW: XI 104.

CHAPTER 3

AMBIGUITY

Inversion by crime—Sultana's reputation as a Robin Hood—crime and insurgency derive from two different codes—reasons why the distinction is not clearly perceived—conspiracy theories—peasant uprisings preceded by increase in rural crime—starvation and banditry—Banjara Singh the Chambal dacoit—the Lodhas of Midnapur—'blurring'—two interpretations of rural crime—ambiguity dispersed by synonymy—outlaws as insurgents—dacoit/rebel—some case histories: the Santal insurrection of 1855 and the jacqueries in UP, 1857–8—a note on historiography.

'Turning things upside down' is a necessary but by no means sufficient condition of the violence of peasant uprisings. In all feudal types of societies there have always been individuals and small groups who were driven by hunger and humiliation to commit acts of violence in such a way as to amount to turning things upside down. These acts were almost invariably designated as 'crime' by the rulers of such societies. For instance, many of the offences prescribed for punishment (*daṇḍa*) in the Smṛti texts constituted crime in so far as they were reversals of the existing codes of deference. Even after the British introduced relatively more modern legal institutions in the subcontinent, political arrangements at the village level were allowed in many cases to continue as of old, so that the local elite went on exercising with impunity their traditional right to discipline members of the lower classes and castes for using the language, dress, transport and other status symbols of their social superiors. For a Chamar to speak like a Rajput, for a Bareia to sport a turban like a Patidar, for a Balahi to ride a horse through a Bundela village, for a peasant not to leave his cot and stand up at the sight of his landlord[1]—were all regarded as acts of in-

[1] Instances of all such inversions have been discussed in detail in the previous chapter. For a landlord's statement about the offence taken and punishment meted out by the members of his class if a peasant failed to get up from his cot as a mark of deference, see Steed: 132.

version and severely punished. By the same token, in eighteenth-century England where 'game was a special currency of class based on the solid standard of landed wealth', poaching was, in the eyes of the landed aristocracy, 'not only stealing a peculiarly valuable kind of social capital' but 'also debasing its coinage'. For it allowed the lower classes to share with the gentry such food and sport as were considered to be the exclusive symbols of privileged status.[2] Consequently the landed aristocracy which was still strong enough to swing the 'rule of law' in line with its own interests, found it necessary to use its authority in order to save the food of the gods from desecration by the underdogs: the draconic Black Act of 1723 (9 George I c. 22) was enacted, on the pretext of an emergency, as a legislation aimed equally against the 'ancient offence' of poaching and the 'displacement of authority' caused by it.[3]

While those in control of the instruments of punishment tend thus to act upon a definition of crime broad enough to permit a defence not only of the material basis of their power but also of their prestige, the more audacious of the outlaws in India and elsewhere have been known, conversely, to add insult to injury in their defiance of authority. Shibeyshani, a notorious dacoit of Nadia at the turn of the nineteenth century, when surprised by a villager and challenged to identify himself, answered back, 'Your father'—an euphemism, in Indian usage, for 'You bastard!' Apprehended, he was made to pay for his robbery compounded by the crime of abusing his upper-caste landlord captor—a serious breach in the code of verbal deference. He had his forearms chopped off and bled to death.[4]

However, it was not in all cases that the inversion effected by crime involved such a crude and frontal assault on codes of deference. Some of the more powerful criminals are known to have brought this about by the knightly device of dealing with the forces of law and order as noble enemies. Sultana, the legendary bandit of Uttar Pradesh, combined a cool disregard for the authorities with humour, hospitality and even chivalry to impose the rhetoric of a combat between equals on a campaign launched by a Special Dacoity Police Force set up for the purpose of destroying him and his gang. He was eventually caught and hanged. Corbett who was one of the small group

[2] Hay: 246–8. [3] Thompson (1975): 191. [4] Mustowfi: 14–15.

that planned and led the police war against him, concludes his account of Sultana's career with a remarkable tribute.

Society demands protection against criminals, and Sultana was a criminal. He was tried under the law of the land, found guilty and executed. Nevertheless, I cannot withhold a great measure of admiration for the little man who set at nought the might of the Government for three long years, and who by his brave demeanour won the respect of those who guarded him in the condemned cell. I could have wished that justice had not demanded that Sultana be exhibited in manacles and leg-irons, and exposed to ridicule from those who trembled at the mere mention of his name while he was at liberty. I could also have wished that he had been given a more lenient sentence, for no other reason than that he had been branded a criminal at birth, and had not had a fair chance; that when power was in his hands he had not oppressed the poor; that when I tracked him to the banyan tree he spared my life and the lives of my friends. And finally, that he went to his meeting with Fredy [Young, the commander of the Special Dacoity Police Force] not armed with a knife or a revolver, but with a water melon in his hands.[5]

Nothing could speak more eloquently of the inversive function of crime than these words. The criminal had in this instance so fully achieved the ultimate objective of rebellion, so thoroughly had he turned things upside down that in the eyes of the custodians of order he was transfigured from an outlaw into a hero and his record remembered no longer as one of offences against the law but that of valour and humanity.

An inversive function of this kind is common to peasant insurgency and certain (though not all) classes of crime. But these two types of violence are clearly distinguished in one important respect. Unlike crime peasant rebellions are necessarily and invariably public and communal events. To generalize, the criminal may be said to stand in the same relation to the insurgent as does what is conspiratorial (or secretive) to what is public (or open), or what is individualistic (or small-group) to what is communal (or mass) in character. In other words, crime and insurgency derive from two very different codes of violence.

The distinction between the two codes is not always easily

[5] Corbett: 130–1.

perceived by observers at the initial stages of a peasant uprising. Used to reading all signs of violence against society under 'normal' conditions as crime, they are inclined at first to read the same set of signs in a violence that has already switched from one code to another. Since the passage from crime to rebellion is not fully comprehended yet, there is a tendency—almost universal on the part of the authorities at the outbreak of an insurrection—to interpret the increased intensity and incidence of violence in quantitative terms alone by attributing it to the secret design of a small number of malefactors rather than the initiative of individual offenders against the law. Insurgency is thus mistaken for that larger type of crime which is produced by conspiracy.

Conspiracy theories figure prominently in the official response to many Indian peasant uprisings. The conspirators are in most of these cases suspected to be members of one or the other rural elite group on the simple assumption that the peasant has no initiative of his own and is a mere instrument of his master. At least one notorious tyrant is known to have escaped the full measure of legal punishment by manipulating precisely such elitist assumptions. Deby Sinha whose oppressions as a revenue farmer of the East India Company goaded the peasantry of northern Bengal into revolt in 1783, argued in self-defence 'that it was the intention of the Zemindars to keep back their revenue for this year and that they had instigated therefore the ryots to rise'.[6] He got away lightly. How keen and predisposed officialdom could be to try and attribute a plot to an event of this kind may be seen from a report written by one of them about his own part in the military action which finally led to Titu Mir's defeat and the fall of his rebel stockade on 19 November 1831. 'On the 20th Instant [that is, November 1831]', he recalled, 'I repaired to the Stockade in order to search for Papers which might have been useful to Government to develop a Plot, if any such existed.'[7]

'To develop a Plot' was also the instinctive response of some of the leading officials to the Kol rebellion of 1831–2. They saw in it the hand of the local chief. The maharaja of Chota Nagpur, wrote one of them, 'may have considered the summary

[6] MDS: 390.

[7] JC, 3 Apr. 1832: Alexander to Barwell (28 Nov. 1831).

expulsion of the Mahajuns and the destruction of their houses, papers, and effects, the most convenient way of squaring all accounts with them, to many of whom he is understood to be much indebted'.[8] However, a fairly thorough investigation carried out by the government produced no direct evidence of any such elite involvement, although Nagvamsi sympathy (as against conspiracy) for the Kols as the enemy of their enemies—the suds—could not be doubted.[9] The outbreak of the Santal rebellion in July 1855 illustrates again how the regime often tended to reach out for a conspiracy theory at the drop of an arrow. Reports received by the Calcutta authorities from their men on the spot during the first fortnight of the hool hinted darkly—and rather hysterically—at invisible strings pulled by hidden hands. Since it was 'evidently a planned and concerted thing' and appeared to be 'long meditated and well organized', and 'as the Sontals [were] generally the most timid people in the world and dreadfully afraid of the Police', it followed 'that all this [was] at the instigation of some one else', that 'they [had] been put up to this'.[10] Even the name of an identifiable conspirator emerged at one point. Meer Abbas Ali, a former Amir of Sind, was suspected of being at the root of all the trouble. But as an official enquiry was soon to establish, it was his passion for sport rather than rebellion that had made him recruit, in the spring of 1855, a large number of Santals as jungle-beaters from the region affected soon afterwards by the uprising. The government was satisfied 'that Meer Abbas Ali Khan had nothing to do with this insurrection'.[11]

To mistake rebellion for crime in the characterstic form of a conspiracy theory is not a matter of mental habit alone. The conceptual inertia that refuses to acknowledge, at first sight, the altered figure of violence, feeds on the sharp increase in criminal activity which often inaugurates a peasant revolt. Quantity again plays a trick on quality. A sudden rise in the incidence of rural violence has been known to herald some of the most massive uprisings in India. The link between the Santal hool

[8] BC 1363 (54227): Blunt's Minute (4 Apr. 1832).

[9] J. C. Jha: 144–9 *passim*.

[10] JP, 19 July 1855: Eden to Grey (9 July 1855); JP, 23 Aug. 1855: Elliott to Grey (19 July 1855). Also see JP, 19 July 1855: Eden to Toogood (9 & 13 July 1855).

[11] K. K. Datta: 50, 125–8.

and the crime wave that preceded it was obvious enough to be noticed by the Lieutenant-Governor of Bengal in his minute of 19 October 1855 three months *after* the outbreak. 'I see no reason to doubt', he wrote, 'that the present disturbance had an *intimate connection* with the so-called Dacoities of 1854 or rather that these Dacoities were *in fact the commencement of the present insurrection*.'[12] We have a clear recognition here of the passage from crime to rebellion, an insight on the part of the peasant's enemies into a process by which violence switched codes. The insight, alas from the official point of view, did not come soon enough. For the process had indeed been building up since 1852 when in one single year dacoities increased by 89 and 58 per cent respectively in Birbhum and Bankura, two districts which were both to be caught up in the insurrection soon afterwards.[13] In Bhagalpur, the other district to burn in 1855, as many as 12 gang dacoities had been committed in the previous year and led to 123 arrests and 74 convictions. 'The occurrence of so many robberies in quick succession within a jurisdiction where such acts of violence had for many years been quite unknown, excited surprise & alarm':[14] these words taken from the Bhagalpur Police Report for 1854 show, incidentally, how difficult it can be for the contemporary observer to identify violence as it transits obscurely through the grey overlap between codes. Too close to the actual events, the Police Commissioner did not have the advantage of hindsight that was to illuminate the Lieutenant-Governor's understanding of crime as the precursor of rebellion.

A somewhat similar pattern of 'preliminary disturbances' could be seen in the jacqueries of Poona and Ahmadnagar districts of Maharashtra twenty years later. The actual outbreak of the riots there in 1875 was preceded by a spate of rural violence during the previous year. Directed invariably against Marwari moneylenders this ranged from what the Deccan Riots Commission called 'social outlawry' and 'petty annoy-

[12] JP, 8 Nov. 1855: Minute by the Lieutenant-Governor of Bengal (19 Oct. 1855).

[13] JP, 17 May 1855 (nos 26 & 27): Police Report for 1852.

[14] Quoted in the Lieutenant-Governor's Minute of 19 October 1855 (JP, 8 Nov. 1855) and hence taken to be more authoritative as well as comprehensive than the lower half-yearly figures given in G. F. Brown's memorial of 12 December 1855 (JP, 20 Dec. 1855).

ance' to dacoities committed by the Koli outlaws in the hills of the western districts of Poona and Nagar.[15] The parallelism between these Indian experiences and the English agricultural labourers' movement of 1830—known popularly as 'Swing'—is close enough to merit some mention here. Hobsbawm has shown how in one particular county, Norfolk, crime increased by at least 30 per cent during the six years ending in 1830, how in the twenty-two counties comprising nearly the entire domain of the Swing movement there was a spectacular rise in crime in 1829 on the eve of the outbreak, and how the incidence of poaching, the most defiant of all rural crimes, 'rose particularly steeply in the years immediately preceding the rising of 1830'.[16]

Statistics such as these usually indicate a lowering threshold of the peasant's tolerance towards the conditions of his existence. Poverty has a way of compelling recognition from all Indian governments—if only as a law and order problem. The British had to take notice of it from the earliest days of the Raj. A district official in Bengal observed how in the spring of 1771 even the honest elements among the tenantry were being driven by hunger to take to banditry: 'Numbers of ryots who have hitherto borne the first of characters among their neighbours, pursue this last resource to procure themselves a subsistence.'[17] The great Bengal famine which followed added dramatically to the number of starving villagers as well as of the banditti.[18] Again, in 1792, another local administrator mentioned 'the last year's scarcity' among the causes that had 'increased the Number of Robberies' in his district.[19] The remaining one and a half centuries of colonial rule followed by more than three decades of government under a successor regime have made little significant change in this causal connection between starvation and violence in the countryside. The account of the restless life and bullet-ridden death of Banjara Singh, as given by a leading police officer of independent India and published with a foreword by the country's Home Minister, is therefore still an integral and authentic part of contemporary history.

[15] DRCR: 2, 54. [16] H & R: 77–81.

[17] Letter of 13 April 1771 from Boughton Rous, Supervisor of Rajshahi, quoted in Hunter (1897): 70. [18] Ibid.: 71.

[19] Keating to Cowper, 13 Oct. 1792 in BDR: 29.

Banjara Singh was a shepherd boy who grew up to be the leader of a formidable band of dacoits in the Chambal region. His father was a poor peasant turned poorer when he pawned half of his small plot of land, sold his flock of sheep and took a loan from the sahukar—all in order to pay for his daughter's wedding. Then he died. And as we learn from the testimony of his adversary and biographer:

> The turning point in Banjara Singh's life was the death of his father. He disposed off the field to fulfil his duties as a devoted son in connection with the last rites of the dead. The *sahukar* turned up to press his demand for the payment of loan. Banjara Singh had no money to give. The *sahukar* remonstrated with abuses. The young man at first kept quiet but later retaliated by uttering abuses in reply. At this, the *sahukar* hit Banjara Singh with his stick. At the first touch of the stick, Banjara was wild and assaulted him with his lathi. The *sahukar* fled. That night Banjara Singh decided to leave his dilapidated house and his semi-deserted village.[20]

Many an outlaw's career begins in almost identical circumstances all over rural India. There are regions of chronic poverty like Banjara Singh's own district where for hundreds of years peasant youths have been slipping out of desolate villages and starvation and bonded labour in order to take to dacoity as a profession. There are demographic masses branded by colonial legislation as 'criminal tribes' (a stigma nominally removed since 1952 but still intact in social practice) for whom the very fact of having been thus classified has made crime the only means left for livelihood. The Lodhas are one such group of the rural poor in western Bengal.[21] A forest people they used to earn their living, traditionally, as hunters, trappers and gatherers of food and fuel from the jungle. But the jungle, their provider, was taken away from them by the zamindar and the sarkar as land hunger and rising birth rates combined to turn more and more of the woodlands of Midnapur into paddy fields and villages. Cut off thus from their principal source of subsistence the Lodhas had, by the turn of the century, adopted robbery

[20] Chaturvedi: 139.

[21] The source of our information on the Lodhas and of all otherwise unacknowledged extracts in this and the next two paragraphs is Bhowmick: 33, 35, 36, 46, 66, 266, 268, 270, 274–5. The statistics on landholding are based on Tables 11 and 12 and those on crime on Table 29 of that work.

and theft as almost a second profession. And then, in 1916, the law stepped in to fasten on them a new identity by naming them officially as a 'criminal tribe'.

The Lodhas had taken to crime rather than agriculture because there was nothing for them in agriculture to take to. They had very little land of their own. A study of landholding by a hundred families in five Midnapur villages showed that an average Lodha family of 4.8 members owned 0.65 acre of land, that is, 0.134 acre per head. Of the families surveyed 57 per cent were landless, 20 per cent owned less than one acre, and 17 per cent more than one acre but less than four. No wonder that the Lodha peasant starves most of the time. 'A few families were found in the course of the enquiry . . . to have no grain of rice for 7 or 8 days at a stretch, and they depended wholly on . . . wild tubers for their food.' Again, in one of the villages 'a good number of families . . . were found to starve or remain without any food for the whole day. This is a common phenomenon in the life of a Lodha here. Even the children are kept starving. Sometimes they are found to collect some edible small or big fruits and leaves to tide over the period of starvation. One woman was found by the writer to swallow a morsel of soil in crushing hunger.' What crime, if any, this particular woman was eventually driven to, we shall never know. But the author of the melancholy monograph from which these facts have been taken does tell us of another woman who was arrested and convicted. She was a widow with four children and the only way she could feed them was by stealing food or articles sold or exchanged for food. Children too had to provide for themselves by similar means. A ten-year old girl was arrested by the police for theft: she had been 'starving for two days and was tempted to lift [a] brass cup with a view to selling it in the market for a little cash by which she could procure some food to eat'.

Hobsbawm has noticed the distinction made by the English rural labourer of 1830 between two classes of crime committed as an escape from poverty. The labourer 'could seek a relief from poverty in crime—in the simple theft of potatoes or turnips which constituted the bulk of the offences which he would himself regard as criminal, and in poaching or smuggling, which he would not'.[22] Hunger has forced the Lodhas of Midnapur to do

[22] H & R: 73.

away with such fine moral distinctions. Parents have to feed their families, and if crime is the only means of access to articles of common consumption, the morality lies with the criminal. Far from being censured for offences against the law, a Lodha punished by the court would often be regarded by his kin as above reproach. 'In a few cases', to quote again from the account mentioned above, 'the wives of the criminals defended their husbands as innocent and spotless in character. They strongly asserted that they knew nothing wrong about their husbands.' Impoverished bread-winners do indeed figure prominently in Lodha crime statistics. In a sample of 180 of them listed as criminals it was found out that 82.2 per cent had no land at all, 12.2 per cent owned one acre or less and 5.6 per cent two acres or more, while 9.4 per cent of the same population belonged to small families of 1 to 3 members each, 46.7 per cent to medium-sized families of 4 to 6 members each, 31.1 per cent to large families of 7 to 9 members and 12.8 per cent to very large families of more than 10 members each. Thus the great majority of Lodha criminals are those who have the largest number of mouths to feed and the least resources. What makes the connection between hunger and crime quite explicit is that it is the practice of Lodha dacoits to carry off from the houses they raid everything they can lay their hands on and exchange it as quickly as possible for food; any foodstuff that can be readily consumed, they consume on the spot during a raid.

Offences of this nature committed in a desperate search for food are not limited to the Lodhas of Midnapur alone. There is nothing in this that is specific to their culture or the region where they belong. Such defiance of the law arises from a common and ubiquitous tradition of resistance to poverty which, at least during the colonial period, received an acknowledgement from the authorities themselves. This was typically expressed in the words of the Police Report of 1852 for the Lower Provinces stating how the number of dacoities in Birbhum district had suddenly increased by about one hundred per cent since the previous year as the direct result of distress following a severe drought:

There appears a considerable increase in the offence of Dacoitee; but bearing in mind that this is one of the districts in which the people suffered most from the want of rain in 1851 and that the nature of the country affords great facility for the perpetration of this offence and the escape of the offenders, such a result might have been expected.[23]

The identification of scarcity as a cause of crime occurs in the administrative literature relating to many other parts of the subcontinent as well. In some districts of Uttar Pradesh, for instance, the authorities saw in dacoity 'the form of crime to which the Bundela Rajput always reverts when pressed by hard times'.[24] The connection between famine conditions in this province and the rise in the incidence of crime during the years of drought and scarcity in the late 1860s was documented by Frederick Henvey. 'In times of famine it is usual to expect an increase in the number of crimes against property', he wrote and went on to show how taking 1867 as the index year the percentage increase for 1868 and 1869 was respectively 175 and 214 in dacoity, 158 and 185 in robbery, 124 and 170 in lurking house-trespass, and 118 and 171 in theft (other than that of cattle).[25]

For the south, too, David Arnold has demonstrated in his excellent study of this subject how drought, dearth and high prices constituted 'the most readily identifiable factor in the incidence of dacoity' in the Madras Presidency in the late nineteenth and early twentieth centuries. The correlation was indeed so clear that the authorities came to rely on it as 'a true index to the state of distress'—a sort of local barometer of the prevailing degree of deprivation—and 'the Inspector-General of Police invariably prefaced his annual report on crime with a summary of the year's rainfall and grain prices'.[26] Again, in the west country hunger often turned peasant into dacoit as witnessed thus by a young Indian civilian in charge of relief

[23] JP, 17 May 1855, no. 26.

[24] Drake-Brockman, *Hamirpur District Gazetteer*, p. 160 quoted in Stokes: 134.

[25] Henvey: 126–7. The percentages, excluding fractions, have been worked out on the basis of the figures given in ibid.: 127 as below:

Year	Dacoities	Robberies	'Lurking House-trespass'	Cattle Thefts	Other Thefts
1867	57	274	13,665	10,218	18,699
1868	100	435	17,071	12,196	22,208
1869	122	509	23,297	6,751	32,090

The decline in cattle-theft in 1869, explains Henvey, was entirely due to the fact 'that a special organization for the suppression of this crime was then in full swing'.

[26] Arnold: 145.

operations in Gujarat devastated by a famine at the turn of the century:

I had set up camp for a few days on the outskirts of a small village some miles away from the nearest railway. Provisions used to be sent up for me by train from the district headquarters. One day it so happened that the entire supply (amounting in fact to eight loaves of bread) was looted on its way to my camp . . . The police blew up the incident out of all proportions. After three days, five Kolis, all skin and bone, were sent up on charges of dacoity for trial at my own court! 'We had nothing to eat for three days in a row', they said without any show of repentance whatsoever. 'Our bellies were burning with hunger. Should we have come across all that food and not eaten it?' Indeed, how were they to let all that food go? But how could I let them go without punishment either? So I worked a bit on the evidence provided by the police and defined the offence as a case of theft rather than dacoity. Then I sentenced them to imprisonment for a day and a fine of half a rupee per head. This was the verdict which I entered in the court records, but felt so embarrassed about the whole business that I said to them, 'Now go away. You are free. Don't steal again.' The fine I paid out of my own pocket.[27]

There is more to this anecdote than a parallelism between the various instances of starvation crime discussed above. It helps to define the ambivalence of the deed on which the young and evidently sympathetic officer was asked to sit in judgment. Was it an offence to be interpreted and punished according to the Indian Penal Code or was it to be justified by a code of social morality that provides for a minimum subsistence as an overriding right? A form of violence against property was obviously switching codes when it was brought before the court and obliged the young officer to produce half an answer to that question in terms of one code and half in another.

The resistance of the rural poor is bound to create dilemmas of this sort for the rulers in any society with a large peasant population, although not all guardians of law and order may turn out to be as conscience-stricken as the young civilian of Gujarat. The mysterious King John's band of 'well-disciplined social rebels' known popularly as the Blacks rode through a part of England in 1723 'administering folk justice' to the evil gentry and inevitably precipitated a lot of 'freelance actions' by

[27] C. Datta: 8.

poachers, smugglers, etc. with whom they had nothing directly to do. But, as E. P. Thompson observes, 'all of these actions were, of course, seen by the authorities, within one common blur, as outrages by the Blacks'.[28] This blur represents classification by a familiar and convenient code. It was obviously convenient for those in power to make no distinction between the activities of the Blacks and others and to lump both kinds of violence as crime—a code which they knew how to handle.

Significantly, however, the peasant's own perception of violence, too, can be and often is characterized by 'blurring' with the difference that with him it operates in reverse. While his foes—landlords, moneylenders and officials—would tend to lump all forms of defiance of the law as crime, the peasant would tend to lump them together as perfectly justifiable—even honourable—acts of social protest. Both points of view are governed by *atideśa* in so far as they both read the signs of one kind of violence into another. But they do so in opposite directions and thereby produce, under conditions of extreme polarization, a categorical conflict so broad and generalized as to amount to a clash between two incompatible theories. Mao Tse-tung's reflections on the antonyms 'terrible' and 'fine' used as contradictory descriptions of the Hunan uprising of 1927 help us to understand the emergence of such mutually hostile theoretical perspectives as the outcome of a peasant revolt.

The fact is that the great masses have risen to fulfil their historic mission [he says in the *Hunan Report*] and that the forces of rural democracy have risen to overthrow the forces of rural feudalism . . . It's fine. It is not 'terrible' at all. It is anything but 'terrible'. 'It's terrible!' is obviously a theory for combating the rise of the peasants in the interests of the landlords; it is obviously a theory of the landlord class for preserving the old order of feudalism and obstructing the establishment of the new order of democracy, it is obviously a counter-revolutionary theory . . . If your revolutionary viewpoint is firmly established and if you have been to the villages and looked around, you will undoubtedly feel thrilled as never before. Countless thousands of the enslaved—the peasants—are striking down the enemies who battened on their flesh. What the peasants are doing is absolutely right; what they are doing is fine! 'It's fine!' is the theory of the peasants and of all other revolutionaries.[29]

[28] Thompson (1975): 145. [29] Mao: I 27.

There must indeed be two different and contradictory ways of looking at the violence of peasant rebellions—the rebel's and his enemy's, giving rise to two different and irreconcilable ways of interpreting and generalizing the experience of that violence —two theories. But even before antagonism in rural society reaches the point of insurrection, elements of the alternative theory already constitute a part of the peasant's perception of the conflict between himself and his foes. These are expressed most commonly in his attitude to certain acts of disregard for the law, especially those committed in response to unbearable degrees of economic deprivation or social humiliation. The Italian woman from Piana dei Greci who during the peasant rising of 1893 justified the admission of petty criminals to the Fascio on the ground that 'if they have stolen a bit of grain they have only done so out of poverty',[30] expressed what is indeed an almost universal tolerance of starvation crimes in all peasant societies. It is again this sort of a linkage between smuggling and poverty that made many rural communities in eighteenth-century Sussex rally not merely to the support but even in defence of 'plebeian gangs' of smugglers, for 'to the common people they were certainly not seen as criminals'.[31] The way the poor villager's 'resentments of decades' allowed the legendary 'King John' of the Blacks to play Robin Hood in Hampshire and 'sheltered him and his band', has been assigned a classic guerilla status: 'His supporters seemed to be able to disappear as easily into the folds of popular concealment as did the Vietcong.'[32] This is how Sultana, 'India's Robin Hood', too, managed to evade the law for a very long time. For 'having known what it was to be poor, really poor . . . he never robbed a pice from a poor man, never refused an appeal for charity'. Consequently, says Corbett, 'his intelligence staff numbered hundreds'.[33] This could be said also of Banjara Singh the bandit who 'ravaged the tract between Jamuna and Chambal rivers and beyond with ruthlessness to the rich and with benevolence to the poor'. He, too, proved to be a most elusive quarry for the police. For, according to the officer who eventually cornered and killed him, he relied for his strength 'on the

[30] Hobsbawm: 183. [31] Winslow: 158, 159.
[32] Thompson (1975): 144–5. [33] Corbett: 101.

support of the many—the many who inhabited the mud-houses . . . on the willingness of the people to aid his struggle against the rich and his vendetta against the Police'.[34]

The peasant appears thus to be ready to put up with and often positively approve of a wide variety of crimes induced by poverty. These may be big or small ranging from petty larceny involving a brass tumbler pilfered by a hungry Lodha child or a handful of grain by a Sicilian pauper to the more spectacular and massive acts of defiance by a band like King John's or Sultana's. Since E. J. Hobsbawm's pioneering formulation of the concept of 'social banditry' an attempt is being increasingly made by historians to distinguish between such offences in terms of the differences in their social content. Sussex smugglers, it has been said, 'were often the rebels of the countryside' who resembled 'social bandits' in the sense that they 'were *not* regarded as simple criminals by public opinion', although in certain other respects they did not conform to Hobsbawm's categories. E. P. Thompson defines the Blacks—the 'armed foresters' of eighteenth-century England—as an intermediate type between 'social bandits' and 'agrarian rebels' sharing 'something of both characters' but identical with neither.[35] But whatever the point of the spectrum to which one assigns an activity of this kind, it has as its core an element of class conflict.

Whether this is more or less evident in any particular instance is of course a function of its relative entropy. Sporadic acts of defiance of this genre are unlikely to have their class character noticed by the rural population. In other words, they fail as signals which transmit poorly because of channel noise or ambiguity or a combination of both. And like all other messages rural crime too requires an adequate level of redundancy or a duplication of the coding system for its class content together with the rest of its meaning to come through clearly enough to make sense. This would explain why it was easy for the Deccan Riots Commission to characterize the events it had been set up to investigate as 'a disturbance arising out of the relations of the agricultural and moneylending classes'.[36] The incidence of

[34] Chaturvedi: 134–5. [35] Winslow: 157, 159; Thompson: 64.
[36] DRCR: 4.

criminal offences committed against moneylenders during the previous thirty years in general and the last five in particular was high enough to make the class character of the jacqueries of 1875 obvious not only to the agrarian population but also to officialdom. They conformed to a clearly recognizable pattern. There were far too many incidents of the same kind involving the same class of offenders and the same class of victims to leave anyone in doubt as to who in rural society was trying to settle scores with whom.

As early as 1845 a large body of Bhils led by Raghu Bhangria had spread terror among the Marwari sahukars by chopping off their ears and noses and plundering their property. Bands of Kolis of the hills between Poona and Thana districts had from time to time murdered, mutilated and robbed moneylenders. Two of the latter were assassinated in broad daylight and in full view of the public during 1852 in widely separated parts of the Bombay Presidency and this was cited by an official as evidence of tolerance, if not approval, of violence against usurers among the rural poor. And the statistics of crime committed against moneylenders during this period in seven districts of the Bombay Presidency—14 murders, 16 dacoities and robberies, 34 thefts, 8 arsons, 39 cases of hurt and wounding and so on adding up to a total of 170 offences in the five and a half years preceding the riots of 1875, an annual rate of about 31 cases—leave nothing unsaid about the focus of the peasant debtor's hostility towards his class enemies.[37] Concentration such as this generates a sort of synonymy[38] which helps to disperse at least some of the ambiguity of this particular type of rural crime. The diversity of violence addressed to one single group of the population —murder, arson, robbery, assault, etc. all directed against moneylenders—has the effect of underscoring not only the wickedness of the objects of such violence but also the morality of the latter as a measure of just retribution in the eyes of the less delinquent members of the agrarian community. There is in this perception the beginnings of the peasants' sense of themselves as a social mass defined not only by a common grievance but also by the possibility of obtaining redress through militant

[37] Ibid.: 4–5.

[38] For the concept of synonymy as used here and its function as an eliminator of semantic noise, see Macy *et al.*: 285–94.

and collective action—the beginnings, if no more than that, of a recognition of their identity as a class-for-itself.

It is precisely the combination of a high frequency of occurrence and a duplication of the coding system that makes the class character of the more powerful and massive peasant uprisings so explicit—explicit at least to the rural masses. For an insurrection incorporates crime such as what has been discussed above and abolishes it thus as a form of social protest: an optimal defiance of authority, it subsumes all other acts of defiance of lesser magnitude by providing them with a total and new context. This is the context of a class war—that is, a struggle in which opposing classes consciously allow force to decide between irreconcilable aims. And just as 'meaning is controlled by the use of language in situations',[39] crime in the new social context comes to signify an integral part of a comprehensive system of defiance—a *parole* in a new *langue*: in short, it changes codes.

This code-switching is seldom overlooked by the peasantry. Tolerant, by tradition, towards crimes of indigence as a necessary aberration rather than as a positive virtue,[40] they now see in rebellion the operations of a *rite de passage* turning criminals into insurgents. This is an experience shared by many agrarian societies. Poor peasants driven to crime by feudal oppression in China rallied to the banner of the hero of *The Water Margin* in his revolt against the Emperor. Some notorious 'bad characters' turned out to be important local leaders of the peasant war in Germany in the sixteenth century.[41] Rudé has noticed how the Swing movement of agricultural labourers in parts of south-eastern England was on some occasions led by smugglers—'a

[39] G. W. Turner: 116.

[40] This is an important distinction. Even the Palermo woman who, as quoted above, would have no objection to admitting to the Fascio those who had been forced by poverty to commit petty crimes, insisted that the aim of this policy was to induce them 'not to commit crimes again', and that 'the object of the Fascio is to give men all the conditions for no longer committing crimes'. Hobsbawm: 183.

[41] Jäcklein Rohrbach, the celebrated leader of the Heilbronn area, was known to be a 'defiant, violent and daring chap' who was suspected to have been involved in the murder of a nobleman, the mayor of Böckingen, and 'he had many debts' (Zimmermann: I 368). For the English and Russian instances cited in the rest of this paragraph see respectively H & R: 105, 106 and Hobsbawm: 27.

natural group of "activists" in this part of the world'. The outlaw has indeed some advantages over others in leading an insurrection: he is less bound by deference to the authorities with whom he has already been at war for some time; and of course he has already acquired a certain amount of expertise in the techniques of defiance. This is why on the outbreak of a revolt existing bands of brigands could be better suited to act as its 'shocktroops', as Hobsbawm puts it. A Russian experience he cites in support of this view illustrates at the same time and very elegantly indeed the formal acknowledgement by the peasantry of the criminal's transformation into the insurgent. Two men who had taken to brigandage after being expelled from an Ukrainian village community as criminals were re-admitted to it when they emerged as the leaders of a local uprising in 1905.

The history of India under British rule is not wanting in instances of those who had once broken the law as individuals or members of small criminal bands and did it all over again on a larger scale as initiators and organizers of rural revolt. There is a reference to a certain Siddoo Sitooba, described as an 'old offender', leading the riots against a moneylender of the village of Pimpalgaon during the anti-usury struggles in Maharashtra in 1875.[42] What particular offence made the Deputy Superintendent of Police of Poona district attach that stigma to Sitooba's name we do not know. But we have on record a curious detail of Titu Mir's career to show how radical the shift from crime to insurgency could be. He was apparently a professional wrestler who, according to a knowledgeable official, 'became a servant to any Zemindar who desired to create Disturbances or to exact from their Ryotts'. Convicted for 'his Service in an affray which took place in the Nuddeah District' he was in prison for some time before going on a pilgrimage to Mecca from where he returned as a disciple of Syed Ahmed and a reformer. When he eventually shot into fame as a leader of the Barasat bidroha he was still mentioned in official correspondence as 'a released convict'.[43] A mercenary who used to

[42] Deputy Superintendent of Police to District Magistrate of Poona (17 June 1875) in DRCR (C) 4.

[43] JC, 3 Apr. 1832: Alexander to Barwell (28 Nov. 1831); JC, 22 Nov. 1831: Barwell to Thomason (14 Nov. 1831).

hire himself out as an instrument of landlord tyranny against the peasantry had obviously turned his own consciousness upside down—a genuine case of *fanshen*—in order to serve as an instrument of popular violence against landlords.

The trajectory of peasant consciousness was not in all instances characterized by such a dramatic change of direction. More often than not it was a matter of robber turned rebel. Two of the principal dacoits of the Kajirhat area were mentioned by Goodlad among the organizers of the dhing of 1783. Again, one knows of Merhai Singh, 'a dacoit who formerly was tried for theft, &c. and was imprisoned in Agra Jail but at the outbreak [of the Mutiny] escaped and [had] ever since been causing a great deal of trouble'. By the time he was captured by De Kantzow in the vicinity of Pawayan and sent back to Agra in the summer of 1859, he was described in the Anglo-Indian press as yet 'another rebel leader' brought to justice.[44] None of their exploits however testifies more fully to such a transformation than the careers of two Santal bandits. The hool, as we have seen, was preceded by a spate of gang robberies. That these were the acts of famished men driven to desperation was obvious even to the authorities. 'In many of the cases entered as Dacoities', wrote the police chief of the province, 'nothing but articles of food were carried off, and the prisoners averred that their sole object was to procure food. Many committed offences against property for the purpose of being put in jail and thus escaping from starvation.'[45] Yet this did not stop the law from dealing most severely with them. The details that we have for a small sample of 42 of such 'dacoits' convicted in Bhagalpur show that 13 of them were sentenced to 16 years each of hard labour in irons and the rest to 10 years each of hard labour also in irons—the terms to be spent, for both categories, in externment away from their home districts. And their age distribution—85.7 per cent in the 25–40 group—makes it clear how hunger and the hand of colonial justice combined to hit the community in the guts, first by turning its most mature male adults into criminals and then by cutting them off

[44] For these two instances see MDS: 324 and FSUP: V 921–2.

[45] JP, 17 May 1855, no. 27. The figures which follow are based on statistics given in JP, 7 June 1855, no. 106.

from their families. Among these 'dacoits' there were, in 1854, two men, Kewala Paramanik of Sindree and Domon Majhi of Hatbanda, who were both to figure prominently in the rebellion.[46] The former, described after his capture as 'the person who was principally concerned in the Sonthal dacoities of last year & who then evaded apprehension', emerged in 1855 as a principal leader of the hool. An exceptionally capable organizer by all accounts he had managed to avoid official attention for most of the time during the rebellion—until in fact his arrest towards the very end of the pacification campaign when the government realized that the man in their custody (who, meanwhile, had assumed a pseudonym) was indeed 'one of the chief instigators & planners of the present insurrection'. He apparently was one of those who had masterminded the two key moves—the communal hunt at Buro Koondee and the march to Hazaribagh in the spring of 1855—which mobilized the Santals and made them ready for the uprising. Then he led the hool in its western sector. Domon Majhi, too, surfaces in the records of the counter-insurgency campaign, but as Domon Daroga. The new designation indicates a change of his role from village head to rebel captain—a change mediated by brigandage and acknowledged both by the Santal high command and the masses who called all their second-ranking war-leaders 'Darogas'—that is, captains of the rank-and-file 'Sipahis'. He was certainly close enough to Kanhu to be trusted, together with Kewala, for the dangerous—and at that particular juncture, politically crucial—mission of executing the traitor who had betrayed Sido to the authorities. An intrepid fighter, his

[46] Both Kewala and Domon were recruited for his own gang by Bir Singh, a regional chief (parganait) of the Santals. He professed to know how to put the inmates of a house to sleep before robbing them. The ability of particularly inspired burglars to cast a sleeping spell on their victims is a folk tradition of long standing in eastern India. But Bir Singh's claim to have been blessed with this magic power only recently by Chando Bonga, the principal deity of his tribe, and its use as a protective device for raids in that critical year, 1854, contain more than a faint suggestion of the morality of breaking into the houses of the Bengali moneylenders. K. K. Datta: 51–2. The direct quotations and the information on Kewala and Domon used in this paragraph have been taken from JP, 4 Oct. 1855: Money to Bidwell (6 Sept. 1855) and Lloyd to GOI (9 Sept. 1855); JP, 8 Nov. 1855: Bidwell to GOB (13 Oct. 1855) and Grey to GOI (31 Oct. 1855); JP, 6 Dec. 1855: 'Statement of Runjeet Pergunnait of Sarmi'. For some further discussion on the circumstances of Domon's death, see Chapter 5 below.

death made some people very happy indeed. 'I rejoice in the death of this man,' wrote a gleeful official on receiving Domon's severed head from a collaborator: 'his death will be a blow to the insurgents.'

The transformation of robbers into rebels made sense to the Santals. Most of the dacoities of 1854 had been committed against the Bengali moneylenders regarded by the peasantry of Damin-i-Koh as their most vicious oppressors. The officials too knew this to be true, as one can see from the Bhagalpur judge's reference in a letter written in the spring of 1855 to 'the fact of some dacoities having occurred at the close of that year which were attributed to the Santals' discontent with the Bengallee Muhajuns'.[47] Thus even as crimes these contained, from the peasant's point of view, an element of moral justification in so far as they represented a desperate attempt by the poor to relieve hunger at the expense of their over-fed exploiters. Yet the law had singled out the Santal for punishment while the mahajan was not merely spared but positively pampered by the police and the courts. The leaders of the hool registered their protest against such iniquity in all their statements. 'I have often complained [about] this to Pontet', said Sido about the way the Damin-i-Koh official of that name had dealt with him, 'but he never listened, I gave him petitions at Burrisuagore, Barhet, Gutcharree, but he will not listen. I also petitioned him at Rajmehal. He only said you have eaten first from the Mahajuns "banchut Sala" now you come to complain "Sala banchut".'[48] It was the use of such double standards which was one of the most important causes of the uprising. Even a myopic officialdom came to see this for itself, albeit rather late in the day, as it was alerted to the rumour which spread soon after the outbreak to the effect that 'avenging the punishment inflicted on their comrades concerned in last year's Dacoities' was the purpose for which the rebels had taken up arms. 'Those Dacoities were committed on the Bengallee Mahajuns who had oppressed them; and they complained that their comrades had been punished, while nothing had been done to the Mahajuns

[47] JP, 17 May 1855: Bell to Registrar, Court of Sadar Dewany Adalat, Ft. William, 28 Apr. 1855.

[48] JP, 8 Nov. 1855: 'Examination of Sedoo Sonthal late Thacoor'. 'Sala' means 'brother-in-law'; 'banchut' means 'sister-fucker'.

whose exactions had compelled them to take the law into their own hands.'[49] It was easy therefore for the Santals to regard the rebellion as a collective bid for social justice already initiated in a small, if rather aberrant, way by the dacoities of the previous year. The hool provided a context in which that limited and somewhat tainted violence of 1854 was transformed into a purer, generalized and just war, cleansing and transforming the previous year's agents too in the process.

There was of course no immediate recognition of this process on the part of the authorities. During the earlier phase of the uprising the official point of view tended to cling on the whole to the familiar penal code, although there was a shade of difference between those in remote control and those on the spot. To the administrators one remove away from the village the Santals were 'rebel dacoits'[50]—an ambiguous expression in which the adjective, though by no means an acknowledgement of a just cause, signifies at least a grudging acceptance of the exceptional nature of this particular 'crime' as an open and collective act of defiance. Their subordinates, however, were far too close to the event and far too tied to routine to notice any difference. Hunter has commented on this combination of insensitivity and inertia among the men on the spot. Some of them, he points out, had reported much progress in the material conditions of the people and a corresponding decline in crime only a few months ago, so that 'it took time for men who had written in this strain in February to realize that their district was the seat of rebellion in July'. Besides, they failed to grasp, at the initial stages at least, that the violence which had just erupted was, despite some apparent similarities, quite different in character from gang robbery so familiar to them.

Night attacks on houses by bands of from five to fifty men had always been common in Bengal, and *it was a difficult matter to pronounce the exact line at which such enterprises cease to be civil offences and become overt insurrection.* A single example will suffice. 'The whole inquiry only tends to prove', wrote the magistrate of Beerbhoom, with regard to the sacking of a Bengali hamlet, 'that it was one of those occurrences common in Bengal, when the Dacoits were bold, adventurous, and determined, the Bengali a coward and helpless, and the village watchmen all

[49] JP, 19 July 1855: Brown to GOB, 9 July 1855.
[50] Ibid.: Eden to Grey, 10 July 1855.

absent from their posts.' It is possible that in this individual case the magistrate may have been right in his conjecture, but in many similar cases there can be no doubt that *he mistook rebellion for robbery.*[51]

The Birbhum Magistrate was not the only one of local officers to mistake rebellion for robbery. To Mahesh Lal Datta, the daroga of Dighee, too, the sullen mass of peasants around him on that July morning looked like dacoits. For twenty years he had grown up with crime (or what he broadly understood to be so) in that area[52] and dealt with it as a chore according to his not too refined notion of law and order. Blinkered by routine he had not noticed the change that had come over the Santals he thought he knew so well, and ended up by paying for this with his life. What happened at that flash point when Sido drew his sword and inaugurated the hool by slaying Mahesh Daroga, is not clear in all respects. As with many other flash points, here too the historian must content himself with an impression which has most of the detail bleached out by over-exposure. Yet the residual outline pieced together from the recollections of one of the protagonists[53] is clear enough to suggest that a clash between the peasants' view of themselves as rebels and a daroga's insistence on dealing with them as criminals is what triggered off the insurrection.

For years it had been Mahesh Daroga's practice to accept bribes from the mahajans in order to harass, arrest and send up the Santals to the nearest district headquarters for detention and trial on false charges of dacoity. He did this so indiscriminately that even the more affluent Santals had turned against him. One of them whose prosperity had made him so much of an object of the mahajans' envy (presumably because it was not easy for them to exploit him) and the daroga's oppression that after being manhandled by the latter he swore: 'We shall see how much twine could the Daroga procure so as to fasten all the

[51] Hunter (1897): 244. Emphasis added. [52] K. K. Datta: 52, 142.

[53] There are four eye-witness accounts on record of the events at Panchkathia on 7 July 1855. Two of these, viz. Woozeer Sheikh's (JP, 19 July 1855: 'The deposition of Woozeer Sheikh taken on oath before the Assistant Magistrate of Aurangabad on the 9th July 1855') and Sido's (JP, 8 Nov. 1855: 'Examination of Sedoo Sonthal late Thacoor') tell us what happened but not how. It is only the two statements taken from Kanhu after his arrest (JP, 20 Dec. 1855: 'Statement of Insurgent Sonthals'; ibid.: 'Examination of Kanoo Sonthal') which help us to get a closer look at the incidents as reconstructed here on the basis of this information.

peaceful Santals whom the wicked Daroga wanted to be sent up.'[54]

The twine with which the innocent peasants of Damin-i-Koh would have their hands tied behind their backs as they were marched under police escort to Bhagalpur on false charges of house-breaking and robbery, had apparently come to be regarded as a hated symbol of official justice. Indeed, the expression 'cart loads of rope' occurs several times in Kanhu's statements. According to him, a man from the police station had called at his house on 6 July 1855 to have a look at a gathering of the Santal chiefs there and 'went away saying he would return the next day with the Darogah and a hundred men with two cart loads of rope to bind them'. He proved true to his word, for, as Kanhu's narrative, taking both the versions together, goes on to say:[55]

> The next morning it was proposed to go out to Shikar. Kanoo, Seedoo, many Manjees and others, amounting to 40 or 50 went out for this purpose, armed as usual for a Shikar. On their way they met the Darogah of Burro, Mohesh Lal, with two Sepoys of the Police and several Mohajuns and two cart loads of rope, and asked where going, replied to Shikar, but the Darogah said, they were intending Dacoitee and were complained against by the Mohajuns accompanying . . . The Mahajuns complained to Buiro Darogah that Seedoo & Kanoo were collecting men to commit a dacoitee. The Mehajuns gave him 100 Rs to come & catch us . . . I said why have you come . . . he said that the 'Moiras have come to complain that you are collecting men for a dacoitee'. I said prove it, if I have committed a theft or Dacoitee . . . said the Mohajuns must be fined 5 rupee each for false complaint . . . The Mahajuns said, 'If it costs us 1000 Rs to your 5, we will do that to get you imprisoned' . . . [Kanhu] saw the cart loads of rope and told the Darogah he had prejudged them, else why the ropes for binding them. An altercation ensued . . . The Mahajuns began to tie Seedoo my brother. Then I drew my sword. Then they left off tying my brother & I cut Manick Modie's head off & Seedoo killed the Darogah & my army killed 5 men . . .

Mahesh Daroga was thus a martyr to his own incomprehension. He could not understand that by refusing to submit to starvation or seek relief in gang robbery, the Santals had transformed

[54] K. K. Datta: 53.

[55] We have collapsed the two statements together here. The reporting, indirect in the first of these and direct in the second one, has been left as in the original. For references see n. 53 above.

themselves into rebels and their consciousness changed codes. This is why the 'cart loads of rope', a punitive message meant to intimidate dacoits and meaningful only in terms of the old penal code, failed to frighten those who had just constituted themselves into an 'army' and were about to declare war against the Raj itself. Those first fatal cuts at Panchkathia were clearly the outcome of a dialogue in which neither of the interlocutors understood the other's language.

Such miscognition was characteristic of a good deal of the official response to the peasant uprisings of the period of the Mutiny too. This is more than amply documented by the reports we have from the district administrators of the time on the disturbances in Uttar Pradesh in 1857–8. What emerges from this vast body of literature is a perception impaled on a single stereotype of rural violence. Unable to distinguish between rebellion and dacoity it tended to classify all 'rebels' as 'dacoits', as if the two words meant the same thing. 'Large hordes of *dacoits* from Rampore and the Moradabad District filled the Bhabur villages of lower Kota', wrote the Commissioner of Kumaun; 'I could not offer any efficient resistance, and the *rebels* having in a few days plundered the villages, the country was left a desert.'[56] Or, take the following extracts from the 'narrative of events' written by R. M. Edwards, Officiating Magistrate of Muzaffarnagar, on the eve of the insurrection there:

On the 15th [of May 1857] or following day information was received that the *people of the neighbouring villages* were collecting in great numbers round the city and proposed attacking and plundering it. On this the Cotewal and the Duffadar of sowars . . . went with a party of district sowars, attacked and completely dispersed the *dacoits* bringing in some 15 or 20 prisoners . . .

In the absence of a jail [destroyed by the insurgents the previous day] *these dacoits* were ordered to be flogged and released . . . The prisoners were caught *with arms in their hands in open resistance to Government authority* and should one and all have been hung on the spot.

. . . we see how effectively a few district sowars drove back and thoroughly dispersed *this large body of dacoits* . . .

[56] This extract and the next are taken from FSUP: V 272 and V 81 respectively. Emphasis added.

Quite clearly Edwards was confronted with a rising of the rural population around the town of Muzaffarnagar. Indeed he came close to acknowledging this to be so when he referred to the participants as villagers 'with arms in their hands in open resistance to Government authority'. However, the habit of identifying any serious violence in the countryside as dacoity won out in the end and an all too familiar term taken from the lexicon of the thana and the *faujdari adalat* was made to describe a very different order of disturbances.

The local leaders of these *émeutes* too were often branded by the same name. They emerged in large numbers in the rural areas as the mutiny of the sepoys in the nearby garrisons detonated pent-up anger against moneylenders, landlords, officials and a host of village tyrants. The jacqueries which thus broke out were led by men with grassroot connections. Inevitably, there were among them a handful of professional dacoits who were tempted to join in the violence only by the prospect of loot or were, as discussed above, re-integrated into the agrarian community by the very force and mass of an insurrection. But it is clear even from the government's own information that the great majority of them were not criminals. More often than not they were members of some of the local subaltern groups and had come to acquire a degree of authority as a result of dislocations in the existing power structure. Or, they belonged to big landed families, and took up arms in order to grab more land, gain a following and settle old scores with rivals or with the sarkar itself if they had any particular grievance against the latter over lost privileges. Whatever their status they were able to mobilize the peasantry in a manner and on a scale quite clearly distinct from dacoity. Yet the distinction was not always grasped by the district and subdivisional authorities. The trauma of these sudden explosions drove them to stigmatize their protagonists indiscriminately as dacoits.

For some fairly representative samples of such 'blurring' one could turn to the contemporary accounts of the disturbances which occurred in Etawah district in 1858.[57] Here the authorities had much difficulty in coping with the activities of Benkut

[57] On the Etawah leaders discussed in this and the next paragraph see FSUP V: 782–3, 802–3 for Benkut Singh; ibid.: 775, 787, 795, 803 for Ganga Singh and Roop Singh; and ibid.: 795, 801, 842 for Niranjan Singh.

Singh. He led a large force of sepoys and armed peasants against the government, clashed with and killed some members of a party headed by Alan Hume, the Magistrate, and sacked a place called Ajitmal. A local leader of considerable standing he was, according to Hume's own estimate, 'assisted by the entire population of the villages of Shahpore, Rajpoorah, Ramnugger and Ayanah'. When the magistrate led a raid into one of these villages, he found it 'entirely deserted, even by women and children', and again, when he and his men were about to withdraw after burning down an insubordinate village, 'the sepoys [i.e. mutineers] and a large force of armed villagers issued' from another. The figure sketched by these details taken from official sources is unmistakably that of a popular leader whose following was large enough to enable him to engage a superior enemy in the classic steps of a guerilla war. And yet with all this evidence before him the Magistrate spoke about Benkut Singh as a dacoit leader and a rebel almost in the same breath in two consecutive paragraphs of his 'narrative'. It was as if the official mind was still undecided as to which of these two descriptions to focus on: pushed by the undoubted fact of insurgency in one direction it was pulled at the same time in the other by the habit of classifying collective acts of rural violence as dacoity according to the book.

There were some other Etawah leaders too for whom the two appellations were used interchangeably in much the same way. One of them, Ganga Singh, claimed to have been 'appointed Nazim of Etawah'. He led 'a well organized attack', though with no success, on the government's forces in an attempt to recover Nimree, 'one of the chief rebel strongholds on the Jumna-Chumbul Doab'. His name is often mentioned together with Niranjan Singh's and Roop Singh's in contemporary accounts. Members of well-established landed families in the district they could hardly be confounded with professional criminals. The former was the Raja of Chakarnagar and the latter an uncle of the minor Raja of Bhurrey. Together they put up the most enduring resistance to British rule in this region during the period of the Mutiny and were recognized by the authorities as having 'maintained the only remaining hostile force in the Etawah District' as late as September 1858. Niranjan Singh eluded the law for a long time before he was finally captured in May 1861. By then, three years after the end of the great rebellion, even the semi-official *Friend of India* had regained enough of its sense of perspective to acknowledge him as the rebel who had 'assumed independent authority and seized the revenue of the district in 1857'. In the official reports of 1858, however, he remains classified as a dacoit leader.

Roop Singh was perhaps the most formidable of all the Etawah insurgents the British had to deal with.[58] He appears to have been the rallying point for many other rebel bands in the region including those led by Benkut Singh, Ganga Singh, Peetam Singh and Niranjan Singh, and for a time there was a ground-swell of support for him from the mass of armed peasants and soldiers on their way back home from mutinous garrisons. By October 1857 he had gathered about a thousand men and was reported to have 'commenced, at the request of the mutineers, a bridge at Sheregurh' to enable the latter to cross the Jamuna. Dalalnagar pargana in the Auraiya tahsil fell to him. His stronghold, a mud fort at Ayanah which 'promised to be of very great strength', according to Hume, and was 'the terror of the neighbourhood', as the colonialist press put it, went on defying the British until April 1858. There could indeed be no doubt about the terror exercised by Roop Singh and his men against those who continued actively to collaborate with the Raj in that part of Uttar Pradesh. As a correspondent from Etawah wrote to the *Bengal Hurkaru and India Gazette* on 9 June 1858:

> The Ajeetmul Thannadar was attacked by a party of Burhee rebels as he was passing the rebel village Bowain, on the Jumna; he and his party escaped, but two of his Burkundazes who were lagging behind were seized, disarmed and murdered at the village, and their heads carried off to Roop Singh at Burhee.
>
> . . . Mr Lance immediately proceeded . . . but before Bowain was reached the rebels had recrossed the Jumna and were comfortably settled in their stronghold, the Burhee fort.[59]

The rebel occupation of the fort at Burhi continued for some time to cause much anxiety to the British. Located at the con-

[58] The source of our information on Roop Singh's career in the account which follows is, unless otherwise stated, FSUP V: 776, 782, 786, 794–6, 798, 799, 803, 804, 835–6, 841–2.

[59] FSUP V: 787–8. For a somewhat different version of the incident see ibid.: 792.

fluence of the Chambal and the Jamuna it commanded the passage of the river and was thus a source of much strategic advantage to whichever party held it. Eventually, in September 1858, it was reduced and in fact blown up in a carefully planned and combined operation of the local troops and the Madras Sappers. Dislodged from his stronghold Roop Singh retreated with his followers and some of the allied bands to the ravines on the Gwalior bank of the Chambal. In this traditional sanctuary for fugitives from the law his support among the people was still large enough to make the British authorities warn the local zamindars who had sheltered him and his men that 'if repeated, their conduct would be punishable'. They also made a representation to the Gwalior Darbar 'with a view to obtaining its consent to a suggestion by the Magistrate of Etawah that he should have authority in effect to punish at his discretion certain villages of the ravines of the Chumbul and Kowaree in Gwalior which had harboured or abetted Roop Singh and other rebel plunderers mostly natives of Etawah'. The British and the Gwalior State governments planned a joint expedition 'to sweep the ill-affected portion of the Gwalior Territory', and a detachment made up of European and Darbar troops was sent out at one point to stop him from joining forces with Man Singh. The last that we hear of him from the records is that a police party led by a Lieutenant Forbes surprised him at a village called Manikpur near Baiswarah on the Chambal, but he gave them the slip.

Nothing more is known about him. However, it should be clear even from this brief sketch based entirely on official sources that there was hardly anything either in Roop Singh's background or in his career during those stormy years to justify characterizing him as a common bandit. Scion of a landed family he emerged as the focal point for rebel mobilization in an entire region—a sort of Kunwar Singh of Etawah district. Even after the initial reverses in his battle against the Raj, even in the period of his retreat into the Chambal ravines he seems to have secured and retained a base among the peasantry strong enough to protect him against the counter-insurgency operations mounted jointly by the colonial and princely armies. There is no evidence at all to show that he ever lost any of this popular support and was forced thereby into a life of crime. Yet the words 'dacoit' and 'rebel' were used almost interchangeably to describe him in the official statements of the time—a fact which goes again to demonstrate how slow the administration could be in its response to the radically changed character of rural violence in conditions of insurgency.

A certain degree of cognitive failure of this kind was of course inevitable during agrarian disturbances under the Raj. It represented that inertia which made it difficult for an alien and authoritarian regime to grasp promptly enough the meaning of a quick change of temper among the habitually docile mass of peasantry. For that stagnant, semi-feudal social order derived its stability from a firm and traditional if tacit agreement between the rulers and the ruled on a mutually acceptable code of dominance and subordination. Any abrupt and extensive deviation of the subaltern masses from this code was bound to take the authorities by surprise, and the almost unavoidable delay on their part in adjusting themselves to a switch of this order had often to be dearly paid for. Indeed it was thus that, as mentioned above, Mahesh Lal Datta, daroga, found himself trapped between two codes, one that was known but moribund and the other emergent, hence unfamiliar, and triggered off that fatal explosion by trying to decipher a message put out in the new language of rebellion in terms of the old one of criminality. Yet his incomprehension is not difficult to explain. It resulted from his failure to read correctly the sign of a change in Santal consciousness at a moment when this change was actually taking place—that critical split-second when a mistake of this sort could not but cause a collision.

Historians however have been known to make the same mistake with less justification and get away with it. It is still very common for many of them to let their source material, almost invariably of an administrative nature, command their view of peasant revolts both in fact and judgement. The reliance on official evidence cannot be helped in most cases because of the absence or inadequacy of information of any other kind. But for a modern scholar to vitiate his work with the subjectivity of the guardians of law and order is to renounce the advantage he has over any contemporary witness of an event—that is, the advantage of looking at it as a past and the corrective influence this has on the bias generated by instantaneous reaction. Colonialist historiography of course abounds in exercises of this kind, but that is hardly surprising in view of the intimate connection that existed between writing history and running the Raj. What is curious is the continuing imitation of this idiom in post-colonial India. Thus, in a study of the Pabna disturbances of 1873, published a hundred years after the event,[60] the historian's voice has been allowed to merge with that of the local sub-divisional officer as he speaks of the 'bad characters' and 'the criminal sections who took advantage of the excitement'. This agrees with the colonialist claim so lucidly formulated by William Hunter at the time when he said that by these struggles 'the rural population have proved themselves quick to appreciate and to act upon the rights which English rule secures to rich and poor . . . and are conducting before our eyes an agrarian revolution by due course of law'.[61] Any act of lawlessness, therefore, has to be explained away as an aberration caused by 'the bad characters who had evidently joined them [the peasantry] for their own gains and induced them in many instances to go far beyond their original intentions'. And to buttress this view the author quotes from a contemporary periodical which stigmatizes all cases of violence during this movement as 'the acts of a number of professional clubmen and thieves joined by the more foolish and ignorant villagers'.[62] An echo of the regime's concern at any critique of high landlordism turning into a 'critique by arms' on the part of the rural masses, this was precisely what had alarmed a district officer forty years ago when he observed how Titu Mir's forces brought about 'the voluntary junctions of all the Dacoyts and bad Characters of the Country to their ranks'.[63]

Why do 'foolish and ignorant villagers' who are usually so peaceful and averse to crime and often preyed upon at other times by clubmen, dacoits and 'bad Characters of the Country' join the latter on such occasions? Because a powerful and sustained class struggle like the resistance of the Barasat or

[60] Sen Gupta.

[61] Hunter (1875): Preface. Sen Gupta quotes this extract, but omits the first boastful sentence about the benefits of British rule. Sen Gupta: 59.

[62] Ibid.: 58 and n. 137.

[63] JC, 6 Dec. 1831: Smith to Money (26 Nov. 1831).

Pabna peasantry tends to invest the disparate attacks on property and person with new meanings and rephrase them as a part of a general discourse of rebellion. Consequently, each of these acts acquires an ambivalence: wired at the same time to two different codes—the code of individualistic or small-group deviance from the law where it originates and that of collective social defiance which adopts it—it bears the twin signs of a birth-mark and a becoming. It is precisely this duplex character which permits it to be interpreted one way or the other depending on the interpreter's point of view. A daroga or a historian who thinks like a daroga would be inclined to interpret it in terms of its past and condemn it. On the contrary, a rebel or a historian who adopts the rebel point of view would tend to seize on its present signification as the highest form of social protest and justify it. In other words, there will be a clash between two ways of looking at it—'It's terrible!'/'It's fine!'—a clash between two theories.

CHAPTER 4

MODALITY

Public character of insurgency—Kol and Santal declarations of war on the Raj—support from public authority claimed in favour of rebellion—investiture of a rebel 'nawab'*—rebellion as a 'collective enterprise'—parleys and panchayats—assemblies: their role in mobilizing peasantry—considered dangerous by the regime—communal and corporate aspects of insurgency—idioms of collective fishing and hunting—working together as families and neighbours—four forms of struggle—wrecking—burning—a critique of economism—eating—looting—plunder as an idiom of peasant war—totality of rebel violence—horizontal and vertical pluralities—postscript on killing.*

What differentiates a peasant rebellion from rural crime is not its inversive function which is common to both and leads people often to mistake one for the other. The confusion, as discussed in the previous chapter, is particularly acute during that twilight phase which separates the actual outbreak of an insurrection from its precursor—the wave of 'preliminary outrages' as it is called in official language. But insurgency soon extricates itself from the placenta of common crime in which it may be initially enmeshed and establishes its own identity as a violence which is *public*, *collective*, *destructive* and *total* in its modalities. Each of these constitutes a distinctive feature in the sense that it has its antithesis in crime, so that the opposition between the two types of violence may be represented as a series of binary contrasts thus—public/secretive, collective/individualistic, destructive/appropriative and total/partial.

To turn to the first of these modalities, rebellion is by its very nature an open and public event. As such, it stands in clear opposition to crime which must rely on secrecy to be effective. It would perhaps not be untrue to say that a tendency towards an open and public affirmation is already evident in certain intermediate types of rural violence, such as the more advanced forms of social banditry, which fall just short of rebellion. The Robin Hoods of many countries have been known to express this tendency in terms of a nonchalance tinged often with a sort of black humour. This is illustrated by a hilarious and authentic anecdote in Jim Corbett's account of Sultana.[1] A contractor who employed a large labour force to fell trees for logging in the jungles of the Terai was induced by the police to invite the dacoit chief and his band to an evening of festivities to begin with a nautch and end with a banquet. Sultana, whose 'intelligence staff numbered hundreds', knew that the invitation was a trap devised by the commander of the Special Dacoity Police Force, but accepted it. On arrival at the contractor's camp in the middle of the forest where the best nautch girls and musicians had been hired for the evening and much food and drink stocked up for the feast to follow, Sultana prevailed upon his host to reverse the scheduled order of merriment and start off with feasting, for, he said, 'his men would enjoy the dance more on full stomachs than on empty ones'. After they had eaten and drunk well, he gathered his band, thanked his host for his hospitality and left regretting that they could not stay for the rest of the entertainment as they had such a long way to go. By the time the drums struck up the signal simultaneously for the nautch to begin and the police party to close in on their quarry, Sultana and his men had slipped away in the darkness.

Not every public act of social banditry is however informed with such witticism. It can take a sombre, declamatory form, too, as it did with 'King John', the legendary chief of the Hampshire Blacks. Alarmed at being mistaken for a Jacobite, he made up his mind to define his position clearly and openly. He 'knew well what he was doing', observes Thompson, 'and took care to make it public'.[2] He made it known that he intended publicly to answer the charge of Jacobitism at a specified date and place. On that day he rode up with a small armed escort to the appointed place, declared his allegiance to the Hanoverian succession before an audience of about three hundred people who had already gathered there, and made it clear at the same time 'that they [the Blacks] had no other design than to do justice, and to see that the rich did not insult or oppress the poor; that they were determined not to leave a

[1] Corbett: 100–2. [2] Thompson (1975): 145.

deer on the Chase, being well assured it was originally designed to feed cattle, and not to fatten deer for the clergy, &c'.[3]

An open affirmation of intent is of course even more characteristic of rebels than of social bandits. Unlike criminals they make no attempt to conceal violence by any pretence to conform to law and order. No criminal can possibly be so matter-of-fact and explicit about the purpose of his visit to the site of his intended crime as were the Russian insurgents of 1905 during a raid on an estate as recalled by its landlord.

> 'Why have you come?' I asked them. 'To demand corn, to make you give us your corn', said several voices simultaneously. 'That is to say, you have come to plunder?' 'If you like, to plunder', said a young lad in the crowd . . .[4]

These are not the voices of thieves operating under the cover of darkness. The Kols of Chota Nagpur too are known to have made a strident avowal when they finally gave up any hope of obtaining justice either from the colonial authorities or from the local chiefs and pledged themselves to annihilate all tax collectors (*thikadars*), wreck all villages and townships including Govindpur itself and 'wash their weapons in the river (the Karroo) which flows past it'.[5] The Santals involved in the hool made no secret either of their intention to slay the rajas of Pakur and Maheshpur as well as all other landlords, mahajans, policemen and white planters, railway engineers and officials they could lay their hands on.[6] Every village they attacked was given an explicit warning well in advance, as the knowledgeable Captain Sherwill found out in the Colgong area. 'The burning of these villages', he wrote with reference to a number of these destroyed by the rebels on 19 and 21 July 1855, 'had been notified four days previously by the sonthals to the zemindars the very hour of the day being mentioned.' He also named seven other villages south of that station which 'had been in a similar manner warned for pillage and burning on or about 26th or 27th July', but were all except one saved by the timely arrival

[3] Ibid.: 145–6. [4] Hobsbawm: 186.

[5] BC 1502 (58891): Dent & Wilkinson to Thomason (16 Nov. 1832).

[6] There are many instances of this in the records. See, for instance, JP, 19 July 1855: Eden to Grey (9 & 10 July 1855); Taylor to Mudge (7 July 1855); Mudge to Eden (8 July 1855); Toogood to Templer (10 July 1855).

of the troops. The plan they had 'to advance by easy marches' towards Bhagalpur and Monghyr and sack these towns one after the other 'was also sent into Colgong by the sonthals for the information of the zemindars and Europeans'.[7] Later on, in September that year, they were to send a bough with three leaves on it to Suri, the headquarters of the Collector of Birbhum, to indicate that they wished to raid that town in three days' time.[8]

What testified even more to the open and public character of the hool was the *parwana* issued by Sido and Kanhu announcing their decision to take up arms. Described as 'The Thacoor's Perwannah', a sort of heavenly ultimatum communicated through the two inspired leaders of the uprising, it read in part:

The Sahibs and the white Soldiers will fight. Kanoo and Seedoo Manjee are not fighting. The Thacoor himself will fight. Therefore you Sahibs and Soldiers fight with the Thacoor himself. Mother Ganges will come to the Thacoor's (assistance). Fire will rain from Heaven . . . I will rain fire and all the Sahibs will be killed by the hand of God in person and Sahibs if you fight with muskets the Sonthal will not be hit by the bullets and the Thacoor will give your Elephants and horses of his own accord to the Sonthals and on seeing this perwannah you will understand all and you will send an answer, and if you fight with the Sonthals two days will be as one day and two nights as one night. This is the order of the Thacoor.[9]

The leaders of the insurrection clearly felt authorized by God himself in declaring war on the Raj. As their adversaries were quick to recognize, it was from this spiritual justification that the hool derived much of its drive and fury. 'It is a war ordered by the gods, they say', observed the Magistrate of Bhagalpur.[10] Some of the implications of such a belief will be discussed later in this work. Here it will suffice to say that in claiming to act on 'the order of the Thacoor' the Santals were merely affirming the public character of their rebellion.

Other rebels and social bandits too have been known to claim the support of higher authorities for themselves. The Bourbon brigands about whom Maffei wrote did not go so far as to invoke the authority of God, but came fairly close to it by

[7] JP, 20 Dec. 1855: Sherwill to Brown (18 Oct. 1855).
[8] BDR: 121. [9] TTP.
[10] JP, 23 Aug. 1855: Richardson to GOB (15 July 1855).

invoking the authority of the Pope when they said, 'We were fighting for the faith and we were blessed by the Pope.' They also believed that they were acting for Francis II, thus staking a claim at a secular counter too for legitimization. In this they conformed to an even wider pattern of rebel activity. For it is very common indeed for a peasant revolt to articulate itself in the name of a secular public authority which in most cases happens to be that of the sovereign. The peasants of the Chernigor Guberniya in 1905 believed that pillage had been authorized by the Tsar. The Swing rebels acted on the conviction that they enjoyed the support of the King and Parliament. The jacqueries against the planters in the indigo districts of Bengal drew some of their considerable striking power from the belief then widespread among the rural masses that the Queen of England herself was on their side. The peasantry involved in the rent agitation in Pabna stretched the meaning of what was a relatively favourable official gesture in the form of the proclamation of 4 July 1873 to imply that 'the government was sympathetic to the resistance movement'. A belief in the alleged intervention of a superior and more just authority against the peasant's immediate oppressors was what fuelled the fury of the Deccan riots too in 1875. Both the versions of this belief as reported to the Commission investigating these disturbances agreed that the peasants acted on the certainty that 'orders had come from England' to force the Marwaris to part with their bonds.[11]

The self-affirmation of a rebellion thus in the name of a public authority carried, appropriately enough, its own sanction in many cases. Armed as it was with a putative approval, blessing, inspiration or support of the highest public authority, insurgent violence assumed, in the eyes of its protagonists, the status of a public service. As such, it had to be paid for. Hence the levy of contributions in food, drink and money by the rebels on *their* public—a feature common to many otherwise different national experiences. The French peasants who participated in the jacqueries of 1789 'often demanded money because they were after all under the impression', says Lefebvre, 'that they were

[11] The instances cited in this paragraph have been taken, unless otherwise mentioned, from Hobsbawm: 180, 187; H & R: 18, 65, 86; Sen Gupta: 38–9; DRCR: 54.

working for the king and they could not work for nothing or wear their shoes out for no return: you had to eat and, above all, you had to drink—you couldn't live on air'.[12] In much the same way the labourers of rural England involved in the Swing movement, especially those of Berkshire and Hampshire 'demanded a fixed monetary contribution, not so much to buy food and drink as a direct payment for services rendered'.[13]

The *dhing-kharcha* (literally, the money to be raised to pay for the cost of the insurrection) imposed on the peasantry by the leaders of the uprising against Deby Sinha appears to have been a levy of the same order.[14] However, the public character of this particular insurrection is even more clearly elucidated by an episode which glows with so much meaning and yet has failed to catch the historian's eye that it may be worth retrieving it from the musty narrative of *The Report of the Rungpore Commission on the Causes of the Insurrection in Rungpore in the Year 1189*. The peasants had elected Derjenarain as their chief—'Nawab' as they called him—presented him with their *nazar* as the formal sign of fealty owing to an overlord, carried him in a palanquin to Balaganj where on the advice of Bara (Baru) Baxey, a local leader, they began to get ready for a march to Demlah. The kachari of Gaurmohan Chaudhuri, a big landlord 'who had three lakhs of rupees malguzari under him'[15] and with whom the peasants had numerous scores to settle, was located here.

The insurgents determined to go to Demlah the next day when Bara Baxey told Derjenarain 'that there were horsemen and Barkandases stationed at Demlah who would attack them and therefore it was to little purpose to go there; . . . however he proposed that the insurgents should go to Demlah, and if they obtained redress, it was very well, but if Gaurmohan should attack them, they would repel his attack'; telling Derjenarain that 'as he was Nabob, he must forgive them for what excesses (*loot mar*), plunder and murder were committed', that Derjenarain considered some time and replied 'that they did not go to fight, but were going for justice; that if Gaurmohan refused them justice and attacked them, . . . they must do the best they could, and that he forgave all excesses (*loot mar*), plunder and murder'. On this the people all shouted and proceeded towards Demlah . . .[16]

[12] Lefebvre (1973): 118. Also see ibid.: 42.

[13] H & R: 197. Also see ibid.: 116.

[14] Kaviraj: 43; Ray (1960): 109.

[15] Kaviraj: 23 n. [16] MDS: 579–80.

What we have in this episode is a rare record of the investiture of a rebellion with public authority. It tells us of the election of the rebel 'nawab' as an alternative source of authority and its formalization by the general body of the insurgents through the ritual presentation of *nazarana*. Even more important is the information it has to offer about the specific manner in which authorization issues from the putative nawab to 'forgive them [the insurgents turned subjects] for what excesses (*loot mar*), plunder and murder were committed'. The prayer for exoneration from guilt, the solemnity with which it was received and considered, and the advice so weightily pronounced granting the prayer to nobody's surprise but everybody's joy correspond to the classic three-step teleology of a Hindu *vrata* in which the uttered wish and its necessary fulfilment by divine grace must be mediated by a ritual worship of the granting deity. The ceremony described above is that of validation—the validation, one could almost say sacralization, of rebel violence as a public service duly authorized by the head of a community and undertaken by its members for their own benefit.

The mass, communal aspect of rebel violence follows thus from its open and public character and differentiates it from the typically individualistic or small-group operation of crime. A rebellion (to borrow Lefebvre's term for the peasant revolts in France in 1789) is indeed a 'collective enterprise'.[17] It uses communal processes and forms of mass mobilization, expresses mass violence in the idiom of communal labour and encourages communal appropriation of the fruits of pillage in many cases. The communal process of mobilization is best witnessed in the parleys and assemblies which inaugurate most agrarian uprisings everywhere. This is how the Peasant War in Germany began in 1525:

> . . . Then six or seven peasants met in a village near Ulm, called Baltringen, and they discussed many things while walking from one village to another, while meeting neighbours and while eating and drinking together as was peasant custom at that time. Those peasants [with whom they had eaten, etc.] went with them [to another village]. If anybody asked them what they wanted and what they were doing, they answered, 'We are collecting the Fastnacht cake'. In this way

[17] Lefebvre (1973): 118.

they travelled all Thursdays and their number increased day by day until they were 400 men. On the 8th day before the real Fastnacht . . . they gathered together at Baltringen. When they saw how many they had become, they told each other: 'There are many of us' . . .[18]

We see a very similar process of consultations and gatherings building up into an insurgent mobilization by the rural masses in Rangpur on the eve of the dhing of 1783. To quote from the official narrative of events:

. . . it appears that the ryots first met at Beedaltur in the perganah of Bamandangah and at Cornarmonah in Tepah. In consequence of a plan concerted then among themselves they assembled and from thence they proceeded to Kyneerry in Tepah where . . . Dirjinarain offered to head them . . . After this the insurgents sent 25 or 30 men to Dakallygange who released such people as were confined there for revenue. The Ryots of the neighbouring talooks assembled and came to them in great numbers . . . Dirjenarain mounted a palanquin and they proceeded to Balagange where by the advice of Baru Baxey it was proposed to go to Demlah . . . The insurgents then circulated letters to the various *talooks* ordering the ryots to assemble and join them . . .[19]

Confer, plan, assemble, attack—the sequence occurs in many an Indian uprising. The initial meeting, often in the form of an extended panchayat of the leaders of the insurgent community, had an important role to play in formulating grievances, defining the course of action and generally preparing the mass of its members for the hostilities soon to ensue. Such a meeting was reported on the eve of Titu Mir's bidroha in which the Muslim weavers (jolas) played an active and militant role. The police at Basirhat received a report from a talukdar of Sarfrazpur (a village which was soon to earn much notoriety in the disturbances that followed) 'to this purport that 20 or 30 Persons had assembled in the House of one Bolaee julah . . . and that he had sent 3 Persons to ascertain the cause of their Congregation; his men, however, were maltreated and one Peadah severely beaten'.[20] A number of such parleys are known to have preceded the Birsaite ulgulan. Some of these were reported by Rev. Hoffmann who appears to have been the voice of the true faith as well as the eyes and ears of the Raj in Munda country. 'I have been informed by a new adept of the village Simbua,' he

[18] Franz: 143. [19] MDS: 579–80.

[20] JC, 3 Apr. 1832: Alexander to Barwell (28 Nov. 1831).

wrote, 'that the attack was planned in the three panchayats on three Sundays before the event. In the two first of these panchayats, only Puranaks were present. There the date was fixed, and bands of three or sometimes four men were designated each to separate places to fire houses and send arrows among the Christian gatherings usually held on Christmas eve. In the last panchayat the nanaks or new adepts were informed of the attack.'[21]

The Kol insurrection of 1831 too had begun with a consultative meeting of this kind. As Bindrai Manki, one of its leaders, was to recall later on: 'We returned home, invited all the Coles (our Brethren and Caste) to assemble at the village of Sankah in Tamar where we had a consultation . . . Our Lives we considered of no Value, and being of one Caste and Brethren it was agreed upon that we should commence to cut, plunder, murder and eat.'[22] For the Santal rebellion we have the words of both Sido and Kanhu testifying to much preliminary cogitation before the actual outbreak. 'Then the Manjees & Purgunnaits assembled in my Verandah', said Sido after his capture, '& we consulted for 2 months.'[23] The information occurs several times in the course of his statement: 'Ever since Chait two months before the Thacoor came, the Manjees had been consulting together to kill the Mahajans.' And again, 'The Manjee & pergunnaits consulted about this in Jait in my house.' It is as if by affirming this fact of frequent communal consultations that Sido was trying to establish what was to him the unquestionable legitimacy of the violence of the hool. Indeed, he came close to saying this in almost so many words: 'All the pergunnaits & manjees consulted & advised me to fight.'

Consultation and advice often figured among the very first steps in popular mobilization in UP too during the peasant revolts of 1857–8.[24] The representatives of a community or a village would meet in a panchayat to decide what course of action the local masses should follow when they rose in arms. It was thus that in May 1857 'Panchayuts were held in the

[21] Singh: 90.

[22] BC 1363 (54227): Cuthbert & Wilkinson to Thomason (12 Feb. 1832).

[23] JP, 8 Nov. 1855: 'Examination of Sedoo Sonthal late Thacoor'.

[24] The facts and the quotations in this paragraph are taken from FSUP: IV 102–4, 284–5, 548–9 & V 41–2, 45, 49.

villages of Cheetee, Deotah, Tilbegumpoor, Dadree, etc in order to loot Secundrabad so that the beams and rafters should not be left.' These were mainly a Gujar affair. But at the panchayat held at Tilbegampur they were joined by Girooas and Gahlot Rajputs to make the insurrection into a broad alliance of the vast majority of the peasants in that part of Bulandshahr district. Again, in Allahabad where 'the Mewatis were the real contrivers of the rebellion of the sepoys and the Risala', a panchayat of the leaders of that community was held on 5 June 1857 at Saif Khan's house in mauza Samadabad and 'all, excepting Saif Khan, decided to rebel the same day'. At about the same time when an *émeute* at Azamgarh acted as a signal for revolt for 'all the loafers and vagabonds of the villages'—official euphemism for the peasantry—in Chiriakot, a pargana to the south of that town, 'the rebels counselled all the night on 4th June on the matter of robbing and that from June 5 they declared a general riot and mutiny'. And further to the east, in Ghazipur, as we shall see later,[25] the rebellion of Meghar Singh of Gahmar was to be inaugurated the following year by a gathering of representatives of all sections of the local population at Biranji on the Karmanasa.

Yet another feature of the risings of 1857–8 was the vast assemblies of the local populations which preceded the actual outbreak of violence in most instances. It was as if the peasants, shaken out of their habitual docility and subservience, turned up in their thousands in response to some invisible, unspoken and yet universally understood signal to meet their enemy in an armed struggle. We know little of the actual mechanics of such autonomous mobilization—the pull of the primordial ties of kinship, community and co-residence, the power of rumour, the compulsion of custom and religion—all of which might have combined in various degrees to make up for the absence of any formal machinery of call-up standing outside and above the rural communities. No real understanding of insurgency in colonial India will ever be achieved without a proper study of this phenomenon. What, however, can be said with certainty at the present state of research is that most of the jacqueries of the period of the Mutiny witnessed large preliminary gatherings

[25] See Chapter 7 below.

of the armed peasantry—Gujars of the villages of Deotah and Til assembling at Cheetee for an attack on the jail at Bulandshahr in order to rescue the prisoners, the assembly of Gujars and others becoming more and more frequent as the revolt gathered momentum in Saharanpur district, massed crowds of Gujars and Rangurs converging on the southern and southwestern parts of Saharanpur pargana prior to the plunder of a village close to the district headquarters and the treasury, Gujars 'assembling in thousands under regular leaders' in Meerut district, large assemblies of 'rustics' in pargana Mandawar leading up to raids on the rich Roh villages in Bijnaur district, and so on, to quote examples chosen at random from western UP alone.[26]

In the case of the Santal hool, too, the parleys among tribal chiefs led eventually to 'an assembly of sonthals at Bagnodee, at which there were many manjees, soobahs and Pergunnàits',[27] as Kanhu was to confirm in his statement when captured. It is this assembly at Bhagnadihi which alarmed the mahajans and the police so much that they lost their nerve and triggered off the revolt by underestimating the peasants' militancy. How unnerving such mobilization often was for the authorities is perhaps best illustrated by a comic incident. The Barasat bidroha (which was itself an occasion for vast gatherings of the rural poor[28]) had just been suppressed when it was rumoured that the 'Moolavies' were assembling again in large numbers—six to seven hundred of them according to one report—in the northern part of Jessore district. The Military Department of the government at Calcutta at once ordered 'a Detachment consisting of one Complete Battalion of the Native Infantry from Barrackpoor and two Six Pounder Horse Artillery Field Pieces manned with the necessary complement of Europeans from the Troop at Dum Dum, with the usual supply of Service Ammunition, the whole under the Command of a Field Officer of Judgment and decision . . . to march . . . by the most direct practicable route towards Jessore'. At the same time the *India Gazette* published a letter from a correspondent 'stating that the

[26] FSUP: V 44, 48, 94, 95, 108, 247, 251, 252.

[27] JP, 20 Dec. 1855: 'Statement of Insurgent Sonthals'.

[28] BC 54222: Metcalfe & Blunt to Court of Directors (10 Apr. 1832), para. 5; JC, 22 Nov. 1831: Smith to Thomason (16 & 17 Nov. 1831), nos 82–4.

Moolavies had broken out afresh a[t] Buttai and Poorahattee'. The panic caught on. During a visit to the Kumarkhali station the Joint Magistrate of Pabna 'found all the Gentlemen there in great alarm—the President had all his Muskets brought out to clean and his people were busily employed in bullet making'. However it soon became clear that the whole thing was a hoax invented by a local planter to amuse himself and induce a friend from a neighbouring station 'to come over and pay me a visit'![29]

The intervention of the custodians of law and order on such occasions is a measure of the fear they shared with their protégés, the rural elite, of any large body of peasants coming together to discuss and air their grievances, however peaceably. Even if no overt acts of violence such as plunder, arson or murder were committed, an assembly of discontented peasantry was often regarded, under the Raj, as a potential threat to the administration. The Pabna ryots' movement of 1873 illustrates this very well indeed. It was officially lauded as an agitation conducted with due respect for the law. Yet the colonial authorities who on the question of tenancy rights had their differences with the landlords, distrusted, as did the latter, any move on the part of the peasantry to mobilize for their rights, particularly when this assumed the form of large gatherings. The Indian Penal Code was used to forbid them from visiting villages in parties of more than ten in order to propagate the aims of the perfectly lawful association they had formed to resist extortion and rack-renting by the zamindars. On one occasion the local magistrate went so far as to override the police who had just released six men from custody for want of evidence and charged them with forming an 'illegal assembly'.[30]

Indeed it would appear that any large and *autonomous* gathering of the peasantry brought about *on their own initiative* to air their grievances unaided by and often in defiance of the rural or administrative elite ran the risk of being regarded as 'illegal' by the colonial authorities for whom its suppression amounted to a veritable principle of government. This was made explicit

[29] JC, 13 Dec. 1831: Casement to Jackson (6 Dec. 1831); Mills to Thomason (8 Dec. 1831); Private Note from Jt. Magistrate of Pabna (7 Dec. 1831); Griffin to Mills (5 Dec. 1831); Griffin to Russell (4 Dec. 1831).

[30] Sen Gupta: 70, 71–2.

in the course of the official discussions on this question following the anti-survey riots in Khandesh in 1852. The attempt made by the government in the winter of that year to introduce a revenue survey in Savda, Raver and Chopda ran into stiff and widespread resistance on the part of the Kunbi peasantry. This took the form of vast assemblies in which the peasants from both sides of the Tapti demonstrated their opposition to the survey. The gatherings assumed their most massive and menacing proportion at Yaval, Savda, Faizpur and Erandol. Peaceful at first they turned violent as more and more people collected at each of these places. Eventually the army was called up and the movement put down by the combined effort of several regiments of the Native Infantry and some companies of the Bhil Corps. Looking at this event in retrospect the authorities were convinced that it was not instigated by the local elite. 'The actors in the disturbances from first to last', wrote Mansfield, Collector of Khandesh and Wingate, Revenue Survey Commissioner, in their joint report, 'were nearly confined to the Coonbee Caste, and among these the two tribes of Pajnee and Telolee Coonbees who form the great mass of the cultivators of the Sowda and Yawul Mahals, were most conspicuous.' Such mobilization, they pointed out, was indeed a part of the tradition of local peasant resistance and this was 'not the first instance of the Coonbees having assembled for the purpose of petitioning and with the object of carrying their point by a demonstration of their number and determination'. Apparently they had done the same thing and with much success on a previous occasion, in 1849, at Dharamgaon in protest of 'the erection of Boundary Marks to indicate the limits of their fields'.[31] Did such a demonstration 'by collecting large numbers of ryots to petition against the survey' constitute a breach of the law? Not so, according to the Magistrate of Khandesh who wrote, 'I know of no law which prevents people from assembling in any numbers for the purpose of petition as long as they conduct themselves inoffensively.' But the view which prevailed at the top of the administration was sterner. As the Governor of Bombay formulated it in his minute of 14 June 1853,

[31] BC 2354 (146775): Mansfield & Wingate to Goldsmid (8 Jan. 1853). I am grateful to Sumit Guha for this reference. My narrative of this event is based on this report as well as on Bombay (1880): 261–2.

It may be necessary here to check the commission of such a crime by severer penalties than would be had recourse to in England and certainly the danger to the ruling power in this Country from a tumultuous assemblage of thousands *is greater* and the measures necessary to meet it involve far more expence and trouble than a corresponding movement by a mob would cause at home.[32]

Nothing could be more explicit as an acknowledgement of the fear inspired by this particular form of autonomous peasant assemblies. It constituted a 'danger to the ruling power in this Country' in the eyes of those who were high enough in the bureaucracy to know which side to choose when consideration for petty legalities clashed with concern for the security of the colonial state. They were right—from their point of view. For when a rebellion set out consciously to mobilize the rural masses for a war on the regime, such *rassemblements* could indeed be a most formidable challenge to the Raj. The Birsaite gatherings which preceded the Munda ulgulan of 1900 were, in this sense, the organs of a peasant war. Soon after his release from jail in November 1897 Birsa and his principal followers met for consultations at Bortodih and planned these rallies as a part of 'an organisation which was necessary to recover their lost rights and to drive out their enemies'.[33] Suresh Singh's authoritative monograph on this subject mentions a very large number of these[34]—far in excess of the official estimate of sixteen[35]—spread over two years between the parley mentioned above and a meeting of about sixty Birsaite gurus in Singhbhum towards the end of December 1899, just a few days before the arrows began to fly. Many of these were addressed by the Munda chief himself. Long before the itinerant agitator was to emerge as a standard feature in the elite politics of the subcontinent, Birsa moved from village to village over an extensive area mobilizing his people. He did not have it all his own way on each of these occasions. Sometimes the Mundas would overrule their leader and impose their collective will on him. Thus at a famous meeting at Simbua hill in March 1898 they firmly and persistently resisted his advice in favour of a religious and reformist

[32] Proceedings, 16 Feb. 1853: Mansfield to Govt. of Bombay (27 Jan. 1853) in BJD 54 (890). BJD 61 (4316): Proceedings, 29 June 1853. Emphasis as in the original.

[33] Singh: 76.

[34] Ibid.: 81–90.

[35] Ibid.: 88, n. 100.

agitational procedure. In fact the cumulative upshot of these assemblies was 'the triumph of the neo-sardars' strategy of revolt over the peaceful means of struggle initially advocated by Birsa'.[36] A genuine instrument of rebellion as a mass event, they mobilized the Munda peasantry for a war on the Raj.

Mobilization of this kind could often assume a religious form. It is well known that in pre-industrial Europe popular uprisings tended to correspond to the Christian calendar of fasts and festivities. Wat Tyler's men entered London on 13 June 1381, the day of the feast of Corpus Christi.[37] The Peasant War in Germany began with Fastnacht, 1525. 'The hour arrived for the fire to be raised', writes Johannes Kessler in his chronicle 'This was on Fastnacht . . . when people tend to gather together.'[38] Lefebvre has identified in this tendency of crowds to gather on feast days and start a riot a 'classic' pattern which repeated itself over and over again during the entire course of the French Revolution: 'Things would begin to stir on a Sunday: throughout the whole period, this day, like feast days in honour of local saints and *baladoires*, was almost a critical day; the peasants would go to mass, then, having nothing else to do, would drift along to the local café: there was nothing like this for starting a riot.'[39] In India the calendar of pujas and *parabs* and the chronicle of rural disturbances did not correlate so directly, although the British authorities were constantly haunted by a fear of this happening during the Mutiny. 'The close of the "Roza" was approaching', wrote the Magistrate of Saharanpur, 'I looked for serious disturbances.' Another officer in that area thought it probable that the local Musalmans 'might take advantage of the Edd [Id] which occurred on the 26th [May 1857] to create a disturbance'. Again, towards the end of July that year all European women and children were evacuated from Nainital in order to ensure their safety in the event of an uprising to coincide with Bakr-Id at Rampur and its spread to that hill station. And at yet another hill station, Mussoorie, all seems to have been well with the white community in those days except for 'an occasional alarm at the native feasts of Eeed, Buqr Eeed, etc.'[40] The Mahommedan festivals passed off without any violence at all these places. But

[36] Ibid.: 81–2. [37] Hilton: 139. [38] Franz: 143.
[39] Lefebvre (1973): 43. [40] FSUP: V 96, 99, 114, 273.

there have been other occasions when religious and rebel gatherings are known to have intersected. Thus, on the eve of the hool the Santals of Bhagnadihi went in a large body to the bazaar at Panchkethia to worship the local deity there and seek her blessing for the ensuing enterprise.[41] The communal visits to 'ancestral places' undertaken by Birsa's followers on his advice exceeded the limits of Sardar revivalism and developed into a series of carefully planned and (as soon as the government came to know of these) risky ceremonial marches to inspire the Mundas for the coming ulgulan. By the time the holy itinerary had been gone through over a period of two years and the 'ancestral possessions' recovered from hallowed sites—the *tulsi* leaves from Chutia, the sandal paste from Jagarnathpur temple and the sanctified water and sacred thread from Naw Rattan—'the psychological preparation for the revolt was complete'.[42] It was already November 1899 with just a few weeks to go before the critical Christmas eve when the uprising was due to begin.

However, it was only rarely that the mobilization of an insurgent peasantry adopted so explicit a religious form in colonial India. There was, of course, a pervasive undertone of religiosity in almost all that happened in village society. But beyond that level of generalization it would be perhaps more true to say that the rather secular idiom of communal festivity and corporate labour was what, more than anything else, characterized the agrarian uprisings of the period. In this respect again the Indian experience had a good deal in common with the European. Lefebvre mentions the 'very strong popular flavour' of some of the jacqueries of 1789. The peasants apparently enjoyed themselves. 'It is easy to see that they were delighted to down tools on the spot and go for a day's outing as though they were setting off to the market or the fair', he observes. 'The whole village would be on foot, the *syndic* leading the way in front of the most important inhabitants, sometimes with drums beating; there would be few guns, but a good number of farming implements and sticks instead of firearms; there were more young people than old . . . There were deafening shouts of "Long live the Third Estate!" '[43] Rudé, too, speaks of the ceremonial aspect of the Swing move-

[41] K. K. Datta: 57. [42] Singh: 77–81. [43] Lefebvre (1973): 119–20.

ment in England, which tended to be increasingly pronounced as the movement gained in strength: 'In the earlier (and later) days, when the militants were more inclined to fear detection, raiding parties might blacken their faces and do their work at night; but as the movement developed, riots took place in open day, and were public performances and at times assumed a festive air.'[44]

Ceremonialism thus emerged as a concomitant of the public and communal character of the Swing. This was true of some of the Indian rebellions too. In Pabna the peasants had started off by trying to mobilize support for their cause by word of mouth sent through individual emissaries, but this was soon given up for more forceful and public demonstrations as the movement acquired momentum and self-confidence. The method they then adopted was to call up large bands of men by sounding the horn, arm them with lathis (and with *polos* as we shall presently discuss), and take them round in imposing columns through the villages along a given route pleading with and if necessary, pressing the local population to join the agrarian league.[45] Again, as Hunter observes, the rising of the Santals 'could not be distinguished at first from one of their great national processions headed by the customary drums and fifes'.[46] The leaders of the hool, like those of the Swing movement, rode at the head of their raiding parties on conspicuous mount—the subahs on horseback and the supreme commanders, Sido and Kanhu, on palanquins and elephants.[47] The French and the English rebels of 1789 and 1830 respectively showed a distinct taste for dressing up for a raid.[48] So did the Santals. We have Sido's own words testifying to the fact that

[44] H & R: 211. [45] Buckland: 545; Saha: II 119.

[46] Hunter (1897): 240.

[47] Balai who was with the plundering Santal army during the first week of the hool referred to five or six palanquins used to carry Sido and Kanhu around. Horses seized during the raid on Putgutteah, he said, served as mounts for the Santal 'darogas'. Kanhu mentioned that he 'was on horse back' when his 'army' attacked and looted Sugrampore, and that '2 Elephants, 2 or 4 palkies' were a part of the booty acquired from the pillage of Pakur. See JP, 19 July 1855: Toogood to Grey (Enclosure, 14 July 1855); JP, 20 Dec. 1855: 'Examination of Kanoo Sonthal'. Also see the song of the hool which begins with the lines: 'Sido and Kanhu in palkis/Chand and Bhaero on horses' (Culshaw & Archer: 221).

[48] Lefebvre (1973): 120; H & R: 211.

during the attack on Maheshpur 'many of the Manjees were dressed in red clothes'. Other armed Santals were variously reported as wearing red *saloo* (a variety of cotton fabric used mostly for festive decoration), white *lungis*, white *dhotis* and *pagris*.[49] The Birsaite march to Khunti for an assault on the police station there had all the marks of a ceremonial procession too: 'their bodies smeared with dust, their arms decorated with *chanwar*, wearing turbans and snow-white *dhoties*', the insurgents arrived at Khunti 'dancing, jumping and brandishing their swords'.[50]

The communal idiom most characteristic of rebel mobilization in India was that of corporate labour. It is often a figure of speech in rebel discourse which illustrates how for the insurgents a jacquerie was simply another way of working together. '*Khunti be rahar jaromakana, dolabu maea*' ('The rahar crop at Khunti is ripe, let's go and harvest it'), cried the Birsaites as they marched on the police station at Khunti.[51] Or, as the formidable Gaya Munda exclaimed when he and his men sighted a posse of police constables, '*Samare hijulenako mar goekope*' ('The sambhar deer have arrived, kill them').[52] The displacement between the primary and secondary referents in these utterances generates that broad, black humour[53] characteristic of peasants out on a raid: '*fricasser ce poulet*' is how the Mâconnais rebels on their way to Pollet's country house described their mission by a play on their victim's name.[54] And the message in each of these Mundari sentences is a measure of the correspondence between its two poles—collective violence against the enemy and co-operation in a task of communal labour such as harvesting or hunting. As we learn from the historian of the ulgulan, the Mundas themselves took their own rhetoric seriously enough to act up to its traditional implications. For when Gaya's party returned home after their successful encounter with the police at Etkedih in the incident mentioned above, 'their women turned out to greet them and wash their feet with water while the men sang hunting songs'[55]

[49] JP, 8 Nov. 1855: 'Examination of Sedoo Sonthal late Thacoor'; K. K. Datta: 102.

[50] Singh: 105. [51] Ibid. [52] Ibid.: 101.

[53] For a discussion of displacement as a joke technique see Freud: Ch. II *et passim*. [54] Lefebvre (1973): 120. [55] Singh: 102.

—all in the customary manner of concluding a good day's shikar.

Or, take this circular issued by the Pabna ryots to mobilize support for their struggle against the zamindars in 1873:

So and so Projas! as soon as you see this circular, hasten over to the side of the insurgent party. If you fail to come within this day, rest assured that we go to fish in the beel, close by your village. We have already fished in the beels of so and so villages. Know this order is peremptory.[56]

The imagery which is meant to mask and by masking drive home the dark message of this notice, relates to a mode of collective work which was as vital to the peasantry of Pabna as hunting was to the Mundas of Chota Nagpur. The *bils* are marshes and swamps which covered a large part of the district—an incomplete list in the *Pabna District Gazetteer* mentions nine of them spread over an area of 215 square miles[57]—and served as reservoirs of fresh water fish ample enough to provide a secondary source of livelihood for a predominantly rice-growing population. A good deal of the corporate life of the villages related therefore to the exploitation of the bils, especially in the form of *polo* fishing, an activity that involved all the peasants in a number of neighbouring hamlets and combined productive labour with much entertainment. 'Besides regular fishing, *polo* fishing is an old pastime indulged in by the villagers in the summer', writes O'Malley.

The villagers are called to the fishing by the blowing of a horn, and men and women and children, sometimes numbering hundreds, troop with *polos* in hand to the nearest *bil*. The *polo* is a bell-shaped split-bamboo trap, with a small opening on the top and no bottom. The fisherman walks into the water, presses down the *polo* in front of him, and then, stooping down, plunges his hands through the opening at the top and gropes in the mud for the fish that are trapped. All are busy catching fish in the shallow water, which is soon churned into liquid mud, and in a few hours the *bil* is despoiled of fish.[58]

[56] Sen Gupta: 41. Unfortunately the original published in the vernacular edition of the *Amrita Bazar Patrika* is not available. The text quoted here is a translation as given in the *Hindoo Patriot*, 14 July 1873.

[57] O'Malley (1923): 3–5. The area of Chalan Bil has been estimated at 88 square miles to include only that portion of it which falls within the Pabna district.

[58] Ibid.: 17–18. The description given in Saha: I 75–6 agrees with this. Accord-

We have quoted this description *in extenso* in order to show how closely the idiom of this particular form of communal labour was replicated in the mobilization of the Pabna ryots for the bidroha of 1873. As in the case of bil fishing a few strident notes on a horn would summon the peasants of some neighbouring villages to an assembly. The time, more often than not, was a late hour of the night, the best time for an abundant catch, too, in the swamps. This nocturnal blowing of the horn was such a dreaded symbol of the movement that in some areas the district authorities issued orders under Section 518 of the Indian Penal Code 'forbidding the ryots to sound horns at night with a view to causing terror'.[59] And just as the members of a party proceeding to a bil would carry polos as their most essential equipment, the peasant agitators, too, would arm themselves with lathis, each capped by a polo, as they marched from village to village agitating for their cause and terrorizing its enemies. The polo in its turn was regarded as a badge of insurgency. It gave to the movement and its participants their respective folk names—'Polo Bidroha' and 'Polowallahs'. To be told 'The Polowallahs are coming!' could indeed panic their opponents as much as did those midnight blasts on the buffalo horn.[60] In this context no one who read the circular quoted above could mistake the peasants' intention 'to fish in the beel close by your village' for anything but the chilling euphemism it was meant to be—that is, a warning to conform to the campaign or be pillaged. It is thus that a set of signs characteristic of mobilization for a mode of communal labour came to be associated with mobilization for an agrarian struggle: the *atideśa* that extended the signs from one domain to the other helped not merely to designate the peasant fishermen as rebels (*bidrohi*)—they were literally known as such—but also to integrate rebellion as a corporate enterprise of the rural masses.

Communal fishing was a part of the Santal tradition, too.[61] But the operative idiom of the hool was that of another corporate activity—shikar. It was a Santal custom for a *dihri*, a man who combined the functions of a master of the hunt

---

ing to that author, the participants in collective fishing of this kind were known as *bahut* and their number, drawn from five to seven villages, could be as high as two to three hundred on some occasions.

[59] Sen Gupta: 70. [60] Saha: I 118–19; III 99. [61] MHKRK: *cxli.*

with those of a priest, to summon all the able-bodied men within a circle of villages at a specified place, usually a jungle or a hill, on a particular day.[62] According to Ranjit Parganait of Sarmi this was precisely how two Santal leaders, Munka Majhi of Chotbazar and Kowleah Majhi of Sindree, mobilized their community for the uprising during the spring of 1855. They 'called together a great number of Sonthals extensibly [sic] for the purposes of Shikar at Buro Koondee. Where [sic] they had assembled these two Manjees told the other Sonthals to assemble at Chotbazar from thence to go to Hazareebagh to consult the Soubah as to their grievances.'[63] Ranjit himself was present at Barakundi. His testimony is confirmed by the somewhat mythified version of the event as recorded in *Mare Hapram Ko Reak Katha* where Jugia, the old Santal, remembers how the word had spread that all should gather for a shikar at Layogarh to celebrate the birth of a Soubah to a virgin girl. 'Layogarh is located in the hills of Hazaribagh. Some people did go there, saw the Soubah and joined him at a hunt in Kanchan forest too.' The Soubah apparently ordered another assembly for shikar to follow at Tirpahar near Deoghar, but this, says Jugia, was never held for reasons not known to him.[64]

It is indeed appropriate that mobilization for a communal hunt should have merged thus with that for the hool. The Santals themselves made the association explicit by a homonymy: they used the word 'fauj' (literally, 'troops') both for the mass of insurgents led by the Soubahs and the parties of armed men led by the dihri at shikar.[65] For it was in either case a matter of arming the entire adult male population for a communal enterprise. After the dihri announced a chase, the villagers would start getting ready. 'They would string their bows, fit arrows with heads ground to a fine point, sharpen the blades of their axes (*tangis*) and fit them to handles, fasten spearheads to long staves and polish their swords to a shine.' And then, on the appointed day, a roll of drums at dawn would start calling them up to the assembly point.[66] This was also how the Santals prepared for war. When the time came, their enemies were quick to identify the hunting equipment by its other

[62] Ibid.
[63] JP, 6 Dec. 1855: 'Statement of Runjeet Pergunnait of Sarmi'.
[64] MHKRK: *clxxvii*. [65] Ibid.: *cxlii*. [66] Ibid.

function and ban it as the insignia of rebellion. As an order issued at the height of the pacification campaign by Major-General Lloyd commanding the Dinapore Division and Santal Field Force put it: 'All villages of the Tribe . . . must be made to deliver up their arms, vizt. Bows and arrows, sword, battle axes & sacrificing knives as well as the Drum called Digdighee used for calling the sonthals together into bodies.'[67] The order appears to have gone down well with the army, and many a gallant officer leading his men against a Santal village or a rebel camp in the jungle proudly reported the seizure of a few bows and arrows, axes, swords, drums, etc. as a part of the day's military achievement.[68]

In one important respect, however, the communality of the hool exceeded that of a hunt. The latter was, among the Santals, an exclusively male undertaking, although it was customary for their women to prepare for them the provisions they took to the jungle[69] and welcome them back home after shikar by ceremonially receiving them at the front door and washing their feet.[70] But men and women would participate together in many other forms of labour essential for their livelihood, such as cutting timber, gathering leaves and harvesting a crop. On such occasions, says the *Reak Katha*, 'Santal men and women greatly enjoyed working together'.[71] They worked together in the hool too. Out on a pillage, the men busied themselves with the rough and heavy job of wrecking enemy property while the women gathered the loot—a replication, no doubt, of the standard division of labour between the sexes at harvest time.

Already in the first week of the rising the planter Maseyk had observed that a party of ten men who attacked and burnt down the village of Monkaparrah had 'a number of women with them to carry off the spoils'.[72] The names of two women, Radha and Heera, both described as wounded, occur in a list of nineteen Santal prisoners produced before the Magistrate of Murshida-

[67] JP, 6 Dec. 1855: 'Copy of a Division Order issued by Major General G. W. A. Lloyd C. B. Comdg. Dinapore Division and Sonthal Field Force' (15 Nov. 1855).

[68] There are many examples of this in the records. See for instance JP, 6 Dec. 1855: Halliday to Gott (25 Nov. 1855); Jenis to Parrott (ibid.); Halliday to Parrott (30 Nov. 1855).

[69] MHKRK: *cxlii.* [70] Bompas: 417. [71] MHKRK: *cxxxvi.*

[72] JP, 23 Aug. 1855: Maseyk to Eden (13 July 1855).

bad on 20 July, a fortnight after the outbreak.[73] And as the insurrection draws to a close in the autumn of 1855, women come up for mention a number of times in the official correspondence about the capture, incarceration and summary trial of the rebels. Thus, a party of four Santals was captured by a Sergeant Gillan near Mohammadbazar on 15 September 1855. The leader, Dhuna Majhi, charged with 'illegally and riotously assembling with offensive weapons for the purpose of plunder and committing a breach of the peace' was sentenced to seven years' imprisonment 'with labour and irons'. His companions, all women, two of them girls of fourteen, 'accompanied the rebels with baskets and bags to carry off grain'. For this the older woman was given one year in jail plus a fine of fifty rupees, and the younger ones six months and a fine of twenty-five rupees each. Dhuna Majhi was transported to Chittagong jail at the other end of the province to serve his sentence while the three females were kept in detention in Birbhum.[74] A rebel family of man, wife and daughters who had been in the hool together, was thus captured, punished and broken up.

Between October and November that year there were at least forty-five Santal women held in Birbhum jail.[75] Some had their children with them. Quite a few of these still fed on the breast and were dying of dropsy and dysentery in the overcrowded and insanitary prison, which moved the Civil Surgeon with pity enough to urge for their immediate release but was regarded by the Officiating Magistrate 'only as the just retribution they have brought upon themselves'. When twenty of these women were brought to trial, thirteen were released. Of the seven others, one 'had accompanied a sonthal force which had gone forth to plunder the village of Deocha' in August and was shot twice in her left leg by the troops; captured and detained since then she had been far too ill to be produced in court and yet apparently regarded as far too dangerous to be released

[73] JP, 15 Nov. 1855: '19 Jonar saotaler kagaj'.

[74] JP, 8 Nov. 1855: Ward to GOB (19 Oct. 1855); Thompson to Ward (15 Oct. 1855); Russell to Ward (25 Oct. 1855); Russell to Offg. Magistrate of Birbhum (ibid.); Russell to Magistrate of Chittagong (ibid.).

[75] For the source of our information here and the rest of the paragraph see JP, 20 Dec. 1855: 'Weekly Sanitary Report of the Civil Surgeon on the State of the prisoners in Beerbhoom Jail for the week ending 10th November 1855'; Thompson to Russell (30 Nov. 1855).

from custody. Five of the women sentenced by the Sessions Judge—three to one year's imprisonment each and two to six months—were 'all convicted on very clear evidence of having actively assisted the Insurgents in plundering and carrying off goods from different villages in this [Birbhum] district'. And one was detained on the order of the Magistrate himself, for she had failed to produce the security for good conduct demanded of her. 'The charge was established against her of having acted not only as a spy for the insurgents, but of having been the means frequently of supplying them, by purchases in this Town [Suri] & elsewhere, with Tobacco, Salt, spirits and other necessaries and provisions.' She obviously was by no means unique, and the entire female population of the Santal districts in 1855 could have been accused of acting as the providers and as the eyes and ears of the rebel forces in precisely the same way.

The records of imprisonment and summary justice throw some light on yet another aspect of Santal collectivity—the co-operation between people of the same village. Mutual aid and co-operative labour among fellow villagers were, according to the *Reak Katha*, an important part of their tradition.[76] Such co-operation was needed and offered when a fairly wide range of skills had to be pooled together as in the construction of a house or when some of the more arduous agricultural operations like ploughing, transplanting and harvesting required more labour power than could be generated by single families working on their own. This apparently was common practice until the rebellion, and there is some evidence to suggest that it featured in the mobilization for the hool to some extent. I have examined three lists of Santal rebels for each of whom the records specify his residence. They were all produced before and found guilty by a Court Martial and a civilian court.[77] Of the seventy-five men from nineteen villages there were only six who were on their own and not accompanied by at least one

[76] MHKRK: *cxxxv*.

[77] JP, 6 Dec. 1855: 'Extracts from the Proceedings of an European Court Martial convened at Camp Jilmillee on the 22nd day of November 1855 etc.'; 'Statement of 20 convicts sentenced by the sessions Judge of Zillah Beerbhoom . . . 3rd December 1855' in BDR: 125–6; 'Statement of 22 convicts sentenced by the S. Judge of Zillah Beerbhoom . . . 3rd Dec. 1855' in ibid.: 129–30. The four non-Santals in the Birbhum lists have not been included in this estimate.

fellow villager. Four villages contributed two men each and another group of four villages three each. The number of participants from the six other villages varied between four and sixteen as shown below.

Table 1 Distribution of Captive Rebels by Neighbourhood

Number of villages grouped according to size of participation	*Number of participants per village in each group*	*Total number of participants per group*
6	1	6
4	2	8
4	3	12
1	4	4
1	5	5
1	11	11
1	13	13
1	16	16
Total: 19	–	75

Two of these lists also specify the thana jurisdiction for each of the ten villages where thirty-seven of the rebels were said to have originated. Bunching them by thanas—ten from the area of Afzalpur thana, twenty-three from Nalhati and four from Nungolia—one can get some idea of local co-operation between groups of neighbouring hamlets within the jurisdiction of a police station. This is further confirmed by what we know about the residence of the participants in one characteristic act of the rebellion. The village Katna in Birbhum was raided and pillaged by sixteen men—five of them from three villages in Nalhati thana and ten from five villages in Afzalpur thana (not counting one from a village for which the thana is not given).[78] And when under the pressure of Captain Pester's operations in that area the Santals were forced to fall back before Afzalpur, they regrouped at Jamjori for an attack on the army unit posted at Jamtara—a move the communal character of which was not lost upon their enemies. 'Almost every Sonthal village is furnishing its quota to Jamtarra', wrote the alarmed commander of the Birbhum and Bankura Field Force to his superiors in the Military Department.[79]

[78] BDR: 129–30. [79] JP, 25 Oct. 1855: Bird to GOI (30 Sept. 1855).

The fruits of corporate activity are communally shared. The portions are by no means equal, headmen, priests, drummers and other special functionaries being entitled to somewhat larger helpings before the remainder is equally divided. But as the Santal book of tradition makes it clear, there is nothing arbitrary about the distribution of reward. Whether it is a communal catch of fish or a communal kill at shikar, there are well defined and universally accepted rules as to who should get how much.[80] The Santals appear to have carried this idiom into their conduct of the hool too. Travelling through the Rajmahal Hills in January 1851 Captain Sherwill had noticed a curious sign in a jungle near a village called Burwa. 'Observing a tuft of straw tied to a tree in the jungle', he wrote in his diary, 'I enquired of the manji the meaning or use of it; he informed me that wherever a Sonthal is desirous of protecting a patch of jungle from the axes of the villagers, or a patch of grass being grazed over, or a newly-sown field from being trespassed upon, he erects a bamboo in his patch of grass or field, to which is affixed a tuft of straw, or in the case of jungle some prominent and lofty tree has the same prohibitory mark attached, which mark is well understood and strictly observed by all parties interested.'[81] Four years later the rebels were to use a variation of the same sign to indicate communal appropriation by pillage. They plundered thirty-four villages in Ooperbandah thana in Birbhum during the insurrection, and as Richardson, the Collector of the district, observed: 'In each plundered Village a bamboo has been fixed in the ground, with a piece of leather affixed, denoting that the Sonthals have obtained possession of the land.'[82]

Since the villages were thus taken over in the name of the community, the loot had to be shared out among the raiders. 'When we attack villages', said Balai Santal after his arrest, 'the people run away and the plunderers take everything.'[83] The cash would then be divided among the members of the party

[80] For such rules of distribution of fish and game gathered by collective effort, see MHKRK: *cxli*, *cxliv–v*.

[81] Sherwill: 40.

[82] JP, 8 Nov. 1855: 'Operations of the Sonthals etc' enclosed in Richardson's Diary (4 Oct. 1855).

[83] JP, 19 July 1855: Toogood to Grey (Enclosure, 14 July 1855).

and all other property handed over to the Soubahs, some of which they were to keep for themselves and the rest for communal use. Kanhu, too, in his statement confirmed that 'the treasure plundered . . . was shared amongst manjees and sonthals', and that he himself received a part of the booty.[84] The portion made over to him as the supreme commander was of course far greater than anything an ordinary 'sipahi' like Balai could expect. 'The three Rupees that were (found) with me', said the latter after his capture, 'I got at the plundering of a Rajah's near Agoonerjah';[85] whereas after the pillage of the princely estate of Pakur, said Kanhu, 'a manjhee brought me two Kulsies [brass pots] of rupees, 2 Elephants, 2 or 4 palkies [palanquins], 2 cloths'.[86] There was nothing egalitarian about this any more than there was about the unequal apportioning of game and fish between the village leaders and the common Santals. What is important however is to note that by insisting on the principle of communal distribution of plunder the rebels placed the hool under the sign of a collective enterprise of the same order as shikar or fishing.

The function of this corporate violence is to undermine the authority of the peasant's enemies by destroying such of their resources as constitute the insignia and instruments of that authority. The means adopted by the rebels for this purpose often vary from event to event and from region to region. But with all its variety there are in this violence certain regularities of emphasis and pattern which have been noticed by some of the most discerning students of the subject. It was thus that Trotsky picked out of the welter of agrarian riots of 1905 in Russia four main 'types' or 'forms of struggle' which 'in different combinations, spread over the country, being adapted to the economic conditions of each region'.[87] Mao Tse-tung, too, in his investigation of the conduct of the peasantry during the Hunan movement in 1927 made it a point to 'closely examine all their activities, one by one, to see what they have actually done' and in his famous report which 'classified and summed

[84] JP, 20 Dec. 1855: 'Statement of Insurgent Sonthals'.
[85] *Vide* n. 83 above.
[86] JP, 20 Dec. 1855: 'Examination of Kanoo Sonthal'.
[87] Trotsky: 202.

up' these activities he identified nine 'methods' governing the very large number of sanctions and coercive measures 'used by the peasants to hit the landlords politically'.[88] The lesson to be learnt from such distinguished exercises is that to fail to investigate and identify these 'methods' and 'forms' of peasant violence is for a historian to be resigned to the point of view which sees in insurgency nothing but chaos, confusion and disorder—'a sort of blindness and madness', as a modern scholar has written of the Kol insurrection echoing the sentiments of the colonial officers who were sent out to suppress it.[89] What this point of view misses out is that there is much order in this apparent 'madness', a great deal of discipline in what looks like pure spontaneity. To quote Lefebvre's memorable words precisely on this question: 'These are not acts of collective madness, as has so often been suggested. The people always has its own way of dealing with things.'[90]

If one examines carefully enough the record of peasant activities during the great rural disturbances under the Raj and combs through the debris of undigested detail stacked in the primary sources, making up an inventory, so to say, of the means and objects of violence, one will probably have no difficulty in concluding that there were *four methods or forms of struggle* which stood out as the most conspicuous and the most prevalent. These were *wrecking*, *burning*, *eating* and *looting*. It is not that each of these figured to the same extent in all the events. On the contrary, it was the want of uniformity in their combinations and the uneven distribution of their relative weightage which helped to distinguish one uprising from another and lent to each its individuality. However, taken together it was these forms which made insurgency so distinctively *destructive* and *political* in its character and put it in a class apart from crime.

To turn first to wrecking, it is well known that the demolition of the symbols of enemy authority was common to all peasant insurrections. In early and modern Europe nothing seemed to the rural poor to express more blatantly the difference between the material conditions of their own life and those of the life of the upper classes than the grandeur and inaccessibility of the residential houses of the latter. The elimination of this measure

[88] Mao: I 34, 36. [89] J. C. Jha: 172. [90] Lefebvre (1973): 119.

of their subalternity was therefore an obvious first step for the insurgents to take towards turning things upside down. Jean de Venette, one of the chroniclers of the Jacquerie of 1358, has observed how eager the peasants were to destroy manor houses;[91] and Trotsky in his account of the jacqueries of 1905 in Russia mentions this particular form of violence to have been so widespread that 'in certain districts the landowners' houses that were left standing could be counted on one's fingers'.[92] Some of the other peasant revolts in Europe during the five centuries between these two dates witnessed the same type of violence as the many references to the destruction of abbeys and castles in Germany in 1525 and of priories and chateaux in France in 1789 testify respectively in Zimmermann's and Lefebvre's histories of those times. Insurgency operated by similar methods in India as well. The wrecking of Deby Sinha's mansion in Rangpur during the dhing was celebrated thus as a mass event in a popular ballad:

Thousands of peasants marched together. They took with them their staves, picks, sickles and choppers. There was no one who wouldn't join. They took on their shoulders heavy carrying poles and yokes used for ploughing. The paupers made their way over fields lying fallow. Indeed the peasants of Rangpur came from all the four directions, while the gentry [*bhadragula*] gathered there simply to witness the fun. They [the peasants] hurled a lot of stones and brickbats which came down thudding on all sides. Some people had their bones broken by the missiles. And Deby Sinha's mansion was reduced to a heap of bricks.[93]

In some of the uprisings the insurgents used wrecking as a weapon to carry out the war into enemy territory. The Kols of Chota Nagpur launched their insurrection by announcing 'that they would destroy every village of the Sonepore Pergunnah',[94] and were almost as good as their word. And in the course of the fituris of 1899 the Saora in a taluk of the Ganjam Agency attacked and razed to the ground 'in the most deliberate manner' the houses of their hated exploiters, the Doms, in some

[91] Hilton: 132. [92] Trotsky: 205.

[93] The text of the ballad is given in full in D. C. Sen (1914): 1413–18. A somewhat different version of the ballad has been reprinted from the *Rangpur Sahitya Parishad Patrika* in Kaviraj: 97–102.

[94] BC 1502 (58891): Dent & Wilkinson to Thomason (16 Nov. 1832).

fifteen villages.[95] The more spectacular acts of demolition in the period under survey had the familiar symbols of British presence in the subcontinent as their targets. The revolt against the tyrannical system of indigo plantation culminated in some instances in the destruction of the factories. Titu Mir's men, for instance, spent a morning demolishing the Burgurreah factory on the Ichamati and did so thorough a job of it that the Magistrate of Nadia had to confess having 'never witnessed a more complete ransack and wanton destruction of property than the empty Bungalow on the shore'.[96] Again in a well-known case the Farazis of Faridpur destroyed a factory at Panch Char belonging to the planter Dunlop in December 1846.[97] During the period of the Mutiny, too, the planters came under attack. As one aggrieved member of this fraternity was to recollect later on, his factories in a part of Ghazipur district of eastern UP were raided jointly by mutineers and the local villagers and destroyed in the course of two nights' work.[98] The Santals wrecked railways and the railroad engineers' bungalows wherever they happened to come across these during the hool.[99] And that unmistakable emblem of colonial authority in rural India, the sadar station, with its bungalows and administrative buildings, met with the same fate when peasants marched into towns as they often did during the disturbances of 1857–8. The destruction of Bulandshahr by the Gujar insurgents provides us with a fairly typical experience in this respect:

> As the Goojurs had entered the station they fired each house, commencing with the Dak Bungalow; and during the four days we were absent the station was completely destroyed, and all property private and public, was carried off and burnt, the city people and those of the neighbouring villages taking a very active part in the work of demolition.[100]

This description taken from an official narrative matches well with Mark Thornhill's account of the sack of Mathura. 'The plunder of the [revenue] office', he wrote, 'was followed by that

[95] Elwin: 254.
[96] JC, 22 Nov. 1831: Smith to Thomason (16 Nov. 1831).
[97] Khan (1965): 34. [98] FSUP: IV 117–19.
[99] JP, 19 July 1855: Toogood to Grey (13 July 1855); Elliott to Grey (15 July 1855); Rose to Elliott (14 July 1855). [100] FSUP: V 39.

of the English houses. In this amusement the villagers spent what remained of the day. The houses contained little that they valued; that little they carried off, the rest they broke to pieces. In the morning they returned and continued the work of destruction. They concluded it by setting fire to the houses.'[101]

The use of fire as a principal instrument of demolition was also by no means exceptional. On the contrary, wrecking and burning almost invariably went together in all great peasant revolts in India as well as abroad. Trotsky noticed the power of this combination in the course of the uprisings in the Russian countryside in 1905. He quoted from a contemporary newspaper to show how a torch set to a landowner's estate at night would often announce the beginning of a jacquerie. The incidence of arson in attacks on farms, stacks and barns in the course of the Swing movement in England in 1830 was so high that Rudé felt justified in characterizing some of the most affected areas as 'incendiary counties'.[102] Lefebvre thought that there was a logic to all this burning. There are instances to show that the peasants often 'proceeded to destroy and burn in a very methodical way'. And according to him, a historian hardly given to generalizing too much, 'All the peasant revolts followed this pattern'. It was, he suggests, as if the rebels exercised a sort of 'right of arson' like what the bourgeois of Flanders enjoyed till the very end of the Middle Ages 'to punish anyone who had injured them or attacked their privileges by burning down his house'.[103]

In rural India it was not so much a sense of right but tradition supported by faith which people living close to nature had in the destructive power of fire that made them adopt arson as a major instrument of rebellion. Its use was frequent—to the point of being almost universal—in the Kol insurrection. In the most recent and detailed account that we have of it there is hardly a case of pillage mentioned without arson.[104] Figures available for four divisions of Chota Nagpur (and those not amongst the most built-up regions) speak of a total of 4,086 houses burnt down.[105]

[101] Thornhill: 87. [102] Trotsky: 205; H & R: 198–203.

[103] Lefebvre (1973): 119. [104] See J. C. Jha: *passim*, but especially Ch. II.

[105] BC 1502 (58891): 'Statement exhibiting the Amount of Property plundered and burnt during the late Insurrection in Chota Nagpoor'. The four divisions are Tori, Lohardagga, Sonepur and Palkote.

These included not only police thanas and mahajans' gadis, but entire residential wards in diku villages and townships as well. The scale of fire-raising by the Kol on this occasion was on a par with that by the Santals in Damin-i-Koh in 1855. They too burned down mahajans' and zamindars' houses everywhere. They reduced to ashes the indigo factory at Balbadda[106] and the railway bungalows at Sreekund and Pakur—in fact, all railway bungalows north of the river Brahmani.[107] Pakur burned particularly high and the blaze could be seen a long way off.[108] Indeed the hool appears never to have stopped burning. It was hardly a week old when an official marching at the head of some troops from Baharampur to Aurangabad found nearly thirty villages burnt down along his route.[109] And 'we could see, as we were marching along, the smoke from 7 or 8 villages distant some 8 or 10 miles from us', he wrote from Kadamsar the following day reporting on what he saw of insurgent activities since leaving Aurangabad.[110] Again, in a memorandum written on 21 July 1855 precisely at the end of the second week of the insurrection Captain Sherwill noted down his observations made during journeys to and from Rajmahal thus: 'Villages all round Colgong have been told off for loot and burning by the Santals . . . Major Burroughs says he will move out this afternoon (21 July) to try and endeavour to stop burning. The villages on fire seem to the East and South-east—and are visible more as I write.'[111] And nine weeks later on 24 September 1855 the Magistrate of Birbhum mentions the burning of over thirty villages in Nangulia and Ooperbandah including the police station at the latter place during the previous fortnight.[112]

Arson played an important role in inaugurating and extending the rebellion of 1857–8. Carey saw a sign of the things to come in a series of fires which destroyed a cantonment, an army

[106] K. K. Datta: 86.

[107] JP, 19 July 1855: 'Statement made before the Assistant Mag^{te}. at Berhampore etc.'; Elliott to Grey (15 July 1855); Hampton to Rose (13 July 1855); Murray to Birbhum Magistrate (14 July 1855).

[108] Ibid.: 'Statement made before the Assistant Mag^{te}. at Berhampore etc.'

[109] Ibid.: Toogood to Grey (13 July 1855).

[110] Ibid.: Same to same (14 July 1855).

[111] K. K. Datta: 80. 'Wrote' in the extract quoted by Datta is obviously an error for 'write'.

[112] JP, 4 Oct. 1855: Rose to Elliott (24 Sept. 1855).

officer's bungalow and a telegraph office at Raniganj and Barrackpore in the last week of January 1857. 'And thus', he wrote in retrospect, 'the Fire King began to demonstrate an inkling of what was in store for almost every station in the North Western Provinces.'[113] The Fire King was indeed much in evidence later on that summer. At Aligarh, for instance, the burning down of a bungalow was the obvious and instantaneous index of the tension generated there by the news of the outbreak at Meerut, and when within a week the sepoys of the local garrison themselves mutinied, the Collector's kachari and the post office, too, went up in flames. At Etawah at about the same time a similar set of buildings, all of them the visible symbols of the Raj—the kachari, the sessions court house, the post office and two bungalows—met the same fate at the hands of incendiaries. Later on, in June, when the mutineers from Jhansi arrived there, the Mewatis felt bold enough to destroy the rest of the bungalows by fire. In Hamirpur, the zamindars of mauza Gohand burnt down the tahsil, its building and its records.[114] It was the same story everywhere with the insurgents setting fire to all administrative buildings and European residential bungalows in district after district throughout Uttar Pradesh.

The same means of destruction was used by the peasants in their struggles in other parts of the country as well—e.g. by the Kunbi as they made bonfires of the Marwari moneylenders' bonds, shops, houses, fodder stacks, etc. during the riots of 1875 in Poona and Ahmadnagar; by the Moplah as they burnt down the landlords' houses and temples again and again in the course of their numerous uprisings in Malabar during the nineteenth century.[115] The last great rebellion of the century, the Birsaite ulgulan too was marked by an 'epidemic of burning and arrow-shooting', particularly in its initial phase.[116] The official statistics of 33 cases in Chakradharpur, 45 in Tamar, 39 in Khunti and 4 in Basia—a total of 121—do not obviously include many

[113] Carey: 9.

[114] FSUP: III 627; V 632, 634, 656–7.

[115] For the Kunbi see DRCR: 2, 3; for the Moplah, Logan: 554, 555, 560, 563, 586, 588 *et passim*.

[116] The details about the ulgulan in this paragraph are taken from Singh: 97, 106, and notes 19 and 68 to Ch. VI of that work.

unreported incidents, and their value for our study of arson is diminished in any case by their being lumped together with arrow-shooting. But since the two forms of violence often occurred at the same time, these figures may perhaps still serve to give some idea of the fairly high incidence of burning. On one of these occasions after a successful attack on a police station the raiders set fire to a few sheds and thatched houses belonging to the police and some of the local moneylenders and danced around the blaze to celebrate their victory. The impact that this relatively minor incident had on a Belgian missionary who witnessed it is a measure of the fear generated by arson. 'It was a terrible night', he wrote, 'to see in the brilliant blaze of this conflagration these hundreds of savage and infuriated Mundas dancing and jumping about with loud shouts and yells and brandishing their terrible battle axe(s).' What made the Munda insurgent dance with joy made T. van der Schueren, S.J., of the Belgian mission shudder. Clearly again a case of two mutually hostile theories interpreting a rebel scenario from opposite points of view—'It's fine!'/'It's terrible!'

It should be emphasized here that destruction by wrecking and burning was by no means limited in any of these cases to 'useless' objects of luxury and conspicuous consumption alone. For if that were the case one would have found it difficult to explain why on so many occasions the rebels chose to demolish things and resources of obviously great economic value to themselves. Take, for instance, the classic case of the destruction of railway works by the Santals during their hool. There can be no doubt about the fact that the introduction of railways added considerably to income and employment in the Santal country. 'High embankments, heavy cuttings, many-arched bridges, created a demand for workmen such as had never been known in the history of India.'[117] For the Santals this provided an opportunity to extricate themselves from the state of landlessness, low wages and bonded labour into which they had fallen thanks to the combination of an administratively engineered rise in the local population—by as much as thirty times in less than fifteen years, according to one authority[118]—and cynical exploitation by mahajans and zamindars under the protection of the Raj.

[117] Hunter (1897): 234. [118] Ibid.

The economic prospect was indeed so radically improved for them that Hunter was persuaded to put the relevant parts of his account in *The Annals of Rural Bengal* under the ecstatic caption: 'The Railway Abolishes Slavery'.[119] Yet when violence actually broke out in July 1855 the beneficiaries seem to have had no hesitation about slaying the goose that laid the golden eggs for them.

The records are quite clear on this point: indeed, railway works were among the very first and most frequently destroyed objects mentioned in the reports received from the disturbed areas within the first week of the uprising. In one of these key reports Richardson identified this particular orientation of the hool and explained this in terms found convincing enough by his superiors as well. 'The object of the Hillmen', he wrote from Suri on 14 July, 'appears to be to destroy everything connected with the Railway works, and their anger has been roused, I have no doubt, by the Railway Officers carrying on intrigues with their women as well as bullying the laborers.' This was corroborated by the Officiating Commissioner of the Burdwan Division who forwarded this report to the authorities in Calcutta saying 'that the Sonthal women have been disgraced and this injury calls amongst them for vengeance'.[120] Quite clearly the Santals had decided that it was not worth their while coming back home to their villages with all the money earned on the railroads—'with their girdles full of coin and their women covered with silver jewellery, "just like Hindus" ', as Hunter put it[121]—if they could not defend the honour of those women and their own dignity as workers against the raping, bullying railway sahibs. In other words, in one of those unpredictable leaps of consciousness prestige suddenly assumed for them an importance exceeding that of money and politics transcended economics.

This was by no means the only instance one could cite. On yet another occasion later on the Santals destroyed all the green crops belonging to Bengali villagers hostile to them in the neighbourhood of Jamjorie in Birbhum district[122] indicating

[119] Ibid.: 235.

[120] JP, 19 July 1855: Richardson to Elliott (14 July 1855); Elliott to Grey (15 July 1855).

[121] Hunter (1897): 235.

[122] JP, 6 Dec. 1855: Bird to Becher (23 Nov. 1855).

once again that they regarded the uprising as a war in which political considerations had to be given a priority over strictly economic ones, the need to destroy the enemy over that of safeguarding economic resources from destruction. The Kols are known to have 'plundered and burned' a little over 29,859 metric tons of gram in four divisions of Chota Nagpur in the course of their insurrection in 1831–2.[123] And to turn to the experience of the year of the Mutiny, the damage done by the rebels to the coal mines at Kotah and their not so successful attempt to wreck those in Rewah, the destruction of canal locks by the peasants in order to prevent Major Reid's battalion from reaching Bulandshahr by boat, the numerous attacks on railways and factories by the rural poor dependent for their livelihood on them in many parts of Uttar Pradesh in those days were all witness to the primacy of politics in Indian peasant rebellions of our period.[124]

There was nothing of course about all this which may be said to have been peculiarly Indian. Parallels abound. During the Peasant War in Germany in 1525 the rebels were known to have damaged crops in fields and barns, destroyed the entire stock of fish in some lakes, burned down a forest and cut down a vineyard ignoring the proprietor's offer of wine, meat, bread and money as inducement to leave him alone.[125] The French jacqueries of 1789 duplicated the pattern: game was killed, woods laid waste, abbey lands ruined, pigeons and dovecotes destroyed, salt pans damaged, and mills, forges and sawmills broken up.[126] On the eve of the Maji Maji rebellion the peasants of Tanganyika defied their leader's advice to continue cultivating cotton for the German colonialists and asked themselves, 'How do we start the war? How do we make the Germans angry? Let us go and uproot their cotton so that war may rise.' They uprooted cotton and thereby inaugurated the revolt.[127] In China in 1927 the Hunan peasantry sought 'outlets for their feelings against those who oppressed them' by slaughtering the pigs and sheep of 'the local tyrants and the evil gentry'.[128] It is

[123] As in n. 105 above. The total amount is given as 822,992 mds. 24 srs. 3/4 chh.
[124] FSUP: IV 32, 556–8; V 32.
[125] Zimmermann: I 171, 303, 374; II 90–1.
[126] Lefebvre (1973): 44, 45, 101, 108, 109, 120.
[127] Gwassa & Iliffe: 14–15. [128] Mao: I 53.

indeed not possible to explain solely or even primarily in terms of economic interests the destruction of so much of productive resources so often by insurgents operating under such widely different circumstances in so many countries.

We thought it fit to insist on this destructive aspect of rebel activities in order to avoid the error of reading purely economic motives in them. For that might tend to blur the distinction between two qualitatively different types of violence—rebel violence which expresses itself in what are essentially political acts intended to turn things upside down and criminal violence against property aimed at transferring economic resources from its victims to its protagonists. This is a functional difference not to emphasize which could lead to a narrowly economistic interpretation of peasant insurgency. Labry's account of the disturbances in the Russian countryside in 1905 provides us with an instructive specimen of precisely such an interpretation. Describing the sacking of the country-houses in the Chernigov Guberniya he writes:

> A very large number of those who took part in these attacks refused to regard their actions as in the least *criminal*, since, as they put it, they had been granted *rights*. They even believed that in acting as they did, they were helping to transfer the lands of the landlords into their own hands, which was the natural consequence of the *rights* they had been granted. Only this explains why on the estates they destroyed orangeries and flower-gardens—which were *useless* to them—with particular fury, and in the houses, pictures and furniture, in a word all that they regarded not as a *necessity of life*, but as a *sign of comfort and luxury*. On the other hand they spared the cattle and took care not to destroy stocks of corn.[129]

Quite clearly it is the author's intention to read in this violence *both* a political and an economic meaning. He starts off by emphasizing the former. The peasants, he says, acted from a consciousness of their own rights, that is, from a political consciousness which, if true, must have had its objects predicated as political. It is thus that they came to regard themselves as involved not in crime but in political action aimed at demolishing the insignia of the landlords' authority. To regard this pillage then as a merely selective attack directed '*par calcul*' against 'useless' and economically unproductive luxuries and

[129] Labry, *Autour du Moujik*, quoted in Hobsbawm: 187. Emphasis added.

suggest, as Hobsbawm does on the basis of this account, that 'destruction is never indiscriminate, what is useful for poor men is spared',[130] is to depoliticize this violence, make it into an economism and consequently render it impossible for us to understand why 'those who took part in these attacks refused to regard their actions as in the least criminal'.

Indeed the correct reading of this experience should be that destruction is 'never indiscriminate' only in the sense that the peasant discriminated between what stands for landlord authority and what does not, and not between what is 'useful' and what is 'useless' in the narrowly economic sense of these words. One can perhaps even go so far as to generalize that the more a violence of this type shifts away from crime towards rebellion the more it comes to be dominated by politics rather than economics, and vice versa. This is why it is often difficult to assign any clear-cut economic motive even to some of the more radical forms of social banditry which come fairly close to rebellion but fall just short of it on the spectrum of rural violence. Blacking, for instance, in most parts of eighteenth-century England could hardly be explained in terms of the poachers' involvement in the illicit venison trade. 'Other motives were *dominant*', says E. P. Thompson. 'The deer killed were often either eaten by the hunters, or their carcasses were left in the parks. Whereas there were distinct venison seasons, with the culling of bucks in midsummer and of hinds in mid-winter, the attacks of the Blacks were at all seasons, at times when the meat would not only be poor, but its attempted sale would attract notice. Above all, the whole pattern of Black actions—the threatening letters, felling of young trees, blackmail of forest officers—disallows a simple economic explanation.'[131] The dominant motive here is clearly political—that of undermining the authority of the gentry by the demolition of its symbols. This inversive function of popular violence is raised to its highest power by insurgency, and destruction becomes in that context the signifier of a consciousness which is as negative in orientation as it is political in content.

No narrowly economic interpretation can explain some of the other forms of rebel activities either, such as eating and looting. There was nothing of the calculus of saving and investment in

[130] Hobsbawm: 26. [131] Thompson (1975): 160–1.

these. Taken together they acted as a foil to the other pair—wrecking and burning, and complemented by expropriation what the latter achieved by demolition, the function of both being to assist insurgency to destroy.

Eating, in this context, must be understood as an integral part of a political process. Neither the gargantuan scale on which it is often organized by the peasants to celebrate a successful jacquerie nor the enormous waste involved makes any sense at all of this as simply a measure of satisfying hunger. On the contrary, its use by the rebels as an instrument of inversion and/or as a penalty imposed on their foes in order to remunerate themselves for 'public services' rendered in the cause of insurgency bears testimony to its political character. It is precisely this meaning that is emphasized by Mao Tse-tung when he identifies this as one of 'the methods used by the peasants to hit the landlords *politically*' during the Hunan movement and characterizes it as a political demonstration thus:

Major demonstrations. A big crowd is rallied to demonstrate against a local tyrant or one of the evil gentry who is an enemy of the [peasant] association. The demonstrators eat at the offender's house, slaughtering his pigs and consuming his grain as a matter of course. Quite a few such cases have occurred. There was a case recently at Machiaho, Hsiangtan County, where a crowd of fifteen thousand peasants went to the houses of six of the evil gentry and demonstrated; the whole affair lasted four days during which more than 130 pigs were killed and eaten. After such demonstrations, the peasants usually impose fines.[132]

Demonstrations of this kind occurred frequently in Germany in 1525, in France in 1789, in England in 1830. However, the Indian parallels I have come across are rather less numerous. There is a reference in Sajon Gazi's ballad to Titu Mir's men feasting on the eve of the battle of Laughati. Again, Bindrai, the Kol leader, mentions that 'it was agreed upon that we should commence to cut, plunder, murder and eat'.[133] Cut, plunder and murder they certainly did, but there is little evidence of the last of those resolutions being acted upon as a 'major demonstration'. Kanhu too says in one of his recorded statements that at

[132] Mao: I 36–7.

[133] Biharilal Sarkar: 30 (I owe this reference to Gautam Bhadra); BC 1363 (54227): Cuthbert & Wilkinson to Thomason (12 Feb. 1832).

Pulsa he and his men 'looted & burnt the Sahib's bungalow & took lots of wine'.[134] We also know that on one occasion, at Umurpore, they were surprised by the troops in the midst of what was obviously a banquet in progress after a successful raid on two neighbouring villages. The Santals escaped leaving behind them 'the remains of an ample feast, a bullock half devoured, quantities of grain, cooking pots and numberless fires where they had just been cooking'.[135] And to go by Krishnadas Ray's near-contemporary verses, they stopped at the house of one Gayaram in another village and 'held a sumptuous feast there'.[136] Elwin in his account of the fituris in Ganjam mentions a case when in the course of a raid on a Pano village the Saora 'took pigs and goats which they killed and ate on the spot—a characteristic touch'.[137]

It should be evident even from these few instances that in India as elsewhere it sometimes happened that the peasants involved in a jacquerie would consume large quantities of edibles seized from their enemies as a method of destroying some of those resources which made the latter so rich and powerful—and indeed so different from themselves. However, it is difficult to decide at the present state of research how widespread this was and whether our want of information on this point is due simply to a gap in the records, or to a failure on the part of historians in extracting this detail from the primary sources if only because they have not grasped its significance, or to the fact that its emergence as a common and popular form of struggle was genuinely inhibited by the fear of ritual pollution through eating even among the non-Hindu peasantry like the Kol and the Santal who had long been influenced by Hindu caste customs.

No such doubt however can occur in the case of the other major type of such destructive activity, viz. looting. Truly ubiquitous, it appears to have made its presence felt in almost all uprisings in every land. In India it featured prominently even in the most 'peaceful' of peasant struggles such as those of Pabna in 1873 where looting occurred in as many as thirty out of the fifty-three

[134] JP, 20 Dec. 1855: 'Examination of Kanoo Sonthal'.
[135] JP, 8 Nov. 2855: Chapman to Bidwell (22 Oct. 1855).
[136] D. C. Sen (1926): 267. [137] Elwin: 255.

(not counting five dismissed as false) recorded cases in the sadar sub-division.[138] In yet another series—the Deccan riots of 1875—noted officially for its moderation the houses, shops and granaries of the Marwari and Gujar sahukars were looted in a number of districts.[139] In the more violent jacqueries plunder and demolition went together in most cases. The ryots who rose against Deby Sinha in northern Bengal in 1783 plundered and burnt down the kacharis in several parganas and on one occasion looted the East India Company's grain stores at the flourishing centre of rice trade at Bhabaniganj.[140]

Looting supported by wrecking and burning—pillage, to call this complex of rebel activities by its composite name—occurred on a massive scale during the Kol insurrection as well. A quick run through its chronology should make this clear. It started with four villages in the Sonepur pargana of Chota Nagpur being raided, plundered and burnt down by a body of seven hundred insurgents on 20 December 1831. This was followed up by the plunder of two other villages on 25 December by three hundred rebels and the sack of three villages on 2–3 January 1832 by a thousand men. On 12 January the entire pargana of Belkudra was looted and set to fire, and so were all villages within the jurisdiction of Govindpur thana as well as Barkagarh pargana and thana by 13 January. Several hundred villages under Jhikuchatti thana ended up in the same way during the next three days and the whole area was abandoned to the rebels by 16 January. All of Armai thana was overrun and pillaged by 24 January and the entire Barwa pargana by the 26th—the date by which the Kols were officially recognized as having taken 'complete possession of the whole of [Chota] Nagpore' excluding some inconsiderable tracts in the southern and north-eastern corners of the region.[141] The value of the property and goods plundered in the four divisions of Tori, Lohardagga, Sonepur and Palkote, for which alone we have complete figures, was estimated at 203,722 rupees not counting 32,494 rupees looted in cash.[142]

[138] JP (P): 'Pubna Riot Case' enclosed in ibid.: Tayler to Mackenzie (23 Aug. 1873).

[139] DRCR: 2, 3. [140] MDS: 323, 564, 582.

[141] BC 1502 (58891): Dent & Wilkinson to Thomason (16 Nov. 1832).

[142] As in n. 105 above.

Pillage, again, emerged as the central modality of the revolt of the Santals in 1855. To Balai Majhi wounded and captured on the seventh day of the hool during a raid by several thousand peasants on Charles Maseyk's indigo factory rebellion *was* pillage. 'I came to plunder', he said simply and succinctly to his interrogator, and then proceeded to fill in the details thus:

After plundering Kudumsha, we looted the residence of the Maheshpore Rajah; then turned back, & went north & plundered all the villages along the back of the river, and we had settled to go as far as Bhaugulpore . . . I was present at the looting of many villages and the three Rupees that were (found) with me I got at the plundering of a Rajah's near Agoonerjah—and we divided all the Rupees. All the other property has been taken to Takoor Sidoo & Kaloor's house . . . and when we attack villages, the people run away and the plunderers take everything . . . The above named Sidoo and Kaloo declared themselves Rajas & [said] they would plunder the whole country and take possession of it—they said also, no one can stop us; for it is the order of Takoor. On this account we have all come with them.[143]

This insurgent view of the hool as one massive plundering expedition was shared by all the local officials too. For them no less than for 'Bullye Sonthal, Manjee, son of Bushye . . . occupation—cultivator, caste—Sonthal, inhabitant of Bahoo or Barah Masseeal, Pergh Zilleagur' the rebellion *was* pillage. 'They go and loot villages daily 4 or 5. They say this is at the order of a God', wrote the sub-divisional administrator of Aurangabad in his first breathless 'demi-official' report two days after the outbreak.[144] And from that point onwards official correspondence on the subject never looks back. There is hardly a despatch from the area that does not mention pillage. It recurs frequently in a diary kept by the Collector of Birbhum at the height of the rising. Thus,

19 September 1855. The Reports from Saruth & Opurbandah are most unsatisfactory—
The Sontals are evidently steadily advancing, looting every village en route.
20 September 1855. Birchunder, a village about 8 miles West of Nugger, has been looted.

[143] JP, 19 July 1855: Toogood to Grey (14 July 1855). 'Kaloor's house' should of course read 'Kanhu's house'.

[144] Ibid.: Eden to Grey (9 July 1855).

21 September 1855. The Sontals are looting to their hearts' content in the Saruth & Opurbandah jurisdictions . . . A report has just come in that the Sontals in very great numbers are at Bindabone . . . & that they have looted Bilkandu.[145]

Within a fortnight, according to this Collector, 'upwards of thirty villages have been plundered and burned by the insurgents in Thannah Operbundha and Nangoolea'.[146] This account of the progress of pillage agrees with despatches from the Commissioner on Special Duty. 'The Sonthals are assembled in large numbers marching & plundering without discrimination all along the South of the Bhaugulpore District N and NW of Beerbhoom and along the foot of the hills', he writes.[147] The insurgents had apparently done so thorough a job already in that part of the country that he had 'no apprehension of any plunder being attempted between this [i.e. Suri] and Rampore Haut for the best of reasons, that the whole of the country to the North of a line drawn between this and that post has been plundered and there is nothing the Sonthals can gain by invading it now'.[148]

It was indeed this sweep and power of pillage which the peasants' enemies feared most. The description of a panic in Burdwan within a fortnight of the Santal uprising was a measure of the extent and intensity of the alarm it had caused. The local correspondent of the *Somprakash* (23 July 1855) wrote:

The rich as well as the poor residents of Burdwan have all been seized with panic here . . . The rich have heard of the depredations of the Santal rebels of the hills and are contemplating various means by which to save their wealth, honour and lives. Thus, some of them have increased the strength of their house-guards by ten times. Some others have hidden all the cash they have in pits dug into the ground and are crying out over and over again, 'O Lord! Save us!' 'O Lord! Save us!' Some others have their eyes glued to the newspapers. And still others are busy gathering news at the railway station about the number of troops sent up by the Company's government. Altogether thus a big furore is being made.[149]

There is clearly a recognition here of the threat to property sensed by those who had most to lose from rebel violence. But

[145] BDR: 120–1. [146] Ibid.: 122.
[147] JP, 4 Oct. 1855: Ward to GOB (16 Sept. 1855).
[148] Ibid.: Ward to Grey (19 Sept. 1855). [149] Ghose: 791.

note how very similar their response was to that of affluent villagers threatened by brigandage—burying cash and jewellery underground was a traditional measure of security against robbery in rural India—and how little this related to the actual practice of looting in the hool. For it was *not* money that was plundered most. 'Grain was our chief plunder and cattle', said Kanhu after his capture; 'many seizures have been made by the Troops, and the remainder are in the Jungles'.[150] This is corroborated fully by the records of the anti-insurgency campaign. Officers would return from their pursuit of the rebels with tales about forest hide-outs stacked with grain and herds of cattle. A Captain Phillips reports on 30 October 1855 from Camp Kurwun that in the course of that day's *dour* he came upon an 'encampment which was in the midst of very heavy jungle' and destroyed the large quantities of grain and other stores he found there 'all by setting fire to the encampment'.[151] A Captain Pester reports on the following day from Camp Jamtarah how his detachment destroyed 'two large encampments and a great quantity of grain'.[152] A Major Hampton reports from Kandra on the same day that he found the two hills near Luckunpore, a large Santal village, 'filled with grain, a great quantity of which was carried off by some 3 or 400 men who crossed the Burrakur and followed my detachment; the remainder was as far as possible destroyed'.[153] The amounts mentioned are impressive. Four to five thousand maunds of grain were destroyed or carried off and 650 heads of cattle seized by the Bengalis (who systematically scavenged on the trail of the army with the latter's encouragement and connivance) from the 1,950 huts burnt down by the forces in twenty-three Santal villages of Birbhum.[154] And at Suburpoor, west of Jamtarah, the troops confiscated 5,000 heads of cattle and destroyed a 'large quantity of grains reported by Captain Nicholls as sufficient to supply a large force [for] at least 2 years'.[155] Looting in the Kol in-

[150] JP, 20 Dec. 1855: 'Statement of Insurgent Sonthals'.

[151] JP, 22 Nov. 1855: Phillips to Parrott (30 Oct. 1855).

[152] Ibid.: Pester to Parrott (31 Oct. 1855).

[153] Ibid.: Hampton to Parrott (31 Oct. 1855).

[154] JP, 8 Nov. 1855: 'Memo. shewing the List of Villages burnt in the Sonthal Districts, as also the quantity of Grain destroyed and removed by the Bengalees on the 10th of October 1855' (12 Oct. 1855).

[155] Ibid.: Ward to GOB (22 Oct. 1855).

surrection, twenty-four years before the hool, had followed the same pattern. It had started off with cattle-lifting, and grain and cattle were the objects pillaged most, as the campaign against the rebels was to demonstrate on that occasion too. Russell, the Jungle Mahal Magistrate, recovered 1,200 heads of cattle and 6,000 maunds of grain in the course of his military operations in one sector alone.[156]

The pattern of plunder thus did not quite correspond to what the men of property had feared it would turn out to be. Their initial response to a *levée en masse* in the countryside clung far too closely to the stereotype of the peasant as a dacoit—a failure on their part to recognize (as we have seen above) that a code-switching had occurred. For the peasant, as a rebel, was out not to rob but to destroy the authority of his enemies by expropriating them. Lefebvre's emphasis on this important distinction has a validity far beyond the particular experience to which it refers. Commenting on the character of insurgent activities in rural France in 1789 he writes:

> These peasants did not band together to go *stealing*: they came to *destroy* and they gave this one *basic aim* their best attention.[157]

Crime had, in his view, very little to do with the jacqueries which broke out in such large numbers in those days. Even brigandage was rare. A certain amount of petty and rather innocuous pilfering would of course occur almost inevitably during a raid on a chateau, and some would help themselves 'to something they fancied and which was often quite valueless'.[158] But by and large the French rebels were positively *not* criminals.

This could be said of their opposite numbers in India too. The storming of the police station at Khunti was a major event of the Birsaite revolt, but the Larakas 'did not touch the money received in the thana the same day' nor did they rob the houses in that town.[159] The evidence that we have of the nature and amount of fortune acquired by some of the Santals during the hool shows how little relation the scale of that vast and violent enterprise bore to the size of individual gains. Balai Majhi's

[156] J. C. Jha: 77.
[157] Lefebvre (1973): 118. Emphasis added.
[158] Ibid.: 117–18. [159] Singh: 107.

share of plunder amounted to 3 rupees;[160] Jata's to some 'silver ornaments and [a] green tin Box he plundered from a Mohajun's house in one of the villages'; and Kanhu Subah's to:

No. 1—A looking glass in a brass case
No. 2—A Wai[s]t plate belonging to the late Lieutt. Toulmin
No. 3—Some silver ornaments
No. 4—Three Pocket Books, and an old Book on locomotive, a few visiting cards of Mr Burn, Engineer, with some torn leaves and envelopes and bits of thin English paper
No. 5 & 6—Two purses containing 12 Rupees and 1 Gold Mohur in the first, and 17 Rupees in the second, and some pice
No. 7—Pieces of silk and Native dresses, Chudders, etc

—all described graphically as 'the property on the table' that is, as objects spread out for quick inspection on the top of a desk in Brigadier L. S. Bird's headquarters at Camp Raniganj. Not counting the twenty rupees in that list which represented Kanhu's own savings 'brought from home and . . . mine', as he said during the interrogation, the remainder was not much indeed to show for the supreme commander of a rebel army that had wiped out the Raj in ten weeks from an area exceeding one thousand square miles in three districts.[161]

No, 'these peasants did not band together to go stealing', as Lefebvre rightly observes. It was not their purpose to appropriate resources by petty crime. Their 'basic aim' was 'to destroy' their enemy's resources and with these his authority by means of a special form of activity of the masses. They distinguished this activity from other types of violence in name by calling it 'ulgulan' in Mundari, 'hool' in Santali, 'dhing' in a dialect of northern Bengal and so on, as well as in practice by imposing on it a rhetoric of war in the form of pillage. In India pillage was not systematized according to the conventions of medieval warfare in the same way as it was done in Germany in 1525.[162] But its war-like figure was never less than obvious.

[160] JP, 19 July 1855: Toogood to Grey (Enclosure, 14 July 1855).

[161] JP, 20 Dec. 1855: 'Statement of Insurgent Sonthals'.

[162] During the Peasant War in Germany the rebels would elect, whenever the occasion arose, one of themselves as *Beutemeister* (Master of the Booty)—a feudal convention they had adopted, democratized and turned the other way round against the nobility. And it was the Beutemeister's task to lead 'the plundering of those houses and palaces which were declared open for pillage'. Zimmermann: II 24, 133.

Major Sutherland, the first official to investigate the uprising of the Kols, remarked that 'they had enriched themselves with the spoils of their enemies for such they considered all foreigners'.[163] In the perception of the insurgents plunder was thus identified as *spoils* rather than as criminal acquisition.

Looting as an extension of war was explicit in the operations of the Santals, too. They used this as a direct instrument of attack, reprisal and self-defence, depending on the occasion that called for it. Major-General Lloyd commanding the Dinapur Division and the Sonthal Field Force emphasized this when he asked the government carefully to consider the pros and cons of the counter-insurgency tactics. 'For every village or store of plunder we destroy, they burn and plunder at least five', he reported.[164] Subsequently, after the hool had passed its peak by the autumn of 1855 looting came to be used by rebels increasingly as the means of self-defence. Burnt out of their villages by the Company's troops and forced to retreat further and further into the jungle, they plundered in order to stockpile provisions for what they obviously expected to be a protracted war. 'It is reported that the depredations now committed by the rebels are mainly for the purpose of plunder in order to supply themselves with the necessaries of life', wrote the Secretary to the Bengal Government, 'for though possessed of money they are unable to purchase supplies owing to the Bengallees flying at their approach. This state of things has produced a new feature in the insurrection the rebels being now stated to come in force at night & carry away the crops which are just ripening'.[165] This is how the troops came upon—and in their own turn, plundered and destroyed—vast granaries and large herds of cattle in the course of their *dours* in the jungle. It was also during this period when the Santals came under heavy enemy pressure that they used plunder as a form of punishment against collaborators. After the capture of Kewala, the bandit who had turned into a leader of the hool, Kanhu with about one thousand of his men raided Londeeha,

[163] BC 1363 (54227): Sutherland's Note to Vice-President's Private Secretary (Mar. 1832).

[164] JP, 4 Oct. 1855: Lloyd to GOI quoting from Col. Liptrap's letter (Sept. 1855).

[165] JP, 8 Nov. 1855: Grey to GOI (31 Oct. 1855).

the village where this happened, and looted it as a punitive measure.[166]

It is precisely because of this quasi-military, hence political, character of plunder that cash and other objects of conspicuous consumption which fell into the hands of the insurgents tended to be treated not as articles of theft but as booty to be shared out amongst all or centralized for use by the leadership in their work for the uprising. The statements of Balai, a rank-and-file insurgent captured at the very beginning of the hool and of Kanhu, its supreme commander captured towards its end, both testify to the fact that all the looted cash was 'shared amongst the manjees and sonthals'.[167] The means of transport seized from the enemy were handed over to the commanders for their use—horses for the middle-ranking darogas and palanquins for the Subahs. And objects which were not immediately distributed or could not be broken up into divisible units for that purpose, were evidently gathered into a sort of communal store and placed under the custody of the supreme command—Sido and Kanhu. It was one such collection of booty 'consisting of Palkees, a Buggy, Brass and Copper utensils, silks, cloths and miscellaneous property' worth four thousand rupees as well as cash amounting to over seven thousand rupees which the rebels looted at Maheshpur but had not yet had the time to share out, that fell into the hands of the troops after they routed the Santals at that village in one of the most critical encounters of the insurrection.[168]

It should be evident from this survey that in its power to destroy, its mass character and its nearly universal use as a form of struggle looting taken in its wider sense as pillage was a quintessential aspect of insurgency. It derived its strength from the collective will of large rural populations acting together to settle accounts with sarkar, sahukar and zamindar. Each plundering expedition of the Kols and the Santals was the work of thousands of people. Even in the relatively less explosive Pabna movement as many as 22,130 ryots were involved in the twenty-five cases of plunder for which figures are given—an average of

[166] Ibid.: Chapman to Bidwell (22 Oct. 1855).

[167] JP, 19 July 1855: Toogood to Grey (Enclosure, 14 July 1855); JP, 20 Dec. 1855: 'Statement of Insurgent Sonthals'.

[168] JP, 23 Aug. 1855: Toogood to Grey (15 July 1855).

885. In eleven out of these twenty-five cases the number of peasants involved ranged between 100 and 500 and in ten between 1,000 and 7,000.[169] And pillage, as we have shown above, moved fast. The cutting edge of the Kol and Santal insurrections, it spread rebel power, however thinly, over the whole of Chota Nagpur in about five weeks and over Damin-i-Koh in ten. There was nothing in the character, mass or velocity of this violence that did not distinguish it clearly from crime.

To conclude this discussion of the distinctive features of insurgency it is perhaps necessary to emphasize that these forms of struggle constitute a *total and integrated violence*. Taken separately each of these would stand for a particular form of crime. In rebellion, however, these four types of destructive activity lose their separate identities and function as mutually connected elements of one single complex. At this level, the distinction between crime and insurgency corresponds to that between two types of violence—partial and total, the former as the expression of the will of a single individual or a small group in any society and the latter as that of the will of the Many.

This distinction is represented clearly in their respective patterns. Crime, as discussed above, expresses itself in two different ways. It is either a singular violence addressed to one particular object or, as it often happens under conditions of acute social conflict, one particular type of violence directed against a variety of objects and conversely, many different kinds of violence against one particular class of objects. The violence of rebellion, however, is conspicuous by its plurality in both respects—in the forms it assumes as well as the objects it chooses. It is the combination of this vertical and horizontal plurality which makes an insurrection so comprehensive in its scope and its articulation so very powerful indeed as ultimately to overcome any ambiguity that it may have at an initial stage. This totality is too obvious to be missed out by any serious student of a rural uprising. Rudé has commented on this aspect of the Swing thus: 'A remarkable feature of the labourers' movement of 1830, distinguishing it from many others of its kind, was its multiformity . . . arson, threatening letters, "in-

[169] This estimate is based on details given in JP(P): 'Pubna Riot Case'.

flammatory" handbills and posters, "robbery", wages meetings, assaults on overseers, parsons and landlords, and the destruction of different types of machinery all played their part.'[170]

This 'multiformity' is clearly another name for 'totality' as defined above—that is, the coming together of many different forms of insurgent activity and its multifarious objects. Even the most casual account of an Indian rebellion, with all its differences of detail indicates a very close similarity, if not identity, of pattern. A comparison of the experiences of three peasant insurrections ranging from the least to the most organized and spanning almost the entire period of colonial rule at fairly even intervals should make this clear. The rising against Deby Sinha in Rangpur and Dinajpur in 1783 had among its targets the persons and properties of landlords and their officials, the East India Company's troops, its granaries, kachari buildings and money and papers found by the insurgents there; the means of violence used by the rebels were arson, killing, armed assault, plunder, physical and ritual humiliation of the enemies, robbery, arrest and forcible detention, rescue of prisoners and looting of grain stores. Again, the violence of the highly disciplined movement of the Pabna peasantry in 1873 counted among its objects landlords' kacharis and estates, houses of zamindari officials and the rural gentry, groceries, police officers, and the person and houses of those who collaborated with the zamindars against the peasant union; the acts of violence ranged from raids on houses and police stations, rescue of prisoners, plunder and extortion of money to rioting, unlawful assembly, intimidation by blowing horns, abuse, theft, trespass and so on—in fact offences covering as many as twenty different sections of the Indian Penal Code in just one subdivision alone. And the violence of the peasant revolt led by the communists in Telengana at the end of the Raj was directed against the landlords, their private armies, the armed forces of the state, moneylenders and collaborators; and it articulated itself in the destruction of landlords' orchards and agricultural tools, social boycott, murder of zamindars, sahukars and *desmukhs*, plunder and destruction of their houses, seizure of their grain stores, standing crops and other articles of consumption, destruction of usurers' bonds, etc.[171]

[170] H & R: 195.

[171] For details see MDS: 213, 323, 326, 330–2, 580, 582; Kaviraj: 21–4, 27–8;

In the case of the most massive and powerful of such uprisings—such as those of the Kols, the Santals and Birsaites which bordered on peasant wars, the range of the rebel attack was so wide, its form so varied and its targets so numerous—the horizontal and vertical pluralities were indeed so well integrated—that in the perception of the colonial authorities the acts of violence often lost their separate identities and merged into a blur to which the law would then assign a name as one undifferentiated crime and deal with it according to the rules of summary justice. This is how all but one of a group of forty-two participants in the hool who were produced before the Sessions Judge of Birbhum and tried in the course of one week in November 1855 came to be convicted of crimes described in almost identical phrases. Twenty insurgents sentenced on 9 November were each convicted of 'illegally and riotously assembling with offensive weapons for the purpose of murder and to commit a breach of peace'; each of the two on 12 November 1855 of 'illegally & riotously assembling with weapons for the purpose of plunder to commit a breach of the peace'; three on 14 November of 'illegally & riotously assembling with weapons for plunder [of] property of parties unknown'; and each of the sixteen on 17 November of 'illegally & riotously assembling with weapons and plundering the village of Katna in Zl Beerbhoom'.[172]

Such want of discrimination was no doubt a symptom of that infirmity of the official mind on some aspects of which Hunter has left us some wry comments in his account of the Santal insurrection.[173] But there was more to this blurred and stereotyped jargon than simply the inertia of administrative perception. It also stood for a groping and hesitant acknowledgement on the part of the court that the offence it was given to adjudicate constituted a totality greater than the sum of the charges. Indeed there were many among the colonial authorities, especially those entrusted to deal with an uprising on a scale larger than that of a single locality, who made no mistake about its comprehensive character. The mutually interacting

Sen Gupta: 160–83; and Sundarayya: 30, 33, 37, 38, 52, 58, 163, 234, 287–9, 292, 297.

[172] BDR: 125–6 and 129–30. The date '7th Novr. 1855' given in BDR: 130 is obviously a copyist's or printer's error for 17th November 1855.

[173] Hunter (1897): 244–5.

processes of its collective violence, its mass and velocity, gave it, in their eyes, the semblance of a 'system'. It was thus that Neave and Russell, two of the principal officers involved in the suppression of the Kol rebellion in 1832, came, respectively, to speak of it as a '*system of burning, plundering and killing*' and a '*system of plunder and outrages*', just as in England at about the same time, their opposite numbers operating against the Swing movement were accusing the peasantry as having established a '*system of pillage*'.[174] Nothing testifies more to the distinction between rural crime and insurgency than such recognition of the systematic, total character of the latter on the part of those to whom it was addressed. It shows that violence, confined no longer to that grey zone where the peasant met his enemy in single combat, had emerged into the open as a war between the classes.

As the reader may have already noticed, the foregoing discussion has not included killing as a principal form or method of struggle. In insisting on this omission we have paid heed to the many references to blood and sword in our evidence and convinced ourselves that these testify less to any considerable loss of life than to the terror which grips the peasants' enemies on the outbreak of an uprising. For the sudden and inversive character of the latter tends to elicit an exaggerated and often hysterical response from those most seriously threatened by it. In so far as the primary sources of our information are made up to a large extent of precisely this kind of response, it is useful perhaps to start by differentiating within this genre of violence between two modes which are often merged in a gory mess in elite perception and hence in elite discourse.

The first of these is the death of members of the armed forces of the Raj or those of its non-official protégés such as white civilians and rural gentry (e.g. those who fought on the side of the government during the Mutiny and the Santal rebellion respectively) caused by peasants in the course of war-like encounters such as those at Mandalghat and Patgong during the Rangpur dhing, at Narkelberia during the Barasat revolt, at Maheshpur and Pakur during the hool in 1855, at Sail Rakab

[174] BC 1362 (54225): Neave to Lambert (10 Feb. 1832); BC 1363 (54226): Russell to Braddon (18 Apr. 1832); H & R: 119. Emphasis added.

during the Birsaite insurrection and at many places throughout Uttar Pradesh in the year of the Mutiny. Most of these battles were fought by the rebels as defensive engagements and decided in favour of the regime by the sheer force of its superior fire power, but not before a few soldiers had been brought down on some occasions by arrows or by the rare volley from a rebel's musket. Yet the very fact that the usually passive and peaceable peasant had, against all expectation, resisted the sarkari troops and even drawn a little blood was blown up into tales of massacre by flustered officers, frightened sepoys and correspondents scared out of their wits as they wrote to the vernacular and English-language press. If anything, it was counter-insurgency rather than insurgency that made of killing a principal modality in such cases, as witness the indiscriminate slaughter of Munda women at Sail Rakab which moved even a brazen Government of India to record a mild regret.[175]

However, the attribution of killing as a characteristic feature of insurgency does not rest primarily on such war-like situations where a peasant mass is driven to defend itself by arms against the troops or some other armed formations acting on behalf of the colonial state. What is at issue here is the notion of violence leading to the annihilation of individuals among the groups or classes hostile to the rebels. The evidence we have on this point is indeed as striking as it is negative. Contrary to the polarized myths of peasant savagery and rebel heroism estimated, in both cases, in terms of the magnitude of killing, the incidence of the latter appears to have been so low indeed as to be negligible. This is true even of the most violent and widespread of Indian peasant revolts. 'Murder has not been *general*', wrote the Collector of Birbhum in his diary recording, at the very height of the hool, the impact of a raid by the Bhagalpur Santals in the course of which 'the Thannah & Village of Operbundah were plundered & burnt'.[176]

This pattern of violence articulated in its most destructive form in plunder and arson but stopping just short of murder, holds for the Kol insurrection too. To quote from an official

[175] Singh: 114–15.

[176] Richardson's Diary (Enclosure, 4 Oct. 1855): 'Operations of the Sonthals during their recent raid into the Operbundah Thanah Jurisdiction' in JP, 8 Nov. 1855.

report on the havoc it caused in a small township inhabited by a large number of those whom the rebels hated most, namely moneylenders:

Boondoonugger was on the 18th [January 1832] taken possession of by the Insurgents. The town being extensive and peopled by wealthy Mohajuns occupied them four days in plundering it and then it was burned to the ground . . . the houses of all the respectable men of the Pergunnah not of the class of Coles were in a few days also destroyed, but the only murders that were committed took place in the Town of Boondoo where 3 Pattons and 2 others were put to death.[177]

Five killings in a town that took four days to sack is perhaps a fair approximation of the incidence of murder as compared to that of the other forms of struggle. This is borne out also by the statistics we have of non-tribal persons (specified as Hindu and Muslim men and women) killed during the entire course of this insurrection in five divisions of Chota Nagpur—3 in Tori, 244 in Lohardagga, 47 in Sonepur, 12 in Palkote and 9 in Tamar and the Five Parganas. A total of 315 this is not much to show in terms of bloodshed for one of the most violent of all rural disturbances which had wiped off the Raj from Chota Nagpur in a matter of weeks. The relative paucity of this phenomenon is further demonstrated by the fact that the total number of houses (presumably belonging to the same groups) burnt down during this period in the first four of the divisions mentioned above was 4,086—that is, one killing for less than fourteen acts of arson.[178]

One wonders if the Indian experience is altogether unique in this respect. Not so, judging by what we know of the French peasant uprisings of the period of the Great Fear in 1789. Lefebvre examined with his customary scruple the charge of atrocities alleged to have been committed during the jacqueries in the Franche-Comté where 'violence was in general more pronounced and was directed mostly at people rather than objects' and concluded that even in this apparently extreme instance 'all in all, though attacks and harassments were many, there were no murders'.[179] And Rudé estimates the number of

[177] BC 1502 (58891): Dent & Wilkinson to Thomason (16 Nov. 1832).

[178] Ibid.: 'Return of Men and Women who were murdered during the Insurrection in Chota Nagpur'. For the statistics on arson see n. 105 above.

[179] Lefebvre (1973): 108.

people murdered by the peasants in all the regions taken together at a total of three. 'Only three landlords are known to have been killed', he writes in his introduction to Lefebvre's great work.[180]

Mao Tse-tung, too, indicates the somewhat exceptional character of this violence when he describes it as 'confined to the worst local tyrants and evil gentry' during the Hunan movement.[181] There is a suggestion here not only of the limited use made of it but also of its logic—a logic of punishment and vengeance. Most of the murders committed by Indian rebels also appear to have been discriminatory. From the cases on record one can see two governing principles at work, one punitive and the other retributive—a distinction which is merely notional and useful for analytic purposes alone, for in real life there was of course a good deal of overlap between the two.

Punitive killing derived its rationale from the exigencies of an ongoing insurrection and its victims were those who resisted it either indirectly by collaboration with the peasants' enemies or directly by arms. Hence the execution of informers was a feature common to many of the events included in our survey. Even a natural ally would not be spared if he worked for the other side, as did that *gwala* whom the Kol would have normally done nothing to harm but ended up by killing because he had betrayed to his master a plan they had to attack him.[182] For much the same reason, again, traitors were singled out for assassination—a question to which we shall return in the next chapter. The taking of life was also the rebels' way of dealing with those who met their force by force either as individuals or as members of official or private armies. 'I ordered', said Kanhu, the Santal leader, 'that all men who fought were to be killed and all who did not fight to be spared.'[183] It was as if he looked upon this particular type of violence as an extension of the peasant war itself and as a measure vital to the defence of the rebellion against efforts to undermine it by counter-violence.

By contrast retributive killing did not derive its rationale from the actuality of a rebellion but from its context. It had its referent in no current project of turning the rural world upside

[180] Ibid.: *xi*. [181] Mao: I 38.

[182] 'Nagpur Trials' (no. 85) in BC 1502 (58893): Master to Reid (22 Oct. 1832).

[183] JP, 20 Dec. 1855: 'Examination of Kanoo Sonthal'.

down but only in the insurgent's past, his prehistory as the subaltern for whom no oppression had been too much to put up with. Murder was thus charged with the memory of wrongs suffered. More often than not the killers and the killed were related as polar elements in the power structure of rural society, as its upper and nether millstones so to say—as landlord and tenant, usurer and debtor, upper-caste and untouchable, and so on. The servant killing the master epitomized the reversal indexed by this violence. The motif occurred again and again. A bondman beheaded his master when the latter was found in his hiding place by a party of Kols during a raid on his village.[184] Jagannath Sirdar joined the hool to slay his former master, the notorious Dindayal Ray of Pakur, and so on.[185] The excessive cruelty of many of these executions was a measure of the bitterness which inspired them. A veritable settling of accounts, the violence was almost codified in some instances—each offending limb of a landlord or moneylender being chopped off by the Santals as punishment for a particular offence of which it was an instrument ('With those offending fingers you counted your interest and ill-begotten wealth!') and each of the seven cuts inflicted by the Kols on any oppressive sud standing for 'the dissatisfaction with some particular tax or duty imposed on them'.[186]

If oppression was what made the peasants wreak vengeance by murder and there was indeed a great deal of oppression around, why were they so sparing in their use of this type of violence? The answer must be sought in two aspects of rebel consciousness—namely, its inertia and its negativity. It was not a liberated consciousness. On the contrary, with all its attempt to reverse the old relations of power it was still trapped in the old culture. That culture imbued the peasant with a sense of reverence for the body of anyone ranked as his superior. For the form of the human body is a symbol, as Hegel said,[187] and its symbolism in the highly semioticized world of traditional India was very

184 'Nagpur Trials' (no. 77). As in n. 182 above.

185 K. K. Datta: 73–4.

186 Ibid.; BC 1363 (54227): 'Note from Major J. Sutherland, etc' (March 1832), para. 15.

187 Hegel (1975): 353.

potent indeed. What was it there that 'ultimately and firmly' distinguished one person from others, we could ask taking a cue from Marx and answer with him, 'The *body*'. There, like in all semi-feudal societies, 'certain dignities, and indeed the highest social dignities' were, as he put it, 'the *dignities of certain bodies predestined by birth*'.[188] Hence in all relationships between the *uttara* (superior) and the *adhara* (inferior) an acknowledgement of the dignity, amounting almost to sanctity, of the former's person was a condition of the latter's subalternity.

This was formalized at Akbar's court by His Majesty's 'mode of showing himself' in the daily ritual of *darsan* 'when', according to *Ain* 73, 'people of all classes can satisfy their eyes and hearts, with the light of his countenance'.[189] This was formalized, too, in his own way by the landlord and headman (Gauda) of a small Andhra village where his infant son's 'mode of showing himself' was a part of his grooming for succession to his father's authority as well as an affirmation of the latter. 'The Gauda's son is eighteen months old', wrote a visiting anthropologist: 'Every morning, a boy employed by the Gauda carries the Gauda's son through the streets of Gopalpur. When the boy is not available to perform this service, a poor relation brought to Gopalpur for that purpose, carries the child . . . When he is carried along the street, the old women stop their ceaseless grinding and pounding of grain and gather around. The Carpenter puts down his tools . . .'[190] For the Gauda's son, no less than for the Grand Mughal, 'his *body* is his *social* right'.[191] This body was still sacrosanct to the peasant even when he was angry and armed. To raise his hands against it was a sin—a notion he shared with his oppressors. As a Chamar beaten up by his Thakur told Cohn, 'How could I have struck him back? He is my Thakur and a Thakur is respected like a father'.[192] Thus an illiterate and untouchable villager spoke in the authentic voice of the sacred texts of the Hindus to assimilate his landlord's authority to his father's after that paradigm by which all superordinate authority was assimilated, in the Dharmaśāstras, to that of the King, the Brahman, the father, the guru and so on. It was the voice of the ruling culture and even an insurgent was not ready to defy it. His violence stopped short of killing

[188] MECW: III 40, 106. [189] Abū-l Fazl: 165. [190] Beals: 60.
[191] MECW: III 106. [192] Cohn: 62.

not out of compassion but because of his failure to overcome fully the spiritual conditions of his subalternity.

But this was not entirely a matter of the inertia of the old culture putting the brakes on murder. It did not figure as a principal modality of struggle also because insurgency did not need it to achieve its general aim. It was not yet equipped with a mature and positive concept of power, hence of an alternative state and a set of laws and codes of punishment to go with it. This is not to deny of course that some of the more radical of the rural revolts of our period did in fact anticipate power at least to a degree and expressed it, albeit feebly and crudely, in terms of a rough justice and punitive violence laced with vengeance. Beyond that however the project in which the rebels had involved themselves was predominantly negative in orientation. Its purpose was not so much to reconstitute the world as to reverse it. This could be done quite effectively indeed by destroying and defying any of that entire range of objects and norms which represented the authority of the elite no less than did their bodies. In a land where the peasant could wreck his superordinate enemy's prestige simply by walking past his house with an umbrella on his head or by substituting *tu* for *vous* in an argument with him, why should insurgency need killing to make its point except in battle?

CHAPTER 5

SOLIDARITY

Emulation—class solidarity overdetermined by other solidarities—religious aspect of insurgent mobilization—ethnicity as a correlate of class solidarity: Kol and Munda rebellions—tribal and inter-tribal alliances in the Santal insurrection—the notion of 'five exempted castes' discussed—the role of Gwalas, Lohars and Doms in the hool—ethics of solidarity—coercion as an instrument of solidarity—visual threats—verbal threats: IPC and ATL—pressing—force as a unifying factor—the concept of betrayal—two types of collaborators: passive and active—official encouragement in favour of treachery—use of decoys—rebel violence against active collaborators—the slaying of Bhagna Majhi.

Insurgency, whatever its modality on any particular occasion, relies for its form and spirit on two closely related patterns of corporate behaviour, namely, emulation and solidarity. These are both exemplified in the annals of almost every peasant revolt. Froissart who saw the eponymous jacquerie in the Beauvais region swelling from 'scarcely a hundred' at the initial stage into a crowd of six thousand and eventually a hundred thousand,[1] reported a classic instance of such emulation. 'When they [the peasants] were asked', he wrote, 'why they did these [violent] things, they replied that they *did not know*; it was because they *saw* others doing them and they *copied* them. They thought that by such means they could destroy all the nobles and gentry in the world, so that there would be no more of them.'[2] To rebel by seeing others engage in rebellion is what the Bhogta and the Ghasi of Tori pargana of Chota Nagpur did during the Kol insurrection of 1832 when, according to the local officials, they burst into an armed uprising '*imitating* the example of the Coles of Nagpore'. And among the Kol themselves resistance extended from one community to another in much the same way. For 'in their immediate neighbourhood

[1] Froissart: 151, 153. [2] Ibid.: 153. Emphasis added.

examples were not wanting to convince them that in any attempt to recover usurped rights much might be gained in the struggle'.[3]

It is precisely to this power of emulation that J. R. Ward, Special Commissioner, paid an indirect tribute when failing to explain the rapid spread of the hool from Bhagalpur to Birbhum district except in terms of the absurd conjecture that 'the whole of the Sonthal population of Beerbhoom' appeared to him 'to have been more or less pressed into rebellion', he went on to say: 'I have failed to ascertain when & how communications had been made prior to Seedoo's first Act [i.e. the assassination of Mahesh Daroga]. Indeed I cannot find that there was any other than the usual intercourse between the Bhaugulpore Sonthals & their fellows of Beerbhoom till the former were in arms.' And it is again the fear of such imitative defiance of authority that made him plead for an imposition of martial law three months after the outbreak lest the 'good deal of restlessness & hesitation' sensed among the Santals to the south of the Grand Trunk Road and 'the lower castes of Bengallees especially those residing in that part of the Country which lies between the Damoodah & Pachate hills', should turn into an open uprising.[4] Emulation of this kind could, of course, inspire either crime or insurgency or as it often happened, both. In the latter case, the generalized violence could stimulate criminal activities—by following the example of their Bhagalpur brethren the Santals of Birbhum had apparently added to the local Magistrate's labour, 'murder, dacoity and highway robbery being very much on the increase and the files very heavy'[5]—and provide at the same time a context to invest some of these with new meanings generating, as we have already noticed, much ambiguity and critically influencing the course of an entire rebellion itself.[6]

From the insurgent's point of view perhaps the most essential aspect of the phenomenon often described as contagion by his

[3] BC 1502 (58891): Dent & Wilkinson to Thomason (16 Nov. 1832); BC 1502 (58893): Master to Thomason (17 Jan. 1833). Emphasis added.

[4] JP, 8 Nov. 1855: Ward to GOB (13 Oct. 1855).

[5] JP, 22 Nov. 1855: Ward to GOB (28 Oct. 1855).

[6] See Chapter 3, *passim*.

foes, is solidarity. This is an important signifier of consciousness in two ways. First, it represents the rebel's consciousness of his own activity: solidarity is, in other words, a figure of his self-consciousness. Secondly, it separates his own consciousness of this activity completely and unequivocally from its cognition by his enemies. These last two are of course implacably opposed. What is regarded by one side as a symptom of disease, immorality and negation of reason is to the other a positive sign of health and spiritual rejuvenation based on the unquestionable right of the oppressed to resist.

Solidarity is thus a categorical imprint of peasant consciousness and there is hardly a rebellion that does not bear it. However, its quality varies from one event to another and from phase to phase within the same event depending on whether its content is a sense of belonging to the same class or any other affinity. Class solidarity and other solidarities are of course not mutually exclusive: their boundaries overlap in most cases, although the *predominance* of one or the other element would tend to determine the *basic character* of a movement. Some of the communist-led agrarian uprisings in India such as the Tebhaga movement of the sharecroppers of Bengal in 1946–7 or the Telengana insurrection of 1947–51—to name only two of the most outstanding events of this kind—were of course distinguished by the solidarity of the peasantry as a class or to be more precise, as a congeries of classes. But even here the sense of fighting together as a class or proximate classes was overdetermined to some extent by other loyalties. The historian of the sharecroppers' struggle has wondered how it all began without preparation or previous organizational work in the area: 'There was no Kisan Sabha in the Duars: the movement began all too suddenly and spontaneously.'[7] It required only a minimal intervention on the part of the communists to come to life, take shape, spread all over the Duars and evoke a quick response among the labourers of the neighbouring tea plantations—all of which testified to a section of the rural poor acting as a class-for-itself and to their alliance with an utterly exploited proletariat.

However, there was more to this than class consciousness alone; otherwise it would not have erupted with such sponta-

[7] S. Sen: 56.

neity. This apparent spontaneity was nothing but a measure of the displacement of class solidarity by ethnic solidarity. It was the militancy of the tribal peasantry—Santals and Oraons—which inaugurated 'the battle for Tebhaga' in that region of northern Bengal, and the plantation workers who fraternized with them were also mainly Santal and Oraon.[8] This displacement was not of course radical enough to let ethnicity prevail over the class character of the event as a whole, but one can hardly overlook its importance if one is to understand some of the otherwise inexplicable aspects of this struggle such as its amazingly rapid extension, its untutored militancy and the promptness with which it armed itself—all distinctive features of the great tribal peasant revolts of the subcontinent. Ethnic solidarity played a part even in the Telengana insurrection, regarded by some as a considerable achievement of revolutionary organization and consciousness. It is clear from Sundarayya's authoritative account that the mobilization of the Koya in favour of that uprising as it spread to the Godavari river forest area, was to no mean extent helped by the support the communists received from the traditional tribal leaders.[9]

Such coexistence of class solidarity and other affinities, as witnessed in the Tebhaga and Telengana struggles, was of course still more explicit in the politically less sophisticated agrarian uprisings of the period before 1900. The dye of a traditional culture was yet to wash off the peasant's consciousness, and its articulation in insurgent violence, directed as it was against the very foundations of that culture, was bound to generate some ambiguity. Many of these earlier instances, therefore, of what essentially was the peasants' resistance to their class enemies, lend themselves to misinterpretation as nothing but communal or racial protest based respectively on sectarian or ethnic attitudes. What is wrong with this type of explanation, often found in historical writings of a reactionary bent, is not that it emphasizes some of the communal or ethnic elements in such combinations of the rural masses, but that it underestimates or even ignores their class character. And yet another brand of historiography, inclined somewhat to the left, often errs in a contrary direction: eager to highlight the class character of insurgency, it tends to underestimate or even over-

[8] Ibid.: 57. [9] Sundarayya: 249.

look altogether the other affinities which help in the process of its mobilization.

The duplex character[10] of this phenomenon is demonstrated again and again in many of the nineteenth-century conflicts between Hindu landlords and Muslim peasantry. The solidarity of the latter as members of a class or proximate classes was often in such cases an expression of a religious brotherhood too. This is why such basic institutions of Islam as the mosque, the congregation and the priesthood had often a lot to do with this genre of agrarian disturbances. The trial of the Wahabis who had been the driving force behind Titu Mir's historic rebellion at Barasat in 1831 and then fought a protracted but losing war for another fifty years against the Raj in the North-Western Frontier Provinces, revealed how the humble *masjids* of rural Bengal used to act as the nerve centres of propaganda and recruitment for the jihad.[11] And we have it on the authority of James Wise, one of the most knowledgeable observers of nineteenth-century Muslim society, that for the Ta'aiyuni, a militant reformist sect of eastern Bengal, Friday, the day of prayer, was also 'a day for popular demonstrations and for forming combinations against the zamindars'.[12] At the other end of the country, in Malabar, the increasing frequency of Moplah peasant uprisings against the jenmi landlords (as many as twenty-four outbreaks in eighteen years between 1836 and 1854) and the more and more explicitly communal character of what was in its essence a militant movement of the rural poor, corresponded to a phenomenal rise in the number of mosques (from 637 in 1831 to 1,058 in 1851) and the emergence of the hitherto inconspicuous Thangals (as the Moplah priests were called) into positions of key local influence. The consequence of this mediation by mosques and Thangals was to promote a vertical alliance between the Moplah poor and their more affluent co-religionists and help thus in modifying the class antagonism of the peasantry by Islamic ideology.[13]

[10] The term 'duplex' has been used here, after Cherry, to indicate 'the simultaneous transmission of two messages over one line without frequency separation'. See Cherry: 37.

[11] This is amply documented in Khan (1961): Ch. III, *passim*.

[12] O'Malley (1925): 46.

[13] See Dhanagare for an excellent study of this question.

There were of course other cases when the rebel consciousness was not so obviously penetrated by religiosity. Even then one must examine the specific determinations of any given experience with the utmost care before attributing a *purely* secular character to peasant solidarity on such occasions. The historiography of the Pabna disturbances of 1873 provides us again with an interesting, if negative, example in this respect. Most of the landlords and the rural gentry economically dependent on them were, in this district, Hindu by faith and constituted only about 9 per cent of the population. Most of the other inhabitants were peasants, and nearly 70 per cent of them Musalmans.[14] The events of 1873 thus shaped up as a convergence of the vertical and horizontal divisions of the rural society in a contest over the producers' surplus. Which of these two antagonisms—class or communal—prevailed and dictated its overall character? The former beyond any doubt. Clearly it was the anti-landlord aims and operations of the peasants' league that gave the movement its basic identity. The size and authority of the league, the impartiality with which it punished Hindu as well as Muslim dissenters,[15] and the absence of any overtly anti-Hindu gestures of violence such as the desecration of temples, forcible conversion to Islam, etc.—all these give the lie to the inspired canard stigmatizing the bidroha as a communal upheaval.[16] But the fact that it developed on the whole as a

[14] Sen Gupta: 8, 9, 51. [15] Ibid.: 52.

[16] Two somewhat spurious arguments put forward by Sen Gupta to demonstrate what he believes to be the secular character of the bidroha are easily dismissed. 'The fact that the two top leaders of the [tenants'] league . . . were caste Hindus' is regarded by him as conclusive evidence of the non-communal character of the agitation (Ibid.: 51–2). By the same token one can deny the anti-landlord character of the league and the movement too, for both these top leaders were also members of the local gentry who, as the author himself observes on the basis of sound contemporary evidence, were closely allied to the landlords and formed a fraction of the small (9 per cent of the population) local elite (Ibid.: 8). The social origin of those who constitute the mass of a rebel peasantry does not coincide in every instance with that of some of their leaders. Such incongruence is common to rural uprisings throughout the world in many historical periods. It is a function of *décalage* which is significant only in a negative sense, that is, as an index of the want of correspondence between the objective character of the mass action of the peasantry and the level of their consciousness. All sorts of historical quirks are possible in these circumstances—a member of the nobility heading an anti-feudal revolt, a Catholic priest leading raids on monasteries, etc. The other argument advanced by

class struggle does not necessarily mean that religiosity played no part in mobilizing the mass of the peasantry for it, as Sen Gupta's account of the event seems to suggest. On the contrary, it is clear from his own reading of the evidence that the 'spirit of combination . . . proceeded to develop quickly in the preponderantly Muhammedan district of Pabna because social alliance was easier among the Muslims than among the Hindus who were divided into innumerable varieties of castes, jealous and distrustful of each other'.[17] Indeed it can hardly be doubted that this spirit of combination was influenced by Farazi sectarianism. The author underplays this factor by alleging that it had already declined in Pabna by 1873.[18] This is difficult to accept in view of the fact that O'Malley writing for the *District Gazetteer* fifty years later in 1923 still found 'the Farazi element . . . strong among the Muhammadans of Sirajganj',[19] the subdivision where the bidroha had in fact originated.[20] Not to face up to the religious aspect of rebel solidarity and ascribe it to a phoney secularism is to falsify the intellectual history of the peasantry and eliminate, by a mere stroke of the pen, the discrepancy that is necessarily there at certain stages of the class struggle between the level of its objective articulation and that of the consciousness of its subjects.

Ethnicity, too, was a correlate of class solidarity in some of the nineteenth-century peasant rebellions. At one extreme it could be expressed, positively, as a ritual affirmation of the tribal identity of the peasantry involved in an uprising. Thus, for a whole year before the ulgulan Birsa led his followers on a pilgrimage to various 'ancestral' sites, collected the relics of what was believed to be their glorious past, and as the party stopped overnight at a particularly holy place called Naw

Sen Gupta is that 'the majority of the inhabitants of Pabna were Muhammedan converts from the lower castes of Hinduism' and 'such men could not rise against the zemindars merely because the latter were Hindus' (Ibid.: 52). Why not? The intensification of Moplah peasant violence corresponded directly to the conversion to Islam of increasing numbers of the Cherumars, members of a Hindu slave caste, throughout the nineteenth century, and there could be little doubt about the fact of their active participation in the jacqueries against the Hindu jenmi landlords (*vide* Dhanagare).

[17] Sen Gupta: 39. [18] Ibid.: 10, 51 (n. 105).

[19] O'Malley (1923): 32. [20] Ibid.: 25.

Rattan, 'those sleeping on the middle floor heard a voice ask: "Are you ready?" There was a reply: "Yes, we are ready".' This, the Mundas believed, indicated that 'the ancestors of the race had blessed Birsa's mission'.[21] At the other end of the spectrum the function of ethnicity could be and often was to help an insurgent group define its identity negatively: not only was the diku to be excluded from it, but he was clearly marked out as the principal object of attack. Such indeed was the logic of the discrimination showed by the Kol rebels in their raids on villages where tribal and non-tribal households lived side by side: the former were invariably spared and the latter alone subjected to violence. As an officer who had witnessed it all was to write soon after the insurrection, 'Throughout the whole of this devastation not a single Cole's life was sacrificed nor a house belonging to them destroyed except by accident.'[22]

Between these polar ends the expression of ethnic solidarity often assumed the form of armed collaboration among the various tribal peoples in rebel areas. Thus, the Dhangar Kols of Sonepur who were the first to rise in that region in 1832, were promptly reinforced by the Larka Kols of Singhbhum, a district still free from disturbances. And to leave no doubt about the authority of this fraternal act the Larkas were led on this occasion by some of their most outstanding chieftains such as Bindrai Manki and Sui Munda.[23] As the insurrection progressed further the Kols were joined by most of the other tribal peasantry of Chota Nagpur and Palamau—the Bhogta and the Ghasi of Tori; the Ho, the Munda and the Oraon of various parts of Chota Nagpur;[24] the Chero, the Kharwar and the Poliar of Palamau.[25] The solidarity of these last named groups must be acknowledged as a particularly self-conscious act of collaboration. For the British colonial authorities had advised the native police officials as well as the landed gentry to arm contingents of tribal peasants within their own localities and use them against the Kols. It is on record that at least in one instance they even financed a local raja to the tune of five

[21] Singh: 77–81.

[22] BC 1502 (58893): Master to Thomason (17 Jan. 1833). Also see J. C. Jha: 176, 183–4.

[23] BC 1502 (58891): Dent & Wilkinson to Thomason (16 Nov. 1832).

[24] Singh: 25. [25] J. C. Jha: 78–83.

hundred rupees—a considerable sum of money in those days—for this purpose. However, when the time came, the tribal recruits refused to open fire on the Kols, turned against the raja and slew a number of what was left of his by now exclusively non-tribal levy. The official campaign to mobilize the Chero, the Kharwar and the Poliar under darogas and *ghatwals*, too, failed, and an allied force made up of the Kols and all the various peoples of Palamau launched a massive offensive in this region on 7 February 1832. 'The attempt to use tribal people to oppose tribal insurgents had thus broken down.'[26]

As mentioned above, one of the ethnic communities to swing into action in support of the Kols in 1832 was the Munda. Later on, in the last decade of the century, when the Mundas in their turn were in a state of revolt, the Kols reciprocated in terms of a militant solidarity. Nearly all of a force of two hundred of them sent under a police officer to apprehend Birsa Munda in August 1895 'went over in a body to the side of Birsa' and foiled this particular attempt to take him prisoner.[27] A week after this incident when the authorities eventually caught up with the rebel leader at his home and put him under arrest, the Kols who served as menials (*dhangar*) in the neighbouring villages withdrew their labour in protest.[28] And as the resentment against Birsa's arrest set in motion a vast and potentially explosive mass of the rural population, all heading towards and converging on his village, Chalkad, the government made it a point to try and ensure that the Kols were not allowed to link up with the Mundas lest such a conjunction should spark off an uprising. The landed magnates of the area, namely, the Thakur of Sarjumdih and the Manki of Tarai as well as the Thakur of Kharsawan and the Deputy Commissioner of Singhbhum were officially directed to prevent the Kols within their respective estates and jurisdictions from joining the assembly at Chalkad.[29]

Subsequently, when after his release from prison Birsa began to prepare for the ulgulan in earnest, the memory of collaboration between his people and the Kols in 1832 played the part of a hallowed tradition. His decision to shift the centre of his

[26] BC 1362 (54223): GOB to Court of Directors (25 Sept. 1832); BC 1362 (54224): Neave to Lambert (4 Feb. 1832), Lambert to Judicial Department, GOB (6 Feb. 1832).

[27] Singh: 55. [28] Ibid.: 63. [29] Ibid.: 64.

campaign from Chalkad to Dombari was apparently influenced by the association the latter had with the Kol rebellion. As a modern historian of the Birsaite revolt has put it: 'The valleys of Icha Hurang, Lango Lor, Domba Ghat and the upland of Jikilata in popular imagination had once resounded with the triumphs (though illusory) of the powerful combination of the Mundas and Laraka Hos against the British [as] commemorated with pride in Munda folk songs.'[30] Many of these songs helped to evoke the theme of solidarity and revolt at the Birsaite meetings of 1898–9. At one such meeting held on Simbua hill in March 1898 the Mundas who were then getting ready for their own insurrection, sang thus about that other event of sixty-six years ago:

> O where are they fighting, shouldering weapons like
> the small ant?
> O where are they shooting arrows, carrying their weapons
> like the big ant?
> O they fight at Bundu
> O they shoot arrows at Tamar.[31]

None of this, however, is meant to suggest that ethnic affinities alone constituted all that there was to rebel solidarity in the Kol and Birsaite uprisings. In both cases the tribal insurgents were careful systematically to spare from violence many of the poorer classes of the non-tribal population with whom they had customary economic and social transactions in the rural communities where they lived as neighbours. Blacksmiths, cowherds and potters had nothing to fear from the Kols even at the height of their insurrection.[32] Apart from them some of the most oppressed among the non-tribal villagers such as bonded labourers and domestic servants helped the rebels actively against their masters.[33] The local officials were quick to identify this as an expression of class solidarity cutting across ethnic divisions among the rural poor. 'The lower classes', wrote one of the British administrators, 'have evidently entered into a

[30] Ibid.: 82. [31] Ibid.: 84.

[32] BC 1502 (58893): Master to Thomason (17 Jan. 1833). Also see 'Nagpur Trials' (nos 38, 85) as in Ch. 4, n. 182 above.

[33] See, for instance, BC 1363 (54226): Russell to Braddon (18 Apr. 1832), para. 12.

combination with the Coles.'[34] The Birsaite ulgulan, too, we are told, was distinguished by 'the absence of an attack on or any bitterness of feeling against certain non-tribal elements socially and economically subordinate to the Mundas', such as barbers, washermen, drummers, weavers, blacksmiths and carpenters.[35]

It is clear that in both these instances ethnicity was only partially modified by class consciousness. The latter never emerged as the principal constituent of rebel solidarity. Although the tolerance shown by the insurgents towards some of the service castes amounted objectively to a horizontal alignment of the most exploited sections of the rural poor, it was primarily their concern to maintain a steady flow of economic and ritual services for their respective communities which motivated the Kols and the Mundas to protect these non-tribal groups so very useful to them. The sense of class was obviously encapsulated in the sense of race, a fact that is worth remembering about these two tribal peasant uprisings in order fully to grasp both their power and their limitations.

Except in one particular respect which, as we shall presently see, was to amount to a critical difference in quality, the mixture of tribalism and class consciousness in the Santal rebellion of 1855 was much the same as in those discussed above. Ethnic solidarity helped considerably in the initial mobilization for the hool by means of communal hunts, mass assemblies and meetings of the elders of the tribe. This was important enough to have been deposited in popular memory as an ancestral tradition. As the *Mare Hapram Ko Reak Katha* has it,[36] an alarm spread through the Santal country on the eve of the uprising to the effect that Lag and Lagin, the He-snake and the She-snake, had set out to devour all the people. The procedure adopted to ward off so painful an end was that the Santals of a number of villages would band together on an evening and visit a group of nearby hamlets. On arriving at the very last of these they would make an offering to Lag and Lagin, invest two of the local bachelors with *poita* (sacred threads), initiate them to the words and music of some traditional songs particularly prescribed for this ceremony and hand over to them a pair of miniature ploughs which these

[34] BC 1362 (54225): Neave to Lambert (10 Feb. 1832).
[35] Singh: 195. [36] MHKRK: *clxxvii.*

two, in their turn, were to pass on to some other villagers after a similar nocturnal round terminating in an identical sequence of serpent worship and the investiture and initiation of two other bachelor youths. Powered and sanctified by a shot of chiliasm the solidarity of the tribe for their coming struggle was thus built up by the relay of a ritual procedure from one neighbourhood to another.

Inter-tribal solidarity, too, featured prominently in this uprising. The two tribal peoples whose involvement was officially acknowledged were the Bhuyan and the Mal, both mentioned in the Santal tradition as the aboriginal rulers of the region.[37] The collaboration of the Mal was particularly significant. For as Captain Sherwill's survey for 1851 showed, the Mal, 'the Rajmahal Hill Tribe' as he named them, constituted nearly 29 per cent of the population of Damin-i-Koh in 38.5 per cent of its villages covering a little over 18 per cent of its area regarded as habitable.[38] By their participation they helped in drawing the entire population into the hool. Qualitatively, too, this enhanced the authority of the rebellion. For the two tribes had not always been on the best of terms. In the course of the previous twenty years the Mals were gradually pushed out of the valleys which had been all theirs until the Santals came in and colonized the land. As Sherwill observed in 1851, 'The hill-men have, with a few exceptions, retired to the hills, being either unwilling to be near the Sonthal, whom the hill-men despise, or, courting that privacy they could not enjoy in a cultivated plain, have yielded up the fertile plain to their more industrious and energetic neighbours.'[39] Consequently, their coexistence had not been always quite so peaceful in the past, and this was indeed what made their solidarity in 1855 all the more impressive.

[37] Ibid.

[38] *Source*: Sherwill: 63. The statistics from which these percentages have been worked out are as follows:

	Population(%)	No. of villages(%)	Area in sq. miles(%)
Mal	33,780 (28.9)	921 (38.5)	56 (18.1)
Santal	83,265 (71.1)	1,473 (61.5)	254 (81.9)
Total	117,045 (100)	2,394 (100)	310 (100)

[39] Ibid.: 45.

There is a great deal of evidence to testify to this inter-tribal collaboration. Already within a fortnight of the uprising the Bhuyans were apprehended by the Bhagalpur police in large numbers for taking up arms and forming unlawful assemblies with the intent of committing riot and plunder.[40] And the Mal came out on the side of the Santals on an even more massive scale. One of the very first rebel statements we have on record is that of a Santal wounded and captured by the troops on the seventh day of the insurrection, and he said that in his particular contingent 'there were with us two or three thousand Pahareeahs and there were of us Sonthals, seven or eight thousand'.[41] It is indeed remarkable how closely the ratio of Mal to Santal in the insurgent forces, as indicated here, corresponded to that in the population of Damin-i-Koh as a whole.[42] Their collaboration was not perhaps altogether free from discord and there might have been some truth in a report about friction between them in the Company Bazar area in September 1855.[43] By then the hool had already lost its momentum, and in view of their past relations it is not surprising that the Mal were keen to disengage themselves from their allies in a period of retreat and mass surrender.[44] None of this however takes away from the extent or the quality of their participation. The point must indeed be made that even according to the authorities the Mal appear to have been motivated by more than greed for a share in the loot. They joined in the plunder of course, but helped in the organization of the rebellion as well. J. R. Ward, Commissioner on Special Duty, wrote to the Government of Bengal about the capture of a Mal who had played an important part in supplying provisions for the Santals. And it is again to the same officer's indignation at abetment on the part of the Mal that we owe an anecdote which has much to say about the spirit of their solidarity.

When Captn. Phillips 63 N.I. came up to Bewa . . . he was informed the Sonthals were then plundering at the other end of the Village,

[40] K. K. Datta: 92. Bhuyan names often occur in the lists of prisoners. For one such list see JP, 8 Nov. 1855: Rose to Ward (12 Oct. 1855).

[41] JP, 19 July 1855: Toogood to Grey (Enclosure, 14 July 1855).

[42] See n. 38 above.

[43] JP, 4 Oct. 1855: Lloyd to Military Department, GOI (15 Sept. 1855).

[44] JP, 8 Nov. 1855: Birbhum Collector's Diary (4 Oct. 1855).

unaware of his arrival. Taking 75 men of his detachment he advanced quickly, & came up to a large pukka house on the doorsteps of which was sitting a man quietly smoking his hooka. Captn. Phillips asked him where the Sonthals were, & was told in reply that they had not come to the Village at all, but he had not got 100 yards further when some 40 or 50 Sonthals rushed from the identical house and attacked the party in the rear, wounding one sepoy. They however were easily repulsed, leaving 8 dead on the field . . . It is to be regretted that the man who misled Captn. Phillips was not also of the number, but he was arrested and sent in to me at Raneegunge. If ever a man deserved hanging it is this scoundrel; but how am I to deal with him? He declares he was not aware there was any one in the house, and if I venture to charge him with complicity in attempt at Murder or rebellion, I must prove the guilty knowledge, for the man is not a Sonthal, tho' a mal, one of the five exempted castes.[45]

This identification of the Mal as 'one of the five exempted castes' was, of course, an error. In fact, the term 'five exempted castes' is itself somewhat suspect. It occurs time and again in the correspondence of the civilian and military officers operating in the region affected by the hool; but, curiously enough, it does not occur even once in any of the several recorded statements of the rebels themselves, although they acknowledge, positively, the collaboration of various non-Santal groups One possible way of unravelling the paradox would perhaps be to read this phrase as a telescoping of two categorically different official perceptions.

It indicates, in the first place, how administrative sociology had anticipated Risley and the Anthropological Survey of India by decades in conceptualizing the rural classes in the subcontinent as simply an array of castes and with nearly the same unhappy consequence. The moment they heard of the uprising the colonial authorities labelled it as an exclusively tribal movement. The very first official reaction on record, a letter from the Magistrate of Bhagalpur written within forty-eight hours of the affray at Bhagnadihi, reads: 'I write a line in a great hurry to let you know that the Sontals of this district aided by a large number from Singhbhoum and other districts have risen to take possession of the country.'[46] The language, breathless as it is,

[45] Ibid: Ward to GOB (13 Oct. 1855).

[46] Richardson to Grey (9 July 1855). This is classified as entry No. 1 in JP,

represents truly the government's view of the character of the insurrection. So when the initial panic subsided and it was noticed that the Santals were careful not to commit violence against the vast majority of the non-tribal population made up mostly of what Hunter was to identify later on as 'the intermediate semi-aboriginal classes between the Santal and the Hindu and indeed several of the very low castes of the Hindus themselves',[47] a rough and ready explanation based on a schematic approach to Indian society was hastily pulled out of the topee. The insurgents, it was said in almost every communication on the subject from the Rajmahal front, would not hurt the 'castes' who 'were obedient to the Santals and helped them in several ways', as Datta's paraphrase of an official document put it.[48] Secondly, the memory of the Kol rebellion of 1832 which never ceased to haunt the authorities during their campaigns against the Santals,[49] may also have encouraged this notion to some extent, for the Kol had indeed spared some of those non-tribal peasant and artisan groups with whom they maintained a sort of *jajmani* relation in their villages. So the classic Hindu model was freely used to explain why a tribal uprising was so consistent in its want of hostility towards the mass of the non-tribal poor. It does not appear to have occurred to the authorities that a horizontal solidarity of all the exploited elements in the given rural society might have had something to do with this phenomenon.

The sociological assumptions in the official correspondence of the time were indeed quite clearly spelt out in an article published in the *Calcutta Review* soon after the hool. Written obviously by someone with access to the despatches received by the Government of Bengal—some of the passages read like direct quotations—it names the 'five exempted castes' as the Lohar (blacksmiths), the Kumar (potters), the Telee (oilmen), the Gwala (milkmen, cowherds) and the carpenters, 'for these were useful to the Sonthal Commissariat'.[50] The apparent

19 July 1855—the very first recorded document on the Santal rebellion in that collection.

[47] Hunter (1897): 250. [48] K. K. Datta: 57.

[49] For some officially invoked parallelisms, see JP, 19 July 1855: Elliott to Grey (15 July 1855); and JP, 8 Nov. 1855: Minute by Lieutenant-Governor of Bengal (19 Oct. 1855). [50] CR: 246.

plausibility of this identification derived from the fact that the local population belonging to these castes lived as artisans and specialists in what were predominantly Santal communities. Yet a close reading of the same official sources also shows how utterly inaccurate this identification was. For most of the reports filed with the Judicial Department of the Bengal Government about the arrest, summary trial and punishment of the insurgents in 1855–6 differentiated meticulously between the Santal and other prisoners as well as between various castes among the latter. These statements make it abundantly clear that almost every commissioner and commander had his own idea as to who constituted the 'exempted castes'.

The category was, in effect, made so elastic as to accommodate any social or ethnic group one wished to describe as 'exempted'. There are at least thirteen such 'exempted caste' names that can be picked out of this collection of records. These are: Bairagi, Bauri, Boya, Carpenter, Dhangar, Dom, Gwala, Hari, Jolaha, Kulwar, Kumar, Lohar and Telee.[51] If one added the Mal to these, as did Ward, the total would amount nearly

[51] For Bairagi, see JP, 22 Nov. 1955: Ward to GOB (28 Oct. 1855); Bauri—ibid. and JP, 4 Oct. 1855: 'Statement of the cases against Sonthal prisoners now in Sooree Jail' (25 Sept. 1855); Boya—ibid. and JP, 22 Nov. 1855: Eden to Bidwell (6 Nov. 1855); Carpenter—CR: 246; Dhangar—JP, 22 Nov. 1855: Ward to GOB (28 Oct. 1855); Dome—JP, 4 Oct. 1855: 'Statement of the cases against Sonthal prisoners now in Sooree Jail' (25 Sept. 1855); JP, 8 Nov. 1855: 'Examination of Sedoo Sonthal late Thacoor'; JP, 22 Nov. 1855: Eden to Bidwell (6 Nov. 1855); Gwala—JP, 25 Oct. 1855: 'Abstract of Police Reports in Bhaugulpore', Bidwell to GOB (3 Oct. 1855); JP, 6 Dec. 1855: Lloyd to Grey (19 Nov. 1855); ibid.: 'Extract Proceedings of a Court Martial assembled at Camp Noni Haut by order of Major General G. W. A. Lloyd . . . on 19th day of November 1855'; K. K. Datta: 57; CR: 246; Hari—JP, 22 Nov. 1855: Ward to GOB (28 Oct. 1855); Jolaha—JP, 4 Oct. 1855: 'Statement of the cases against Sonthal prisoners now in Sooree Jail' (25 Sept. 1855); JP, 22 Nov. 1855: Eden to Bidwell (6 Nov. 1855); Kulwar—JP, 22 Nov. 1855: Bird to Military Department, GOI (6 Nov. 1855); JP, 22 Nov. 1855: Ward to GOB (8 Nov. 1855); Kumar—JP, 4 Oct. 1855: Ward to GOB (16 Sept. 1855); JP, 8 Nov. 1855: 'Examination of Sedoo Sonthal late Thacoor'; JP, 22 Nov. 1855: Ward to GOB (28 Oct. 1855); ibid.: (8 Nov. 1855); ibid.: Bird to Military Department, GOI (6 Nov. 1855); CR: 246; Lohar—ibid.; JP, 19 July 1855: Toogood to Grey (Enclosure, 14 July 1855); JP, 4 Oct. 1855: Ward to Grey (19 Sept. 1855); JP, 25 Oct. 1855: Birbhum Collector's Diary (2 Oct. 1855); CR: 246; Teli—ibid.; JP, 8 Nov. 1855: 'Examination of Sedoo Sonthal late Thacoor'; JP, 22 Nov. 1855: Bird to Military Department, GOI (6 Nov. 1855); ibid.: Ward to GOB (8 Nov. 1855); ibid.: Eden to Bidwell (6 Nov. 1855).

to the entire non-Santal population of Damin-i-Koh minus the handful of the elite made up of zamindars and mahajans. The term 'five exempted castes' thus dissolves in the light of evidence. Far from providing an accurate description of the hool as a vast alliance of peasants and rural artisans of all ethnic groups it narrows down and falsifies our vision of this historic event. The only value it may be said to have is to illustrate how the official mind committed a priori to a perception of Indian society in caste categories fails to understand even the most explicit evidence about the class character of peasant activity and ends up with an erroneous identification of the actors—an epistemological legacy which colonialism was to bequeath to the discipline of social anthropology in the next century.

The term 'five exempted castes' misrepresents the mobilization for the hool not merely in a quantitative sense. It also stands for a perceptual error on the part of the authorities about the quality of that mobilization. The suggestion it conveys of the non-tribal peasantry standing by passively to watch the rebels carry fire and sword through the countryside might have been true to some extent of the Kol uprising but not of the Santal. In the latter case there was no section of the rural poor, tribal or otherwise, that can be said to have abstained from the mass violence of the hool or from active collaboration with its initiators and leaders, the Santals. They were *all* rebels. The ethnic distribution could of course vary widely between any two samples of them: it all depended on where they came from. As many as twenty-four out of sixty prisoners taken by a Captain Pester in a raid on two neighbouring villages, Ludna and Tulberiga, on 2 November 1855 were non-Santals 'all of whom', he said in his report, 'assisted the insurgents in every way in supplying them with the different articles they each manufacture'.[52] As against this proportion of 40 per cent the non-tribal component was a mere 10 per cent in the group of twenty from two villages within the Nalhati thana, who were summarily sentenced by the Sessions Judge of Birbhum on 3 December 1855.[53]

The want of uniformity in the composition of the rebel bands

[52] JP, 22 Nov. 1855: Bird to Military Department, GOI (6 Nov. 1855).
[53] BDR: 125–6.

was matched by the uneven quality of their collaboration too. Reports came in from time to time about the Santals being given the cold shoulder by a local peasant or artisan community that had been consistently loyal until then. One such instance involving the Mal has already been noticed above.[54] Again, the Kumars mentioned by Sido himself as one of the artisan groups (the other being the Telees) most friendly to the Santals and proved as such by their inclusion in almost every official list of rebel prisoners and convicts, were said to have withdrawn from the alliance in some parts of Birbhum in September 1855.[55] The level of co-operation appears to have varied not merely between the local groups of the same caste or community, but also between some castes and others. The Gwala, the Lohar and the Dom emerge from the evidence as the most active non-tribal participants in the hool. The first of these are specified as one of the 'five exempted castes' in many despatches. A Bhagalpur police report for Doomka thana indicates that in September 1855 the Gwalas came out in support of the Santals in Belputtah and 'towards the confines of Beerbhoom'.[56] But the most spectacular information we have on their solidarity derives from a report sent in by Major-General Lloyd, Commanding the Dinapore Division and Sonthal Field Force, on the capture of Bechoo Raout. It merits being quoted *in extenso*:

The day before yesterday on arrival at Hasdiha I received information that only three or four days previously Kanoo Majhee with his Brothers and Followers had visited Bechoo Raout a gwallah the head of the village of Sooria Haut about 3 coss from my camp, that they had

[54] See *supra*: 150.

[55] For Sido's statement, see JP, 8 Nov. 1855: 'Examination of Sedoo Sonthal late Thacoor'. For some other evidence of Kumar participation see JP, 22 Nov. 1855: Ward to GOB (28 Oct. 1855); and ibid.: (8 Nov. 1855); ibid.: Bird to Military Department, GOI (6 Nov. 1855); 'Statement of 22 convicts sentenced . . . dated 3rd Dec. 1855' in BDR: 129. On the discord between Santals and Kumars J. R. Ward wrote from Suri, Birbhum, on 16 September 1855 to the Secretary, GOB: 'There can be little doubt of the truth of the report that they [the Santals] are suffering much for want of proper food . . . and unfortunately for them the Insurgents have fallen out with the Koomars one of the 5 excepted classes and cannot procure cooking pots—which add greatly to their difficulties but for all that there is no sign of an inclination to submit.' JP, 4 Oct. 1855.

[56] JP, 25 Oct. 1855: 'Abstract of Police Reports in Bhaugulpore', Bidwell to GOB (3 Oct. 1855).

been entertained and Housed by him, that Kanoo had created him a Soobah and as a Symbol of the rank conferred had bound a turban on his head, that the Rebel Sonthals had gone thence to plunder two villages some little distance to the south, returned with their plunder to Bechoo's village . . . On receiving the above information I at once despatched a small party under Lieutt Briggs of the 40 N.I. to apprehend the gwallah which was effected; a number of arms were found in his Thakoor Buree as well as in his and the adjacent houses and very fortunately he himself happened at the moment of his seizure to be in the act of holding a kind of Court in the market place in the Exercise of his office as Soobah surrounded by a large concourse of people & assuming all the airs and consequence of a Ruler.[57]

A few days after his arrest Bechoo Raout was produced before a court martial at Camp Noni Hat, found guilty of 'an overt act of rebellion against the State', and sentenced 'to be hanged by the neck till he be dead at such time and place as Major-General Lloyd Command may be pleased to direct'. The latter ordered the hanging to take place 'in the nearer neighbourhood of his [Bechoo Raout's] Village'. At the same court martial a death sentence, commuted eventually to seven years' hard labour, was passed on Juttoo Rai, a peasant of the same village, who 'opposed by force of arms a party of troops sent for the apprehension of Bechoo Raot gwallah'.[58]

The Lohar (blacksmiths), also referred to as Lohar Mistrees, figure, like the Gwala, in all enumeration of the so-called 'exempted castes'. However, the records make it quite clear that the Santals were more dependent on them than on any other group of their allies. The reason obviously was that these metal workers on whose skill the Santals relied so much for the manufacture of their agricultural and domestic implements in times of peace, became even more valuable to them in a war requiring a steady supply of weapons for the tens of thousands of peasants who constituted their fauj. As one such combatant, who had fallen into enemy hands was to testify: 'We had all swords; some of us had made new ones.'[59] This was indeed where the Lohar came in. They moved around with the rebel forces as so many ubiquitous arsenals. 'The Sonthals are very

[57] JP, 6 Dec. 1855: Lloyd to Grey (19 Nov. 1855).

[58] Ibid.: 'Extract Proceedings of a Court Martial assembled at Camp Noni Haut by order of Major General G. W. A. Lloyd . . . on 19th day of November 1855.'

[59] JP, 19 July 1855: Toogood to Grey (Enclosure, 14 July 1855).

busy making arms at Bunbatee and other places. They are headed by Ram Manjee and Gooloo Manjee, and have smiths with them hard at work.'[60] This entry for 2 October 1855 in the Birbhum Collector's diary indicates a feature of the mobile Santal warfare to which the authorities were, for understandable reasons, particularly sensitive. Some weeks later when an officer commanding a detachment of native infantry reported the arrest of three Lohar Mistrees, he claimed to have 'witnesses to prove that these men made arms for the use of the Sonthals assembled at Subbunpore'.[61] He also added that one of these had a thigh wound received during an attack on that officer's own camp a few nights ago—a detail which illustrates how these artisans could also be trusted to act as auxiliaries in the guerilla army when the occasion arose.

In fact, neither the civilian nor the military authorities treated the blacksmiths as anything but insurgents. Two of them from the village of Geriapani, arrested together with their Santal neighbours, were, like the latter, summarily tried on 3 December 1855 for 'illegally and riotously assembling with offensive weapons' and sentenced to hard labour by the Sessions Judge of Birbhum.[62] On the same day an officer returning with his regiment from a counter-insurgency operation near the Phuljhuri Hills ran into a party of twenty Lohar Mistrees migrating to Kumirabad with their families and their cattle. 'They had their working tools with them and also a few arrow heads; I therefore think they must have been in some Sonthal assembly, employed [in] making weapons.' Q.E.D., and the despatch ends by stating, 'I seized all the cattle and intend selling them by auction'.[63] Apparently thus in their hurry to put down the rebellion with the least possible delay and utmost severity the local magistrates and army captains seldom paused to distinguish between the Santal and the Lohar. Indeed the violence of the insurgent had blended so well with the artisan's skill that at a higher level of the administration this was regarded as the most serious obstacle to disarming the Santals. 'To

[60] JP, 25 Oct. 1855: Birbhum Collector's Diary (2 Oct. 1855).

[61] JP, 6 Dec. 1855: Phillips to Major of Brigade, Raniganj (10 Nov. 1855).

[62] 'Statement of 20 convicts sentenced . . . dated 3rd December 1855' in BDR: 125–6.

[63] JP, 20 Dec. 1855: Phillips to Parrott (4 Dec. 1855).

disarm the Sonthals appears to me a measure which might follow submission, but I do not see how it is to be carried out till they are subdued', wrote the Commissioner on Special Duty to the Secretary of the Government of Bengal: 'The facilities too for procuring fresh arms are great. They have very clever workmen in the hills and plenty of material. There is scarcely a Sonthal female who is not covered with ornaments of different kinds, which bear evidence to the abundance of metal and the skill of the workmen.'[64] What a splendid, if unintentional, compliment this to the solidarity of the oppressed that had joined the skill of fashioning trinkets to the art of making an insurrection!

The alliance of the Dom, unlike that of the Lohar, would, however, bear no explanation in terms of any particular military or economic use this might have had for the Santals (apart from the obvious fact that strength lay in numbers). They, too, figure on the official lists of prisoners and convicts like the members of those other groups mentioned above. But in one striking (and little known) respect their collaboration was positively acknowledged by both the principal rebel leaders, Sido and Kanhu. They were convinced that in launching the insurrection they were acting on divine command. A god, claimed Sido, had descended from heaven in the shape of a cartwheel and ordered him to take up arms. It was a command written on a piece of paper that fell on his head. 'I could not read', he admitted, 'but Chand & Seheree and a Dhome read it; they said, "The Thacoor has written to you to fight the Mahajens & then you will have justice".'[65] Subsequently Kanhu, in his turn, was to mention a Dom as one of the three scribes who wrote out for him the parwanas he sent out to 'the Burra Sahib at Calcutta' and to the officials and principal landlords of Birbhum and Rajmahal. 'These perwannahs', he said, 'were written by Lehra & Kritu of Suckrigulli & Soona Dhome.'[66] It is indeed a remarkable fact about this uprising that its supreme commanders should speak thus of the Dom primarily as a sort of rebel intelligentsia. Nothing could be a more complete inversion of their status in Hindu society as its most backward, oppressed

[64] JP, 4 Oct. 1855: Ward to Grey (19 Sept. 1855).

[65] JP, 8 Nov. 1855: 'Examination of Sedoo Sonthal late Thacoor'.

[66] JP, 20 Dec. 1855: 'Examination of Kanoo Sonthal'.

and polluted caste. It is this latter image of them which, *pace* Sido and Kanhu, is recorded in the *Reak Katha* as a part of the collective Santal memory of the events of 1855. According to a rumour that gained currency at the time of the rebellion the Dom, persecuted as untouchables, were fleeing *en masse* to the jungle where they 'dressed up as Santals and lived in Santal houses'[67]—a figure of imagination which poignantly represents the union of two of the most exploited sections of the rural population in a common resistance irrespective of ethnic differences.

Indeed what makes the hool stand apart from the rest of the series of tribal peasant rebellions of the nineteenth century—apart even from the Kol insurrection and the Birsaite ulgulan—is precisely the fact that class solidarity triumphed over ethnicity here more decisively than in any of the others. The most handsome tribute ever paid to this distinction came from one of the commanders of the colonial army sent to put down the revolt. For Major-General Lloyd it was not enough to have a martial law to deal with the insurgents themselves; pleading for its extension to cover their allies too, he wrote to the Government of Bengal: 'With all due deference to the opinions of superior authority I consider that the advantages of Martial Law would be much strengthened and increased if . . . its Exercise was not restricted only to those taken in the actual commission of any overt act of rebellion but the penalties it authorizes Extended to any against whom proof can be adduced of any recent covert acts of rebellion such as harbouring, aiding and abetting or sharing the booty of the Rebels. Of such there are very many Tribes, gwallahs &ca well known to be guilty of such acts and yet whom it would seldom be practicable to take in their *actual commission*.'[68] Written in the latter half of November 1855 when the insurrection had already passed its peak, this indicates the still formidable power of a rebel consciousness projected well beyond the sense of tribe and caste.

Solidarity produces an ethic: to rebel is good, not to rebel is bad. This follows directly from the communal character of rebellion: in so far as the latter is an expression of the will of the Many,

[67] MHKRK: *clxxvii*.

[68] JP, 6 Dec. 1855: Lloyd to Grey (19 Nov. 1855).

rebel solidarity functions both as an expression and an instrument of communal authority—as its standard as well as its sword. How the morality of Islam was identified in one instance with that of rebel solidarity, is illustrated in a planter's evidence before the Indigo Commission in 1860. The local peasants, he testified, had entered into a combination against his factory. A leading Muslim ryot who started having second thoughts about it all and wanted to withdraw, was unable to do so, because he, like the others, had pledged his support by kissing the Koran.[69] Popular resistance inspired by a common faith was a feature of the anti-British mobilization in 1857–8 as well. 'The Mahommedan population is ever against us', wrote the Magistrate of Saharanpur: 'I am told that in this and the Moozuffurnuggur districts they are bound by oath not to give decisive evidence against each other.'[70] But it was not religion alone that brought people together in that great struggle, for, as the loyalist press observed with some chagrin at the time, the Kurmis of Bareilly region, 'formerly the chief Hindoo population', not only refused to help the authorities with intelligence against Khan Bahadur Khan's rebel forces but even sheltered the latter from the government's counter-insurgency operations.[71]

It was precisely because it was a representation of popular conscience that solidarity such as this could stand up to much strain. Binay Chaudhuri has shown how the combination of the Pabna *bidrohis* in 1873 survived not only the severity of official repression but the many attempts made on behalf of the landlords to divide the movement by tempting ryots to settle with them by separate agreements. However, 'within a village the peasants seem to have been still bound by a kind of oath' not to do so, although the central organization of their union had for all practical purposes been put out of action by then. The Magistrate found out that even those among the tenantry who 'had nothing really to complain of' as individuals, 'were simply determined to refuse rents so long as the majority of ryots did so'. This was indeed a remarkable demonstration of solidarity, of what Chaudhuri describes as 'the strength of the peasants' convictions', especially in view of the fact that a considerable

[69] RIC: para. 2213 quoted in Kling: 86.
[70] FSUP: I 474. [71] FSUP: V 486.

number of them were 'not firmly committed to the rebel cause'.[72] In other words politics had managed to triumph over economics so that differences concerning particular aspects of the rent question yielded to a general consensus born out of the peasants' awareness of themselves as a community opposed actively to the community of their oppressors, the zamindars.

Unity such as this depended for its strength on two types of communal sanctions—cultural and physical. The first of these was imposed usually as a threat to one's status within the community either by defilement or by social boycott. The leaders of the anti-survey movement in Khandesh were said to have summoned the Kunbis to a vast demonstration at Fyzpoor by orders issued to the village Mahars 'to defile the household of any person who refused to obey them, by throwing down bones at his threshold'.[73] More often, however, the price of dissidence from a common action would be the denial of co-operation by fellow villagers. This could ruin a peasant economically as well as socially. The power of this particular form of sanction is brought out very clearly indeed by some of the articles of agreement in a *Sama Patra* executed by the inhabitants of Kallas in Poona district during the Deccan riots. It was resolved that no villager, male or female, should serve a Guzar, that is, a moneylender in any form whatsoever: 'Any person cultivating fields belonging to Guzars, or serving them, will be denied service by the village barber, washerman, carpenter, ironsmith, shoemaker and other Ballutas (village servants).' To go against this decision could cost a villager his livelihood: if he was a Mahar he was to forfeit his customary share of bread and straw, a priest his traditional right to perform ritual worship for clients served by his ancestors and even the Mokadam Patel all his hereditary privileges. And the ultimate penalty of being put out of caste was held out against all dissidents: 'Any one acting to the contrary will neither be allowed to come to caste-dinners nor intermarry amongst his own society. Such a person should be considered an outcast[e].'[74]

Rarely, however, would sanctions against breach of solidarity remain confined to a purely non-violent exercise in social boy-

[72] B. B. Chaudhuri (1973): 228–9.
[73] BC 2354 (146775): Mansfield & Wingate to Goldsmid (8 Jan. 1853), para. 18.
[74] DRCR(C): 208–9.

cott. It was common for the latter to be accompanied by threats of physical violence, too. Two villagers from Akola who had come to Kallas to work for the Guzars there in the teeth of local opposition found this out soon enough. 'The Patel and Kulkarnees are threatening to drive us away and to beat us in case we continue to serve the Guzars', they explained: 'We have also been warned that the community will put us out of caste.'[75]

The threat of violence against the person or property of anyone suspected of undermining solidarity could be conveyed visually or verbally. The struggles of the tenant-cultivators of Tripura who formed themselves into a league in 1872–3 in order to resist rack-renting, provide us with a striking example of visual intimidation. 'The unionists had a peculiar way of intimidating the minority into joining the union', writes Sen Gupta. 'If any ryot was bold enough to withstand the league, he received a solemn warning. A bundle of straw shaped like a torch was placed in front of his house, an action which signified that if he continued to hold out, his house would be burnt.'[76] One has merely to recall a well-known practice of the German rebels of 1525 to realize how close the Indian experience was in this respect to that of some other countries. It was customary for the insurgents then to plant a pole in front of the house of any peasant who vacillated in his support to the war against the castles and the abbeys.[77]

The parallelism applies to verbal threats too. Here is an example of the sort of language often used during the peasant war in Germany to persuade a rural community to overcome its hesitation in joining forces with their brethren who had already taken up arms. 'You should come to us, the [rebel] army', said a notice served on the peasants of Hall at Ottendorf on the Kocher; 'we shall be very pleased, if you agree to do so.

[75] Ibid.: 211.

[76] Sen Gupta: 110–11. The threat of arson was also used by the peasants of Sandip to dissuade people from offering hospitality to the *amins* (surveyors) during an anti-survey movement there in 1870. The threat was vividly formulated in the following line of a folk song: 'Lal bolod lagai dium zeter barit amin ase', meaning, 'We shall set the red bulls on the houses of those with whom the surveyors lodge' (Grierson: 257–9). 'Lal bolod', a red bull, was, of course, an euphemism for the incendiary's torch. See Ray (1966): 414–15.

[77] Zimmermann: II 100.

If not, we shall call on you in such a manner that we're afraid it may not do you any good.'[78] Join us, or else face the consequences: the structure of this message—an appeal for common action backed up by a threat—is identical to that of some of the communiqués issued by the north Bengal insurgents to mobilize support for the dhing in 1783. And the menacing punchlines of these texts (which survive, alas, only in the official English rendering of what must have been vivid eighteenth-century Bengali prose) read so much like a paraphrase of the German circular quoted above that one realizes how central the notion of solidarity is to rebel consciousness even when its subjects vary widely in culture and age. As a local leader (sardar) of the dhing, a certain Israel Khan, stated in a parwana:

This is of consequence. We have all joined and assembled at Jarbana. You are our brothers. Do you join with all expedition. If you do not join us on our arrival you will repent it. When you join us we will consult what is best to be done. If you do not come we will burn your houses. You have warning.

Or, as the peasants of Kazirhat in Rangpur wrote to those of Pinjirah in Dinajpur:

We have made an insurrection . . . All Coochwanah (Rangpur) are coming forth. Do you do the same and join us. We have surrounded the Raja at Rangpur with the nazir's people. The rest is left to chance. Do you pay no more revenue. In this letter we give you information. If you come, it is well: if not you will repent it, after which you must not blame us.[79]

The universality of this figure of verbal threat within the Indian tradition of insurgency is affirmed by its recurrence in another peasant revolt at the very other end of the Bengal Presidency and among a very different kind of peasantry, namely, the Santals. Formulated in the same binary terms, that is a call for help followed by intimidation if the addressee failed to respond,

[78] Ibid.: I 361.

[79] Kaviraj: 40–1. Communications of this particular type appear to have been frequently used. As the *Report of the Rungpore Commission on the Causes of the Insurrection in Rungpore in the year 1189* put it: 'The insurgents then circulated letters to the various *talooks* ordering the ryots to assemble and join them, and threatening to burn their houses and destroy their crops in case of their refusal and delay.' MDS: 580.

it occurs in some of the *hukumnamahs* issued by the leaders of the hool. One of these summoning a certain Shobha Majhi of Monabari, for instance, says: '[At] the sight of Perwannah you all must be in attendance. If you do not attend, your head will be cut off.'[80]

There is some superficial resemblance between this form of intimidation and that used in such anonymous letters as were addressed to their intended victims by the swadeshi dacoits of Bengal and the English smugglers and poachers of the eighteenth century. Yet it would be wrong to lose sight of some of the important differences between these two kinds of discourse which, for the purposes of our discussion here, we shall call 'insurgent peasant communication' and 'anonymous threatening letter'—IPC and ATL for short, respectively. E. P. Thompson who has studied the latter in much detail, has described it as 'a characteristic form of social protest in any society which has crossed a certain threshold of literacy, in which forms of collective organized defence are weak, and in which individuals who can be identified as the organizers of protest are liable to immediate victimization'.[81] One can use this definition as the basis of a comparison between ATL and IPC and distinguish between them in at least two respects.

First, ATL is secret and private in form while IPC is open and public. This corresponds to a set of basic distinctions between crime and rebellion which we have already discussed above,[82] and explains why the two types operate, on the whole, in separate domains in spite of some occasional overlaps. This is also why the specific character of IPC would be rather inadequately represented if we were to assign to it the term 'letter' with all its association of a private exchange of messages between individuals. For, the form of IPC is essentially that of the public notice, the circular, the parwana. As such it claims to speak in the name of the authority assumed and exercised by the rebels on a site left vacant by the old established order, a vacancy which testifies by itself to the presence of the rebellion and puts its participants beyond any liability to 'immediate victimization'. Far from being a symptom of weakness in 'collective organized defence', it is a public demonstration of the will of an

[80] JP, 6 Sept. 1855: 'Hookumnamah of Sree Kanoo Thakoor Sidoo Thakoor etc.'
[81] Hay *et al.*: 255. [82] See Chapter 4 above.

armed mass of the peasantry to impose itself peremptorily and by force, if necessary, on vacillators and fence-sitters of all kinds. The strength of IPC is indicated by the form of a mandamus it invariably adopts and its liberal use of the imperatives while its corporate character is made explicit by the sign of the first person plural: '*We* have all joined and assembled at Jarbana'; '*We* have made an insurrection'.

However, these two types of discourse differ not merely in authorship. They represent rather different, almost contrasting, relationships between their authors and addressees. ATL is addressed only to enemies. Whether the grievance is 'private' or 'social', makes no difference in this respect.[33] Thompson's list of ATL recipients includes members of the gentry and the nobility, tradesmen, millers, mayors, magistrates, farmers, clergymen, excise officials, blacklegs, etc. The threats held out to them range from murder and mutilation to arson, wrecking of houses, maiming of stock, felling of trees, and so on—the destruction of life and property, in short.[34] Clearly, the recipients are marked out as enemies and the function of ATL is to convey to them the authors' intention to punish them in various ways. Even when the penalty is commuted for a sum of money, that is, imposed as a fine, it hardly alters the essentially punitive character of the communication. The addressee is offered no choice: he is a foe with whom scores must be settled one way or another. By contrast, the recipients of IPC stand in a non-antagonistic relation to their communicators. Indeed the parties are potential allies. The aim of IPC is to mobilize the still uncommitted members of the rural community for the rebel cause and not to chastise them. The threat of punishment is, of course, a part of the message, but unlike in the case of ATL—and this is a basic distinction between the two types—it is prefaced by a call for help. A rebel circular is not issued as a verdict on some wrong done and a resolution to bring the offender to book. On the contrary, its purpose is to win support by appealing to the

[33] This is how E. P. Thompson differentiates between the two major classes of grievances that inspired the ATL specimens examined by him (Thompson: 258). He mentions dismissed servants among authors of ATL generated by 'private' grievance. His list of 'social' grievances includes those relating to bread and corn prices, industrial and agricultural wages, smuggling, poaching, enclosures, etc. (Ibid.: 260). [34] Ibid.: 259.

mutuality of interest between those who have already taken up arms and others who are yet to do so: 'You are our brothers. Do you join with all expedition'—as the Rangpur parwana says. Or, as the villagers of Kallas wrote to those of Akola mildly reproving the latter for not doing enough to promote the struggle against their common enemy, the moneylenders, during the Deccan riots of 1875:

After compliments. It is very wrong of your people to keep communication with persons who are deemed as excluded from the community of this village. Unanimity is very important at this time . . . It would be better if you should come to our village and get yourself informed of the whole matter for the information of your village people. Please do not hesitate to do so, as the time is very critical . . . For the good of all of us it is necessary that we should cooperate with each other. As we consider Kallas and Akola as one village, we have made the above suggestions to you . . . The villagers of Palasdeo are assisting us this time, and since we think you do not treat us similarly, we pray you to see us to-morrow . . . Please do not fail . . .[85]

Clearly the function of communiqués of this kind is to emphasize the need for unanimity, co-operation and common action, to plead for solidarity rather than to discipline opponents.

There is yet another instrument of solidarity which operates on a mixture of intimidation and persuasion in a manner even more explicit than it is the case with IPC. This is what is known as pressing—the form in which the insurgents use their presence in large numbers to win over to their side the recalcitrants and vacillators within their own community. The practice is almost universal. It has been noticed by Zimmermann in his history of the Peasant War in Germany, by Rudé in his account of the Swing in England, and so on.[86] Everywhere it is a combination of the moral prestige of solidarity and elements of public authority accruing to the insurgents at such junctures which encourages them to put on these impressive shows of rebel power for the benefit of their less stout-hearted brethren.

[85] 'Substance of a Letter addressed to the Mokadam Patel and the Village Community of Akola by four persons of the village of Kallas on behalf of the whole community', in DRCR (C): 210.

[86] For some of these instances see Zimmermann: I 354 and H & R: 107, 108, 111, 112, 113, 212.

Everywhere indeed they use it as 'an essential measure' of mobilization, that is, as Rudé said of the English agricultural labourers of 1830—'to muster a sufficiently imposing force'.[87] Thus, when the peasants of Kazirhat, Kakina and Tepa rose in arms against Deby Sinha, 'they pressed all the villages round to join them [and] collected in a more formidable body'. Afterwards, as we gather from the Rangpur Collector's report on the dhing, 'they assembled in different bodies in different parts of the District. One body went into Cooch-Behar and obliged the ryots to join them; another went into Dinagepore by the western border through Boda; another went into the Pergunnahs of Andewah etc to the northward . . . there were few ryots but what willingly joined them and those who showed the least resistance were compelled to it.'[88] Pressing also helped in the massive mobilization for the Kol insurrection of 1831–2. According to a correspondent of the *Bengal Hurkaru*, the rebels 'proceeded from village to village burning and massacring every respectable person and every foreigner, and forcing every Cole by the fear of instant death to join their standards'.[89] The same method of inducement was used by the Santals as well. The Collector of Birbhum made some notes about this in his diary thus:

30 September 1855. Captain Terry reports that the Sonthals are in large numbers at a place about 14 miles north East of Rumpore Hath, that they have surrounded two large villages and insist upon the villagers joining them in plundering, burning etc.

2 October 1855 . . . Since the 23rd July the Sonthals have occupied Juggutpore. Seedoo joined on the 23rd Sept. since which day the villagers have been seized in order to help in plundering villages.[90]

It has been said that 'the typical agent of propagation' of the Swing movement in England was 'the itinerant band which marched from farm to farm, swelling its number by "pressing" the labourers working in the fields or in their cottages at night'.[91] In much the same way the Pabna bidroha of 1873 was propagated by roving bands of peasants who went the rounds of the villages blowing on their buffalo horns and calling on their

[87] H & R: 212. [88] MDS: 323, 325. [89] J. C. Jha: 179.

[90] JP, 4 Oct. 1855: Birbhum Collector's Diary (30 Sept. 1855); JP, 25 Oct. 1855: ibid. (2 Oct. 1855). [91] H & R: 209.

fellow ryots to join them. Those who agreed to do so were left in peace; those who did not, were harassed. On one occasion the unionists, wrote Nolan, defied an official ban to assemble in large numbers at Sallop and marched 'in a threatening manner to some villages which had not hitherto joined'.[92] In the Uttarshahpur estates of Dacca, the following year, the peasants formed a union to resist a landlord who had just purchased that property and 'on many occasions even forced some of the other ryots to join the union against their will'.[93]

Using force to generate solidarity: this apparent contradiction in terms makes pressing easily a most misunderstood figure of insurgency. The peasant's enemies tend altogether to ignore its unifying function: they look upon it as nothing but a sign of the coercive character of rebellion. Such an interpretation agrees with their view of the peasant as by 'nature' averse to turning against his superiors with whom he is supposed to be attached by a 'natural' bond of affection and loyalty, so that when he does in fact rebel, it is comfortable to explain so 'unnatural' an event as having occurred under duress. It is thus that landlords, administrators, officers out on anti-insurgency missions, informers, white settlers frightened by jacqueries—all go on talking *exclusively* about the peasants being 'forced', 'seized', 'compelled', in short, drafted against their will into the rebel contingents. This is a misrepresentation of the character of pressing because it is one-sided: what it fails to grasp is precisely the duality of this phenomenon and its inherent contradiction symptomatic of the want of uniformity in peasant consciousness. For no class or community is ever so monolithic as completely to rule out lags or disparities in its members' response to a rebellion. Some of its constituent groups or individuals are bound to rise to the call of an insurrection more readily than the others. They are also the ones most likely to use some of the public authority appropriated by force in order to mobilize their less militant brethren to the common cause. If this is true even of the most advanced revolutionary classes (e.g. the Russian proletariat on the eve of the October Revolution, as witness the disparity between Moscow and Petrograd workers and that between sections of the Petrograd

[92] Saha: II 118–19; JP(P): Nolan to Pabna Magistrate (1 July 1873).

[93] Sen Gupta: 105.

workers themselves in their readiness for armed insurrection), it is all the more so of the loosely structured and not so class-conscious peasantry in a pre-industrial society.

Among the latter difference in the degree of militancy between their relatively advanced and backward sections determines the extent to which rebel solidarity is likely to be more or less voluntary. In the event of an uprising it is of course the radical elements who are the first to come forward. In the village, 'the centre and starting-point of all "Swing's" multiform activities', says Rudé, 'a nucleus of militants initiated action and built up support, by persuasion or intimidation'.[94] And between villages, too, the more militant ones would try, 'by persuasion or intimidation', to rally the others to the standard of the rebellion—Kazirhat calling on Pinjirah, 'We have made an insurrection . . . All Coochwanah are come forth. Do you do the same and join us . . . If you come, it is well; if not you will repent it . . . People are therefore sent to you.'[95] Pressing, in this context, is primarily an instrument of solidarity, that is, of unification and not of punishment. 'One and all, one and all, we'll stand by one another', shouted the Sussex agricultural labourers as they moved from farm to farm in November 1830 pressing those who had not yet struck work.[96] There, as in those other instances cited above, they were using their mass and militancy thus to resolve a contradiction among the people themselves, not between the people and their enemies.

However, in no peasant rebellion does the relation among the people remain non-antagonistic all the time. The peasantry produce not only rebels but also collaborators, informers, traitors. These latter personify the irreducible dregs of a backward consciousness which even the force of an insurrection cannot fully flush out. They stand for the servility, fear of change, fatalism and urge for self-preservation at any price which go with the petty proprietor's mentality everywhere. Peasants themselves, they turn against their class and community at the critical hour and act as the instruments of their own oppressors. And it is thus that a contradiction among the people themselves turns into a contradiction between the people and their enemies. The insurgents are remarkably quick to recognize this. In the

[94] H & R: 209. [95] Kaviraj: 41. [96] H & R: 108.

Peasant War in Germany it was customary for them to mark out the houses of enemies *as well as* of enemy collaborators by the sign of the pole—a sign of equation, so to say. 'Those who were not with them', wrote Zimmermann, 'were to be treated as *traitors* to the common cause and a pole was to be placed in front of their houses *as if they were enemies*.'[97] This transformation of attitude corresponds directly to the reversal of solidarity into betrayal, and as the Santal tradition of the hool suggests, the antinomy Solidarity/Betrayal constitutes a well-defined element of rebel consciousness:

> Then there was yet another hearsay. According to this, any two women who had the same number of children, were to adopt each other as ritual friends. They were also to exchange gifts of clothing and interdine. No one knew why. Perhaps this was done to ensure solidarity through ritual kinship, so that no one might turn traitor in the event of an uprising and so that all messages could be kept secret.[98]

Here, as in so many other domains of Indian culture, what is socially desirable, is helped by ritual to acquire a quasi-religious quality—a sort of 'spiritualization of politics', to use a Gandhian phrase, which makes any transgression reprehensible not only in terms of social morality, but the latter compounded by religiosity. Betrayal, thus, becomes a 'sin' meriting the severest sanction.

The chastisement of traitors, therefore, figures prominently in most of the peasant uprisings of our period. But who is a traitor? In effect, the notion of betrayal tends to acquire a certain degree of elasticity at the height of a peasant insurrection when the usual thresholds of tolerance are considerably lowered and all neutral markings erased between sharply polarized positions. Under such conditions the insurgents do not often care to discriminate between the various shades of dissidence, non-conformity and downright treachery. All who fail to co-operate with them one way or another, are lumped together as traitors. However, judging from the instances I have come across, betrayal appears in rebel perception to stand for two forms of collaboration with the enemy—passive and active. The former is almost always identified by the insurgents as a negative response on the part of those whose duty it is supposed to

[97] Zimmermann: I 278. Emphasis added. [98] MHKRK: *clxxvii*.

be to participate in the common struggle together with the other members of the group. Indifference, vacillation, fence-sitting are all regarded as tantamount to hostility: the conflict is indeed so acute that anyone not actively in favour of the movement risks being classified as an enemy. The point was clearly made in a poster in Hindi, Urdu and Persian which appeared in Lucknow on the eve of the Mutiny 'inviting Hindoo[s] and Mussulmans to unite and exterminate all Europeans—some of them as inflammable as language can make them—denouncing all who remain passive as born of the pigs of Europeans, born of crows, despised by the Gods, hated and spat at by all true sons of Mahabeer Jee, and of Mahomed'.[99] What the hostile correspondent of the *Bengal Hurkaru and India Gazette* saw in this 'proclamation' simply as rhetoric, was in fact a statement of the principle by which the rebels distinguished between allies and traitors.

Passive collaboration expresses itself either as a refusal to resist the enemy or as a refusal to join forces with the rebels. Not to oppose the enemy when such opposition is due, is regarded by the insurgents as withdrawal of co-operation from their 'collective enterprise' and therefore liable to punishment. Kanhu, the supreme commander of the hool, is known to have led a thousand men including his brothers, Bhairab and Chand, on a raid on two villages where Kowleah, the bandit turned a rebel chief, was captured by the troops and the villagers had done nothing to prevent this. The Santal fauj pillaged these villages and took away some thirty of their inhabitants as 'prisoners'. The demi-official report of an action by the infantry which then set out in pursuit of the rebels but failed to make contact (although they found and released the captives left behind by the guerilla army in its haste to get away), testifies to the strictly punitive character of Kanhu's operation. 'I received intelligence from various quarters', wrote the British officer in charge, 'that the Soubah [i.e. Kanhu] had come to Pidra, a place 12 Cos from this. It appears that he marched yesterday with about 1000 followers to Londeeha near Kuturia, both of which villages he plundered, bound and carried off 30 or 40 of the Inhabitants *as punishment for allowing Kowleah to be captured.*'[100]

[99] FSUP: II 7–8.

[100] JP, 8 Nov. 1855: Bidwell to GOB (20 Oct. 1855). Emphasis added.

However, the more usual form of passive collaboration was non-conformity—that is, refusal by peasants as individuals or groups, to join in an uprising. Anyone identified as a traitor in these terms was liable to be subjected to violence in precisely the same manner as the enemy. That the insurgents made no fine distinctions between classificatory foes and real ones on such occasions was clear for all to see in the course of the jacqueries that broke out in the wake of the Mutiny. It was thus that the villagers of Gohand in Hamirpur district of Uttar Pradesh threatened other villages in the area with plunder if the latter failed to conform to their advice not to pay up any revenue due to the government.[101] And in the Gaya region Kunwar Singh was said to be 'burning all villages which do not join him'.[102] The following case history of an *émeute* involving indigo growers in a Bengal village may help to elucidate the point further.

> On May 11th, 1858, about 80 inhabitants of the village of Betai [Nadia district] attacked Mr. A. Hill's cutcherry in that village, took several papers, wounded a Government peada and chowkeydar, then went to another quarter of the village and plundered there and severely wounded 6 men. *This last attack was made, because the sufferers would not join them against the factory.*[103]

The punishment of dissidents was a part of the experience of the Pabna bidroha, too. One of the most violent incidents to mark its course was a punitive raid by the people of Nakalia, a militant village, on those of Sagtollah, a village which had held back from the movement. The attack, it has been suggested, 'was an exceptional case where the league was misused for the purpose of intimidation'.[104] Misused by whom? By a couple of designing *ijaradars* perhaps who had something to gain by stirring up trouble, but *not*, as the knowledgeable Assistant Magistrate of Sirajganj wrote at the time, by 'the ryots who executed the design because they [the Sagtollah villagers] would not join the league'.[105] In fact, there is good reason to believe that in acting as they did the Nakalia peasants were being true

[101] FSUP: III 626. [102] FSUP: IV 464.

[103] IRC: Appendix 11, Case no. 18 of 1858. Emphasis added.

[104] Sen Gupta: 56.

[105] JP(P): Nolan's Diary (Entry for 2 July 1873).

to a well-established local convention. For some of the cases which came up for trial in connection with the bidroha arose from attacks alleged to have been made on the persons and properties of those who had sided with the zamindars against the unionists.[106] It did not fail to register on their enemies that the peasants were prevented by no sectarian consideration in dealing with passive collaborators in their midst. 'When a Hindu ryot of any village refuses to join the rebels', wrote the *Amrita Bazar Patrika*, 'his house is plundered. Should the recusant ryot be a Muhammadan, his house is plundered.'[107] Indeed, it would seem that far from 'misusing' the strength they derived from their union it was precisely in applying it as a deterrent against passive collaborators that the Pabna ryots came to join a world-wide tradition of peasant insurgency. 'At Betwar [Bettberg] in Ostheim', wrote the historian of the German Peasant War, 'some refused to join the rebels. Their houses were ransacked'; and in some other areas 'those who did not join the people's union [*Volksbund*], had to pay heavy fines'.[108]

Active collaboration is also of two kinds in both of which it figures as a replication of peasant subalternity. In the first of these the replication appears as a persistence of the traditional political relationship between the peasant and his enemy—the relationship between servant and master. Since it is the object, in fact the fundamental object, of a rebellion to destroy this very relationship, any member of the insurgent community who chooses to continue in such subalternity is regarded as hostile towards the inversive process initiated by the struggle and hence as being on the enemy's side. In the villages of Bengal in the nineteenth century a landlord's authority found its most characteristic expression in his power to extract rent from his *proja*. So when in the 1870s and 1880s rack-renting emerged as the focal issue of the anti-zamindari struggles in Lower Bengal and rent-strikes as their principal form, any ryot who persisted in paying rents was liable to be subjected to violence by the

[106] Ibid.: 'Pubna Riot Case'. See, for instance, 'remarks' on cases arising from the complaints of Rohim Molla (Shernagur) and Bainjshaik (Barbala).

[107] *Amrita Bazar Patrika*, 25–26 June 1873, quoted in Sen Gupta: 52.

[108] Zimmermann: I 278.

others as a collaborator. 'The defendants, 30 men, fell upon the house of the complainant [and] assaulted him in consequence of his having paid rents to the zamindars': thus reads the pithy summary of a case that came up before a sub-divisional

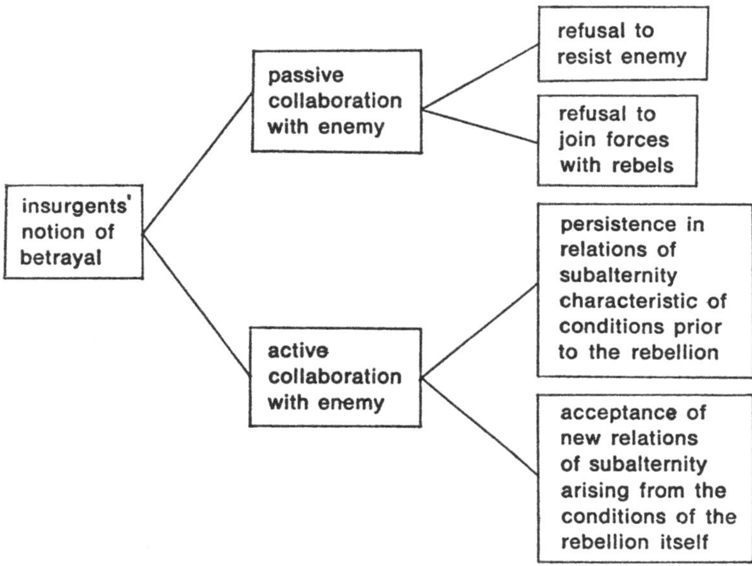

Figure 1 The Insurgent's Notion of Betrayal.

court relating to an attack by the Pabna bidrohis on the property and person of Shabun Pramanick, a ryot of village Chachkea.[109] Again, in 1881, the peasants of Hoshainpur in Mymensingh 'made unions and maltreated all who *sided with the landlord or paid any rent*'[110] without bothering to distinguish between the two acts of collaboration whatsoever.

The identification of collaborators in these terms represents the limit beyond which the rebels are unwilling to put up with the conditions of their subalternity. This is a critical threshold which acts as an index of the differentiated levels of consciousness at such times and sorts out the peasantry into relatively advanced and backward elements according to the degree of

[109] JP(P): 'Pubna Riot Case'.
[110] B. B. Chaudhuri (1967): 289. Emphasis added.

their willingness to cross it. We have it on record that during a phase of the civil war in China in 1946 some peasants of a particular village which had been already liberated by the communists and gone through the Land Distribution Movement, were so frightened by a sudden turn in the war in favour of the Kuomintang 'that they secretly sent back to landlord families the property and clothing they had received in the distribution, or they began to pay a little rent for the use of expropriated land'. And the tradition of subalternity reasserted itself with a vengeance not only with regard to rent and property, but along the entire range of attitudes characteristic of the old feudal relations. 'The wife of one village chairman', wrote Hinton to whom we owe this information, 'even hired herself out as an unpaid servant in an ex-landlord's household in return for a promise of protection when the gentry again took power.'[111] Collaboration feeds precisely on this tendency of the weaker elements of a rebel community to continue in their submission to landlordism and other forms of enemy authority even when time is ripe for *fanshen*.

The other type of active collaboration involves a somewhat different order of subalternity. This expresses itself not in terms of a continuation of traditional forms of subservience antecedent to the rebellion, but in those contingent on it. Members of the rebel community who act as the enemy's agents are its most typical and notorious representatives. Active collaboration is thus sired by insurgency no less than is rebel solidarity itself and complements the latter both as its twin and its reverse. There is indeed a necessary connection between the two. The stronger the insurgents feel in their solidarity the more pressed their adversaries are to recruit collaborators from the rebel ranks. This is why spies, approvers and agents of various kinds figured so prominently in some of the most vigorous pacification campaigns under the Raj. The meticulously engineered plan to use Man Singh to apprehend his friend and confidant Tatya Tope, the great leader of the Mutiny, shows how cynical and indeed how effective the official promotion of perfidy could be.[112] How-

[111] Hinton: 206.

[112] For some details of this plan see FSUP: III 558–64 and S. N. Sen: 377–8. One has to read the shocked recollection of this event thirty years later by Lieutenant-General Showers, Political Resident in Mewas State of Rajputana at the time of

ever, in this respect, as in many others, the war waged by the colonial regime on the Santals in 1855 was a dress rehearsal of the other and bigger war of two years later. The impression this policy made at the time on the defeated and demoralized rebels is recorded thus in Jugia Sardar's narrative of the terminal phase of the hool:

All of us male Santals, that is those already taken captive, were put in custody and removed, one by one, to Dhasnia Rajgram . . . At that time the European officers gave us all sorts of false assurance. 'Why must you suffer?' they said, 'tell us the names of your Subahs and we'll let you off straightaway'. So many of our people squeaked and the sahebs arrested the Subahs. Some of those captured thus were hanged on the spot; some others were sent to penal colonies.[113]

The official inducement to treachery in 1855 was of course much more elaborately worked out than this simple peasant imagined. It originated piecemeal out of the desperate need of the local civil and military authorities to cope with the thrust of a spreading insurrection and was eventually generalized as a part of the government's strategy for the suppression of the rebellion. The many initiatives which were launched in this process added up to a search for three categories of active collaborators. First, there were the spies. The routine despatches from the area of the uprising offer us occasional glimpses of these sleuths at work—spies sent out on 1 October to find out what happened 'at a grand meeting of the Santhal Chiefs . . . held yesterday at Raneebehal', Sergeant Gillen's spies watching whether the rebels would actually act up to 'their intention to loot Raneegaon, Jehanabad, Jypore' in Birbhum, spies reporting a large Santal force crossing the Grand Trunk Road, information received from a spy about Kanhu's presence at an important meeting at Kumirabad on 27 October, verifying intelligence received from some spies about the setting up of a rebel camp at Chamoapara,[114] and so on.

---

the Mutiny, to realize how unethical this policy appeared to be even in the eyes of some of the highest British officials in India. Showers: 146–7.

[113] MHKRK: *clxxviii*.

[114] For these instances see JP, 4 Oct. 1855: Birbhum Collector's Diary (1 Oct. 1855); JP, 8 Nov. 1855: Bidwell to GOB (Enclosure, 20 Oct. 1855); JP, 22 Nov. 1855: Ward to GOB (30 Oct. 1855); and Richardson to Burney (n.d.) in BDR: 123.

These informers were poor villagers themselves. 'A bill for Contingent expenses incurred by the Coll^{r} of Beerbhoom in connection with the Sonthal Insurrection' exhibits a total payment of one rupee 'to Kenaram Mal and 25 other informers on account of their diet.'[115] Who but the poorest could be trusted to subsist on food worth one-twentysixth fraction of a rupee for two meals a day even in 1855? However, judging by the far too few names actually mentioned in the sources—they figure only as items on the expense accounts of officers on duty in the Birbhum area—the spies who worked for the government were all non-Santals (e.g. Nabi Baksh, Chand Mallik, Abhoy Surak, Kenaram Mal, etc).[116] It is possible (though by no means certain) that ethnic solidarity proved firm enough to frustrate attempts made by the authorities to recruit informers from the rebel community itself, which would explain partly at least the poor quality of much of the intelligence they received and their failure to contain the hool by timely interception at an early stage. One wonders whether the obsessive reference to 'Santal spies' in official communications and the large number of prisoners accused of spying for the insurgents were not indeed a measure of the triumph of popular counter-intelligence over the operations of the army in the disturbed areas at the time.[117] There is no doubt in any case that such counter-intelligence was to prove a serious obstacle for the Raj in its efforts to suppress the uprisings inspired by the Mutiny two years later. The experience of the Magistrate of Saharanpur was fairly typical in this respect. He led a raid on the village of Manuckpur in order to arrest its headman, Umrao Singh, who 'had been very forward, calling himself Raja, and levying money from the

[115] JP, 8 Nov. 1855.

[116] Ibid.; JP, 4 Oct. 1855: 'Contingent Bill of the Office of Special Commissioner in the District of Beerbhoom for the month of August 1855'.

[117] There are many references to Santal 'spies' in the official records of the hool. Ward's letter to Grey of 25 September 1855 may be read as a representative sample of the counter-insurgency authorities' obsession in this respect and the summary manner of dealing with this problem. Three Santals 'who arrived as I was leaving Sooree', he reports, 'were headmen who had given up a few unserviceable bows and arrows to Mr. Lock six weeks ago, and had gone out promising in 4 days to bring other Chiefs to Sooree. They evidently had come as spies, and I immediately put them in irons.' (JP, 4 Oct. 1855). For some other examples see JP, 4 Oct. 1855: Richardson's Diary (26 Sept. 1855); JP, 8 Nov. 1855: Ward to GOB, para. 15 (13 Oct. 1855); JP, 20 Dec. 1855: Hawes to Parrott (11 Dec. 1855).

surrounding villages'. The government had declared a 'large reward' for his apprehension, and yet, wrote a very frustrated officer, 'His intelligence was too good for us, and we found the village all but deserted'.[118] There was obviously no one ready to sell the insurgent's head to Spankie for a handful of silver.

The use of rebel prisoners as approvers to denounce other rebels, free or captive, constituted a second category of active collaboration encouraged by the government. It is thus that Gurucharan Das, a non-Santal, described as a Bairagi, earned a place for himself in official correspondence. He had joined in the uprising and was taken prisoner. 'It might be desirable to make him an approver', wrote Ward, the Special Commissioner, 'though I will not recommend the measure unless I find very good grounds for so doing.'[119] Whether the Bairagi finally came up to Ward's expectation and ratted on fellow insurgents, we shall never know. But the same officer's efforts to find yet another approver is more fully documented. A skirmish between the troops and the Santals on 15 September 1855 near Mahomed Bazar had resulted in the capture of a peasant family of four—Dhona Majhi, his wife Sona who had been shot through the knee during the fight, and their two young daughters, Soomee and Dilgee. Reporting the incident to the Government of Bengal, Ward wrote:

> Dhona will, I think, confess. I have ordered him to be kept in solitary confinement and have given him to understand that in 24 hours I shall be prepared to give him some hope of pardon if he chooses to denounce his associates and their leaders.[120]

Dhona Majhi did not oblige. A month later, on 15 October he and his family were charged with 'illegally and riotously assembling with offensive weapons for the purpose of plunder and committing a breach of the peace', and the Sessions Court at Birbhum sentenced 'Dhuna Manjhee Sonthal to 7 years' imprisonment with labor and irons; Sona Manjhian Sonthalian to one year's D^o^ and to pay a fine of Rs. 50 in lieu of labor—Soonee Manjhian and Dilgee Manjhian Sonthalian each to six months' imprisonment and to pay a fine of Rs. 25 in lieu of

[118] FSUP: V 96.
[119] JP, 22 Nov. 1855: Ward to GOB (28 Oct. 1855).
[120] JP, 4 Oct. 1855: Ward to GOB (16 Sept. 1855).

labor'. After the case was reported to him the Lieutenant-Governor ordered Dhona to be separated from the rest of his family and transported to Chittagong jail, that is, as far east (within the Presidency) as possible from his tribal habitat.[121] In this exemplary punishment for a rebel who refused to buy his freedom by turning approver we have yet another instance of the solidarity of the Santals defying attempts to recruit collaborators within their community.

Neither of these forms of active collaboration was as valuable to the authorities as the services rendered by decoys. A few defections in rebel ranks had already by the middle of August 1855 set some of the local army commanders thinking in terms of the use they could make of these breakaway elements in order to apprehend any of the still unrepentant participants in the uprising. 'At Pakour', it was reported, '4 Head men amongst the rebels had given themselves up and promised to bring in others.'[122] And we know of a Captain Birch 'halting at Amrapara negotiating with some of the Sonthal for the delivery into his hands of the rebels'.[123] But it was only after Sido was betrayed and delivered into their hands without requiring any exertion at all on their part that the advantages of this particular stratagem became altogether obvious to the authorities. The incident was reported thus by Major Shuckburgh, commander of a regiment of native infantry, from Camp Gutiari on 20 August 1855:

> On our road here yesterday about 3 miles from this a Sonthal Runjunnite Bhugun Manjee of the village Punderha Pergunnah Pusye voluntarily came to me and said he had never joined the Insurgent party and would assist in quelling the insurrection . . .
>
> Shortly after our arrival in Camp a man came in to say that he had got the Head Chief Seedoo Manjee bound in cords in a neighbouring village and if ordered to bring him in he would do so. It was done and the celebrated Robber Chief and Rebel is now a prisoner in Camp and will be sent to Bhaugulpore . . .

[121] JP, 8 Nov. 1855: Ward to GOB (19 Oct. 1855); Thompson to Ward (15 Oct. 1855); Russell to Ward (25 Oct. 1855); Russell to Officiating Magistrate, Birbhum (ibid.); Russell to Officiating Magistrate, Chittagong (ibid.).

[122] JP, 4 Oct. 1855: Lloyd to Military Department, GOI (9 Sept. 1855).

[123] Ibid.

> The name of the person who brought Seedoo into Camp was Nazea Manjee he and the Manjee Bhugun (who joined us on the road) are gone to see if they cannot bring in the other chiefs Kanoo Chundeae Byzoo Manjees and Thakoor.[124]

The practice of using decoys sprouted directly out of this act of treachery. For Major Shuckburgh goes on to say in the same despatch that he and W. J. Money, a civilian officer accompanying him, 'both think that to advance further at present would be of little use and that it would be better to wait and give time for these Sonthals to capture their Chiefs themselves'.

The idea caught on. Vigorously advocated at the highest levels of the army as well as of the civilian administration, it was soon integrated into the general strategy of suppression of the hool. In its fully developed form this operated as a policy of securing the collaboration of decoys for a two-fold reward. First, it offered various sums of money for assistance rendered to the authorities in capturing the leaders of the insurrection. When Major-General Lloyd noticed that the rebels were 'ill disposed and disinclined to surrender themselves' and that this might have been due to the presence in that neighbourhood of their principal leaders, Kanhu, Bhairab and Chand, he felt that 'perhaps a high reward offered for the capture of the three chiefs might induce their followers to give them up'.[125] The reward originally declared by the government was very high indeed—5,000 rupees for the arrest of any of the ringleaders, 'but as this was considered excessive it was reduced by the Special Commissioner' to the still quite substantial sums of 500 rupees for the apprehension of Kanhu and 200 for that of each of his two younger brothers.[126]

The other reward for successful decoys was official pardon. Its terms were rigorously laid down. When the leader of a rebel force operating in the Telabuni area and some other *majhis* surrendered to the Magistrate of Birbhum in October 1855, the Special Commissioner warned the latter against leniency. These

[124] JP, 4 Oct. 1855: Shuckburgh to Becher (20 Sept. 1855). 'Runjunnite' refers, presumably, to a follower of Runjit Parganait, a Santal chief who was to surrender later on. JP, 6 Dec. 1855: Lloyd to Grey (23 Nov. 1855). The personal names are all so wrongly spelt in this despatch as to be almost unrecognizable. Read 'Mazea' for 'Nazea', 'Chand' for 'Chundae' and 'Bhairab' for 'Byzoo'.

[125] JP, 4 Oct. 1855: Lloyd to Military Department, GOI (9 Sept. 1855).

[126] JP, 20 Dec. 1855: Eden to Grey (12 Dec. 1855).

rebels were 'not entitled to pardon on surrender' unless they agreed to seize and deliver Kanhu, their commander, within a fortnight. 'The leader must be given up Kanoo Manjee or Thakoor is certainly known to them—and you should insist on his being made over to you.' Thus reads the stern instruction issued to the Magistrate concerned, and it goes on meticulously to specify the mechanics of betrayal as required by the government:

Of course it will be necessary for you to release some of the men who surrender, for the purpose of bringing Kanoo in but you will first have carefully examined them all and if nothing is said to those, whom you may intend to release for this purpose, till after examination, it will not be difficult hereafter from the account they gave of themselves, their residence &ca to trace them and punish their want of faith, if they do not hold to the conditions on which they were released which should be recorded, a time being fixed within which you will receive the leader Kanoo 15 days would be ample but you will judge for yourself taking the distance of his present residence into consideration.[127]

The care for detail in this official advice on the use of perfidy as an instrument of pacification is indeed a measure of the distance the colonial government had traversed since the days of 'liberal imperialism'. In 1832 Buddhu Bhagat, the leader of the Kol insurrection, was killed not by a traitor's ruse but in a pitched battle (although it was an unequal encounter between tribal axes and bows and arrows on one side and the guns and sabres of the British colonial army on the other). Yet when a sum of one thousand rupees was distributed among a number of non-commissioned officers and privates as their reward for delivering Bhagat's severed head to the authorities, the latter were revolted enough to put an end at once to 'the practice of offering rewards for delivering the insurgent leaders dead or alive, as had been done in the case of Buddhu Bhagat'.[128] A far cry that from the no-nonsense administration of a quarter of a century later when a Lieutenant-Governor's first thoughts on hearing about the arrest of the leader of the hool were to ascertain 'by whom the original information was given which led to it who the Baboo is who seems to have been immediately in-

[127] JP, 8 Nov. 1855: Ward to Birbhum Magistrate (16 Oct. 1855).
[128] J. C. Jha: 99–100, 102–3.

strumental in effecting it and whether he is considered to be deserving of reward for what he has done',[129] and when an estate, the size of a small kingdom, was the prize awarded by the Raj to a collaborator for double-crossing his friend, a leader of the Mutiny and handing him over for summary trial and execution.[130]

The official use of decoys was, in 1855, an extension of the military campaign itself as well as a partial recognition of its failure. Major-General Lloyd said this in almost so many words when he observed with some bitterness that large masses of the Santals 'evidently . . . acting under the orders of their Soubahs, Kanoo and his brothers' were still holding out as late as November that year. 'I have little hope of being able to seize these leaders by means of the Troops', he admits and goes on to affirm his dependence on collaborators thus: 'We are endeavouring to secure them by the aid of some of our Prisoners.'[131] This however proved to be of little avail. When Kanhu was captured soon afterwards, this was achieved neither by force of arms nor by that of deception. (He and a few of his companions fell by sheer chance into the hands of some Ghatwals who made them over to the authorities.[132]) In fact, nothing happened at all to confirm W. J. Money's prediction, made immediately after Sido's arrest on 19 August, that 'the other Chiefs may be captured in a fortnight or three weeks'.[133]

To regard this simply as an error of judgement on an individual's part will be wrong. For the administration as a whole and even at the highest level appears to have grossly underestimated the strength of the hool which to many officials

[129] JP, 6 Dec. 1855: Grey to Bird (5 Dec. 1855).

[130] Major Meade who was primarily responsible for Man Singh's betrayal of his friend Tatya Tope wrote thus about the price asked by the traitor for his services: 'I learnt . . . that Maun Singh would do as I wished, but that he was desirous of having Sir R. Hamilton's general assurance of consideration for such a service . . . and that his ambition was to have Shahabad, Powrie or some other portion of the Ancient Raj of Nuswn guaranteed to him in the event of his efforts to apprehend Tantia Topee being successful.' FSUP: III 561.

[131] JP, 20 Dec. 1855: Lloyd to Grey (28 Nov. 1855).

[132] JP, 20 Dec. 1855: Bird to GOB (9 Dec. 1855); Eden to GOB (12 Dec. 1855). The authorities trusted the Ghatwals to remain loyal during the hool as they had indeed been during Ganganarain's insurrection in 1832. See JP, 15 Nov. 1855: Allen to Grey (31 Oct. 1855). Their trust was not misplaced.

[133] JP, 4 Oct. 1855: Shuckburgh to Becher (20 Aug. 1855).

including the Lieutenant-Governor himself looked like a short-lived local disturbance.[134] Barely a month had passed before the Santals appeared to them 'in a great measure to have abandoned active opposition to the Troops sent against them'.[135] It was this that led the government to issue, early in August 1855, a proclamation promising pardon for all who would surrender within ten days. Only the leaders of the uprising and those actually involved in acts of murder were not covered by this proclamation which also threatened at the same time to put down all further resistance with the utmost severity.[136] The aim of this policy of carrots and sticks was, to quote the Lieutenant-Governor's own words, 'to give every opening to the misguided mass of the Sonthals to detach themselves from their more able instigators & leaders'[137]—that is, to encourage defection and treachery in the insurgent ranks. The betrayal of a commander of the hool, coming as it did soon after the proclamation, was, therefore, seen by the authorities as a sign of its success as well as the begining of the end of Santal resistance.

They had, however, reckoned without their host. For the rebel leaders, on their part, were quick to recognize in this policy a serious threat to the morale and solidarity of their ranks, and Sido's arrest confirmed their worst fears. Kanhu, therefore, made it known that any positive response to the proclamation would be treated by his side as treachery and therefore liable to punishment. 'He is aware of these proclamations and kills everybody who offers us assistance or even hints at surrendering', wrote the same Money on 10 September considerably chastened already by the fact that with all his efforts to make it widely known at Mohanpur and in the neighbourhood of Noni Hat, 'no one on the force of the proclamation has yet come in to surrender'.[138] In the weeks that followed the same sort of concern was voiced by some other civilian officers too—even by those of Birbhum where the Santals were said to have been unwilling to fight the troops and about to surrender in

[134] See the two minutes of 12 & 16 July 1855 by the Lieutenant-Governor of Bengal in JP, 19 July 1855.

[135] GOB to Bidwell (6 Aug. 1855) in BDR: 134.

[136] BDR: 133–4.

[137] JP, 8 Nov. 1855: Minute by Lieutenant-Governor of Bengal (19 Oct. 1855).

[138] JP, 4 Oct. 1855: Money to Bidwell (10 Sept. 1855).

response to the proclamation.[139] In a letter written soon afterwards the Magistrate of that district mentioned some 'recent reports' from the daroga of Nungolea saying 'that the copies of the Government Proclamation issued on the 18th Instant have been treated in the most contemptuous manner by the rebels who attribute their circulation to fear and have no intention of yielding themselves'.[140] An entry for 2 October in the Birbhum Collector's diary confirms this. 'When the sonthals got the Proclamation', it reads, 'they said they would rather be cut in pieces than give in . . . The Proclamation seems to have been received in all quarters with supreme contempt, many of the copies were torn up and thrown in the faces of those who brought them to the Sonthals.'[141]

It was not long before local intelligence of this kind forced a reappraisal of this policy at the highest level of the administration. A spokesman for the Military Department of the Government of India was soon to observe that the number of insurgents to take advantage of the clemency offered by the proclamation was 'quite insignificant' indeed, and 'by the latest reports the rebellion continues in as great force as ever',[142] a view corroborated by the Lieutenant-Governor's own minute of 19 October acknowledging that 'these [proclamations] though know[n] to be widely disseminated among them [the rebels] have hardly produced any effect & have indeed been generally treated by them as an evidence of the weakness of the Govt. & an encouraging token of the success of the rebellion'.[143] When this admission of failure was followed up, three days later, by yet another of his minutes enclosing a draft proclamation of martial law,[144] it was demonstrated beyond doubt that the solidarity of the rebels had triumphed over the official attempt to lure them into surrender and collaboration.

The history of the Mutiny, too, offers some striking examples of the power of solidarity. Maulvi Liaqat Ali's rebel government in the Allahabad region collapsed on 16 June 1857 after his

139 GOB to Bidwell (6 Aug. 1855) in BDR: 134.
140 JP, 4 Oct. 1855: Rose to Elliott (24 Sept. 1855).
141 JP, 25 Oct. 1855.
142 JP, 8 Nov. 1855: Atkinson to GOB (19 Oct. 1855).
143 JP, 8 Nov. 1855: Minute by Lieutenant-Governor of Bengal (19 Oct. 1855).
144 Ibid.: Minute (22 Oct. 1855).

defeat in a battle with the British army the previous day. But all attempt made by the restored colonial authorities to gather incriminating evidence—'to collect real facts and the names of culprits'—was systematically stonewalled by the local people. 'The residents of this pargana', complained the officials of Chail, 'so combined that none was prepared to disclose the facts at the time of enquiry . . . There is no doubt that the residents of the villages . . . were accomplices of Liaqat Ali, the rebel, but they have all conspired to hide facts.' It was decided as a measure of sheer desperation that the inhabitants of Chail pargana as well as of Allahabad city should be punished 'with fines on account of suppression of facts'.[145] The Proceedings of the Government of the North-Western Provinces for 1859 contain a remarkably candid admission of the failure of the policy to induce betrayal by large pecuniary rewards. It reads:

> . . . the Lieutenant-Governor deprecated the offer of large rewards for leading rebels. During the rebellion notwithstanding the enormous sums that were offered for offenders, there was, His Honour believed, not a single instance on record of one man having been brought to justice by these means. On the other hand, the offer of large rewards gave the proclaimed rebel an exaggerated notion of his own importance and tended to exalt him in the eyes of his followers and of all around him; while the futile offer was significant of the weakness of Government, or at all events that it did not possess the sympathy of its subjects.[146]

One can hardly think of a better tribute than this to rebel solidarity!

The insurgents' defence of their solidarity assumed its most dramatic expression in their violence against active collaborators of all kinds. In this respect the peasant rebels of India were no different from those of any other country. In eighteenth-century England, too, no one who informed against smugglers and poachers could feel altogether secure.[147] 'The pressure against informing was great.' A Sussex smuggler who was condemned to death 'had often said that he did not think it a crime to kill an informer', and another maintained, even as he was

[145] FSUP: V 551. [146] FSUP: III 609.

[147] The instances and extracts in this paragraph are taken from Hay *et al.*: 144, 145, 166, 198 and Thompson (1975): 143.

being led to the tree from which he was to be hanged, that he 'was not guilty of the murder of which he was accused . . . though if he had he should not have thought it any crime to destroy such informing rogues'. Poachers, too, 'took measures against informers'. A farmer near Waltham Chase who had informed upon 'King John', the leader of the Blacks and his band of 'Hunters', had his fences destroyed, the gates to his fields thrown open and cattle driven into his standing corn. Such acts of reprisal were by no means the work of these rural 'criminals' alone. 'The informer faced not only direct retaliation by the smugglers but also the open wrath of the entire community.' A man was chased through the streets of Hastings 'for informing against several persons' and in Kent an excise officer and his sleuth were followed by a violent mob armed with missiles and shouting, 'Informers, they ought to be hanged. It is no sin to kill them.'

'No sin to kill them': that seems to have been how the peasant rebels of India, too, felt about spies and all other active collaborators. Even a gwala (cowherd and milkman), a member of one of the groups considered as firm allies, was killed by the Kols for having informed against them.[148] Again, four men found spying for the British in Pasgawan during the very last phase of the great rebellion of 1857–8 had their noses chopped off and one of them was shot dead by insurgents acting on behalf of Khan Ali Khan.[149] Sometimes an entire village was the object of popular wrath for co-operating with the enemy. Nizam Ali, a leader of the Bareilly region in this period, 'intended to make a *Chupa* [i.e. *chhapa*, an attack] on Ishurpoor and burn it in revenge for the assistance given by the inhabitants in arresting some rebels in Pootkunea'.[150] The Santals, for their part, subjected collaborators to the utmost violence as well. One of these was so frightened when Kanhu 'sent him word that he will take vengeance on him for giving information', that he promptly sought asylum in the camp of a counter-insurgency official.[151] The rebels also 'swore to revenge themselves upon the families of Doorga Manjee', apparently a collaborator.[152]

[148] 'Nagpur Trials' (no. 85) in BC 1502 (58893): Master to Reid (22 Oct. 1832).
[149] FSUP: II 513. [150] FSUP: V 498.
[151] JP, 8 Nov. 1855: Bidwell to GOB (Enclosure, 20 Oct. 1855).
[152] JP, 4 Oct. 1855: Lloyd to Military Department, GOI (9 Sept. 1855).

Harma Majhi of Seetasal who surrendered and 'was sent out to bring in other head men', brought upon himself the swift retribution meted out to decoys. He 'was attacked by the rebels, his village destroyed, and property plundered, he himself narrowly escaping—because he had set such a bad example'.[153] Harma escaped with his life. Another traitor, Bhagna Majhi, did not. His story deserves to be told in some detail if only because it represents in one single episode of the hool all its drama of treachery, terror and counter-terror.[154]

Bhagna Majhi, a Santal of a village called Pindeah in pargana Pusye, was recruited as an agent by the police daroga of Bousee some three weeks after the beginning of the insurrection and introduced by him to W. J. Money, the civilian officer mentioned above. 'I caused letters to be written to him', recalled Money, 'assuring him that [he] need fear no attacks and assuring him that I should be thankful to him for any assistance that he could render'. The assistance rendered proved to be as valuable to the authorities as it was spectacular. On 19 August Bhagna approached Major Shuckburgh as the latter was leading a regiment of native infantry not far from Gutiari and offered to 'assist in quelling the insurrection'. Later on that day he and an accomplice, Majea Majhi, brought Sido 'bound in cords' to the Major's camp. 'The celebrated Robber Chief and Rebel is now a Prisoner in Camp and will be sent immediately to Bhaugulpore', wrote Shuckburgh reporting this marvellous windfall in a despatch the following day. Meanwhile, encouraged by the ease with which they had taken their captive, the two traitors went off for yet another and hopefully larger haul—'to see if they cannot bring in the other chiefs', that is, Kanhu, Chand and Bhairab, too. But they had no such luck the second time. On the contrary, this one act of betrayal did more than anything else to make Bhagna[155] and all other

[153] Ward to Birbhum Collector (9 Sept. 1855) in BDR: 137. Also see JP, 27 Sept. 1855: 'Extract from a letter from Mr. Ward . . . 9th September 1855'.

[154] The sources for the narratives in the next two paragraphs are as follows. JP, 4 Oct. 1855: Money to Bidwell (6 Sept. 1855); Lloyd to Military Department, GOI (9 Sept. 1855); Shuckburgh to Becher (20 Aug. 1855). JP, 8 Nov. 1855: 'Examination of Sedoo Sonthal late Thacoor' (17 Sept. 1855). JP, 20 Dec. 1855: 'Examination of Kanoo Sonthal'.

[155] We have no information at all on the fate of Majea Majhi. He seems to have disappeared from the records and from history. Money's letter of 6 September 1855

collaborators the object of Kanhu's implacable vengeance. 'I had ordered that the man who had captured Seedoo should be killed', he said in a statement after his own arrest; 'the Gurriapanee people brought news of this man then Doomun Darogah cut off the head of that man & others who had aided in his capture'. The details of this incident can be pieced together from some of the official correspondence which followed. It appears that on hearing of 'the services that Bugna Manjee had rendered' to the authorities, the rebel leaders decided to seize him. They 'secured his son & kept him as a hostage until the arrival of his father'. It was not long before Bhagna was 'inveigled' into Kanhu's camp and there 'he was killed by a slow process of crimpling' on Domon Daroga's order.

This act of exemplary violence was matched by an equally cruel sequel for Domon himself. An inhabitant of Hatbanda in Lachmipur, he was alleged to have been active in a series of dacoities committed on the houses of some affluent dikus in 1854 under the leadership of Bir Singh, Parganait of Sasan.[156] Like Kowleah, another member of the same gang of social bandits, he too emerged as a prominent figure in the hool, the title 'Daroga' indicating the relatively senior rank he had come to occupy in Kanhu's fauj. 'His name struck terror into the heart of every Sonthal, whether rebel or not, and his death will be a blow to the insurgents', wrote Money after his murder, indicating, in spite of himself, that Domon must have been more of a menace to collaborators than to rebels if his death was indeed such a loss to the latter. In any case, the action which cost him his life was a punitive raid against a Santal collaborator called Bijnath Majhi, Bhagna's son-in-law, who had been captured by Kanhu's *sipahis* either for refusing to join in the in-

---

to Bidwell describing what happened to Bhagna refers thus to Majea: 'Of Majjeea Manjee I have heard nothing, but I should imagine that he was too careful a man to be easily seized' (JP, 4 Oct. 1855). One of the mysteries surrounding the circumstances of Sido's arrest is the fact that Majea Majhi, though mentioned by both W. J. Money and Major Shuckburgh, the two officers who directly dealt with the agents responsible for the capture, does not figure at all in either Sido's statement or Kanhu's. JP, 8 Nov. 1855: 'Examination of Sedoo Sonthal late Thacoor' (17 Sept. 1855); JP, 20 Dec. 1855: 'Examination of Kanoo Sonthal'. The former named Tulsi Majhi as his captor; the latter did not mention the captor by name, but his reference to Domon's victim pointed clearly to Bhagna Majhi.

[156] K. K. Datta: 52.

surrection, that is, as a passive collaborator, or simply as an affine of a notorious traitor and hence classified as a traitor himself.[157] Rescued by his friends, he was presented to W. J. Money who gave him leave to return home to his family when his house was attacked by a party led by Domon Daroga. 'To my surprise', wrote Money in his report on the incident, 'on the following morning he [Bijnath Majhi] returned . . . bringing with him the Head of Domun Darogah.' Collaborator beheaded by rebel beheaded by collaborator—it is thus that the two sharp movements of an encounter between Solidarity and Betrayal closed on each other in a figure of perfect symmetry.

This is a figure of irony—a 'representation by the opposite'.[158] By feigning to demonstrate an identity of manner between a rebel's destruction and a collaborator's it helps on the whole to illuminate their mutual opposition. To regard this opposition as simply a difference of degrees in peasant consciousness would be to miss its specificity. For the contrast between rebel and collaborator is the function of a double displacement. A displacement occurs when a peasant revolts against anyone in the position of a master, and the peasant-servant set free from the traditional coupling of dominance and subordination by the force of this reversal is transformed into the peasant-rebel. This transformation affects not only the militant members of a community but also the relatively backward. When, therefore, any of the latter break away and collaborate with the enemy, a new displacement occurs: the peasant-rebel reverts to the peasant-servant. In other words, since rebellion stands for a positive rupture in the peasant's relation with his master, it follows that collaboration, child of insurgency and its antithesis, makes sense only as a geometry of transformation, that is, as a displacement displaced.

It is the recognition of this double displacement which alone can help us adequately to understand both the general character and the particular bitterness of the rebel's hostility towards

[157] The source is open to interpretation either way. The relevant passage reads thus: 'In the mean while Kanoos "Sepohis" were scouring the countryside for recruits, killing all who refused to join Kanoos army. Two of these men came to seize Bijnath Manjee a son in law of Bugna Manjee's and succeeded in detaining him some time.' JP, 4 Oct. 1855: Money to Bidwell (6 Sept. 1855).

[158] Freud: 73, 174.

the traitor. In its general character that hostility is an articulation of class consciousness. It shows that this consciousness has learnt to identify the peasant's enemy not merely by the insignia of the latter's authority. For the peasant-collaborator is as poor and powerless as the peasant-rebel himself. He does not command such resources as fields, cattle, granaries, women fattened by leisure, mansions, silks, jewellery, etc., all of which stand for the status of his overlord. When his house is pillaged, as during the Pabna bidroha, it is only a few items of cheap earthenware constituting all his domestic possessions which get smashed up.[159] The insurgents regard him as a classificatory foe not because of his wealth or authority, but because he is the carrier of a corrupt consciousness in their own ranks. Rebel violence functions therefore as a defence of class consciousness against its perversion, as a necessary act of spiritual fratricide in which a brother must be sacrificed for the sake of solidarity. As such it represents the peasant-rebel's war on alienation within his own class and against his *alter ego*. A radical if still immature consciousness, it operates, under the sign of Cain, as a class hatred laced with an element of self-hatred. It cannot afford to be sweet and forgiving.

[159] JP(P): 'Pubna Riot Case'. See 'remarks' on the case arising from the complaint of Jooman Sirkar (Hati).

CHAPTER 6

TRANSMISSION

Insurgency regarded as 'contagion' by the elite—imageries of poison and infection—suggestion of irrationality—suddenness, speed and simultaneity—conspiracy theories—oppression as the objective basis of insurgency and its transmission—instruments of transmission—aural transmission—visual transmission—iconic signs—symbolic signs: messenger boughs, tel-sindur, *chapati —verbal transmission—graphic and non-graphic modes—transparency and opacity—authored and anonymous utterances—rumour: its universality and necessity—anonymity and transitivity of rumour—rumour and rebel consciousness.*

While the peasants regard rebellion as a form of collective enterprise, their enemies describe it and deal with it as a contagion—which goes to show again how such violence tends to evoke contradictory interpretations from its perpetrators and its victims. 'Contagion': the word occurs so often and so persistently in the official and pro-landlord accounts of agrarian uprisings in so many different places and times that it has acquired almost the status of a convention, that is, of a stereotyped figure of consciousness among those least likely to sympathize with disturbances of this kind. It was considered by 'clergymen, overseers of the poor and others not notably identified with the labourers' as one of the causes of the riots of 1830 in rural England.[1]

In colonial India the authorities acknowledged its power in no uncertain terms. The spread of the sepoy and peasant rebellions of 1857–8 was often described as a function of contagion and infection in official statements. 'Most of the mutineers from Azimgurh, Jaunpore and Benares', wrote Lieutenant-General McLeod Innes in his account of the events in Awadh, 'had . . . moved on Fyzabad and spread the *contagion* there.' Or, to quote from the proceedings of a case before a court: 'The mutiny

[1] H & R: 81–2.

broke out in Benares, Allahabad and Jounpore about the 4th or 5th of June 1857. Pergunnah Bhurdohee which is bounded on three sides by those districts became *infected* on the 7th or 8th.' The District Magistrate of Satara, too, expressed his fear in similar terms: 'Our frontier near Beejapore where there is a large Mahommedan population requires to be watched. *Infection* may be expected to spread quickly.' Almost any extensive disturbance, especially in the rural parts, made the authorities reach out for this particular imagery. They remarked how on the outbreak of the Kol uprising of 1832 'the people of Toree . . . (though not themselves Coles) had also caught the *infection* and risen in arms'. The potential of the Santal insurrection too was described in those terms: 'Revolt is *contagious* & it is impossible to foresee the extent to which the evil might spread.' On that occasion the Lieutenant-Governor of Bengal himself mentioned 'the *contagious* character of insurrection in this country' in his minute of 19 October 1855 on the yet unchecked career of the hool.[2]

The collocation speaks for itself. A rebellion—any rebellion—is, in the eyes of its adversaries, a disease. The words of a provincial chief of the military police bear witness to this view of politics regarded as a pathology. 'The mutiny [of 1857] spread through the Bengal Army (already in a highly excited and dissatisfied state) like any *infectious disease* in a vitiated atmosphere', he wrote about a year after the event. 'The *contagion* being allowed to spread from Meerut unchecked and without the prompt and stern retribution the exigencies of the case required, even the cutting off root and branch of the *diseased* member, corps after corps caught the *infection*.'[3] The analogy of the *corps* consumed by an uncontrollable virus could hardly be stretched further. When, therefore, the virus hit the countryside it was almost invariably regarded by the gentry as a morbid poison bound to destroy the peasant's healthy sense of loyalty to his master and undermine thus the moral edifice of the latter's authority. As the Officiating Commissioner of the

[2] In this paragraph the references are as follows: to the Mu'tiny—FSUP: IV 78, I 366; to the Kol insurrection—BC 1362 (54223): Metcalfe & Blunt to Court of Directors (25 Sept. 1832); to the Santal hool—JP, 8 Nov. 1855: Ward to GOB (13 Oct. 1855); Minute by the Lt.-Governor of Bengal (19 Oct. 1855).

[3] FSUP: V 20. Emphasis added.

Burdwan Division remarked on the way the Santal jacqueries had been enveloping the western districts of Bengal in the second week of July 1855, 'This shows that *distant* parts of the country inhabited by the Sonthals, to which I hoped the evil would not extend, are already *tainted*'.[4] There is a distinct suggestion here in the emphasized words—emphasized as in the original—of a spiritual defilement as well as of the externality of its agent. It is being insinuated that the peasants, even those in the remotest areas, have lost their innocence thanks to the irruption of outsiders—an idea on which it is easy to hang both a conspiracy theory and the image of an uncorrupted tenantry blissfully reconciled to landlord rule.

Clearly, too, the metaphor carries with it the notion of irrationality. This has two moments. It implies in the first place that contagion affects such disparate elements of the rural population as are linked by no common grievances. A. C. Logan's recollections of an *émeute* which broke out in the Thana district of Bombay Presidency in 1897–8 provide us with a typical example of elite incomprehension of the processes by which the apparently unrelated segments of a rural society are integrated into a common uprising. As the officer entrusted with its suppression he wrote, long after the event but with a sense of bewilderment hardly modified by time, recalling how 'the grievance which started the troubles was confined to a few hundred forest people'. The latter depended for their livelihood on the customary right to gather firewood in the forests and sell it in Bassein and other coastal villages. When the administration put a ban on this trade, they 'defied the interdict, overpowered the forest guards and brought their loads to Bassein with riotous demonstrations'. However, the failure of the authorities to respond at once to this disturbance with punitive measures produced, according to Logan, 'a contagion of lawlessness which soon infected the whole district'. And this is how that 'contagion' spread to other subaltern groups in the region:

> . . . forest tribes though in general unconnected with the particular trade described, rose everywhere and for a while ousted the jurisdiction of the forest department: even the European officers were assaulted and had to be withdrawn to headquarters. The Koli fishermen who had absolutely nothing to do with the forests and who owing to

[4] JP, 19 July 1855: Elliott to Grey (15 July 1855).

their trade in Bombay are an exceptionally prosperous class, rose to the cry of free liquor and free salt, and stormed a Deputy Collector's camp demanding (and getting) orders from him to the liquor shopkeepers to supply liquor gratis. The Agris or cultivating class became turbulent and threatening in demands for various concessions, and all the guards of the subdivisional officers had to be posted to secure their personal safety. In the meantime a plot, no doubt under skilled guidance, was being formed for the advance of three mobs from different directions on the headquarters town . . . One of these mobs consisting of several thousand persons rose before its time and attacked the town of Mahim with the intention of plundering the treasury.[5]

Nothing could be more typical as an official response to what was regarded as a spreading epidemic about to destroy a body politic. From its emphasis on the very small beginnings of these riots to its belief in the existence of 'a plot, no doubt under skilled guidance' it has all the characteristic markings of an elitist perception. What however appears to have flummoxed Logan most is the manner in which groups and grievances scarcely connected with what had triggered off these disturbances in the first place, entered the list as the situation developed.

His incomprehension is understandable, for he had obviously never seen anything like that before. But as a matter of fact what happened in Thana district in 1897–8 conforms all too well to a familiar pattern. For when a rural society is polarized so sharply as it appears to have been on this occasion, it often leads to a generalization of violence making the individuality of other local conflicts merge in the overall confrontation between the subaltern classes and their enemies. No pre-existing tension or dispute remains outside the scope of the insurrection under such circumstances and all antagonisms start functioning as if in an altogether new context. This is why paupers' riots, tithe riots, wage riots and food riots which had nothing directly to do with the English agricultural labourers' movement of 1830, were all absorbed in the latter as it reached its peak.[6] This is why, again, 'the news of the formation of the [peasants'] league' in Pabna 'revived' many old rivalries 'not even remotely connected with the agrarian movement' and 'brought these out in the open'.[7] In other words, these were all en-

[5] BSM: II 637–8. [6] H & R: 130. [7] Sen Gupta: 57.

capsulated in the bidroha of 1873 although each of them was antecedent to it. It is this *process of encapsulation* which is characterized as 'contagion' by those who are hostile to the peasantry.

The suggestion of irrationality in this metaphor has yet another moment made up of the closely related notions of suddenness, speed and simultaneity. From the days of Jacques Bonhomme and Wat Tyler to those of Kanhu Santal and Birsa Munda no peasant revolt has ever failed to shock its upper class contemporaries by its abrupt beginning and rapid thrust. Some of that trauma as registered in the evidence (often the only available evidence) originating from elite sources and representing the elite point of view tends to filter into the historian's discourse as well. And it is thus that imageries based on the destructive forces of nature are used as a common literary device for the description of rural uprisings. The Birsaite ulgulan is said to have been 'spontaneous, sudden in its eruption, elemental in its character like a volcanic outburst', the Kol insurrection to have spread 'like wildfire', and so on.[8]

From the notion of spontaneity and speed it is but a short step to that of simultaneity. In many, though by no means all cases the rebellions coursed through their respective territories very quickly indeed. It was only a matter of three to four weeks before the greater part of Chota Nagpur and Palamau was overrun by the Kols and most of Damin-i-Koh and Birbhum by the Santals. Such phenomenal spread involving people geared to an unhurried pace of life in an age of relatively slow communication generated among observers outside the rebel communities the illusion of a *levée en masse* everywhere at the same time in a given region. Co-territoriality thus came to acquire a semblance of contemporaneity. The fallacy was noticed by Gramsci. Commenting on the argument among historians about the character of the Sicilian Vespers he observed how this was 'a spontaneous rising of the Sicilian people against their Provençal rulers which spread so rapidly that it gave the impression of simultaneity'.[9] Lefebvre, too, deals with this notion in almost identical terms in his study of the Great Fear: 'The fear streamed across the kingdom in a limited number of currents, but most of France was affected: this suggests that the Great Fear was universal; the currents moved with great

[8] Singh: 193; J. C. Jha: 65, 80, 179. [9] Gramsci: 199.

speed: hence the impression that the Great Fear broke out everywhere simultaneously "almost at the same time". Both these ideas are wrong. They represent contemporary opinion and have been passed on without question.'[10]

Simultaneity, they both point out, was a convenient peg on which to hang a conspiracy theory. 'Once it had been decided', writes Lefebvre, 'that the Great Fear must have broken out everywhere at the same time, it followed logically that everyone should think it the work of secret agents working together in a general conspiracy.' It is not difficult to see how this idea has its source in the psychosis of dominant social groups confronted suddenly by a revolt of those whose loyalty had been taken for granted. Yet there is perhaps an element of truth in this fantasy of 'preconcertation', as Gramsci calls it. It reflects an intuitive recognition of an organizing principle behind what looks like the world being turned upside down. However, this is not an intuition which can overcome the constraints of elitist outlook and it ends up inevitably with a false attribution—that is, by blaming the inversion on a pre-existing plot.

What the pillars of society fail to grasp is that the organizing principle lies in nothing other than their own dominance. For it is the subjection of the rural masses to a common source of exploitation and oppression that makes them rebel even before they learn how to combine in peasant associations. And once a struggle has been engaged it is again this negative condition of their social existence rather than any revolutionary consciousness which enables the peasantry to rise above localism and unite in opposition to their common enemies. 'In eliminating localism, reasoning can at best produce only limited results', wrote Mao Tse-tung in 1928 reflecting on the situation in the Hunan-Kiangsi border area under communist control, 'and it takes White oppression, which is by no means localized, to do much more. For instance, it is only when counter-revolutionary "joint suppression" campaigns by the two provinces make the people share a common lot in struggle that their localism is gradually broken down.'[11]

In colonial India, too, exploitation and oppression helped to promote resistance among the peasantry long before the advent

[10] Lefebvre (1973): 137; also see ibid: 52–6, 141.

[11] Mao: I 93.

of party politics in the countryside. The baffled response of the Raj to the rapid progress of some of these struggles produced the usual crop of conspiracy theories. As one officer wrote to another in a state of shock during the Kol disturbances, 'Certainly if the insurgents were not urged on and supported by such [an] influential Individual [as the Raja of Chota Nagpur], it is difficult to account for the insurrection so *extensive* and *simultaneous*.'[12] Speculations such as these were a measure of the failure of the official mind to come to terms with the fact that an uprising on that scale required no secret plots but only the open and overbearing presence of the colonial power to stimulate it. For by building a highly centralized state in the subcontinent the British had unified and brought into focus the refracted moments of semi-feudalism in the countryside in a manner unprecedented in Indian history. And one of its direct consequences, that is, the fusion of the landlord's and the moneylender's authority with that of the sarkar, was what provided insurgency with the objective conditions of its development and transmission.

The spread of peasant violence in such conditions was achieved by a variety of means which were all specific to a pre-literate culture or, to be more precise, a pre-literate culture transiting slowly—very slowly indeed—towards literacy. This implied that rebel messages circulated more by spoken utterance than by writing, a phenomenon which, as we shall presently see, constituted a distinctive feature of this genre of conflict in rural India. It also made for the use of some traditional and relatively archaic forms of communication which, rooted as they were in a culture unfamiliar to the colonial authorities, helped merely to emphasize the distance between the latter and the mass of the native population. Not infrequently therefore the British officials felt perplexed and mystified as much by the speed of an uprising as by the mode of its transmission. It is thus that one of them mentioned, almost under his breath, that 'signals were made and given' in the course of the indigo riots of 1860, just as, according to Logan, 'occult symbols flew from village to village' in the Thana district during the events

[12] BC 1363 (54226): Russell to Braddon (18 Apr. 1832). Emphasis as in the original. For a more detailed discussion on this point see Chapter 3.

described above.[13] There are many such statements to be found in the records indicating an acute sense of alienation on the part of the regime whenever the peasantry managed to slip out of its patriarchal embrace. Secondly, in studying this question it may be of some help to bear in mind that all rebel messages, whatever the means of their transmission, had the dual function of informing and mobilizing at the same time. It was not often that a local community involved in an *émeute* made any public announcement about this to its neighbours without calling upon the latter for help and emulation at the same time. 'We have made an insurrection; join us'—this customary formula, a declaration followed by an appeal, as used by the rebels in their parwanas, governed most of their other forms of communication too.

Insurgency spread by verbal and nonverbal means. The latter were of two kinds—aural and visual. Such distinctions are, of course, purely schematic and stated here for analytic reasons alone. For in rebellion, as in other circumstances of real life, human communication operates eclectically by a mixture of signs. Thus there were nonverbal messages which were relayed by sight and sound at the same time such as in the movement called *hadun* when, according to Chotrae Desmanjhi, 'the people of one village went dancing to another with buttock and anklet bells' on the eve of the hool, or when the Santals looted the bazaars at Narainpur and Gunpura to the sound of drums and horns.[14] The same was true of the Pabna ryots' parades in 1873 carrying lathis and polos on their shoulders and blowing on their buffalo horns to make their bidroha known in such a way as could be seen as well as heard. Or take the pilgrimage of the Birsaites to their ancestral sites and the pageantry of their assault on Khunti all dressed up for the occasion and 'dancing, jumping and brandishing their swords'. Each of these apparently nonverbal demonstrations relied to no small extent on words to clarify its meaning—on their leader's aphorisms and lessons in one case and on belligerent war-cries (e.g. 'The *rahar* crop is ripe, etc.') in the other. Indeed, a rebel assembly, whether it was a battle formation as that of the Santals at Pealapur and Maheshpur in 1855 or a rally to inaugurate an uprising such as the one organized by Meghar Singh at Dewal in eastern Ghazipur in 1858 or

[13] Kling: 93; BSM: 638. [14] Desmanjhi: 233–4.

a quasi-religious congregation like any of those Munda prayer meetings on Dombari Hill in 1898–9, transmitted its message by a combination of verbal and nonverbal signs, and within the latter category, of aural and visual signs. However, to appreciate fully the power and intricacy of such combinations one can do no better than to study the operations of each of these semiotic systems in actual historical instances.

The drum, the flute and the horn were the instruments most used for the aural transmission of insurgency. They formed a class apart from verbal media in the sense that they helped to realize what Jakobson has called transmutation, that is, 'an interpretation of verbal signs by means of signs of nonverbal sign systems'.[15] As such they acted as a surrogate of human speech and were independent enough of the latter to permit the decoding of messages directly rather than through linguistic symbolism. In terms of the volume and variety of messages the operation of such a 'substitutive system' was perhaps not nearly so elaborate in our country as it was in Africa.[16] Yet in both the regions it served equally to emphasize the family likeness between fighting and other forms of communal labour. We have it on Nadel's authority that in the Nupe kingdom of Nigeria drums and wind instruments like trumpets and flutes were used to assemble people for war as well as for the *egbe* type of collective labour for agriculture and other forms of large-scale co-operation required for the community as a whole.[17] At the other end of the continent the Kiganda drums 'which announced to the people that there was urgent work to be done at the chief's place', were used to pick up the beats on the royal war-drum and relay these across the entire country to summon armed men to war within four days. Again, among the Tumba who lived on the east side of the Congo River it was customary for messages to be beaten out on the drum, to call people together to fight, to warn them 'during the rubber war days if

[15] Jakobson (1971): 261.

[16] We owe the term 'substitutive system' to Sebeok & Umiker-Sebeok: *xiv*. The collection of papers in this volume indicates some of the wealth of the African material and the research that has gone into it. There are no such studies for the Indian subcontinent.

[17] Nadel: 111, 248–9.

soldiers were coming', to summon them for a hunt or any other kind of collective work such as roofing houses.[18]

Much the same kind of semiotic correspondence existed in India, too, between labour and insurgency. The sound of the buffalo horn which, as we have already seen, brought the villagers together for polo fishing in the marshes of Pabna, was also the aural sign used by the tenant-cultivators of that district to rally people for the bidroha of 1873. The Santals, on their part, mobilized for the rebellion of 1855 at the sound of drums, horns and flutes just as they did for a communal hunt. The organization of the latter is described thus in the *Mare Hapram Ko Reak Katha*:

> At dawn on the day scheduled for the hunt a few men leave before the others for an open space where the entire male population of the village is to be called together. They take with them some large drums (*nagra*), flutes and horns, and then go on beating *dubu-dubu* on the drums, playing *shorong-shorong* on the flutes and blasting *tutu-tutu* on the horns . . . until all the villagers come out there. When they have all assembled there, they would give a loud shout and then proceed to the spot marked out for the formal gathering for shikar.[19]

An identical role was played by the same instruments in calling up the Santals for the hool, as Major Burroughs found out within four days of its outbreak. Justifying his reluctance to deplete his forces engaged in operations in the Colgong area he wrote to the Commissioner of Bhagalpur on 11 July 1855: 'We hear that the insurgents move about in very small parties but on their drums sounding they assemble in parties up to 10,000 men each for the purpose of plundering.'[20] When by the end of that year the insurrection had nearly spent its force and the troops were busy chasing and harassing the Santals, the latter tried from time to time to collect their scattered fauj in the jungle by the beat of the drum for skirmishes with the enemy. Whether one believes the Birbhum balladeer's complaint about the incessant beating of the drums as 'a regular nuisance' or a captive rebel's claim to have seen over a hundred and fifty drums at the Bhagnadihi house of the Santal leaders,[21] the

[18] Lush: 469, 473; Clarke: 418–33.

[19] MHKRK: *cxlii*. [20] K. K. Datta: 62.

[21] JP, 6 Sept. 1855: 'Deposition of Dhunwa Manjhee etc.'; JP, 20 Dec. 1855: Hawes to Parrott (11 Dec. 1855); D. C. Sen (1926): 266.

importance of that humble instrument can hardly be overestimated.

Indeed in an age of poor communication and nearly total illiteracy in the countryside the pressing need for mobilization made the use of such aural signs almost imperative in most of our peasant uprisings, tribal as well as non-tribal. It was the insurgent drum which called up the ryots taluk by taluk for the dhing against Deby Sinha in 1783.[22] The sound of the *nagra* carried the message of the Kol insurrection all over Chota Nagpur and Palamau in 1832.[23] The uprisings in rural UP in 1857 also relied partly on the same device. Dunlop of the Khakee Ressallah mentions how on one occasion when the troops approached a village in the Meerut region, 'its inhabitants thinking themselves doomed to destruction, commenced beating their dhôl, or Indian war-drum, and turning out in numbers'.[24] Again, as the special investigator appointed by the Lieutenant-Governor to probe into the indigo peasants' revolt of 1860 found out, 'A regular league was . . . formed against indigo cultivation . . . Ryots of one village were called upon, by beat of drum, to assist those of another . . . villagers turned out by the beat of drum and proceeded in large bodies to any alleged threatened spot.'[25]

The colonial government on its part was far from indifferent to the power of these rustic means of transmission. It is not merely that in times of trouble they broadcast messages of defiance, but their 'language', known only to the members of the community which produced it, was itself evidence of the failure of an alien authority fully to understand, hence control, the native population under its rule. An instance cited by Burridge of official hostility to certain uses of the slit-gong in a region of New Guinea under Australian control illuminates the attitude of colonialists everywhere. Here a community of Kanaka people known as the Tangu used this instrument customarily to communicate among themselves by sound signals not generally intelligible to outsiders. After the district passed under Australian administration, they were for some time forbidden to sound the slit-gongs when a white officer ap-

[22] Kaviraj: 41.

[23] J. C. Jha: 177; BC 1362 (54225): 'Statement of Buhardar Singh etc.'.

[24] Dunlop: 114. [25] Kling: 93.

proached any particular neighbourhood. 'In this way [so ran the theory] he could see what the villages were like when he was not there. The villagers would have had no warning of his approach.'[26] In other words the ban on a vital medium of indigenous communication was for the authorities an essential condition of their knowledge of that society, and a system of aural signs came thus to symbolize at once an epistemological and political opposition between the rulers and the ruled. When such opposition matured to the point of provoking mass peasant violence, as it often did under the Raj, even the most innocuous means of aural transmission among the people could assume in the eyes of the regime the status of instruments of rebellion and were treated as such.

It was thus that the drum and the buffalo horn, especially the latter, came to be an object of official hostility during the Pabna bidroha. In some parts of the district the local administration resorted to the Indian Penal Code forbidding 'the use of musical instruments for the purpose of invoking assemblies, intimidating union, or causing terror'. At least six peasants were sentenced to three months of rigorous imprisonment each on a charge of forming, at Ghasgali, 'an illegal assembly in which horns were blown to make a demonstration and intimidate a village which had not joined the combination'.[27] In much the same way the prohibition and destruction of Santal drums and flutes became an integral part of the policy adopted by the Government of Bengal for the suppression of the hool. These were identified as instruments of rebellion when Bidwell, a Special Commissioner in charge of the counter-insurgency campaign, urged the government to bring in a law making it a penal offence for a Santal to possess bows and arrows, swords, battle axes, sacrificing knives (*chhora*) 'as well as the Drum called by them Digdighee and used for collecting the Sonthals in bodies'.[28] Ward, another high-ranking official, disagreed. 'To disarm the Sonthal race would be almost cruel', he argued; 'it

[26] Burridge: 48, 128–9.

[27] JP(P): Nolan to Pabna Magistrate, Letter no. 321 (1 July 1873); 'Pubna Riot Case' (case no. 850). Also see ibid.: Nolan to Pabna Magistrate, Letter no. 1 Ct. (1 July 1873). For a Bolivian parallel of the use of wind instruments—'intimidatory incantations of the *pututus* or deep-sounding bamboo pipes', see Pearse: 133.

[28] JP, 8 Nov. 1855: Bidwell to GOB (26 Sept. 1855).

would certainly greatly effect [sic] their future prosperity by interfering with their intercourse with neighbouring tribes & among themselves; to many these are the only means of livelihood, besides these arms are not of a nature of which the Govt. should be afraid.' The humane alternative advocated by him was the introduction of martial law giving the army the right to dispense summary justice unfettered by the niceties of civilian legislation.[29]

In the event the Santals got martial law. This, however, did nothing to save their primitive means of aural transmission, nor, of course, their crude peasant arms. For within less than a week after its proclamation on 10 November 1855 Major-General Lloyd, commanding the Dinapore Division and Sonthal Field Force, issued an order on the same lines as Bidwell had recommended earlier and almost in the same words. 'All villages of the Tribe', it read, 'must be made to deliver up their arms vizt. Bows and arrows, sword[s], battle axes & sacrificing knives as well as the Drum called Digdighee used for calling the sonthals into bodies.'[30] After that the drum (in both varieties, that is, the larger nagra and the small *digdigi* or *doogdoogi*) and the flute—although the latter was not named in the order at all—came to rank as routine targets in all military operations against the Santals. The reports sent in by the officers repeat this information over and over again. A summary of the record for the fortnight following that divisional order may give some idea of this war waged by the colonial army on such objects:[31]

17 November 1855. Captain Halliday orders the Santals of Jagadishpur to surrender all their arms, plundered property and *doogdoogis*.

19 November 1855. Dissatisfied with the peasants' response to the above order Halliday invades Jagadishpur with a detachment of native infantry and recovers some flutes and drums among other things.

[29] Ibid.: Ward to GOB (13 Oct. 1855).

[30] JP, 6 Dec. 1855: 'Copy of a Division order issued by Major General G. W. A. Lloyd C.B. Comdg. Dinapore Division and Sonthal Field Force' (15 Nov. 1855).

[31] The sources for this summary are JP, 6 Dec. 1855: Halliday to Adjutant, 56th Reg. N.I., Suri (19 Nov. 1855); Lister to Parrott (20 Nov. 1855); Halliday to Gott (25 Nov. 1855); Ryall to Parrott (29 Nov. 1855); Hawes to Parrott (28 Nov. 1855); and JP, 20 Dec. 1855: Hawes to Parrott (1 Dec. 1855); Rubie to Shuckburgh (29 Nov. 1855); Halliday to Adjutant 56th Regt. N.I., Suri (19 Nov. 1855); Ryall to Parrott (27 Nov. 1855).

20 November 1855. Captain Lister raids some villages east of Uporbandha and failing to find any plundered property there takes away 'some bows, arrows, Drums and Doogdoogees'. A raid by a party of sepoys led by another officer on a number of villages six miles west of Uporbandha yields 'a good Bundle' of the prohibited articles and 'some Drums and Doogdoogees'.

25 November 1855. Captain Halliday surprises a large body of insurgents assembled at Moorguthole and Amjharee and captures some arms and heads of cattle as well as a few *doogdoogis.*

27 November 1855. Lt. Hawes attacks a Santal camp in the jungle on the Phuljhuri Hills and seizes a quantity of paddy and arms and four drums. Lt. Ryall commanding an infantry regiment searches a village called Suttulpur in the Jamtara region and seizes 'quantities of Bows, arrows, fulsas and Drums'.

28 November 1855. Troops led by Ensign Harrington pursue a body of rebels in the jungles of Bilmee Pahar and secure a *doogdoogi* and some weapons. Lt. Rubie's infantry detachment on its way to Palasi stops at a village called Amdaha and destroys some grain, arms and drums found in the house of a majhi reported to have left the village that morning.

29 November 1855. A search by troops under Lt. Hawes along the base and up some of the ridges on the eastern side of the Phuljhuri Hills yields a quantity of hidden arms as well as one *nagra* and two *doogdoogis.* A *dour* against the rebels in the jungles near Bagmarra results in the capture of arms and thirteen tribal drums.

And thus until the end of the hool the army went on dealing with these primitive instruments of aural transmission as if they were yet another set of weapons used by the rebels.

Another class of nonverbal transmitters used for the propagation of insurgency was made up of a number of visual signs—iconic and symbolic. The best known example of the former was the arrow of war used by the Kol. Its role as a means of rebel mobilization was made widely known by Dalton in his *Descriptive Ethnology of Bengal* published forty years after the event: 'An arrow passed from village to village is the summons to arm and sent to any one in authority it is an open declaration of war.' On the eve of the 1832 uprising such arrows circulated 'like the fiery cross' in that region, so that by the time it got under way by the middle of January that year 'the Mundaris and Oraons had all entered with zeal into the spirit of the insurrection'.[32] A reference to the primary sources can help us with an insight into this mode of communication from a new angle. Major Sutherland who investigated the causes and course of the uprising even before it had been completely suppressed mentions how he was told by the Maharaja and other knowledgeable informants 'that this system prevailed among the Larka Coles of Singhbhoom, but it had never before extended to the Danger Coles of Nagpoor and its dependencies'. He was to take up the point again in a detailed statement prepared for Metcalfe, the Vice-President of the Council. 'This is a custom of the Lurka Coles and had never before been generally adopted by the Dângar Coles', he wrote. 'In the present instance it seems to have extended throughout the country of the Dângars.'[33] In other words, the latter had borrowed it from the Larka Kols of Singhbhum and used it for the first time in the course of this insurrection beginning with Sonepur pargana and then elsewhere in Chota Nagpur and Palamau. The pressure of insurgent mobilization appears thus to have helped a sign to extend its domain beyond its traditional boundaries. The fact that it was still in circulation in that region in 1857, according to Dalton,[34] indicates how it struck root in the adopted community and continued to function as an integral part of its 'vocabulary'.

If insurgency added to the territorial range of this particular sign, there were others of the same class, but symbols rather than icons, which it helped to expand in semantic range. One such sign which the Kol insurrection rescued from the obscurity of custom and ushered into history was the messenger bough. Known as the *dhauree* or *dheori*, this was 'despatched from one party of Coles to another as a signal from them to join expeditiously and to engage in any contemplated exploit'. The receiving party was then 'expected to unite with the one issuing the Summons before the leaves of the branch fade[d] away'.[35] It was the mango tree which they preferred for this purpose. By contrast, the Santals of Birbhum and the Saora of Jaypur

[32] Dalton: 171–2.

[33] BC 1363 (54227): Sutherland's Note (11 Mar. 1832); Note from Major Sutherland enclosed in Metcalfe's Minute (27 Mar. 1832).

[34] Dalton: 171 n.

[35] BC 1502 (58893): 'Nagpur Trials' (no. 22) in Master to Reid (22 Oct. 1832).

taluk in the Ganjam Agency were to use sāl and jack branches to rally their fellow tribesmen for rebellion later on in the century. Diversity such as this did nothing however to weaken the symbolism common to all of them. Verrier Elwin identified the Saora jack branch as 'a well-recognized form of the fiery cross summoning villagers . . . to assemble at a fixed time and place', and the anonymous author of the *Calcutta Review* (1856) article on the hool described the sāl bough as 'a symbol which like the fiery torch in old Highland gatherings, appears to have had, either by a general ancient custom, or more probably a preconcerted recognition, a secret attached meaning'.[36] The sign in both instances was categorized as one that had its meaning assigned to it by convention, that is, as a symbol and as such, was evocative, for all British observers, of the most celebrated symbol of that kind within their own tradition.

This rather unimaginative assimilation of so many varieties of insurgent signals in an alien land to the single stereotype of the fiery cross was their way of trying to understand an unfamiliar and disturbing message by translating it into a code they knew. The attempt did not quite succeed in every case. At least for the correspondent of the *Calcutta Review* (1856) it appears to have failed to clarify the 'secret attached meaning' of the Santal missive. This made him speculate about 'a preconcerted recognition' demonstrating once again how the official mind retreated into conspiracy theories whenever it was unable to penetrate the language and mechanics of peasant insurgency. What is curious about his incomprehension is that the authorities at the centre—his informants—should continue to puzzle over this particular transmitter of the hool long after the local administration had grasped what it was all about. A reminder, one wonders, that the capital, whether Calcutta or Delhi, is always so far away (*dur ast*)?

The messenger bough makes its appearance in the records of the Santal uprising for the first time in the form of an entry in the Birbhum Collector's diary of 20 September 1855. It reads:

A branch of a Saul Tree has just been sent in to me by the Nugger Police Zemadar who received it from Goluck Chowkeedar of Afzool-

[36] Elwin: 254; CR: 244.

pore. This man states it was made over to him by Shiboo Gope Mundle of Champoora with the message that the Sontals would shortly proceed to Sooree for the purpose of having a meeting with the authorities. Shiboo Gope states he does not know who brought the branch but the messenger expressed a hope that the ryots would not run from their villages on the approach of the Soobah.[37]

It seems that the rebels had 'stopped the Dak running from Deoghur to Sooree', that is, disrupted the country post, and 'ill used the runners'. This last phrase was an euphemism for the fact that they had seized one of the official couriers and forced him, ironically enough, to run an errand for them.[38] But what did the 'Saul twig with 3 leaves upon it' mean for the head of the district to whom it was addressed? Richardson got little out of the Santal prisoners by way of an answer 'except that the three leaves express the intention of the sender to come at the third day'. He was obviously not amused at the prospect of a rendezvous imposed on him by this 'person calling himself the Soobah Baboo' and asked the commander of the sadar station to take all the necessary military precautions. 'I for my part', he wrote, 'shall send no answer to the message, it being my intention to put the Soobah . . . in irons on his arrival. The question as to whether he is about to come in peacefully to submit, or try his strength with us, must remain for the present a matter of doubt'.[39]

Indeed the question must remain unanswered for all time. For the Subah never arrived and we have no way of knowing why. It is possible that the Santal leadership had planned a spectacular march on that sadar station, but circumstances or second thoughts made them give it up. Or perhaps it was all a gigantic hoax played for a laugh at the expense of the all-powerful sahibs. Boldness and black humour have both been known to play their part in a peasant war, for each could be highly effective in its own way as an instrument of inversion. What is certain is that the insurgents' use of the twig with the three leaves as the carrier of an ultimatum was clearly an iconic adaptation—'each leaf signifying a day that is to elapse

[37] BDR: 121.

[38] JP, 4 Oct. 1855: Rose to Elliott (24 Sept. 1855). The version of this letter as published in BDR: 122 omits a part of the original.

[39] Richardson to Burney (21 Sept. 1855) in BDR: 121.

before their arrival'[40]—of a traditional symbol which meant, by convention, a summons to a communal assembly. The Santals in Suri jail whom the Collector found 'unwilling or unable to give any information in the matter', could hardly have failed to recognize in this the all too familiar *dheora* used to call up all able-bodied men for collective fishing and hunting. As the *Reak Katha* has it:

Fishing, too, is work that we enjoy . . . The majhi of the village where the fishing ground is located, has it as his task to launch a *dheora* (that is, to go around carrying a branch in order to make the announcement). And on the scheduled day we the people of the neighbourhood assemble there at noon.

Formerly it was customary for a messenger bough to circulate from village to village as summons to a communal hunt. But since the days of our first settlement in Shikar country we have been sending out the message at the time of the Festival of Leaves (*Pata Parob*) . . . There is a *dihri* (that is, a priest who presides at hunting ceremonies) for each area (*desh*). As he goes around carrying a branch at the time of the Festival of Leaves, the local people ask: 'What is that *dheora* for?' He then names a forest and says that we should assemble at such and such a place in such and such a forest, indicating at the same time where people could stop over for the night. We, the males of the community, then go home and talk over among ourselves the arrangements for the hunt scheduled to commence on such and such a day in such and such a forest or on a hill.[41]

The circulation of a branch was thus a commonly understood signal for communal action. Its use in the course of the hool emphasized, once again, the character of the uprising as a form of corporate activity. Just as a dheora would be sent out to collect men for a big job of fishing or hunting, so 'when the Thacoor came', said Sido, 'I sent a sal branch to the Sonthals to collect them together, then all the Sonthals were collected at my home at Bhugnadihee'.[42] And the dheora, so useful at this initial stage in mobilizing for the rebellion, continued to operate at its height as the principal means of communication between the various rebel groups. 'Messages are passing daily between

[40] JP, 4 Oct. 1855: Rose to Elliott (24 Sept. 1855). For a discussion of the iconic and indexical constituents of symbols see Jakobson (1971): 345–59, especially p. 357 where he quotes Peirce to say that 'a symbol may have an icon or an index incorporated into it'.

[41] MHKRK: *cxli–cxlii*.

[42] JP, 8 Nov. 1855: 'Examination of Sedoo Sonthal late Thacoor'.

the Mangees at Telobonee and those looting in the direction of Ooperbundah', wrote Richardson in his diary on 26 September 1855, 'the communication is carried on by messengers with small branches of trees'.[43]

It was thus that insurgency helped an old, established sign to extend its semantic range. An improvisation in the use of *tel-sindur* on the eve of the hool provides us with yet another instance of this kind. Unlike the dheora, neither *tel* (oil) nor *sindur* (vermilion powder) was known to have any transmissive function prior to this event. Together they constituted for the Santals, as for the Hindus, a propitiatory gift for ritual purposes. Whether offered by a newly-wed girl to the gods to seek their blessing for her married life, or by the diseased in order to pacify the spirits through a witch-doctor's (*jan*'s) mediation, or applied by a peasant on the horns of his cows to make sure of divine protection for the herd, or addressed as a gesture of supplication to various deities during the sohrai baha and karom festivals[44] the gift was meant, in each case, to neutralize the malignity of the supernatural powers and coax a boon out of them if possible. This no doubt was the intention of the leaders of the hool as we learn from Chotrae Desmanjhi's account of its preparation. 'Before the rebellion started', he said, 'oil and vermilion in leaf cups were sent by Sido and Kanhu and taken round from village to village to placate the bongas so that they might help in the fight'.[45] Considering the outcome of the fight it is by no means certain that the *bongas* were sufficiently placated. What however is beyond doubt is that these objects put thus in circulation were understood to convey not only a propitiatory message addressed to the spirits but a militant message addressed to the Santals to prepare for resistance. In this manner a traditional symbol was fitted with a new meaning. This homonymy helped not merely to propagate the insurrection but also brought to the latter a touch of the ritual sanctity implicit in its original function.

The pacification of the Santal districts had been hardly completed when in another part of the country the government was

[43] JP, 4 Oct. 1855.

[44] For these and other uses of tel-sindur in Santal tradition, see MHKRK: *ciii, cxx, cli, clix, clx, clxii, clxvi.*

[45] Desmanjhi: 232.

alerted by a signal even more widespread and less comprehensible than anything witnessed during the hool. This was the chapati, the flat unleavened bread made of wheat, maize or barley flour, which constitutes a staple of the popular diet in many regions of the subcontinent. Its circulation during the winter of 1856–7, in what was then the North-Western Provinces, the scene of the great disturbances of the next two years, has been publicized more than any other sign of an Indian rebellion for reasons not only of its intrinsic importance but also of a historic miscognition. A symptom of collective anxiety and uneasiness in an agrarian society poised on the brink of a violent upheaval, it was regarded by some as the index of a conspiracy behind the Mutiny. This error has however had its uses: by mistaking the sign of a spreading unrest among the peasantry for that of a sepoy rebellion it has helped to underline the ambiguity generated by their overlap.

The essentially peasant character of this phenomenon is acknowledged in all accounts. According to one of these, 'A chowkeedar appears in the village adjoining his own with two small chupattees, which he delivers to his brother chowkeedar, with an injunction to make six others—to be then delivered by him, two and two, to the chowkeedars of the adjacent villages with instructions to act in a similar manner: each chowkeedar was to keep two for presentation to the hakim or "when called for". Obedience was paid to the instructions and the cakes were passed on rapidly from village to village.'[46] Not all observers agreed about the number of chapatis alleged to have changed hands at each point of the relay, but the fact that it increased by geometric progression and coursed with the utmost speed through much of upper India, has never been doubted.

There is, however, nothing in contemporary evidence to tell us what the circulating chapati meant. There is no trace left in the records of the interpretation put on it by the peasants *at the time*. As for the authorities, they identified it as a signal as soon as it appeared, but did not know how to read its message. The reaction of the Magistrate of Gurgaon was typical of the initial sense of bewilderment among the local administrators. 'I have the honour to inform you', he wrote to the Commissioner of Delhi on 19 February 1857 reporting one of the earlier

[46] Carey: 10.

official sightings, 'that a signal has passed through [a] number of villages of this district, the purport of which has not yet transpired.'[47] A fortnight later the *Friend of India*, that faithful echo of Anglo-Indian opinion, was still wondering, 'What does it mean?' And after a week when the circulation had already reached Awadh, it was obviously no wiser and referred to the matter as 'still a mystery'.[48]

All this should make it clear that there is no way at all of knowing whether or not the chapati had anything to do with the uprisings of 1857. Yet the attempt on the part of some bureaucrats and scholars to decipher it after the event and the size of the literature this has inspired are a measure of the urge for an understanding of insurgency in terms of the processes of its transmission. At a certain official level this urge expressed itself in the search for a prime cause and helped by an obvious predilection, spawned a conspiracy theory. It was then easy to read into this hitherto inexplicable relay a meaning appropriate to that theory and brand it, in retrospect, as the signal of the troubles just experienced. Before the Mutiny contemporary opinion close to government circles appears to have denied itself the temptation 'to detect a fiery cross in these local substitutes for a hot-cross bun'.[49] But once the post-mortem began, the analogy was quick to insinuate its way into some, though by no means all, of the most influential writings on the subject, as, for instance, into Holmes's classic account which described the chapatis as passing 'from village to village through the length and breadth of the North-Western Provinces like the fiery cross that summoned the clans-men of Roderick to battle'.[50]

This is worth some reflection as more than a simple literary curiosity. It represents the misreading of a *symbol* as an *index*. Jakobson, following Peirce, distinguishes between the two types of signs by saying that 'the index acts chiefly by a factual, existential contiguity between its signans and signatum', whereas

[47] Ibid.: 9. [48] FSUP: I 390–1. [49] Carey: 10.

[50] Holmes: 90. Like many others who subscribed to a modified version of the conspiracy theory Holmes identified the chapati not as what triggered off the uprising directly but as a signal which alarmed the Indians about the subversion of their religions by official policy and helped thus to generalize the discontent that led to the rebellion of 1857. 'The meaning of the portent has never been positively discovered', he wrote, 'but it is certain that many of the natives regarded it as a warning that Government was plotting the overthrow of their religion.' (Ibid.)

'the symbol acts chiefly by imputed, learned contiguity between signans and signatum', that is, by a conventional rule. 'The knowledge of this conventional rule is obligatory for the interpreter of any given symbol, and solely and simply because of this rule will the sign actually be interpreted.'[51] The colonial administrators and British writers close to them were not familiar with the rule by which the symbol of the circulating chapati could be identified. Some of them therefore sought to extract its meaning in terms of a convention pertinent to their own culture and rooted in their own history, and ended up by identifying it as the index of a preconcerted design to destroy the Raj. It is as a symptom of this miscognition that the 'fiery cross' haunts their discourse.

Yet for every official or semi-official statement to this effect there were others which dismissed this entire notion as fanciful. These came mostly from local administrators who, hardly wiser about the meaning of this phenomenon themselves, were clear-headed enough to see through the retrospective character of its designation as a cause of the Mutiny. In one such statement published within a year of the rebellion R. H. W. Dunlop, a magistrate who had found chapatis going round his district, Meerut, in February–March 1857, commented on these attempts 'to connect this cake distribution with our disturbances' as 'without any sufficient grounds'. It was his view that 'if any connexion existed it was accidental and the relationship acknowledged by either designing or ignorant persons was consequent upon the distribution and did not cause or precede it'. The point was made even more strongly and lucidly by yet another district magistrate—that of Budaon. 'I truly believe', he wrote in July 1857, 'that the rural population of all classes, among whom these cakes spread, were as ignorant as I was myself of their real object; but it was clear they were a secret sign to be on the alert, and the minds of the people were through them kept watchful and excited. As soon as the disturbances broke out at Meerut and Delhi, the cakes explained themselves, and the people at once perceived what was expected of them.'[52] Scepticism such as this has been fully vindicated by all subsequent research, and historians like Majumdar and Sen have

[51] Jakobson (1971): 347.
[52] Dunlop: 26; Edwards: 15–16.

established beyond doubt that the chapati was more of a red herring than a fiery cross.

However, the proof of there being no causal connection between the relay of chapatis and the outbreak of the rebellion, as dreamt up in some Anglo-Indian circles, does not exhaust the question of their mutual association. For many others who lived through those times also linked the distribution with the disturbances, and did so retrospectively as well. But their perception differed in two important respects. First, the former ascribed a preterite function to the sign: it was, as they understood it, an index of some pre-existing plot. By contrast, those other observers regarded it as predictive, in fact as an omen the purpose of which, according to Toporov, is 'the reduction of entropy in the language of events'—that is, to anticipate the future, so that 'no event can be considered absolutely unexpected and independent from the viewpoint of the most powerful of possible semiotic analyzers'.[53] In other words, its 'mode of being' was that of a symbol which, to put it in Peirce's words, 'enables us to predict the future' as against an index which 'has the being of a present experience'.[54] Secondly, it is important to recognize that these conflicting interpretations derived from two utterly different cultural codes which had little in common between them. The 'conventional rule' used by the British to interpret the sign was based on the tradition of popular mobilization in rural Scotland; that used by other contemporaries, mostly Indians, on the ritual of immunization against epidemics.

A cholera epidemic had swept through much of what corresponds to the modern Indian states of Uttar Pradesh and Madhya Pradesh during the year before the Mutiny. It had nearly spent its force in some regions while in others it was either still quite active or simply lingering on and the fear of its recrudescence was very much alive indeed when the chapatis began to circulate.[55] The latter, occurring as it did in this context, was interpreted by many at the time as a traditional technique of disease prevention which was fairly widespread in northern India. 'Its real origin was', according to Dunlop, 'a superstitious attempt to prevent any return of the fearful visita-

[53] Toporov: 159, 160. [54] Jakobson (1971): 358.

[55] For some contemporary evidence about this see Dunlop: 24–6; S. A. Khan: 3; and Keating to Hamilton quoted in S. N. Sen: 400.

tion of epidemic cholera'.[56] The superstition was not uniquely Indian and is known to have existed in a number of other pre-industrial societies, too. Its practice in northern India, described in much detail by William Crooke,[57] involved the symbolic use of a ritually consecrated object or animal to act as the carrier of an epidemic which had broken out in a locality or was about to do so, and push it beyond its boundaries. This, it was believed, would guarantee recovery or protection from the actual or the potential disease by transferring it from the protagonists to the community next door.

This technique was known, appropriately enough, as *chalawa* 'which', says Crooke, 'means passing on the malady'. It was so structured as to permit the use of a variety of transmitters for passing on the same pestilence irrespective of whether its victims were people or cattle and conversely, the use of the same transmitter for passing on a number of different epidemics.[58] Thus, taking the region as a whole, the range of

[56] Dunlop: 26.

[57] Our information on disease transference is based on Crooke (1968): I 141–2, 144, 146, 164–70. Crooke's work on this subject has, apart from its intrinsic merit, the added historical value of a record of beliefs collected within a few decades of the Mutiny in regions both affected by the cholera and involved in the distribution of chapati in 1856–7.

[58] An analysis of fifteen cases of *chalawa* described by Crooke (ibid.: 142–4, 166–7, 169–70) indicates the following pattern of correspondence between the diseases and their transmitters:

(*A*) *Disease* → *Transmitter*

disease	*transmitter*
cattle disease	buffalo skull etc., fowl
cholera	buffalo, fowl, goat; Chamar; filth, image, rice
influenza	buffalo
smallpox	pig; filth

(*B*) *Transmitter* → *Disease*

transmitter	*disease*
buffalo	cattle disease, cholera, influenza
Chamar	cholera
filth	cholera, smallpox
fowl	cattle disease, cholera
goat	cholera
image	cholera
pig	smallpox
rice	cholera

instruments for the transfer of cholera could include images of the cholera goddess, doles of rice collected from the local residents, filth and sweepings picked up from the affected villages, domestic animals such as goats, buffaloes and fowl, or as in the case of an exceptionally cruel custom reported from Punjab, Chamars 'branded on the buttocks and turned out of the village'.[59] Clearly, in the mechanics of this paradigmatic substitution where man and beast and inanimate object could stand in for each other as a signal for the same message, the chapati had come to acquire a place for itself as yet another vehicle of chalawa by 1856. In fact it was identified precisely as such and by this very name by a contemporary northern Indian observer whom Sen quotes as saying that the chapatis 'were mere chalawas to stop the progress of some disease'.[60]

However, the procedure provided for substitutability the other way round too, and the same carrier could be put to work for the transference of more than one disease—buffalo for influenza, cholera and cattle disease, fowl for cholera and rinderpest, village filth for smallpox and cholera, and so on. This helped, in certain contexts, to expand the symbolic meaning of these instruments. How this happened in the case of the chapati which had by this time gained currency as a magical transmitter too, may be illustrated by the testimony of an Indian thanadar at Paharganj just outside the city of Delhi. Recorded after the event like other statements of this kind it reads in part:

> I received an order from Sir Theophilus Metcalfe, then Joint Magistrate at Delhi, to report privately what I believed to be the origin of the matter [i.e. the distribution of chapatis]. I wrote that I had heard from my father how, in the downfall of the Mahratta power, a sprig of china (or millet) and a morsel of bread had passed from village to village, and that it was more than probable that the distribution of this bread was significant of some great disturbance which would follow immediately.[61]

Clearly we have an instance here of a visual sign acquiring a new meaning in much the same way as 'shifts in application' of words and figurative usage tend to generate polysemy in natural languages.[62] The power of analogy seems to have helped to shift the sense of the circulating chapati from pathology to

[59] Ibid.: 170.
[60] S. N. Sen: 399.
[61] Metcalfe: 40–1.
[62] Ullmann: 159–61.

politics: a carrier of one kind of catastrophe it came now to symbolize, by a semantic slide, a catastrophe of an altogether different kind and the calamity that had overtaken the Maratha empire was believed to be about to visit the British too. The sign was thus assigned a predictive function—the function of an omen exuding evil forebodings. However, it is by no means clear what was being predicted in this case except that it was an unspecified kind of 'some great disturbance'. Such vagueness of meaning which arises from the multiplicity of the aspects of a sign and makes for polysemy,[63] is indeed an essential characteristic of an omen. For the latter, as Toporov has defined it, is a 'signal . . . in which the true signal . . . is hidden, masked or distorted by . . . noise' creating, among other things, a sense of 'indefiniteness' about it.[64] This is why omens appear in 'moments of collision' when the generally accepted semioticization of a social or political order comes under question and unforeseen options are opened up, when for instance the foundations of a ruling power are seriously threatened as were those of the German and Austrian monarchies by the peasant wars of the sixteenth century[65] or of the Raj by the revolt of 1857.

It is also as a function of the noise in their signalling systems that omens tend to attract different and often mutually conflicting interpretations. In this respect they are, contrary to R. C. Majumdar's ingenious suggestion, very unlike indeed the so-called 'chain letters' current in many parts of India.[66] Unsolicited and of unknown origin as a rule, one of these bearing usually a religious (or occasionally, a religio-political) message would reach an addressee by post with the command that he should, on pain of dire consequences, make a stated number of copies of the text and send each of these to a friend or relative. The 'chain' in the case of this curious and as Majumdar says, powerful device operates in just the same way as the chapatis did on the eve of the Mutiny, that is, by geometrical progression. But there the similarity ends. The manner in which the system of meanings in the two missives works, is altogether different. The graphic character of the 'chain letter' keeps its

[63] Ibid.: 124–5, 159–60. [64] Toporov: 160–1.

[65] For some instances of the sighting of omens during the peasant wars of the sixteenth century, see Zimmermann: I 87, 184.

[66] Majumdar: 209.

meaning firmly tied to the text: in fact, the addressee is specifically warned by his anonymous correspondent not to alter the message in the least, which is precisely what makes it the very reverse of the omen. The vague and indefinite character of the message carried by the latter keeps it wide open to various degrees of semantic modification at each point of its passage between communicators.

It is no wonder, therefore, that the circulating chapati, as a witness at Bahadur Shah's trial testified, 'had different meanings for different people'.[67] Zimmermann too has remarked how during the peasant revolts of 1525 in central Europe popular excitement was caused as much by the reported sightings of 'unusual phenomena in the sky and on earth'—rings round the sun and the moon, the mark of torches and crosses on the surface of these heavenly bodies, deformed animal births, aerial battles fought between flocks of birds, and so on—as by their confused interpretations.[68] Similarly the welter of meanings read in the relay of chapatis, too, produced more smoke than light and helped to darken the minds of men by a premonition of some impending disaster. The thanadar of Paharganj remembered it as 'an event which undoubtedly created a feeling of great alarm in the native mind throughout Hindoostan'.[69] And Sherer who lived through those times, confirmed this impression. 'If the transmission of these cakes was only intended to create a mysterious uneasiness', he wrote, 'that object was gained.'[70] Evidently, the chapati, though by no means a cause of the disturbances of 1857–8, was still not altogether unrelated to them. The symbolic agent of an epidemic in the countryside it took on an added meaning as the carrier of an imminent but undefined political holocaust. No index of any kind of conspiracy, it connected neither with the past nor with the present. As an omen it looked ahead of events, and in an atmosphere charged with growing unrest in agrarian communities and army barracks it transmitted the rebellion in anticipation by sounding a tocsin for all to hear but none yet to understand why.

The verbal transmission of insurgency was of course inseparable in practice from the aural and the visual and yet distinctive

[67] S. N. Sen: 399. [68] Zimmermann: I 184.
[69] Metcalfe: 39. [70] Sherer: 7–8.

enough to constitute a class by itself. Of its modalities, graphic and non-graphic, the former varied in articulation according to whether its constitutive messages were more or less opaque and subject to corresponding degrees of semantic change. The propagation of a rebellion was sometimes sought to be achieved by a clearly motivated kind of writing. To this category belonged the letters circulated by the Rangpur insurgents in 1783 'ordering the ryots to assemble and join them and threatening to burn their houses and destroy their crops in case of their refusal and delay'.[71] Nothing, again, could be more transparent than the 'treasonable document' found on the person of a Santal courier as he was arrested by the colonial authorities while crossing the Barakar river on 22 September 1855. Described as 'a perwannah or order from one Thakoor to another' it read in translation: 'The bearer will give you the particulars. The man has come here & been well beaten. Send the two men. The power is now ours, for the past what of it, & for the future there is no fear. Take notice.'[72]

Rebel communication by means of such written messages was of course not widely prevalent in a country where illiteracy was as high as in rural India under the Raj. Writing was socially privileged. The production of verbal messages in graphic form for purposes of insurgency was feasible only when individuals of elite origin were induced by circumstance or conscience or a combination of both to make common cause with the peasantry, or when a few among the latter had managed, against all odds, to acquire the rudiments of literacy and put these at the service of an uprising. Occasionally one comes across instances of both kinds in the history of our peasant movements: some members of the impoverished rural gentry were indeed involved in the Rangpur dhing, the indigo rebellion, the Pabna bidroha and so on, while a few persons—one of them a Dom and another a 'Joolha'—are mentioned in the records of the hool as having helped the Santals with reading and writing.[73] But the in-

[71] MDS: 580.

[72] JP, 8 Nov. 1855: Ward to GOB (13 Oct. 1855).

[73] The names of Dirjenarain, Mathuranath Acharya and Ishanchandra Ray come readily to one's mind as members of the gentry who distinguished themselves by siding with the peasants in the dhing, the indigo rebellion and the Pabna movement respectively. See MDS: 579–80; S. C. Mitra: II 790; JP(P): Tayler to Commissioner (July 1873). For the names of some of those who helped the Santals in

cidence of such elite participation or subaltern literacy was not high enough to make the written propagation of rebellion anything but exceptional.

However, it was not only the production of writing for insurgency that was adversely affected by illiteracy. The want of literacy also made the peasants relate occasionally to a written utterance in such a way as to destroy its original motivation by deverbalizing it and exploit the resulting opacity in order to provide that graphic representation with new 'signifieds' (*signifiés*). Lefebvre has cited some classic instances of this genre. During the French Revolution, he says, 'the rebels were rather tempted to support their claims by showing printed or handwritten posters to peasants who could not read'. On one occasion, stolen copies of some seventy-year old official decrees were displayed 'to encourage the listening crowd', and on another, a printed booklet about legal matters concerning a particular property was flaunted as 'the King's orders' justifying the uprising.[74]

In the Santal rebellion of 1855 too we have an example of such separation between the content of a verbal message and its graphic expression and the uses made of the latter for the transmission of insurgency. For some of the papers which were supposed to have conveyed the Thakur's own command in writing to launch the hool and carried by Kanhu on his person as both an emblem of authority and an instrument of mobilization, proved on scrutiny to contain among other things 'an old Book on locomotive[s], a few visiting cards of Mr Burn Engineer' and if the testimony of the semi-official *Calcutta Review* (1856) article is to be believed, a translation in some Indian language of the Gospel according to St John.[75] What is even more remarkable is that the rest of the papers said to have dropped from heaven and regarded by the Santal leaders as evidence of divine support for the insurrection had nothing in-

---

this respect see JP, 6 Sept. 1855: 'Deposition of Dhunwa Manjhee etc.'; J.P., 8 Nov. 1855: 'Examination of Sedoo Sonthal late Thacoor'.

[74] Lefebvre (1973): 96.

[75] JP, 20 Dec. 1855: 'Statement of Insurgent Sonthals'; CR: 245. Also see Bidwell to Richardson (30 Aug. 1855) in JP, 6 Sept. 1855: 'The Sonthal priest taken yesterday produced part of the New Testament in Hindee which he had been using in the performance of all his religious rites.'

scribed on them at all either in writing or in print. 'All the blank papers fell from heaven & the book in which all the pages are blank also fell from heaven', said Kanhu.[76] Clearly thus the conditions of a pre-literate culture made it possible for insurgency to propagate itself not only by means of the graphic form of an utterance divorced from its content but indeed by the writing material acting on its own unscored by graphemes. The principle governing such extension was essentially the same as that of the 'drinking of the word' known in some of the islamicized parts of Africa. There the ink or the pigment used for inscribing holy or magical formulae on paper, papyrus, slate or skin and believed to be invested by the sanctity of the message itself, would be washed off and swallowed as a cure for certain ailments.[77] However, there was a difference. While the metonymic projection of supernatural faculties from written word to writing material was used in such instances to leave the cure of physical illness to Allah's grace, the Santals used it merely to legitimize their attempt to remedy the ills of the world by their own arms.

One paradoxical outcome of this extension was to convert a verbal signal into a purely visual one. This was possible because of the two-dimensional character of written utterances, which, as Vachek has argued, distinguishes them clearly from spoken utterances.[78] But although the acoustic material which constituted the latter would permit no manipulation of meaning in quite the same way, the propagation of insurgency by speech could also be subject, on its part, to cognitive hazards. This can be demonstrated by a comparison between the two principal types of this discourse which, like those in the previous category, differed according to the degree of their transparency.

The more transparent of spoken utterances of this kind included much of the common currency of non-graphic verbal exchange used by the peasants to mobilize themselves for an uprising. It was made up mostly of declarative and deontic statements of various kinds aimed at altering, informing and commanding a local population. It could be cool and deliberate like the announcements made by the Kol and Santal tribal councils to launch their respective insurrections in 1831 and 1855 or the

[76] JP, 20 Dec. 1855: 'Examination of Kanoo Sonthal'.

[77] Goody: 230–1. [78] Vachek (1964): 454.

purely factual messages about enemy troop movements communicated by rebels to their leaders; or hot and excited like the traditional night cries by which the villagers were warned and rallied during the 'blue mutiny' in the indigo districts of Bengal in 1860. The transmissive function of the latter was noticed thus in the columns of a journal during the Pabna bidroha of 1873 in terms of a historic parallel:

Those who were in India during the indigo disturbances often described the peculiar effect of the night cry in the villages which were opposed to the planters. It is a shout given by all the inhabitants of a village at night in chorus and taken up by . . . hamlet after hamlet. In some of the places where the agrarian question is most hot this shout may now be heard at night and very impressive effect it has showing more clearly than anything else the numbers and unanimity of the ryots.[79]

What all such discourses had in common despite variations of tone and idiom was that they related to one or the other of the practical aspects of insurgency and sought to mobilize the rural masses by means of clearly motivated messages. It was this firm empiricism which saved rebel communication of this particular type from any excessive semantic slide.

By contrast the other type of speech which helped to spread insurgency was characterized by a relatively higher degree of opacity. The most common of all means used for the propagation of mass peasant violence in any pre-industrial society it was suited, both by expression and content, to serve as a particularly powerful vehicle of subaltern politics. It was made up of two kinds of utterances which were often telescoped in practice and may be broadly classified, for the convenience of description, as authored and anonymous. The former was distinguished by the fact that its origin could be traced to one or more known individuals. Many charismatic leaders of peasant rebellions in all lands and ages have contributed to the historic repertoire of this genre of spoken utterance. More often than not, it was indeed this kind of speech which formed the most effective component of their charisma. For unlike the other type of non-graphic discourse the relation it had to an uprising was not a strictly empirical one. It was made up of words and expressions which had their referents in a universe beyond the lived,

[79] *Indian Daily News* quoted in *Indian Observer*, 28 June 1873 (Sen Gupta: 40).

practical domain of an insurrection and represented the urge for a change in the conditions of this world as a kind of other-worldliness. Its function was thus to shift the context of a rebellion from the real and the empirical towards the surreal and the mythical just as the feline subject of Baudelaire's well-known sonnet, made doubly famous by Jakobson and Lévi-Strauss, is winched out of domesticity by some figures of speech and fitted into a cosmic, astral frame.[80] Thanks to the referential opacity characteristic of such discourse the mediation of the practical and social aspects of insurgency by myth articulated itself as a mediation of the ideology of class struggle by religion. In India, as elsewhere, therefore, the leaders of some of the mightiest peasant revolts spoke in the inspired language of prophets and reformers—Titu Mir of an Islamic kingdom to come, Sido and Kanhu of the hool as a project fabricated in heaven, Birsa of his war on the Raj as an exercise in a new ethic and the harbinger of an Era of Truth (*Satjug*). This is one reason why the politics of our peasant rebellions was almost invariably expressed in sacred idioms and some of the most militant movements of the rural masses, such as those of the Satnamis, Farazis, Birsaites, etc., ended up, apotheosized, as faiths and sects.

None of the signals discussed so far helped more to spread an insurrection than anonymous speech in its classic form—rumour. This was of course by no means a uniquely Indian experience. One would perhaps be quite justified in saying that rumour is both a *universal* and *necessary* carrier of insurgency in any pre-industrial, pre-literate society. An unmistakable, if indirect, acknowledgement of its power is the historically known concern for its suppression and control on the part of those who in all such societies had the most to lose by rebellion. The Roman emperors were sensitive enough to rumour to engage an entire cadre of officials—*delatores*—in collecting and reporting it, while in 1789 the French farmers found it to their advantage to want 'to put a stop to the rumours, excitements and seditious chatter on the part of the lower orders in the

[80] Jakobson & Lévi-Strauss, '*Les Chats* de Charles Baudelaire' in Jakobson (1973): 401–19. See especially p. 416 for the correspondence between *empirique/mythologique* and *réel/irréel-surréel* which is the sense in which we have used these terms in this section.

market place'. In India governmental anxiety about rumours can be traced as far back as the Kautilyan state. 'Spies shall also know the rumours prevalent in the state', prescribes the *Arthaśāstra*.[81] Many centuries later gathering rumours was still a routine chore with the colonial bureaucracy, especially in periods of war and unsettled political conditions as witness that familiar rubric in the weekly and fortnightly intelligence reports in the *Home (Political) Series* at the National Archives of India.

Vigilance such as this on the part of the authorities was of course fully justified from *their* point of view. For in no country with a predominantly illiterate population has subaltern protest of any significant strength ever exploded without its charge being conducted over vast areas by rumour. The phenomenon has indeed been found to be so common and its incidence so large as to look like 'a law of social psychology' to some scholars. As Allport and Postman have put it in their well-known study of the subject, '*No riot ever occurs without rumours to incite, accompany and intensify the violence*.'[82] All historical accounts of violent crowd behaviour from Livy to Lefebvre would tend to confirm this. The former has left us with some memorable evidence of the play of rumour on popular passions in the course of the many conflicts between patricians and plebeians in ancient Rome.[83] For the Middle Ages too we have an indication from Froissart that, thanks to rumour, 'the things he [John Ball] was doing and saying [in Kent] came to the ears of the common people of London, who were envious of the nobles and the rich' and mobilized them for the peasant revolt of 1381 led by Wat Tyler. Blum has observed how rumour helped to rally the Russian serfs to Pugachev's standard in 1773–5. In France, as Rudé has demonstrated it, many of the grain riots of the decade preceding the Great Revolution were stimulated by rumour while the Swing movement of the English agricultural labourers in 1830 too was enlarged in scope by the same verbal means. In Tanzania a spate of rumours concerning a 'magic medicine' and the extraordinary powers of its dispenser, Kinjikitile of Ngarambe, prepared the ground for the Maji Maji rebellion of

[81] Allport and Postman: 159; Lefebvre (1973): 27; Kauṭilya: 23.

[82] Allport & Postman: 193. Emphasis as in the original.

[83] For a typical sample see Livy: 178–9.

1905.[84] One could go on piling up instances of this truly ubiquitous form of insurgent communication in many lands at many times. But for our present purpose it may suffice to represent the spirit of them all by an extract from Lefebvre's great work on the power of rumour as manifested in the uprisings in rural France in 1789. He wrote:

The vast majority of the French people depended entirely on oral tradition for the dissemination of news . . . But for the government and the aristocracy, this means of transmission was a great deal more dangerous than freedom of the press. It goes without saying that it favoured the spread of false reports, the distortion and exaggeration of fact, the growth of legends . . . In the empty silence of the provinces, every word had the most extraordinary resonance and was taken as gospel. In due course, the rumour would reach the ears of a journalist who would imbue it with new strength by putting it into print . . . Indeed, what was the Great Fear if not one gigantic rumour?[85]

In many respects the panic that spread in the wake of some of the rural uprisings in colonial India too was the work of a series of gigantic rumours. The alarm caused by the Kol insurrection of 1832 led to the desertion of villagers even from those parts of Palamau district which were not implicated in the rebellion at all. In the Jungle Mahals many of the propertied people buried their wealth underground fearing for the worst. Towns as far removed from the area affected by insurgency as Mirzapur and Banaras were caught up in the panic. Totally unfounded reports about the sack of Mirzapur, an uprising in Azimgarh and even of Maratha reinforcements on the rebel side—all duly duplicated in the press and endowed thereby with a spurious authority—added further to consternation among the suds and flight from the countryside.[86]

One such panic which seized Pakur at the outbreak of the Santal hool has been vividly described by a contemporary who, as a child, had lived through it all.

Then [he recalled] there arose loud wailings of the females, children shrieked and screamed, men talked nonsense and rushed hither and thither without any fixed aim; fathers left aside their crying children

[84] Froissart: 213; Blum: 556; Rudé's 'Introduction' to Lefebvre (1973): *xiv-xv*; H & R: 198–200, 215–19; Gwassa & Iliffe: 11–12.

[85] Lefebvre (1973): 73–4.

[86] BC 1363 (54226): Russell to Braddon (18 Apr. 1832).

unheeded; no one cared for the old, the infirm and the sickly. There was tying and untying of bundles, everything turned upside down and mixed up helter and skelter promiscuously. In short, a confused and heart-rending scene ensued which can be better imagined than described . . . The fear and anxiety with which the terrible long night passed away, beggar any description. But long before the day dawned almost the whole village became empty . . . In this sad plight the villagers left their homes not knowing where to go, what food to give to the children when they would cry from hunger. All the eatables, all the money, utensils, furniture, in short, everything they possessed was left behind, their only aim and only object being to put as much distance as possible between the Santals and themselves.[87]

Something like the same 'indescribable panic' swept through Khunti and Ranchi, too, during the Birsaite revolt of 1900.[88] And to avoid the facile misconception that all this was merely the diku's response to tribal violence, one should refer to similar instances of fear generated by the Barasat and Pabna bidrohas. On the former occasion the authorities apprehended the desertion of all the police darogas from their posts in the neighbourhood 'now that this panic has spread abroad', while on the latter the local gentry sought official protection against their own Bengali projas, for, they complained, 'neither life, property, nor the family honour of the people is safe. The feeling of insecurity pervading the villages is so great that danger is apprehended at every place and every moment' and 'it has become difficult for gentlemen to protect their families and keep their honour any longer'.[89] Clearly the panic caused by rumour during any demonstration of peasant militancy cuts across ethnic lines.

However to emphasize only the alarmist aspect of rumour would be to miss its positive and indeed more important function in mobilizing for rebellion. In each of the instances mentioned above the anonymous verbal signal helped not merely to frighten those against whom a particular insurrection or jacquerie was directed, but above all, to spread the message of

[87] K. K. Datta: 71–2. For some instances of official acknowledgement of panic caused by the hool among civilians and troops at Murshidabad and Suri see JP, 4 Oct. 1855: Macgregor to Grey (18 Sept. 1855) and Ward to GOB (30 Sept. 1855). [88] Singh: 107–8.

[89] JC, 22 Nov. 1831: Smith to Thomason (17 Nov. 1831); JP(P): Tagore to GOB (1 July 1873); ibid.: Chuckurbutty, Rae & Bhowmic to GOB (1 July 1873).

revolt among the people. This was certainly true of the rebellion of 1857 which to many of its contemporaries was nothing but a direct outcome of the rumours that had preceded it throughout northern India. Typical of such an oversimplified view of what was indeed a complex happening were causal explanations of the kind mentioned below.

Previous to the outbreak, rumours to the following effect very generally prevailed:-

1st. That 2,000 sets of irons were being made by the sepoys.

2nd. That by order of government, attah mixed with bones was to be sold.

3rd. That the sepoys were to be deprived of the charge of their arms and ammunition.

These reports caused the disturbance.[90]

With all its naivety this deposition by Mohur Singh, a Deputy Collector of Meerut, came close to identifying what by all accounts was one of the most powerful factors in the mobilization of the subaltern masses for that event. For current after powerful current (to use Lefebvre's aquatic metaphor) of unfounded and unverifiable reports about greased cartridges, flour polluted by bone meal and forcible conversion to Christianity, about the disarming of native soldiers and official prohibition of agricultural work, about the coming end of British rule and the advent of a deliverer—about issues touching on indigenous sentiment at profound depths—merged into 'one gigantic rumour' and transformed the many disparate elements of popular grievance against the Raj into a war of sepoys and peasants.

In this respect 1857 was no exception. The statements of some of the Maratha peasants convicted of rioting against local moneylenders in 1875 illustrate the role of rumour in inspiring jacqueries. Here are a few extracts:

News came from Aligaon about a riot against the Wanis. People [of Supa] said that if we go to the Wanis they will give back our bonds. The first rumour was that they would give back a Rs. 100 bond and take one for Rs. 50 . . .

The villagers [of Ghospuri], hearing that the residents of the neigh-

[90] FSUP: I 392–3.

bouring villages have got back from sowkars their bonds by force, they also one day collected themselves and went to the shop of Moolchand Hakumchand and demanded from him all the bonds . . .

About 5 or 6 days before the row in my village [Sonsangwi] the villagers had heard that the residents of Kurdi Nimone have got back by force their bonds from the banias, and since then the villagers were thinking of doing the same in my village, which they ultimately did . . .

No wonder that the Commission appointed to investigate these disturbances came to the conclusion that '*in almost every case* the riot is stated to have commenced on news arriving of bonds having been extorted in some neighbouring village with the usual story that the Government approved of the rioters' action'.[91] In most other instances, too, of rural insurgency during the period under discussion rumour proved to be a powerful vehicle of the hopes and fears, of visions of doomsdays and golden ages, of secular objectives and religious longings, all of which made up the stuff that fired the minds of men.

It is precisely in this role of the trigger and mobilizer that rumour becomes a necessary instrument of rebel transmission. The necessity derives of course from the cultural conditions in which it operates. For the want of literacy in a pre-capitalist society makes its subaltern population depend almost exclusively on visual and non-graphic verbal signals for communication among themselves, and between these two again rather more on the latter because of the relatively greater degree of its versatility and comprehensibility. But it is also by virtue of its character as a type of speech that rumour serves as the most 'natural' and indeed indispensable vehicle of insurgency. This point needs some emphasis, for it is only by working out its implications for an agrarian disturbance that one can come fully to appreciate the contribution of rumour in developing it into a mass event and influencing its ideology.

Rumour is spoken utterance *par excellence*, and speaking, as linguists say, differs from writing not merely in material, that is, by the fact of its acoustic rather than graphic realization, but in function. It is this aspect of the difference which is the 'more profound and more essential' according to Vachek.

[91] DRCR: 3; 'Depositions of Convicted Rioters at Present in the Poona and Yerauda Jails' in DRCR (B): 3, 9, 14.

Speech, he says, responds to any given stimulus more urgently, emotionally and dynamically than written utterance.[92] It is this functional immediacy which develops in rumour its characteristic drive to seize upon important issues in periods of social tension[93] and create a large public audience for them. Prasad in his well-known study of the reactions to the Bihar earthquake of 1934 noticed how anyone who heard a rumour at that time had an 'almost uncontrollable impulse to pass it on to another person', and Schachter and Burdick too, working on American material, have found rumour to be 'a chain pattern of communication' in which the 'possession of the item of information' by an individual 'seems to create a force to communicate further'.[94] This force or impulse is what makes rumour bring people together. 'Passing on a rumour involves a desire on the part of the transmitter to affect other people's behavior, to bring their perspectives in line with his own, or, at the very minimum, to share a valuable bit of information.'[95] That is, 'the communication of a report to other members of the group implies an underlying bond of community among the members'. It helps to evoke a 'comradeship response' which, as was observed during the Bihar disaster, made the community 'less one in which superiors confronted inferiors and more one in which all people were pretty much on an equality'.[96]

The solidarity generated thus by the 'uncontrollable' force of its transmission confers on rumour two of its characteristic tendencies as realized in time and space. First, it is precisely to this socializing process that rumour owes its phenomenal speed. This, according to Prasad, was at least 'a part of the explanation of the rapid transmission of the stories and prophecies of disaster' which followed the Bihar earthquake. Rumours about man-made cataclysms, too, travelled equally fast. The news of the anti-usury riots in Poona district in September 1875 were known to have triggered off similar disturbances in almost no time at Kukrur in the Satara collectorate

[92] Vachek (1966): 153, 154.

[93] Allport and Postman have identified importance as one of the two essential conditions of rumour, the other being ambiguity (Allport & Postman: 33–4, 36 *et passim*). See also Schachter & Burdick: 296. For the prevalence of rumour during social crises, see Vansina: 118.

[94] Prasad: 11. [95] Lang & Lang: 65. [96] Prasad: 11, 14.

over a hundred miles away.[97] Kaye who, as a historian of the sepoy war, had to deal with some of the vast collections of rumour produced by that event, commented, in some despair, about 'a certain description of news, which travels in India, from one station to another, with a rapidity almost electric' and which, dismissed lightly by the English officers, 'had travelled another hundred miles whilst the white gentlemen, with bland scepticism, were shaking their heads over the lies of the Bazaar'.[98]

To describe rumour as 'the lies of the Bazaar' is to wrap up in a pejorative the truth about its other tendency which is to originate in places where people assemble in large numbers. Since it is at the market-place where perhaps more than anywhere else in a pre-industrial society people gather regularly at frequent intervals and *en masse* for trade and certain forms of folk entertainment, the socializing process of rumour too tends to operate most actively there. It is thus that the verbal exchange which, as discussed above, constitutes the transitive function of rumour, comes to affirm its own identity as a type of popular discourse by virtue of its intimate association with economic exchange so essential to the life of the people. Lefebvre whose keen eye missed nothing that was significant in inciting the jacqueries of the year of the Great French Revolution, emphasized the importance of this association. The tales taken back by the country labourers from the markets, especially after outbreaks of riot there, and told in their own villages, would often, he wrote, 'spread revolt among their fellows and fear among the farmers'.[99]

In India the bazaar was clearly identified in colonialist thinking with the origin and dissemination of rumour. As the intelligence records of the Raj so amply testify, official espionage kept its ears firmly glued to the bazaars throughout India and at all levels from the village upwards. For much more than in the council chambers and lecture halls ringing with elite voices it was there that the government could get 'some idea of the standpoint from which they [the masses] regard the actions of their foreign rulers'.[100] Sensitivity to 'bazaar gup' was, of course, at its most acute among the officials when the regime

[97] DRCR: 3. [98] K & M: I 361, 362.
[99] Lefebvre (1973): 27. [100] Oman: 218.

felt seriously threatened by enemies abroad as in times of war or by those within as in times of popular revolt. No wonder therefore that this is mentioned so often and indeed so obsessively in Kaye's celebrated history of the rebellion of 1857, written from a point of view identified with imperialist interests. The talk of the market-place, he insists, was an authentic register of a great deal of the most useful intelligence 'especially if the news imported something disastrous to the British'.[101] So in his narrative he draws liberally on material linking the rumours in circulation at the local bazaars with the spreading disaffection in sepoy 'lines' on the eve of each of the series of massive explosions—at Barrackpore, at Meerut, at Kanpur and so on—which reverberate throughout that monumental work.[102] We have thus in the life of that great rebellion as well as in its reconstitution in historiography a clear acknowledgement of the correspondence between the public discourse of rumour and the popular act of insurrection, that is, of the collaterality of word and deed issuing from a common will of the people.

To regard rumour as lying is not merely a measure of the distance between a typical site of collective discourse and an ideal seat of official truth—between the bazaar and the bungalow, so to say. But it is also the result of an ill-conceived assimilation of rumour to news. Kaye in characterizing the former as 'a certain description of news' shares with other elitist writers the fairly common error of lumping these together and identifying one as merely a corrupted version of the other. In fact, however, no two kinds of verbal communication could be more different. They differ in two important respects.[103] In the first place, the source of news is necessarily identifiable: its message is open to verification by being retraced to the point of its origin and the bearer is considered accountable for its accuracy in most cases. By contrast, rumour is necessarily anonymous and its origin unknown (even though on occasions,

[101] K & M: I 361.

[102] The instances are far too numerous to cite, but see K & M: I 394–5, 415, 417–18 *et passim*.

[103] There is a fairly elaborate discussion of the distinction between rumour and news in Lang & Lang: 58–64. My understanding of the distinction agrees with theirs on the question of source; however, what they describe as a distinction of channel is perhaps more of a distinction of process.

as we shall presently see, a fictive source may be assigned to it). Hence, its message cannot be authenticated by any reference to a source nor can its purveyor be asked to guarantee its accuracy or answer for its effects in any way. Secondly, the process of transmission implies, in the case of news, a necessary distinction between the communicator and his audience. No such distinction exists in the case of rumours which are passed on 'from a teller to a hearer who himself becomes a teller'—an instance of absolute transitivity. In other words, the encoding and decoding of rumour are collapsed, unlike news, at each point of its relay.

Quite clearly rumour belongs to a class apart from news. An autonomous type of popular discourse, it may perhaps be more properly regarded as one of those 'intermediate forms' which lie, according to Lévi-Strauss, between the two poles of tale and myth.[104] The characteristic they all have in common is ambiguity. This, it has been said, is essential to the making of a rumour[105]—a generalization amply confirmed by the experience of some of the great insurrectionary movements in the colonial world. The story which spread, for instance, on the eve of the Maji Maji rebellion about a wonder drug passed on by a snake-like spirit to a medicine man of Ngarambe was apparently 'understood in a rather hazy way by the many people who made pilgrimage to the medicine man'.[106] There was much the same kind of 'cognitive unclarity' too about the 'vague reports of some coming danger which no one could define' as they circulated in northern India just before and during the Mutiny and the peasant revolts detonated by it. Kaye mentioned the 'expressive' vernacular saying, 'It is in the air', as an index of this elusive but inflammable haziness. 'It often happened', he writes, 'that an uneasy feeling—an impression that something had happened, though they "could not discern the shape thereof"—persuaded men's minds.'[107] Ambiguity such as this is indeed what makes rumour a mobile and explosive agent of insurgency, and it is a function precisely of those distinctive features which constitute its originality—namely, its anonymity and transitivity.

[104] Lévi-Strauss (1978): 130.

[105] Allport & Postman: 33–4 *et passim*; Schachter & Burdick: 296.

[106] Gwassa & Iliffe: 12.

[107] K & M: I 355, 361.

Anonymity gives rumour its openness, transitivity its freedom. Being of unknown origin rumour is not impaled on a given meaning for good in the same way as a discourse with a pedigree often is. 'To give a text an Author is to impose a limit on that text, to furnish it with a final signified, to close the writing.' This perceptive comment which we owe to Roland Barthes,[108] is of course true of spoken utterance as well. It explains why rumour, by contrast, is not sealed off by any 'final signified' emanating from a primal source, but remains open as a receptacle of new inputs of meaning. This openness is indeed the objective basis of that spontaneity which is exploited so well and so naturally by speech. For, as Vygotsky has observed, 'The speed of oral speech is unfavourable to a complicated process of formulation—it does not leave time for deliberation and choice. Dialogue implies immediate unpremeditated utterance. It consists of replies, repartees; it is a chain of reactions.'[109] This could be said of rumour too. Indeed, it has all those qualities of speed, immediacy, disposition for unreflecting response to stimulus, etc. developed more fully within it than perhaps in any other type of spontaneous discourse. And the 'uncontrollable impulse' which drives any of its interlocutors to pass it on to the next person in the relay, makes it a most perfect 'chain of reactions'.

Thanks to such transitivity and the social tension in which it operates, rumour functions as a free form liable to a considerable degree of improvisation as it leaps from tongue to tongue. The aperture which it has built into it by virtue of anonymity permits its message to be contaminated by the subjectivity of each of its speakers and modified as often as any of them would want to embellish or amend it in the course of transmission. The outcome of all this is a plasticity that enables it to undergo transformations similar to, though perhaps not to the same extent as, those which occur, according to Propp, in fairy tales.[110] The importance of these for the spread of mass disturbances can hardly be exaggerated. The additions, cuts and twists introduced into a rumour in the course of its circulation

[108] Barthes (1977): 147. [109] Vygotsky: 144.

[110] Some aspects of the transformation of rumour are described in Allport & Postman: *passim*. But these are not as numerous or varied as those analysed in Vladimir Propp's classic study, 'Les Transformations des Contes Fantastiques'.

transform its message (often just minimally) by such degrees as to adjust it to the variations within a given ideology or mode of popular expression and by doing so broaden the range of its address. In other words, improvisation contributes directly to the efficacy of rumour for rebel mobilization.

Since rumour is 'immediate unpremeditated utterance' (to recall Vygotsky once more), it is improvised within the rebel community not as a conscious device to rally the people, but spontaneously, without deliberation, that is, by the force of ideology alone, so far as the insurgents themselves are concerned. However, seen from the other side, from the standpoint of their adversaries, this transformative process could appear to be highly motivated. Fairly representative of such a standpoint is what Kaye wrote about a group of pollution rumours of 1857.[111] The most celebrated of these was the one relating to greased cartridges, which has passed into history as having triggered off the Mutiny. But fears about officially induced impurity and the consequent loss of faith 'were not confined to the military classes', we are told, 'but were disquieting also the general community'. He mentions the prevalence of 'a belief that the English designed to defile both Hindus and Muhammadans by polluting with unclean matter the daily food of the people'. However, in spite of the technical difference between the alleged media of defilement in the two sectors—cartridges for the army and food for the civilians—it was by no means two distinct sets of rumours but *variations of the same rumour* which generated the suspicions both among the sepoys and the public and mobilized them respectively for mutinies and jacqueries. To quote:

Now the disturbing rumour, cunningly circulated, took *many portentous shapes*. It was said that the officers of the British Government, under command from the Company and the Queen, had mixed *ground bones* with the *flour* and the *salt* sold in the Bazaars; that they had adulterated all the *ghi* with *animal fat*; that *bones had been burnt* with the common *sugar* of the country; and that not only *bone-dust flour*, but the *flesh* of *cows* and *pigs*, had been thrown into the wells to pollute the *drinking water* of the people. *Of this great imaginary scheme of contamination the matter of the greased cartridges was but a part, especially*

[111] The source of all direct quotations in this paragraph including the long extract at its end is K & M: I 416–17. Emphasis added.

addressed to one part of the community. All classes, it was believed, were to be defiled at the same time; and the story ran that the 'bara sahibs', or great English lords, had commanded all princes, nobles, landholders, merchants, and cultivators of the land, to feed together upon *English bread.*

Thus the variations on that single theme of defilement were addressed to all sections of the indigenous population (see Figure 2 below) and appeared, in the eyes of the authorities, as

Animal extracts as polluting agents	*Media of oral defilement*		*Sections of population affected by impurity*
	non-edible	*edible*	
fat	cartridge	. . . .	. . . . sepoys
fat	. . . .	ghee	. . . . all
flesh	. . . .	water	. . . . all
bone: burnt . . .	. . . .	country sugar	. . . . all
bone: ground	. . . .	flour and salt	. . . . all
all above	. . . .	'English bread'	. . . . all

Figure 2 Elements of a Pollution Rumour of 1857.

a shrewd unifying stratagem. Sepoys and civilians were brought together by a common suspicion—that of being polluted by oral contact with animal fat applied, inedibly, to cartridges in one case, and edibly, to ghee in the other. Then the amplitude of impurity was further extended: two other agents of animal extraction were included to cover four other edibles—flesh added to drinking water and bone burnt into country sugar as well as ground into flour and salt. Altogether five essential components of the common diet of all classes of people were thus represented as liable to pollution by three substances extracted from each of the two animals most prohibited under Hindu and Islamic alimentary rules. The threat to the 'general community' could not be more comprehensive. However, to leave nothing to chance the most impure of all food, 'English bread', believed to contain each of the five unclean ingredients, i.e. flour, salt, sugar, fat and water, and hence optimally defiled, was mentioned as the ultimate instrument of the official 'scheme of contamination' enforced on all from the highest to the lowest in native society. The unity of all Indians and the opposition between them and their alien rulers were thus expressed in terms of a single theme—that of ritual pollution—phrased as a rumour in 'many portentous shapes'. That a little fear could spread so far by means of simple verbal manipulation—it could all be said in six short sentences—was what made this type of popular discourse so alarming to those who found themselves on the wrong side of an insurrection.

Improvisations such as these testify to the freedom of the rumour process. However, this freedom is not unlimited. A rumour can be improvised only to the extent that the relevant codes of the culture in which it operates permit. In this respect it follows the logic of the 'effort after meaning' mentioned by Bartlett as characteristic of every human cognitive reaction. 'Certain of the tendencies', he wrote in explanation of this term, 'which the subject brings with him into the situation with which he is called upon to deal are utilised so as to make his reaction the "easiest", or the least disagreeable, or the quickest and least obstructed that is at the time possible.' And thus 'in certain cases of great structural simplicity, or of structural regularity, or of extreme familiarity, the immediate data are at once fitted to, or matched with, a perceptual pattern which appears to be pre-existent so far as the particular perceptual act is concerned. This pre-formed setting, scheme, or pattern is utilised in a completely unreflecting, unanalytical and unwitting manner. Because it is utilised the immediate perceptual data have meaning, can be dealt with, and are assimilated.'[112]

Rumour, as Allport and Postman have shown, represents precisely such an effort after meaning.[113] Instantaneous and unreflecting by its very constitution this type of spoken utterance is of course ideally suited for assimilation in an 'unanalytical and unwitting manner' to pre-existing ideological patterns. In conditions of insurgency it represents an attempt on the part of its interlocutors to make sense of a challenge to an established authority by matching their perception of the by then inevitably strained or already modified relations of power with a 'pre-formed scheme' or code of political thinking.

During the first hundred and fifty years of colonial rule and

[112] Bartlett: 44–5.

[113] Allport & Postman: 37, 40, 121, 206 *et passim.*

indeed for long afterwards this code was a measure of the still relatively immature view, half-realistic and half-fantastic, that the peasants had of politics. In part it was based on their knowledge of the values and relations of power in the world they lived in. The rumours which circulated, for instance, in Rohilkhand in 1857 'to the effect that the cultivation of the fields has been prohibited by the British Government',[114] were of course silly and unfounded. But the alarm to which they gave voice had its referent in the undoubted fact of the agrarian policies of the Raj being regarded at the time as less than helpful towards the peasantry. Again, the word that spread 'in the shops of the money-changers and in the vestibules of the Palace' in Delhi during the Mutiny about British reverses in the Persian Gulf region or about the Persian army marching towards India through the Bolan Pass[115] had, with all its exaggeration characteristic of wishful thinking, some of the actualities of international political conflict as its premise.

However, in conformity with the semi-feudal conditions of his existence the peasant's code of political thinking in this period also involved conceptualizing all higher authority such as that of kings, landlords, priests, elders, males, etc. as quasi-divine. Consequently, he tended to look upon man's domination of man not as a process governed by the laws of this world but by those of the other world. Instead of seeing in it the operation of human will he saw an expression of divine will. Politics took on the appearance therefore of Providence, its routines of rituals, its temporal articulations of a kind of timeless sacred history. In other words, his understanding of the relations, institutions and processes of power were identified with or at least considerably overdetermined by religion. During an uprising, that most political of all events, he was led spontaneously to interpret its vicissitudes by this quasi-religious code, and the more backward the material and spiritual conditions of his social being the more obscurantist that interpretation tended to be. Rumours in circulation at such times often acted both as the register of this political consciousness suffused with religiosity and as the media of its transmission among the subaltern masses in the countryside.

Some of the rumours which were current on the eve of the

[114] FSUP: V 531. [115] K & M: II 26.

Santal and the Munda rebellions illustrate how this consciousness gave a semblance of ritual to what was essentially political action. A rumour which helped to promote a ritual of friendship among Santal mothers before the outbreak of the hool, has already been noticed: explicitly political in motivation, it aimed at building up an ethic of solidarity household by household within the would-be rebel community by means of interdining and exchange of gifts between any two women who had the same number of children. An even more powerful instance of such ritualization of the political process as aided by rumour is recorded in the *Reak Katha*. 'Then it was heard that a Subah Thakur had been born at Bhognadi in the Par country', it says. 'On hearing this, people began to set off, each with a *pai* [measure] of *atap* rice and the milk of a cow. There they found that an altar had been built with a railing which enclosed it on all sides. In the middle the Thakur himself was seated in the guise of Sido of that village. People worshipped him (*puja*) by prostrating themselves in his presence and put together all the rice and milk at one place as an offering to him.'[116] It was thus that the mobilization for a peasant war commenced with rumours about the advent and apotheosis of a rebel leader and assumed the form of a pilgrimage and ritual worship.

Forty-five years later the historic ulgulan of the Mundas, too, began in a very similar manner. 'The stories of Birsa as a healer, a miracle-worker, and a preacher spread, exaggerated out of all proportions to facts', writes Singh[117] and a great mass of Mundas, Oraons and Kharias set out for the remote and almost inaccessible hamlet of Chalkad where the new prophet had arisen. They were pilgrims and described as such by many contemporaries. Their songs about the distance, the hazards and yet the irresistible attraction of this journey towards Dharati Aba's seat rang with the longing of the traditional Indian devotee.[118] However, the politics of that pilgrimage was soon to become apparent to those who had most to fear from the consequences of large and potentially hostile tribal gatherings. Rev. Hoffmann spoke for all of them when he wrote:

[116] MHKRK: *clxxviii*. [117] Singh: 46.

[118] See, for instance, the excerpt from *News from Murhu* in Singh: 47 for a contemporary description of the pilgrimage. Singh also quotes some Birsaite songs on this theme. (Ibid.: 47–8).

I distinctly remember how the known sardars were urging the common people to go on pilgrimage to 'Birsa Bhagwan' . . . Rumours of miraculous cures and the resuscitation of dead men were diligently spread . . . crowds of the Mundas, especially of the known sardari villages, were constantly going armed. I got certain news, too, that the religious colouring of Chalkad was fading more and more, and that the real political aims were coming out clearer as Chalkad was getting more and more crowded with armed men, permanently settled there with provisions for many a day.[119]

Quite clearly a religious enthusiasm fanned by rumour had laid the basis for a massive and armed mobilization of the Munda peasantry, and the holy father, acting as a spiritual gendarme of colonialism, was quite understandably alarmed to see a sacred, if heathen, assembly turning so profane, so obviously political!

If political action was sacralized thus, so was political thinking. This was represented quite transparently in some rumours such as those which gained wide currency at the time of the Vellore mutiny of 1807 and again fifty years later during the sepoy rebellion to the effect that the government had plans to convert all Indians to Christianity. On the former occasion the story went round the bazaars in southern India that the Company's officers had sprinkled all the newly-manufactured salt with the blood of pigs and cows and 'then sent it to be sold throughout the country for the pollution and the desecration of Muhammadans and Hindus [so] that all might be brought to one caste and to one religion like the English'.[120] The 1857 versions of that story have been discussed earlier in this chapter. Again, it was rumoured in the south in 1807 that the government had ordered a church 'to be erected in every town and every village in the country'. This corresponded to the panic caused in some parts of the North-Western Provinces in 1857 by reports about an official policy forcibly to baptize all uncircumcised Muslim infants and led to hundreds of them being rushed through that rite in Bareilly and Rampur in order 'to save them from the hands of the Missionaries'.[121]

Kaye who was more sensitive than most writers about the influence of rumour on insurrections, comments on the absurdity of the Vellore stories circulated at a time 'when there

[119] Ibid.: 51. [120] K & M: I 181. [121] FSUP: V 576.

were no indications on the part of Government of any especial concern for the interests of Christianity', and accounts for them by the fact that 'in a state of panic men do not pause to reason'. This, of course, hardly constitutes an explanation. For it still begs the question why people in a state of panic expressed their alarm in those particular terms. However, the author himself comes close to producing an answer, apparently without being aware of its implications, when he suggests that these rumours were perhaps inspired by the belief 'that the English gentlemen cared only to destroy the religions of the country, and to make the people all of one or of no caste, in order that they might make their soldiers and servants do everything they wished'.[122] In other words, at a time of quickening mass anxiety those figments of popular imagination had translated politics instinctively by a religious code and come to express an antagonism towards the Raj as a fear of the cultural hegemony of the Christian rulers, a sense of loss of freedom as an apprehension about loss of faith.

It was this consciousness, an unquestionably false consciousness if ever there was one, which also generated a certain kind of alienation: it made the subject look upon his destiny not as a function of his own will and action, but as that of forces outside and independent of himself. The thinking which filled the void created thus by the displacement of the subject was, in its most general sense, religious—that is, to put it in Marx's words, 'a product of self-alienation'.[123] This was true not merely when the alienated will was attributed (as often done) to gods, godlings and jinns or mythical heroes and monsters, but equally when attributed to real, empirical people seen as the bearers of super-human and super-natural powers. What was political came thus to be regarded as religious. Rumour, again, acted as the carrier of this consciousness, although the messages transmitted by it could often be a shade more opaque than those about involuntary defilement and enforced conversion as cited above.

Even a small sample of the folklore of fear and hope known to have been current during the Indian peasant rebellions of the eighteenth and nineteenth centuries should make this clear. It

[122] K & M: I 182. [123] MECW: III 339.

was this genre of discourse which often registered the peasant's anticipation of the political outcome of an uprising—an outcome mediated invariably by forces other than himself. Such mediators could be either purely mythical or they could be empirical ones with mythic functions assigned to them. The former figured in some of the rumours of the hool. One of these relating to the apocalypse of Lag and Lagin had, as we have seen, inspired a set of propitiatory rituals. Yet another chiliastic rumour which made the rounds, concerned a buffalo said to have been on its way to the Santal country. 'Wherever it found grass growing in the open space in front of one's house', recalled Jugia Harom, 'it would stop over to graze and rest there and would not leave until all the members of that family had died.'[124] Whereas the harbingers of doom in these two instances were derived from a bestiary made up in equal parts of Santal and Hindu fantasy, a harbinger of deliverance, a Subah, whose advent too was reported at the time, was believed to be human, though no less mythical: as rumour had it, he was born of a virgin at Layogar, somewhere beyond Hazaribagh. Kanhu himself referred to this as if it were a real event and did so in a manner that made no distinction between fact and fancy. Thus:

> The sonthals went for Shikar to Charichunaro . . . 1 man, 1 woman & one girl/a virgin/were there & cut the Lyo/a sort of grass/they rubbed it & threw it about & it became Lyo fort or Lyghur the girl had a son who grew up at once and began to talk & became a soubah.[125]

Apart from such mythical instruments of political change the mind of the rebel had room in it for empirical ones too, that is, for real human beings and institutions. But this did not prevent the latter from being brought, in their turn, into line with those in the other category of mediators by having mythic functions attributed to them. These functions varied of course according to events and the cultures specific to the subaltern populations concerned. However, taking together the elements common to them all, these could be said to belong to four notionally distinct though in fact imbricated types—divine, martial, monarchical and sacerdotal. Rumours relating to the first of these have already been mentioned in connection with the apotheosis of

[124] MHKRK: *clxxvii.*

[125] Ibid.: JP, 20 Dec. 1855: 'Examination of Kanoo Sonthal'.

Sido and Birsa on the eve of the revolts led by them. Like them the mediators of the martial type, too, were real people, but unlike the former, not transformed into divinities. The mythopoeic imagination of the rebels endowed them with exceptional and indeed magical powers, a pathetic device by which a poorly armed peasantry compensated themselves in fantasy for what they actually lacked in military equipment and organization. The belief generated by rumour about the Santal and Munda leaders' ability to turn British bullets into water cost their credulous rank and file many lives during the decisive battles at Maheshpur and Sail Rakab respectively.[126]

But it was not the tribal peasantry alone who were prone to conjuring up the image of the deliverer as gifted with a striking power superior to that of the enemy. Among the 'wild reports' said to be 'assiduously spread through the district' of Bareilly in June 1858 'evidently to unsettle men's minds and to destroy confidence in our Government' the battered colonial administration listed one to the effect 'that Khan Bahadur Khan will re-enter Bareilly under [the] shelter of a miraculous dust-storm and annihilate his enemies'.[127] In fact this wishful tendency to exaggerate the strength of the enemy's enemy and to make a potential liberator of him gave even the relatively transparent speculations based on Anglo-Persian hostilities a touch of myth when it was rumoured 'that the Shah of Persia had for five generations been accumulating munitions of war and heaping up treasure for the purpose of conquering India and that the time had now come for action', and that he had obtained the assistance in this venture not only of the Tsar and the Amir but also of the French and Turkish emperors. In the communication of all this, wrote Kaye, an 'ambiguous, enigmatical language suited the occasion', and in Delhi in the spring of 1857 'the talk was still of a something coming'.[128]

It was thus that with all their practical involvement in a rebellion the masses could still be tricked by a false consciousness into trusting the magical faculties of warrior heroes to win it for them. This process of vicarious substitution was even better exemplified in the kingly function often attributed by

[126] CR: 247; Singh: 111–12.

[127] FSUP: V 531–2.

[128] K & M: II 26–7, 31.

rumour to yet another class of these quasi-religious mediators. These, too, like the types previously mentioned, had a real, empirical existence as human beings and institutions. They stood in fact for the political system which dominated the very conditions of the peasant's life and was indeed the object of his revolt. Yet by a curious turn of self-estrangement it was from them rather than from his own will and initiative that he sought validation for his desperate act of defiance. Representatives of the Raj at various levels these mediators came to be regarded by the rebel as a source of sovereign authority more just and partial towards the peasantry than it was in real life as the custodian of order and protector of landlords, moneylenders and village tyrants of all kinds. The experience of rural insurgency in all countries amply illustrates this mentality. In pre-revolutionary Russia the muzhiks rose in revolt again and again in the Tsar's name at least since the days of Pugachev; in France during the jacqueries of 1789 the peasants burnt and pillaged in the belief that they had royal support for what they did; in England in 1830 the country labourers claimed authorization by the Crown for their riots.[129]

In India too the peasantry involved in the 'blue mutiny' of 1860, the Pabna bidroha of 1873, the widespread struggle against rack-renting in eastern Bengal during the 1880s—all acted in the name of the Maharani, the Lat Saheb, the Sarkar, the 'New Law', and so on. In each of these instances it was the force of rumour which did most to spread the illusion. 'All sorts of rumours which agreed with the peasants' longing for better days were circulating: the despotic power of zamindars would be soon gone for ever . . . rent rate would be reduced everywhere and Government legislation would deprive zamindars of all powers to enhance it, etc.'[130] This description of the role of hearsay in generalizing the Bengali tenants' resistance to high landlordism in the eastern districts during the 1880s was indeed typical of many other situations of agrarian conflict. In such cases oral communications of this kind could serve both to

[129] These are fairly well documented facts of history. For some of the most authoritative statements, see Field: *passim*; Lefebvre (1973): 38–40, 42, 94–7, 118, 214; H & R: 18.

[130] B. B. Chaudhuri (1967): 289.

disseminate ideology and trigger off militant action as the following excerpt from the Deccan Riot Commission's report shows:

A circumstance which perhaps more than any other precipitated the outbreak was the circulation of a story which would seem too absurd to obtain belief even among the most ignorant . . . The most popular form of the story was that an English *sahib* who had been sold up by a Marwari creditor, had petitioned Her Majesty the Queen on the subject and that she had sent out orders that the Marwaris were to give up their bonds. As more briefly told and largely believed even by the more educated people of the village the story was condensed into the simple form that, on a report from India, orders had come from England that the Marwaris were to have their bonds taken from them. In some form or other this report was circulated and a belief established that, acting under orders from England, the Government officers would connive at the extortion of their bonds from the sowkars.[131]

It was thus that the Maratha peasant was driven by self-alienation into a paradox: what he did was the very opposite of what he thought he was doing. Engaged in violently undermining a central pillar of colonialism in rural India, i.e. the authority of the moneylender, he claimed validation for that very destructive enterprise from the highest level of the colonial government itself. As in all thinking of a religious kind he 'estranged his own activity from himself' and came to confer the attributes of what should have been his own will and initiative on people and institutions 'other than and differentiated from himself'[132]—that is, on mediators. Indeed like his brethren

[131] DRCR: 54. The extract ends thus: 'It is somewhat remarkable that a somewhat similar belief was entertained by the Sonthals whose rebellion in 1855 originated in similar causes.' The collection of Santal rebellion papers in JP which I have used in this work does not contain anything at all to testify to such a belief. Nor does K. K. Datta's monograph based on the Bhagalpur records of the hool. The source for this particular idea may be CR: 245 where it is said that 'the order of the Thakoor was remarkable; it expressly disclaimed all intentions against the government'. This is obviously wrong, for in TTP, that key document, the Thakur appeared clearly to be dissatisfied with the way that the sarkar had been supporting zamindars and mahajans against the Santals and He quite explicitly ordered the sahibs to quit Santal territory and withdraw to the other side of the Ganges or face the Thakur's rain of fire. This speaks for the emphatically anti-colonialist character of the hool.

[132] MECW: III 279.

operating elsewhere under similar circumstances he modelled this particular set of mediators according to his idea of a Good King—Queen, to be precise, the gender lending it a touch of spurious authenticity as well as some motherly sanctity—the very source of an abstract and universal Justice, an image based clearly on the Indian feudal concept (known to some other cultures too) of the divinity of the sovereign ruler. This image came to be foisted on all believed by the rebel to be higher in authority than his immediate adversaries. As such, the mediator could be any instrument of British power ranging from Parliament to the district level administration, from the Queen to the Collector. To describe this process as a legitimizing device (as is customary in learned discourse) would be correct only if it were made *absolutely* clear that for the subject, that is, the insurgent himself the legitimizing of his action derived *not* from the positive laws, institutions, personnel, etc. of any empirical government in Calcutta or Whitehall but from the sanctions of that heavenly kingship in which all other authority was thought to have been subsumed.

Rumour has also been known to propagate the mentality which makes the rebel have recourse to the type of mediation characterized above as sacerdotal in the broadest sense of that term. It included the functions of the priest, saint, healer, preacher, prophet, etc., some, if not all, of which the insurgents would ascribe to their leaders at critical moments just before or in the actual course of an uprising. This again was symptomatic of a consciousness that proved far too feeble to cope with its own project and left it to be completed by the intervention of a superior wisdom. The African peoples' struggles against foreign rule in many parts of that continent provide some outstanding examples of such mediation. Isaacman has documented the crucial importance of spirit mediums in the tradition of peasant resistance in Mozambique. The miracles, charms and prophecies they produced were in many cases among the most powerful influences in inspiring and sustaining the peasants' fight against the Portuguese. Again, in Tanzania it was Kinjikitile's prophecies and his eponymous medicine which helped as much as anything else to convert anti-German feelings into the Maji Maji uprising.[133]

[133] See Gwassa & Iliffe; Isaacman.

In colonial India this particular type of mediation played a relatively less conspicuous part in mobilizing for rebellion but was by no means unknown. A certain amount of sanctity and prophetic vision was attributed by rumour to both the Santal brothers who led the hool. But it was in the career of Birsa Munda that the functions of the seer, saint, healer and preacher were all clearly and comprehensively combined.[134] From that moment on a mid-summer day in 1895 when, as a Munda song had it, 'deep amidst [the] wild forest on [a] burnt and cleared upland Singbonga entered [his] heart', the word went round about his being the repository of a revealed wisdom, a miracle man who could walk on water and cure by incantation, a preacher with the message of a new cult, a prophet who spoke of the coming deliverance of his people from the demon-queen Mandodori's yoke. Saintly rather than miraculous was the function that mediators of this type had in the non-tribal uprisings of our period, which may perhaps have something to do with the importance of the sadhu and the fakir in the Hindu and Islamic traditions respectively. The fracas which occurred at Fyzabad in February 1857 between the military authorities and a fakir, Maulvi Ahmadullah Shah, who said 'that he was prepared to wage a holy war with the help of Mussulmans and Hindoos against the English' and the peregrinations of a sadhu in the spring of that year between Meerut and Ambalah—'one of the many emissaries who were moving about the country'—were to be mentioned later on as possible influences on the outbreak of the Mutiny and the civilian disturbances in those regions.[135]

One of these holy men, Hasan Askari, 'a Muhammadan Priest of the Hereditary Priesthood', who lived near Delhi Gate, made a name for himself in 1857 by prophesying that the Shah of Persia would conquer India and restore the Mughals to power. He even performed 'propitiatory ceremonies to expedite the arrival of the Persians and the expulsion of the Christians'. A variation of this, according to which the would-be liberator was an Arab rather than a Persian, was ascribed to a saint called

[134] All information on this particular point is based on Singh: Ch. III and Appendix H.

[135] FSUP: I 381–8, 397–9.

Shah Mamat-ullah. 'After the fire-worshippers and Christians shall have held sway over the whole of Hindustan for a hundred years and when injustice and oppression shall prevail in their Government', he predicted, 'an Arab prince shall be born, who will ride forth triumphantly to slay them.'[136] However, it was not merely Islamic fantasy which forecast the end of the Raj in its hundreth year. Hindu speculations to the same effect were also in currency before and during the Mutiny. Harvey, Commissioner of Agra, referred to a 'Hindoo prophecy limiting British rule to a centenary of years'.[137] Again, the mediating functions of the partly deified leaders of the Santal and Munda rebellions were also known to have included predictions about imminent encounters with the Raj in chiliastic terms. 'Fire will rain from Heaven', declared Sido and Kanhu in their parwana; and Birsa caused a stampede into his village Chalkad and a run on the stocks of cloth in the local markets when he announced that on a specified day fire and brimstone would pour down from heaven and destroy all on earth except those who were with him at that time and remembered to put on new clothes for the occasion as advised by him.[138]

Prophecies of this kind, whether based on what saints, oracles or quasi-divine leaders actually said or (as it often happened) fabricated by the collective imagination of the rebel community, were a concomitant of popular uprisings in many other pre-industrial societies too. On the eve of the Maji Maji rebellion in east Africa they spread by the dozen charged with the foreboding of doom and deliverance—a great flood to destroy everything, the sea to overflow and 'devour all whites on the coast', the earth to open up and 'swallow all whites inland' together with their native collaborators, a messiah soon to appear in the guise of an ape or a chicken or a man riding a dog, or even the advent of a god—the god of the Saramo—believed to have set up an empire at Kisangire, '8 hours from Maneromango', as an alternative to the German colonial regime and a refuge for all from the hated rule of foreigners.[139]

Europe too was no stranger to this genre of discourse. Keith Thomas has shown how England seethed with prophecies in

[136] K & M: II 28, 27 n. [137] FSUP: I 392. Also see FSUP: V 9.
[138] JP, 4 Oct. 1855 (no. 20); Singh: 48.
[139] Wehrmeister: 88; Schumann: 63; Berliner Missionsberichte: 462–3.

periods of heightened social tension both in the Middle Ages and early modern times. These were powerful enough to make the circulation of such utterances by medieval Welsh bards and the Lollards a penal offence under various governments. Later on the Tudors were to be constantly on the look out for political prophecies of all kinds in order to suppress them by acts of parliament, Privy Council orders, instructions to J.P.s, etc. For 'prophecies of one kind or another were employed in virtually every rebellion or popular rising which disturbed the Tudor state'. In fact, the association between prophecy and insurgency continued through the entire series of sixteenth-century rebellions—the risings in the North and East Ridings in Yorkshire, those led by Robert Kett in Norfolk and so on—until the Civil War. The authorities were never far from the truth in describing 'vain prophecies' and 'seditious, false or untrue rumours' as 'the very foundation of all rebellion'.[140]

Rumour was of course an ideal instrument for making the sacerdotal function of the mediators known to the masses. For miracles, spiritual healing, revelations, etc. lent themselves more easily to being talked about than experienced in real life. Supernatural and occult phenomena, they lived only in words. As a part of the semiotic of insurgency they were realized not in terms of the visuality which imagination endowed them with, but *only* verbally. However, in one particular instance, that is prophecies, the sign of the sacerdotal function was not transubstantiated in any sense: the material which constituted it did not alter by propagation. The mediator's words predicting a golden age or an imminent end to the world, the coming of a messiah or an apocalypse passed from mouth to mouth exactly as they originated, that is, as verbal messages.

Yet if such utterances were subjected to no material change in the course of transmission, they were still modified in another way. Rumour separated them from all the other linguistic messages circulating in the rebel community, attributed to them an authoritativeness derived from the elevated status of their speakers and bestowed on them the significance of truth—in short, *textualized* them.[141] Distinguished thus from the mass of

140 Thomas: 470–2, 478–9, 505, and Ch. 13 *passim*.

141 The notion of text and non-text and its implications for the study of culture as used in this paragraph is based on Lotman & Pjatigorskij.

all other discourses—non-texts—current within that collective, these were represented as 'displaying traits of an expressiveness that [was] complementary and meaningful in the cultural system'. According to Lotman and Pjatigorskij, this distinction between text and non-text corresponds to that between 'closed' and 'open' cultures. A text acquires meaning in the latter 'because it has a definite sense that defines its functional value' and results in an 'absolutization of historical experience'. By contrast in 'closed' cultures a text tends to be 'meaningful', 'sacred', because it is a text and is characterized, accordingly, by 'an absolutization of prophecy and hence of eschatology'. Indeed, the contrast becomes quite evident when with the transition of a culture from a 'closed' to an 'open' state the notion of cyclical time begins increasingly to yield to that of linear time and prophecy declines with the growth of historical criticism as it did in England by the end of the seventeenth century.[142] By its ahistorical character prophecy is thus ideally adapted to religious thinking in which man's destiny appears not as what it is, that is, a product of his own activity but as determined for him by forces standing outside history, as a future beyond his own control but programmed in the prescience of saints and seers mediating for him. The circulation of prophetic rumours in the course of the events discussed above was thus symptomatic of self-estrangement on the part of the typical peasant rebel of our period: it testified to that false consciousness which made him look upon his own acts of resistance as a manifestation of another's will.

[142] Thomas: 507–14.

CHAPTER 7

TERRITORIALITY

Localism denounced by revolutionaries—territoriality defined—local character of tribal peasant revolts—ethnic space—physical space—time as a correlate of space—territoriality and consciousness among non-tribal peasantry: caste, locality and culture—Kunbi territorial ties and Maratha peasant movements—territoriality of the uprisings of 1857–8 as recognized by counter-insurgency—peasant violence focused on local enemies: local administration and local moneylenders—local units as the social base of violence: Rajputs, Mewatis, Gujars—local revolts seen as caste revolts—uprisings in single-caste villages in support of mutineers of respective castes—ethnic solidarity as an instrument of rebel mobilization—the political aspect of caste ambition as a factor of insurgency: Gujars, Palwars, Monas—intercaste mobilization at the local level: some instances—Meghar Singh's rebellion: its course and character—intersection of ethnic and physical space—territoriality as a positive aspect of insurgency.

How far can insurgency spread? Is there a natural limit beyond which it cannot carry in spite of its speed and the versatility of the means of its transmission? This is a question which some of the great rebellions in history forced their leaders to ask. They were disappointed to find that even the most powerful of peasant uprisings were often unable to exceed local boundaries. Trotsky gave voice to a common exasperation in this respect when he commented on the failure of the Russian revolution of 1905 to generalize itself in the countryside. 'Local cretinism is history's curse on all peasant riots', he wrote.[1] Even Mao Tse-tung who took on the whole a more positive view of peasant militancy found peasant 'localism' a serious impediment to party-building in the Hunan-Kiangsi border area in 1928, that critical year of retreat and regrouping in the career of the Chinese revolution.[2] Ten years later, at the beginning of the war of resistance against Japan, he was still unhappy about the existence of localism in

[1] Trotsky: 65. [2] Mao: I 93.

peasant guerilla units and guerilla bases 'which are frequently preoccupied with local considerations to the neglect of the general interest'.[3]

These observations link both these leaders directly to a historiographical tradition going back to Engels. The latter in his famous work on the German Peasant War of 1525 dwells again and again on this particular limitation and shows how the want of co-operation between the armed peasantry of neighbouring regions led often to their defeat. Words and imageries signifying the peasants' inability to rise above local considerations abound in his text. 'The mass of the peasants never overstepped the boundaries of local relations and local outlook.' They were 'confined to their local horizon'. Indeed, what 'ruined the Peasant War' was, according to him, their 'stubborn provincialism' and 'appalling narrow-mindedness', qualities which he described as 'always inevitable among the peasant masses'.[4]

What is this consciousness which is so bitterly denounced by revolutionaries as a limiting factor of peasant insurgency? It is made up, in its Indian form, of a sense of belonging to a common lineage as well as to a common habitat—an intersection of two primordial referents which, for the purpose of the present discussion, we shall call *territoriality*. The relation between its two components, consanguinity and contiguity, was the subject of an argument among scholars for a long time. Maine, and following him Morgan, had attributed to the former a sort of historical precedence and structural primacy until R. H. Lowie demolished this theory to prove that 'the two principles . . . however antithetical, are not of necessity mutually exclusive'. He showed that in the historically earlier social formations 'both the bilateral (family) and the unilateral (clan, sib, moiety) unit are rooted in a local as well as a consanguine factor'. Our use of the concept of territoriality in this chapter and elsewhere in this work agrees with his conclusion that 'the two types of union'—by blood tie and local bond—'are in reality intertwined'.[5] In this we conform to the practice of Indian sociology, especially in the field of village studies where the notion, if not the term

[3] Mao: II 108.

[4] Engels (1926): 36, 116, 130 *et passim*.

[5] Maine: 105–9; Lowie: 53, 66, 73 *et passim*.

itself, often occurs in descriptions of unity and discord. What we intend to do however is to try and extend its application to the series of larger and more intense, hence qualitatively different, rural conflicts which rocked the subcontinent under the Raj from time to time.

With the exception of the uprisings triggered off by the Mutiny (to which we shall turn later on in this chapter) the most extensive disturbances of this type until 1900 were those caused by tribal peasant revolts. Even these were *on the whole* local in character—a fact which appears to have impressed many observers close to those events. The Birsaite ulgulan ranged over an area of 400 square miles, yet in retrospect the *General Administration Report of Chotanagpur Division for 1899–1900* could describe it as no more than a 'localised affair'.[6] In much the same vein the Lieutenant-Governor of Bengal commented on the hool as it was still sweeping irresistibly through Damin-i-Koh: 'I do not see reason to believe that the rising is any but a local one'; and again, 'Every thing that has been heard confirms me in the conviction that this rising is merely local.'[7] Dalton, too, in his account of the Kol insurrection of 1832, noticed a tendency on the part of the rebels not to operate beyond their immediate neighbourhoods. 'It does not appear that the Kols in their work of destruction moved far from their own homesteads', he wrote.[8]

In each of these instances the range of the rebellion was contingent on a whole set of material conditions relating to the economic life of the populations concerned, the terrain on which they fought, their strength in arms and men as against that of their foes and so on. The force and combination of these factors differed from one local event to another and gave each of them its particular character. What was common to them all, however, was the manner in which the rebels' view of the enemy as an alien provided the domain of an uprising with its subjective determinations. These latter were made up of two categories of concepts denoting ethnic space and physical space, each of which again had a negative and positive aspect

[6] Singh: 194.

[7] JP, 19 July 1855: Lieutenant-Governor's Minutes (12 & 16 July 1855).

[8] Dalton: 172.

depending on whether it sought to define the domain in terms of the otherness of the alien or in those of the self-identity of the insurgents themselves.

Hostility towards 'foreigners' which was such a prominent feature of the rebellions mentioned above, antedates them by a considerable length of time. In the Chota Nagpur plateau it was perhaps as old as the last quarter of the seventeenth century when the jagirdari system was first introduced there.[9] In Damin-i-Koh, too, thanks to the intrusion of Hindu landlords and moneylenders into what was originally designed as a Santal sanctuary,[10] it had at least two full decades to mature before the outbreak of the hool. In the event the term diku, used generically in the local tribal languages to describe anyone belonging to 'non-tribal out-groups', came to acquire a meaning which indicated at the same time both the ethnic and the class aspects of the exploitation of the peasantry of these regions. The semantic range assigned to this lexeme in Hoffmann's *Encyclopaedia Mundarica* and Bödding's *Santal Dictionary* clearly brings this out. Diku in these works stands for 'a Hindu', 'a Hindu landlord', 'Hindi or Sadani', 'a Hindu or Bengali of the better class', etc., and *diku-n*—'to become the landlord of a village'. It has also been noticed that in at least one language of the Mundari group *di* means 'that' and the plural diku—'those', a telling deixis which leaves little room for doubt about the speaker's insistence on his own separate identity. Linguistic evidence such as this was recorded by missionaries and administrators at a time when the memory of some of these tribal insurrections was still quite vivid. Yet nearly sixty-seven years after the last of these great revolts and twenty years after the end of the Raj the pejorative associations of the term were found to be still quite firmly embedded in popular mentality among the adivasis of Chota Nagpur. A survey conducted by a group of sociologists[11] in this area in 1967 showed that it had not only retained its dual function of signifying the non-autochthones (such as Hindus, Musalmans, Europeans, Marwaris, Biharis, Bengalis, etc.) and class enemies (such as rural

[9] Roy: 165. [10] Hunter (1897): 222–3.

[11] See Sinha *et al.* Much of our argument on this particular point is based on the results of this survey and on the linguistic information presented in this excellent article.

capitalists, banias, moneylenders, rajas, zamindars and landlords' servants), but had acquired for itself a new and expressive moral connotation. Diku, said many of the Munda, Oraon and Ho informants, deriving, ironically enough, from an alien etymology, meant for them 'trouble-makers' (*dik dik karnewale*). The stereotype which was thus established was backed by a host of other words, phrases, imageries and adages to emphasize the malevolence, avarice, meanness and generally the negative qualities of the outsider. Looter, deceiver, exploiter—such were the epithets predicated on him. He was unreliable and fearsome. His eyes (*diku med*) were like those of a dog, for he fawned on his master for small favours and snarled at all others to keep them away. He was unfriendly: he would not recognize his own neighbour. 'A *deko* friend a thorn tree; they prick': so ran a Santal proverb. When a Munda oppressed another, he was said to be—*dikuing*. And if he set himself up as a zamindar and lived off rents extracted from other Mundas, he was regarded as *dikuized*.

No wonder then that the diku figured as a major target of violence when the time came for the tribal peoples of Damin-i-Koh and Chota Nagpur to settle scores with traders, moneylenders, landlords and their staff. This was indeed so conspicuous a feature of these insurrections that their essentially anti-colonial character was often overlooked by some observers who regarded these as nothing but a conflict between some of the exploiting and exploited sections of the Indian population itself. Yet the very error of this perception was itself an authentic register of their impact on contemporaries if only because it has a lot to tell us about the way these uprisings *looked* at the time (as different from what they *were*). For there could be no mistake about the fact that resentment against the alien intruders was what provided, for each of these massive explosions, the spark that ignited the fuse. Bindrai, the Kol leader, spoke for all tribal insurgents of the nineteenth century when he explained why his people had taken to arms in 1832:

The Pathans had taken our Hoormut and the Sing our Sisters and the Koour, Harnath Sah had forcibly deprived us of our Estates of Twelve Villages which he had given to the Sing. Our Lives we considered of no Value, and being of one Caste and Brethren, it was agreed upon that we should commence to cut, plunder, murder and eat . . . It is with this resolution that we have been murdering and plundering those who have deprived us of both honour & homes . . .[12]

The selective violence of that rebellion measured up to the bitterness and anger of these words. In villages where the tribal people and the dikus lived together as neighbours, it was on the latter that the Kols concentrated their attack.[13] To the local representatives of the Raj this looked clearly like a movement aimed at the expulsion of the diku. 'The whole of the Moondas and Coles', they said in a report on the progress of the insurrection, 'have taken up arms against the respectable inhabitants of the country, burnt and plundered their houses and property, and expelled them.'[14] Their superiors in the Calcutta Council too acknowledged that the 'extermination or expulsion of every inhabitant of the Country, who came under the designation of Foreigner' was what the rebels wanted, although, more aware than their subordinates of the overall implications of the uprising, they mentioned 'the utter annihilation of the Government' as its other objective.[15]

Even the violence of the Santal hool which made no distinction between the sarkar and the diku and focused on both with equal intensity from the very outset, was considered by some observers as exclusively directed against the latter in its early stages. This can be clearly seen, for instance, in the demi-official account, 'The Sonthal Rebellion', published in the *Calcutta Review* of 1856 and regarded as one of the most important sources of information about that event. There is much internal evidence to show that its author had access to the reports received by the Bengal Government about the uprising and its initial thrust in Damin-i-Koh, all of which spoke emphatically of the rebels' hostility both towards the government and towards zamindars and mahajans. He had also read or been told about the parwana issued by Sido and Kanhu on the eve of the hool. It accused the dikus as well as the sahibs of 'sins' committed against the Santals, announced the end of the Raj ('the Thacoor has ordered me saying that the country is not the Sahibs') and asked the white men to retire to the other

[12] BC 1363 (54227): Cuthbert & Wilkinson to Thomason (12 Feb. 1832).

[13] BC 1502 (58893): Master to Thomason (17 Jan. 1833).

[14] BC 1362 (54224): Cuthbert & Wilkinson to Bowen (9 Feb. 1832).

[15] BC 1363 (54227): Vice-President's Minute (30 Mar. 1832).

side of the Ganges failing which, it said, there would be war: 'The Sahibs and the white Soldiers will fight . . . The Thacoor himself will fight. Therefore you Sahibs and Soldiers [will] fight the Thacoor himself.'[16] One could hardly mistake this as anything but a clear declaration of belligerence addressed both to the colonial authorities and their protégés, the native exploiters of the tribal peasantry. Yet the author of the *Calcutta Review* article read in this text nothing but the Santals' determination 'to banish the traders and zamindars and all rich Bengalees from their country' and to commit 'the instant slaughter of all the muhajuns, of the Darogahs'. The parwana, he wrote, 'expressly disclaimed all intentions against the government',[17] an error echoed a decade later by William Hunter when he wrote that even on 7 July 1855, the day the hool broke out at Bhagnadihi, the Santals 'do not seem to have contemplated armed opposition to the Government'.[18]

What generated such optic illusion it is difficult to say. Perhaps a degree of official complacency made many nineteenth-century administrators look away when confronted with the evidence of failure in the machine they were given to run with a sense of historic mission. For the Raj had by this time come to believe firmly in its role as protector and benefactor of the peasantry, so that whenever a jacquerie occurred it was comfortable for the authorities to look upon it simply as a revolt of the underdog against his native oppressor rather than against the colonial government. Whatever the reason, the blind spot which had thus developed inspired a false historiography dedicated to absolving the regime of any responsibility for making the life of the tribal peoples too miserable to bear. Its filiation was by no means limited to the school of British administrator-historians like Hunter. Indian scholars such as S. C. Roy too ignored the anti-colonialist content of these uprisings and helped to perpetuate the myth that they were

[16] TTP. [17] CR: 245.

[18] Hunter (1897): 240. Hunter (ibid.: 238 n. 69) says that he never came across a copy of this parwana ('one of those curious missives'), but relies on the authority of 'an accurate contemporary writer with the whole facts before him'—presumably the anonymous author of CR to say: 'The ultimatum is said to have insisted chiefly on the regulation of usury, on a new arrangement of the revenues and on the expulsion, or as some say, the massacre, of all Hindu extortioners in the Santal country.'

nothing but demonstrations of ethnic antagonism. Suresh Singh is right in joining issue with the latter on this point and insisting on the predominantly political and anti-colonialist character of the Birsaite ulgulan. Yet as he himself points out, even this, perhaps the least racially oriented of all the great tribal rebellions of the nineteenth century, was marked by 'an under-current of hostility against *Dikus*' particularly in its earlier and preparatory phase.[19]

Going by Hoffmann's testimony it is clear that the malevolence of the diku had already been codified by this time in such imageries as snakes (*bing*), witches (*najom*) and tigers (*kula*) in Mundari usage.[20] It was to be expected therefore that sentiments of fear and hatred such as these would be used to power any violent mobilization of the masses in this region. Indeed it is not difficult to locate this as an important element in Birsaite agitation on the eve of the ulgulan. The Munda leader's parable of stones and clods related during his visit to the Chutia temple in 1898 provides an example. He pointed to a structure of stones topped by clods of earth to serve as a crude stove of the kind often used in the country for cooking outdoors, and apparently made his followers believe that the stones and clods changed places before their very eyes, just as Mundas and dikus, he told them, were bound to do one day.[21] Again, at an important assembly of the tribe at Dombari hill the following year he unfurled a two-coloured flag with its white symbolizing the purity of the Munda and red the exploitation by the diku and prophesied that 'there was going to be a fight with the *dikus*, the ground would be as red as the red flag with their blood'.[22]

Thus the domain of the rebellion defined itself negatively by exclusion of the diku just as the tribe defined itself in terms of the otherness of the alien. But the parallelism extends even further. There are many ideas relating to *ethnos* used by a tribe positively to assert its own identity. One of these, the notion of an ethnic space, occurs in all the tribal revolts discussed above. In each of them the domain of insurgency was considered to be as large as the tribe itself, a *coincidence* emphasized in all those preparatory acts (discussed in Chapter 4) of ritual

[19] Singh: 191. [20] Ibid.: 190 and n. 25.
[21] Ibid.: 79. [22] Ibid.: 85, 147.

solidarity, ceremonial gathering and gerontic consultation as well as in the tendency of that violence, once it broke out, to permeate the entire tribal diaspora. The Santal insurrection was hardly a fortnight old when the authorities were alerted to the contact it had already established 'with the numerous population of the same tribe which inhabit[ed] the districts of Pachete, Manbhoom, Singbhoom and other districts south of the Grand Trunk Road', and feared 'that the insurrection [might] spread from Beerbhoom to those districts which [were] the original site of the Sonthal tribe'.[23] In this respect Major Sutherland's perceptive comment on the Kol disturbances of 1832 could apply to the whole genre. One of the officials most knowledgeable about Chota Nagpur and the first amongst them to examine the nature of that event, he wrote:

> The insurrection had no limit but that which it found in the class of people by which it was instigated. Had the Country between Chota Nagpoor and Calcutta on the one hand and Benares on the other been inhabited by Dânger Coles, the insurrection would have spread to those places. The Coles are one large family which can unite for any purpose good or bad. It is perhaps fortunate for us that they are not more extensive, and that there are not many such families in India.[24]

The tribe, in other words, was not merely the initiator of the rebellion but was its site as well. Its consciousness of itself as a body of insurgents was thus indistinguishable from its recognition of its ethnic self. 'The tribe remained the boundary for man, in relation to himself as well as to outsiders':[25] this observation made by Engels about the Iroquois was true of the Indian adivasis, too, not merely when they lived in peace with themselves and the Raj, but even more so when they took up arms both as a positive and a negative affirmation of their ethnicity.

Corresponding to ethnic space there was also their notion of physical space which figured prominently in every tribal rebellion and constituted an important element of its territoriality. Its function was to enable the insurgents to assert their own

[23] JP, 23 Aug. 1855: Grey to GOI (21 July 1855).

[24] BC 1363 (54227): Sutherland's Note to Vice-President's Private Secretary (Mar. 1832).

[25] Engels (1968): 529.

identity in terms of what they claimed to be their homeland. As with the category of *ethnos*, antagonism towards the diku provided it with its negative determination. It had its roots in the undoubted fact of the expropriation of the adivasis. 'They have taken away from us our trees, fishes, lands and jagirs', said Singrai, the Kol.[26] The massive alienation of tribal lands to outsiders in the years preceding the insurrection which he led, testified to the truth of his indictment and was indeed officially acknowledged as one of its primary causes: 'We have reason to believe that lands were taken by the Rajah and the Jageerdars from Coles or Raoteeas and given to Farmers for an increase of Revenue, and it is easy to understand that the ousted parties would try by all means to recover their lands.'[27] This was confirmed by a well-informed administrator who, commenting on the event seven years later, ascribed it to 'no one cause so much as the dispossession of the Moondas and Mankies who are the Bhoonears of Sonepoor of their lands'.[28]

These dispossessed *bhumihars* were among the more active participants in the Bhumij rebellion and the Sardar agitation which formed the most important links between the revolt of the Kol and that of the Birsaites at the end of the century. Bindrai, one of the mankis responsible for inspiring the Kol to rise in arms, joined forces with Ganganarayan in the Bhumij rebellion in 1833, while from 1858 onwards the 'class of uprooted *bhumihars*' constituted, according to Singh, 'the core of the Sardar movement'.[29] Both represented the uneasy response of the tribal peasantry of Chota Nagpur to the combined impact of the diku and the colonial government on an agrarian order which was the very basis of their livelihood as well as of their way of life. The protracted campaign of the Sardars was in fact called *mulkui larai*, meaning, literally, the fight for the land.[30] Spread over a period of forty years the larai exceeded the purely economic objective it had assigned itself in the initial stages, and what was originally conceived as a struggle for land assumed, by a series of transformations, the character of a struggle for a homeland. When, therefore, the hour struck for

[26] BC 1363 (54226): 'The Translation of the Statement of Sing Rai . . . taken at Inchagur . . . on the 14th of February and subsequent dates'.

[27] BC 1363 (54227): Vice-President's Minute (30 Mar. 1832).

[28] J. C. Jha: 151. [29] Singh: 26. [30] Ibid.

the ulgulan, the ritual chants of the Mundas rang with lament for a lost primordial *disum*. Here are some stanzas from Suresh Singh's translation:[31]

The land given to us in the beginning [of Creation] by Singbonga
was snatched away by our enemies
We shall assemble in large numbers with weapons in our hands
The new sun of religion was born, the hill and valley were lit up
The zamindars harassed and put us to trouble

Birsa Bhagwan is our leader . . .
We shall not be afraid of the monkeys
We shall not leave the zamindars, moneylenders and shopkeepers
[alone]
They occupied our land
We shall not give up our *khutkatti* rights
From leopards and snakes we reclaimed our land
The happy land was seized by them

O Birsa, our land is afloat
Our country drifts away . . .
The big enemy, the sahebs donning the hat
Seized our land

But the notion of an 'original home' was more than a mere zero sign of rebel consciousness. Neither the Kols nor the Mundas resigned themselves to mourning an absence. Territoriality expressed as a sense of physical space had also a positive side to it. In the insurrection of the Kols this was indicated by the fact of their 'never having attempted to cross the Subarnareeka [Subarnarekha] River (which at that season is nearly dry) into the adjacent Pergunnahs of Patcoom and Seldah of the Jungle Mehals, which while those Pergunnahs presented every temptation to plunder from the opulence of the many Inhabitants, were wholly unprotected and could not, it appears, at that time have offered any resistance'.[32] Obviously for them that river was the frontier by which the realm of insurgency defined itself—a sort of geopolitical sign of the aims of the uprising, similar to what the Ganges was to be for the Santal hool later on in the century.

This positive spatial aspect of territoriality was even more

[31] Ibid., Appendix H. The translation has been slightly modified.

[32] BC 1363 (54227): Blunt's Minute (4 Apr. 1832). The same point is made in his earlier minute of 28 January 1832 as well.

clearly emphasized in the ulgulan. The recovery of the lost homeland of the tribe (*ekasi piri tirasi badi*, to mention it by its picturesque name) was a central aim of Birsa's campaign, and he educated his people for this task by ceremonial visits to their ancestral sites and his emphasis on recovering the tribal 're- cords of rights'. The idea was obviously powerful enough to be incorporated into their religion. Some Birsaite hymns like the one cited below bear witness to this:

> O Lord, Chutia Garh was our ancestral place . . . The Lord [Birsa] on his return from Jagarnathpur took brothers and sisters to Chutia Temple. He went there to bring the records of rights, manners and customs for us to support our ancestral rights which had been taken away by the enemy. Now we shall worship the Tulsi plant . . . We shall live according to the religion in our lands and spread it all over.[33]

What had begun thus as a simple declaration of spiritual faith absorbed in the course of the ulgulan some of the anxieties generated by that conflict. 'O Dharati Aba', they chanted then, 'help us today/ . . . With your strength turn bullets to water/ Let all enemies fall prostrate/O Dharati Aba, ours is the land, ours the country.'[34]

The adivasi view of the otherness of the diku in spatial terms was an element of the territoriality of the hool too. The self-differentiation of the autochthones in this particular respect is perhaps more clearly enunciated in the *Mare Hapram Ko Reak Katha*[35] than in any other recorded tribal tradition. Its account of the early history of the Santals sets them apart from the dikus by their residence in clearly demarcated areas even when there was no hostility between them: 'They settled in the more open parts, we in the hills and the jungles.' But that was a long time ago when they lived together in peace in the legendary land of Champa. Since then however their relation had been one of continuous antagonism. Wherever the tribe settled down in the course of their restless wanderings they invariably clashed with the 'others', that is, Hindus and Musalmans. They lost Champa to the former who followed close on their heels into

[33] Singh: Appendix K.

[34] Ibid.: Appendix H. Slightly modified.

[35] MHKRK: *xci–xciii*, *clxxvi–clxxvii*.

the plains (*tandi desh*) and ousted them from there. The Santals pushed on still further but only to come into contact with the Musalmans (*Turuks*) and flee in fear. 'We moved on and on like caterpillars.' In the 'Shikar country', they cleared the king's jungles and acquired some villages for themselves. 'But the Hindus chased us away even from there and seized our lands and settlements.' Eventually they came down to the plains again, and were 'driven by Hindu oppression and hunger' to cross the Ajay and spread over the hilly tracts to the north and east up to the Ganges. 'We had to fight many a battle with the dekos', says the *Reak Katha*; 'and we are not reconciled to them even today. Wherever we clear up some land for a settlement, the dekos come and grab it.' Inevitably, therefore, this grievous sense of loss formed a part of the complex motivation for the uprising of 1855. As a Santal folk song has it:

> Sido, why are you bathed in blood?
> Kanhu, why do you cry *Hul, Hul*?
> For our people we have bathed in blood
> For the trader thieves
> Have robbed us of our land.[36]

However, in the hool, no less than it was in the ulgulan, the fight for land merged in the general struggle for a homeland. According to Dalton, the region between the Ganges and the Kasai was regarded by the Santals as their 'fatherland'.[37] Sherwill mentioned Monghyr as its westernmost point. This was confirmed by yet another officer who wrote about their plan to march 'via Bhaugulpore to Monghyr to take possession of the Fort, which they affirmed to be the western boundary of a Kingdom once their own'.[38] Whatever its precise geographical boundaries (as a country of the mind it didn't *need* any) its presence as an ideological factor in their rebellion was obvious. Even before it actually broke out, 'mysterious allusions' were often made to a certain Morgo Raja of the Pareshnath hills who, it was believed, would set up 'an independent kingdom of the south country, meaning the original country of the Sonthal tribe'.[39] And in the third week of July 1855 when the hool was

[36] Archer: 207. [37] Dalton: 208.

[38] JP, 20 Dec. 1855: Sherwill to Brown (18 Oct. 1855); Barnes to Brown (8 Nov. 1855). [39] CR: 242.

still going strong, the colonial authorities were alarmed at the prospect 'that the insurrection may spread from Beerbhoom to those districts which are the original site of the Sonthal tribe'.[40] The insurgents themselves referred to the Ganges as a frontier of this 'original site'. In the parwana issued by Sido and Kanhu on the eve of the insurrection, they asked the Europeans to retire to the other side of that river. 'If you are satisfied with the Thacoor then you must go to the other side of the Ganges', they advised.[41] This, according to the *Reak Katha*, was to apply to all other outsiders as well. One of the elders whose testimony is recorded there, mentions that 'the Ganges was regarded as our frontier at the time of the rebellion' and the dikus would have been driven beyond it but for the intervention of the sahibs on their behalf. Old man Jugia's reminiscences, too, confirmed this. 'Sido and Kanhu then commanded', he said, 'we shall slay all the rajas and mahajans, and chase away all other Hindus beyond the Ganges; we shall then rule ourselves.'[42] The insurrection was thus a consciously defined space for them.

A correlate of the category of space was a sense of time. As such, this also entered into the subjective determination of territoriality as one of its elements and helped a tribal rebellion to define its domain in terms of the insurgents' relation to the diku. Expressed in its most generalized form as a contrasted pair of times (*then/now*), a good past negated by a bad present, its function was to endow the struggle against the alien with the mission of recovering the past as a future.

The traditions of the Santals are overlaid with nostalgia. Collected as folklore fifty years after the hool, some of these refer to a state of grace from which they are believed to have fallen by sinning against God (Thakur Baba).[43] Others, recorded closer to the event, in 1871, are informed by a more secular vision. They look back to an age of relatively greater affluence and purer ethical conduct. The decline since then is said to have been caused by factors of two different kinds—those which are internal to the tribe itself and those for which the responsibility lies with the dikus. 'Times have degenerated

[40] JP, 23 Aug. 1855: Grey to GOI, Military Department (21 July 1855).
[41] TTP. [42] MHKRK: *xci, clxxviii.*
[43] For some specimens see Bompas: 401–2.

now': the Santals no longer observe the customary norms of deference due from women to men, from daughters to mothers, sons to fathers, and the youth to the elders; the majhis have lost their ancient authority; disputes, so rare in the past, are common even among affines; there is no longer that peace and accord with which people used to live together in former times; the high standards of sexual morality once based on religion and maintained by the fear of reprisal and communal sanctions have given way to seduction and promiscuity; industry which in the past made the people produce what they needed for their own immediate consumption has disappeared and sloth taken over; and so on.[44] As against these there are some other symptoms of moral and material decline attributable directly to the intrusion of the dikus into Santal life. Some of these are vices acquired by the Santals when they came into contact with the aliens. Specified in the *Reak Katha*[45] these are as follows:

Begging: 'Formerly there were no beggars. The few who go around begging in the villages nowadays have learnt to do so from the dikus. This is generally disliked. Nor is this necessary. For whoever is willing to work can find enough subsistence within the village.'

Stealing: 'Formerly the Hor Hapans (Santals) never stole. But nowadays they have learnt to do even this in emulation of the dikus.'

Quarrelling: The Santals often fight among themselves over land and quarrels break out over the use of boundaries between fields. 'These two forms of dispute have now spread all over our land, thanks to the example set by the *deko hapans* (Hindus). There were no such disputes in the past.' It is the dikus 'who are making us fight between ourselves and grab each other's properties. Where they are, there's no amity . . . Had the 'deko pusis'[46] not been there amongst us, we the Santals would have been better off morally.'

Lying: 'From the very beginning until the other day we the Santals didn't know how to tell a lie; we said only what we saw with our own eyes, whether this concerned our enemies or our own brethren. Since the advent of the sahebs some of our people have been hanged to death only because they owned up to the truth . . . It was not customary with us to produce the witnesses one after the other before our

[44] MHKRK: *cxxxvii–cxxxviii.* [45] Ibid.: *cxxxv, cxlvi, cxlvii.*

[46] According to Bödding, the term 'deko pushi' means 'a Hindu cat, a term of contempt (said to be due to the Hindus, like cats, being particularly fond of milk and fish)'. As a Santal saying goes, 'You may pass with a Santal, you will never pass with a Deko-cat (i.e. you may deceive a Santal, but not a Hindu)'. Sinha *et al.*: 127.

own tribunals; they were all presented together and made to face each other. And yet no one would commit perjury. But the Santals have now learnt the language of intrigue from the dikus and like them are selling off their life and honour for a tumbler of country liquor.'

The dikus, however, were held responsible not merely for the moral corruption of the Santals but also for the loss of their material prosperity. The intrusion of the moneylender and trader in the economic life of the tribe was recorded in its tradition as a watershed dividing a happy past and a poor present. The phenomenon was integrated into the legends of its early wanderings and assigned a place in popular imagination by many a hostile proverb and imagery. 'Formerly no one borrowed from the mahajans', said Kaloyan, the wise old man of the race, in his ancestral account,[47] 'nor indeed were there any mahajans around. It was only in Shikar country that they latched on to us for the first time . . . Since then until this very day we have been in their clutches and they are tearing away at us like vultures . . . As the saying goes: . . . "The Hindu *sahukar* will chew up even the dry bones of the aged and the decrepit." As a matter of fact it was their extortion which put us on the run again from Shikar as well. However, at the beginning they were not so unscrupulous about charging interests . . . but their oppression increased as time passed . . . We, too, on our part have to take some of the blame. People fall into the mahajans' clutches without considering the pros and cons of what they are doing [while transacting with them].'

A sense of time expressed in terms of a *then/now* distinction may be said to have been implicit in the Santal hool if for no other reason than that it was a determined and conscious attempt to end the tyranny of the diku. However, it would be reading too much into the evidence to say that the termination of an unbearable present was regarded by the rebels as the means of recovering the past. We know that the establishment of some kind of a political kingdom was a part of their stated aims, and that the parwana issued by their leaders had, indeed, announced the advent of 'the reign of Truth' and 'True justice'.[48] But it would be rash to suggest that this rather hazy vision of the shape of things to come was to any significant degree invested with the qualities of an idealized past. By con-

[47] MHKRK: *cxxxix*. [48] Ibid.: *xci*; TTP.

trast, the temporal component was more fully developed in the Birsaite ulgulan. Its spatial objective, the purloined *disum*, was assigned a place in time not only as a memorable past but also as a desirable future in the Munda imagination. The domain of rebellion extended thus in both directions from the subject's locus in an embattled present.

A tendency to look back in time had featured in the Sardar agitation too, but it was only under Birsa's leadership that the distinction between past and present came to acquire a decisive ideological function.[49] Codified in the form of the antinomy Satjug/Kaljug, it derived at the same time from the Hindu myth of the four epochs (*yugas: Satya, Treta, Dvapara, Kali*) and Judaeo-Christian millenarism, imbibed respectively from the Vaishnava contacts of his early youth and his schooling at a missionary institution as a child. Whatever its origin, the opposition between the two *jugs* figured most prominently in the religious discourses and rituals by which he prepared his tribe for the uprising of 1899–1900.

In the Birsaite homiletics the difference between the past and the present conditions of the Mundas is represented as a contrast between conditions characteristic of Satjug and Kaljug. The comparison ranges over all the salient aspects of material and spiritual life. In Satjug the Mundas were directly ruled by Niranjan, the creator of the universe. In Kaljug they are ruled by Queen Mandodari, the spouse of the mythical demon-king and archetypal evil, Ravana. The contrast between life under divine rule and subjection under the Raj presided over by Queen Victoria could not be more clearly stated.

Land constituted the material basis of the blissful life of the Mundas in Satjug. Their ancestors cleared the jungle and made the land habitable for man. They lived in harmony with nature and with the wild beasts around them. They set up colonies, controlled floods, excavated wells and tanks and learnt the use of natural springs for the supply of fresh water. They introduced agriculture and made the earth ready to bear the grains and fruits they needed. In Kaljug the Mundas have been expropriated of this land which once belonged to them. They have been robbed by zamindars and mahajans who have

[49] For our information on this subject as given in this section we have relied entirely on Singh: 27, 36, 147, 160–3 & Appendix K.

made their way in their midst like 'a substance smooth like oil' and ruined them. In general, the natural economy of their Golden Age has been replaced by a money economy, industry and commerce, their freedom and self-sufficiency by the tyranny and exploitation of the dikus. As a result they have nothing left of their ancient prosperity. In Satjug they used to gather seven harvests from each sowing; in Kaljug they have only one harvest per sowing. In that happy ancestral past they used to eat their meals out of gold and silver dishes. Now they starve to death. In the old days no one died of disease. Now it is common to suffer from and die of illness. Gone is the time when there was no sorrow on earth.

This decline in material well-being corresponds to a moral degeneration. Thanks to the dikus, Munda society has been penetrated by alien influences. The prevalence of *karam* and *paika* dances is symptomatic of a general and widespread corruption of their race in Kaljug. A high standard of social and spiritual morality was characteristic of their culture in Satjug. The Mundas in those days would commit no violence against their kinsmen. Sexual morality was strictly observed and unlike the dikus, men would not exceed the socially prescribed degree of joking with women. Spiritually, Satjug was characterized by an emphasis on religious faith and ritual observance. The rules of purity were taken seriously. No one would eat or drink before taking his bath. Alcohol was forbidden. People wore the sacred thread on their person and sanctified themselves by sandal paste marks. They prayed and made ritual offerings at their ancestral temple. They turned away from the anti-gods (Asur) and worshipped the sacred *tulsi* plant twice every day. All this has disappeared from Munda life in Kaljug.

This contrast between the two jugs was used by Birsa to encourage his people not only to reject their inglorious present but also to fight for a better future and Satjug was his blueprint for that future. He prophesied the end of Kaljug in chiliastic terms: 'O men, beware! This world will not end like this . . . it will end in great misery. I will turn deep waters into outlets. I will crush the hills.' And the reign of the enemies of the Mundas was to be 'destroyed in a violent conflict'. All 'the Romans, Germans, British, Rajas and Zamindars, Satans and devils' would be driven away from the land. 'The Zamindars are now very happy and they laugh at us. But their allotted period, their time-limit is over.' The land was to regain its former purity when washed with the sacrificial blood of 'a white goat', that is, the white men. The Mundas would then march to Delhi, occupy the 'throne', and 'rule in the land'. Eventually, 'when they win back our kingdom, they will make merry and their happiness will never end'. This was to be the beginning of yet another Satjug, a recapitulation of the original: 'And the cultivation of only one field will do for us. The people will not take land even if it is tied to their neck. There will be no war in the land. All will be done in accordance with religion. Just as our ancestors ruled according to their religion, so shall we reign.'

The coming end of Kaljug and advent of Satjug was a theme on which Birsa played again and again in his sermons at mass congregations and parables told to smaller groups of disciples. At Thakurdura, for instance, he looked into a dried up well and 'exclaimed that Satjug had arrived and Kaljug was on its way out'. The termination of the bad present was ritually enacted at some of the larger gatherings of his people on the eve of the ulgulan. A contemporary account of the Birsaite assembly at Dombari in February 1898 offers us a glimpse of this picturesque ceremony:

> . . . to perform the last rites of the enemies an artificial grove was improvised on Dombari hill. And they cut a banyan tree in the name of the Queen and observed the Holi festival. They placed the earthen lamps all over the tree and pitched a red and white flag near it. Then they danced the *Karma* dance of Kaljug. They chopped it from one side. A red flag was pitched on one side a white flag on the other. For the faithful, all the Birsaites, an artificial enclosure was built and the white flag pitched. All customs and manners, dance, garland, bangle, flowery finger ring and flower comb of Kaljug were prohibited and given up . . . And he [Birsa] put them [his enemies] to death. He danced on the dancing ground to the accompaniment of drum beats and declared that the Empire of the British Queen had come to an end. They proclaimed that in the name of the Queen they would shoot arrows at her effigy. They set the plantain tree on fire and cut it down and did away with it in her name.

It was thus that the wicked epoch and its institutionalized form, the Raj, were symbolically destroyed to make way for a return to Satjug and Munda rule. The Hindu festival of Holi celebrated by burning the effigy of Holika, the she-demon, to mark the end of the old year and usher in the new, was its ritual equivalent. And since the function of mime is to make a wish come true, the ulgulan when it came darkening the sky with arrows and dotting the land with columns of fire, was to be the actualization of that ceremony performed at Dombari hill. Enmeshed as it was in the fantasy of a Satjug, it was nevertheless a step forward in the direction of a *real* future. In that future the Mundas were not destined to walk on earth as twenty-one foot tall giants like the fabled supermen of the Golden Age dreamed up by Birsa. However, thanks to this dream they gained immensely in stature as rebels fighting for a life free from the domination of foreign and native oppressors.

It will be wrong to deduce from what has been said above that territoriality was characteristic of the outlook and uprisings of the tribal peasantry alone. On the contrary, this was an element of consciousness common to all of the rural populations including Hindus and Muslims and deeply ingrained in their view of society, politics and culture secular as well as religious. The growth and consolidation of a colonial empire with its centralized bureaucracy, army and legal system, its institutions to purvey a western-style education, its railways, roads and postal communication, and above all the emergence of an all-India market economy did much to undermine the force of territoriality. Yet the habit of thinking and acting on a small local scale, continued throughout the colonial period and particularly until the end of the nineteenth century: the nationalization of politics on a sub-continental scale was still to take some time fully to develop.

It is generally believed that the *Pax Britannica* contributed much to the reinforcement of casteism at the expense of territoriality.[50] Yet in a curiously paradoxical way it was this very process which guaranteed the survival of the latter and most caste populations, including, as Dumont points out, even the widely distributed Brahman castes of Uttar Pradesh, tended to

[50] Facts and words quoted in this paragraph are taken from Srinivas (1962): 16; Miller: 410, 418; Dumont: 199, 200; Mayer: 151, 212–13, 271–2; Pocock: 131, 159; and Inden & Nicholas: 33.

concentrate in a few districts as their respective foci. For territoriality, though by no means identical with caste consciousness, was still for a long time to count as one of its basic components. Miller's observation about the system of territorial segmentation in Malabar as 'a necessary correlate of a rigid caste system' could be said to apply to all of India, for everywhere, as in Malabar, it was the function of these small local units to promote intercaste relations and sustain the caste hierarchy at the village level. They represented the villager's notion of the size and spread of his own subcaste—a correspondence so direct, indeed, that in many cases a subcaste was known by the name of its locality. The range of affinal links of a village subcaste group was yet another instance of such correspondence. Described by Mayer as a 'subcaste's region' it acted, among other things, as a catchment area for marital transactions involving its members. Pocock's study of such transactions among the Patidar of Gujarat shows how until recently the territorial factor used to be a determining influence on marriage alliances concluded by the members of an *ekada*. And one may cite linguistic usages such as *parasamparke bhai* ('neighbourhood-related brother'), *gramsamparke kaka* ('village-related father's younger brother'), etc., in Bengali as further evidence of the link between kinship and locality. Altogether it is difficult not to accept Mayer's observation that at 'the level of the effective caste group and subcaste group . . . we step down to purely local relationships'.

Caste, of course, is pre-eminently Hindu and casteism alien to canonical Islam. Yet in the local societies where Hindus and Muslims live together the latter, too, are assigned ranks, rights and obligations in what amounts virtually to caste terms. This, according to Imtiaz Ahmad, involves them in an actual recognition of caste distinctions and its rationalization in religious terms. No wonder, then, that the divisions within Muslim society too are partly conditioned and the relations between them governed by territoriality. Thus, the Muslim Meos of Rajasthan and Haryana parallel the Bengali practice mentioned above in attributing an imaginary kinship to fellow villagers: 'The entire community is visualized as an extended family and members of each generation born in the village are believed to be like siblings, unless, of course, they are actually closely related in a different way.' A study of a local Muslim population in a West Bengal district has shown how it regards itself as an aggregate of ethnic communities called *jats* (meaning castes in colloquial Bengali) with a single jat living on its own in each of the ten villages out of a group of thirteen and two living together in each of the remaining three villages, but with one jat vastly outnumbering the other in every case even there. A clear pattern of territorial segmentation has been noticed among the Muslims of south India too. In Malabar the division between the father-right and mother-right Moplahs who 'usually form two different compartments', corresponds, in spite of a certain overlap, to fairly distinct regional concentrations—the former in the interior of South Malabar and the latter in the coastal regions of North and South Malabar and Mangalore. In Tamil Nadu the four subdivisions of the Muslim community 'appear to be distributed within territorially distinct parts of the state' with Kayalars and Marakayars located primarily along the Coromandel coast and Labbais and Rawthers in the interior. The division between the last two groups again corresponds to that between a predominantly southern and a northern cluster. With all four endogamy helps to reinforce their separate identities in both kinship and territorial terms. Very much the same pattern holds for Uttar Pradesh where local Sheikh Siddique groups (which for all practical purposes act as subcastes) assert their identity positively in terms of endogamy and common habitation within a particular circle of villages and negatively by refusing to acknowledge by intermarriage or otherwise the rest of the Sheikh Siddiques in that neighbourhood as members of their own caste. Finally, it may be in order to mention that over 60 per cent of Meo marriage alliances in a Rajasthan village were found to have been contracted within a radius of twenty miles and over 90 per cent within a radius of thirty miles[51]—clearly a case of 'kinship enforced by propinquity' (to quote Lowie's happy phrase[52]) and a close parallel to the Patidar practice cited above.

Territoriality thus is no less essential to the Hindu and Muslim way of thinking and acting in society than it is to that of the

[51] Facts and citations in this paragraph up to this point are taken from Ahmad: *xxvii*, 36, 39, 49, 51, 63, 65, 66, 113, 117a, 169. [52] Lowie: 69.

tribal peasantry. Indeed, this is what links even the local administrative units, such as the village and the *nād* as Srinivas says of Coorg, to 'the sentiments of the people'.[53] Such sentiments permeate all levels of the superstructure. In politics these can be traced back to a period of about a thousand years beginning with the later Vedic age when petty kingdoms were slowly evolving out of local tribal settlements—*grāmas* amalgamating into *rāshṭras*—and tribal chiefs transforming themselves into kings,[54] a process ritualized, for instance, in the picturesque Hiraṇya-garbha ('Golden Womb') ceremony which, conducted by Brahman priests, helped the chieftains of the *āṭavika* tribes to be 'reborn' into another caste or even into a caste for the first time. 'Royal prerogative', writes Kosambi of the earlier part of this period, was still 'seriously restricted by tribal custom and tribal law' and territoriality, that hallmark of tribal polity, was made explicit by such punishments as ostracism—that is, by actually cutting off the territorial bond between an offender and his local community or as the term *aparuddha* implies, by pronouncing him to be a person denied the right of access. Subsequently as castes began to emerge 'the essentials of tribal society were retained in this transition, namely endogamy' and 'expulsion from the *jāti* remained the most potent and dreaded punishment, as expulsion from the *gens* or tribe had been earlier'. Vestiges of such correspondence between politics and territoriality are still to be found both in the authority of the local caste panchayats and in such expressions of rural justice as the temporary banishment of a man beyond the village boundary in order to punish him for the highly polluting offence of causing the death of a cow.[55]

In many parts of colonial India the village boundary was and perhaps is even today a particularly sacred mark of territoriality. A host of godlings and rituals were its ubiquitous symbols. Srinivas mentions a 'familiar deity in Telugu and Tamil villages' whose name, Ellamma, literally means 'boundary-mother'. Poleramma and Kalamman were two other boundary goddesses listed by Whitehead in his account

[53] Srinivas (1952): 57.

[54] This and other observations on ancient India in this paragraph are based on Kosambi (1972): 51, 87–8, 171 *et passim*, and Kosambi (1975): 148–62, 318 *et passim*.

[55] See Dumont: 220 and Mayer: 265.

of the village gods of south India. He also describes the worship of the boundary stone, *ellai-kal*, which 'is very commonly regarded as a habitation of a local deity, and might be called a shrine or symbol with equal propriety'. In one such village near Puddukkottai he found an elaborate ceremony involving as many as nine boundary stones. The central Indian village studied by Mayer, too, had a number of shrines of this kind—three of them devoted to Adyapal Maharaj, the lord of the southern, western and eastern gates of the village, two to Bisesa Maharaj and Udeyrao Maharaj, deities who presided over its northern and south-eastern borders respectively and one to Chira, a holy stone that divided the village from a neighbouring hamlet. And in Coorg the nād-boundary was the ritual site for the customary 'plantain honour' done to a groom on his way to the bride's village as well as for offerings made on the outbreak of an epidemic to Mariamma, the goddess of pestilence.[56]

Suffused thus with religiosity the territorial sentiment itself tended to be spiritualized to some extent. In Coorg, for instance, 'it was common for deities to be identified with their *nāds*' and consequently, for chauvinism with religion. 'A patriot', says Srinivas, 'was also a devotee.' Raiding and defending temples, 'the most sensitive part of a *nād*', victories and defeats in such encounters and deeds of great daring on such occasions were the stuff of which the folklore of local patriotism and the legendary reputation of individual heroes was made. At the hour of the birth of a hero in a nād, it was believed, the tower of the most important temple in its rival nād would crack.[57]

However, local solidarity was not made up merely of feuding over temples even in Coorg. The closing up of ranks by all villagers irrespective of caste in the face of a natural calamity befalling any one *okka*, the ritual mourning by all of bereavement in any single household, the village dance which concluded the harvest festival, the communal hunt which followed and the terminal feast, literally called 'village harmony', on the occasion of certain festivals, were all highly formalized expressions of a territorial tie which was no less secular than religious. In Malabar, too, Miller found this tie to be very strong indeed:

[56] For the information cited here see Srinivas (1952): 180, 204; Whitehead: 24, 32, 33, 35, 101–4; Mayer: 102.

[57] Srinivas (1952): 69, 203.

'The *desam* was the locus of nearly all intercaste relations from the lower (non-military) Nayar subcastes downwards.'[58] So was the 'village region' in Malwa. A correlate of the subcaste's region but less obviously articulated in institutional terms, it was a significant element of the villager's idea of himself as a member of a local community. As Mayer defined it:

This [village] region is never made manifest, for the village as such never invites guests or acts as a body in this way . . . Nevertheless the village region to some extent exists because villagers do think of an area in which they are at home, *where people are not felt to be strangers.* In the same way as a subcaste member coming from a distance is not admitted until he can claim some connection with 'recognized' relatives, so *villagers see the people outside their region as strangers,* with different customs, different ways of speech, etc.[59]

It is important to notice how the villager's self-identity in terms of his own region was negatively defined. If solidarity was one axis of territoriality, exclusion was another, and the latter had many determinations depending on the context in which it functioned. It could take the form, as it did in Malabar, of denying immigrant astrologers or barbers a *desam avakasam*—that is, the right to practise their traditional occupation in a desam without the approval of the family which had the hereditary privilege to render these services in that particular area. Or it could find expression in a tragic dilemma like that of the Coorg physician, Kunge, dramatized customarily at harvest festivals. He was split between his sense of duty to attend to a severely wounded man from a friendly nād and his obligation to heed his mother's injunction not to do so on the ground that the man belonged to a village traditionally hostile to her native nād and the wound had been received during a feud between the two. The mother prevailed and the warrior died testifying to the fact that a non-tribal villager's hatred of an 'outsider' could fully match a Santal's or a Munda's antagonism towards a diku.[60]

One such outburst of hatred, historic rather than legendary, was witnessed in the Deccan riots of 1875. Moneylenders were

[58] Ibid.: 61–2, 202; Miller: 414.
[59] Mayer: 213. Emphasis added.
[60] Miller: 413; Srinivas (1952): 203.

the invariable targets of these jacqueries of the Kunbi peasantry. Their attempt, in all cases, to seize and destroy the bonds, decrees and other related documents held by their creditors, their willingness to spare the latter any further violence once the incriminating papers were obtained and resort to physical assault only if the bonds were not surrendered, leave no doubt about the precise character of the riots as a conflict between moneyed capitalists and the agriculturists exploited by them through usurious transactions. Yet this conflict was so overdetermined by territoriality that it was, for the peasant, no less a resistance to 'foreigners' than a struggle against oppressors.

The great majority of the moneylenders—*vanis*, as they were locally known—were, indeed, not natives of Maharashtra. They had migrated from Gujarat and Rajasthan and settled in the Kunbi villages of Ahmadnagar and Poona districts. The power of their purse made them indispensable to the local peasant economy without, however, assimilating them into the local society. Their insistence on maintaining intact all affinal and ritual ties with their native provinces, their aggressive techniques of money-making and above all their indifference to local sentiment had done nothing over the decades—centuries in the case of the older immigrant families—to endear them to the Kunbis even during Maratha rule. What, however, had been until then a state of uneasy symbiosis broke down altogether under the combined impact of the ryotwari system and the judicial procedure introduced by the British. It helped the vani to enmesh the peasant even further in usury and displace at the same time the village community and the traditional elite who under the old regime mediated between the state and the cultivator as well as between the latter and his creditor.[61] No wonder then that within two decades of British rule the moneylenders came to be regarded not merely as ruthless exploiters of the peasantry but also as elements who stood clearly outside the local tradition and subverted it. This image was not made up of peasant prejudice alone. In official statements, too, they could be represented as 'chiefly foreigners, different in religion from their clients, entirely out of sympathy with them, and accustomed to retire with their profits after a sufficiently long

[61] Kumar: 34–5, 151–5.

course of business to their homes in Rajputana'.[62] As for the Kunbis themselves the idea of the vani as an outsider appears to have been a directive principle of their violence in 1875. It was aimed almost exclusively at moneylenders, but within that class it discriminated carefully between the 'indigenous' and the 'alien', as the Deccan Riots Commission observed:

> The Marwari and Gujur sowkars were almost exclusively the victims of the riots, and in villages where sowkars of the Brahmin and other castes shared the money lending business with Marwaris it was usual to find that the latter only were molested.[63]

A negatively defined territoriality was thus as basic to Maratha peasant insurgency as it was to the tribal uprisings above. However, there is some evidence to suggest that the territorial tie operated among the Kunbis not merely as a measure of exclusion. They also appear to have used it, as did the Santals and the Mundas, to promote solidarity between neighbouring villages against their common foe. A letter sent by the inhabitants of Kallas in the summer of 1875 to those of Akola reproaching them for not joining in the campaign of excommunication against Marwaris 'who are deemed as excluded from the community of this village', appealed for co-operation, 'for the good of all of us . . . *as we consider Kallas and Akola as one village*.'[64] One wonders if in sending out this appeal the Kunbis of Taluka Indapur were drawing consciously on a tradition of Maratha peasant militancy based on co-territoriality. For the latter is known to have played an important part in popular resistance to fiscal surveys in Khandesh in 1852. This movement derived its strength from the solidarity of the Pajna and Tilole Kunbis who lived in the Savda and Yaval regions of that district. As the officials most concerned with this event wrote at the time, 'The fact of all the chief men of the Pajnee and Teelolee castes to which the mass of the cultivators in the Yawul and Sowda districts belong, being residents of the villages of Sowda Mahal, accounts for the

[62] *Selections from the Records of the Government of India, Home Department, no. cccxlii* (Calcutta 1897), vol. II, p. 256, quoted in Stokes: 245.

[63] DRCR: 3.

[64] DRCR(C): 210.

agitation having originated and attained its greatest development there.'[65]

Nothing brings out more clearly the role of territoriality as a positive factor of rebel mobilization among the non-tribal peasantry than the massive jacqueries triggered off by the Mutiny. What made insubordination within the army particularly dangerous for the Raj was its linkage with peasant violence especially in large areas of what is now known as Uttar Pradesh and Madhya Pradesh. Here the insurrection of the sepoys boiled over and spread beyond barracks, cantonments and sadar stations into the surrounding countryside to acquire innumerable local bases for its articulation. These figure in many accounts of the rebellion as an acknowledgement of its territoriality by those who had the most to lose from it. As many as sixty-two villages were named by Qazi Kamaluddin, Munshi Lachhman Sarup and Shivabans Rai Vakil, three pillars of Sikandarabad society in their statements describing the sack of that town by the populace from its immediate neighbourhood.[66] The colonial authorities, too, were keen on tracing the agrarian violence to its local roots. Many amongst them were completely taken aback by the outbreak of these jacqueries and their force and extent. H. D. Robertson, Assistant Magistrate of Saharanpur, who had toured the tranquil countryside around Deoband on official business in April 1857 wrote thus in utter astonishment at what he saw there on his return six weeks later: 'Troops might mutiny, but I could hardly realize this rapid change among peaceful villagers.'[67] His words echoed the sentiments of those who functioned at the lowest levels of the administration close to the villages. And it is their response to the sudden rise in the local temperature that summer which explains more than anything else why their narratives of the Mutiny exude such a strong sense of place.

A most authentic source of our information of what happened in the rural districts of northern and central India in those days, these local reports and despatches bristle with place-names—the names of parganas and mauzas, particles of geography

[65] BC 2354 (146775): Mansfield & Wingate to Goldsmid (8 Jan. 1853).
[66] FSUP: V 40–51. [67] Stokes: 164.

caught in a beam of history. An extract from a Collector's report on the disturbances in a Rohilkhand district may serve to illustrate this. 'When the mutineers came to Budaon from Bareilly', he wrote, 'the inhabitants of Surai Jullundri, Surai Miran, Naee Surai and Surai Nahr Khan and mohulla Brahempoor—all mohullas in the city of Budaon, and those of Nugla Shurkee, Rusoolpoor and of other adjoining villages united with them in plundering the furniture and property in the bungalows of the European officers and residents in the station . . . The villagers of Nugla Shurkee also in unison with the residents of the Brahempoor, Puttialee Surai and Naee Surai—mohullas of Budaon, plundered and destroyed the records of the Moonsiffees as also those of the Kotwalee. On the news of the outbreak at the Sudder Station becoming known in the pergunnahs of the district disturbances broke out in every direction.' And he went on to list forty-five inhabitants of thirty-four villages in ten parganas as 'individuals and villages [that] would appear to have been conspicuous in their own respective localities'.[68]

But perhaps the most impressive tribute paid by the Raj to the territoriality of that rebellion was to pick out its rural sites as the focus of the counter-insurgency campaigns of 1857–8. These were military forays in which fire was as important an instrument of pacification as the sword—a pattern common to all British attempts to deal with the peasant wars of nineteenth-century India. Small mobile segments of what remained of the colonial army, often reinforced by all adult white men in a given area, penetrated into the countryside in Uttar Pradesh, just as they had done in Bihar and western Bengal two years earlier to suppress the Santal hool, and as on that occasion crowned most of the punitive raids on villages with exemplary acts of arson, execution and arrest. The activities of R. Spankie, Magistrate of Saharanpur, were fairly representative in this respect and deserve therefore to be recalled in some detail. This is how he described these in an official letter to the Commissioner of Meerut Division:[69]

On the 21st May [1857] a large assemblage of Goojurs and Rangurs took place on the south and south-west of pergunnah Saharunpore.

[68] FSUP: V 222, 224–5. [69] Ibid.: 95–7.

The village of Mullypore was looted close to the station and treasury. Some signal example was necessary. All the Europeans of the place accompanied me with the district sowars and twenty men of the 29th, with a view to disperse the assembly. The villagers would not meet us, and scattered, deserting their villages, three of which were burnt . . . a number of prisoners were captured and brought into Saharanpore.

. . . I determined on the 22nd May to march to the village of Gurhow some 7 miles from the station. I found it deserted . . . I went on to Nagul, three miles further, and thence to a round of villages on the right; they were all deserted. I managed however to find the Lumberdars of mauza Kunkuri and Phoraur. These men had refused to pay their revenue. I brought them into Saharanpore . . .

On the 23rd May I visited several villages on the Deobund Road and off it. On this occasion I was also accompanied by several gentlemen of the station. I burnt one village . . .

On the 30th May I went down towards Munglour accompanied by Messrs. Trench, Plowden and Edwards, and by Captain Garstin. We were joined at midnight at a given point by Mr. Robertson and Captain Wyld . . . Our intention was to attack the village of Manuckpore . . . we found the village all but deserted. It was burnt, and we captured a few prisoners . . .

On the 3rd of June the Goorkhas under Major Bagot arrived . . . On the same evening I took a portion of the Goorkhas and some of the 4th Light Cavalry to attack and disperse a body of Goojurs . . . The Cavalry pursued them for some distance . . . A few men were cut up, and some prisoners were made. Two villages were burnt. In this affair I was joined by Mr. Brownlow and most of the residents, and of course by my own officers . . .

A report on some of the auxiliary operations carried out in the same district by another officer, W. C. Plowden, fills in some of the details of this campaign—how on 21 May 1857 he and his troops punished the village Chowree by flogging its headmen and destroying their houses and how two days later they raided the village Tarpah in order to seize Bukshee, a rebel leader. 'But though Bukshee remained at large, the object of our expedition was in a measure attained. The village of Tarpah was burnt to the ground. The headmen were secured and a quantity of cattle was captured.'[70] A year later, almost to the day, the village of Chit Baragaon, the principal seat of the Kausik Rajputs in Ghazipur district, which had provided a strong local base for

[70] For the source of our information and the extracts cited in this paragraph see Nevill (1907*): 183; FSUP: IV 269–70, 487 and V 98, 99.

Kunwar Singh, was given the same summary treatment. When the army attacked it after some hesitation—'the village was so strong'—it was found to be empty. 'Two of the notorious ringleaders were, however, fortunately caught lurking in the neighbouring ravines and immediately tied and executed; their houses and those of the other ringleaders were levelled to the ground.' Soon afterwards Brigadier Douglas's force reached Gahmar in the same district in pursuit of Amar Singh only to find him gone; so he 'burnt it, the villagers having openly sided with the rebels'.

What the pacification campaign sought to achieve thus by taking on the offending villages one by one was to cope with the concrete articulation of the rebellion, for territoriality as the intersection of geographical and social space was indeed what constituted this concreteness. The jacqueries of 1857–8 were strictly local affairs: they operated within discrete local vicinages and had their social bases in local units with clearly recognized boundaries.

To take up the first of these two aspects, the domain of each jacquerie coincided with the domain of the peasants' relationship with their local enemies—official as well as non-official. More often than not the villagers would turn on the nearest seat of government as the foremost and immediate object of their attack. In their eyes, a sadar station—the Anglo-Indian term for district headquarters—stood for sarkar itself. Situated usually in a small town its official buildings housed the court, the treasury, the police station, the jail and so on, and were the visible symbols of an authority which the peasants regarded with fear rather than affection at the best of times. Now that this authority had weakened and become vulnerable—a mutiny in a local garrison was often believed to be the signal of the end of the Raj—country literally invaded town to settle scores with tax collectors, court officials, policemen and not the least, those sinister files which ruined the cultivator by expensive and unintelligible legal processes.

Sadar stations therefore ranked high on the list of casualties in all accounts of the rebellion in the northern provinces.[71] Mathura provided a typical case. Here a detachment of native

[71] Our sources for the facts and direct citations used in this and the next para-

infantry mutinied in the afternoon of 30 May 1857. They killed a European officer, set fire to the administrative buildings, destroyed the public records, plundered the treasury, released all prisoners and then marched out of the town in the direction of Delhi. 'This state of things continued until the afternoon of the 31st [May] when the inhabitants of the surrounding villages made an inroad into the Sudder Station and plundered all the inhabited bungalows of the entire property belonging to the residents and from those which were not occupied they removed the doors and *chowkuts*, including those of the Government buildings; a few of the bungalows have also been burnt down by the insurgents.' Elsewhere in that district the people of Nohjhil and their neighbours pillaged a tax collector's office and destroyed all documents they found there. At Raya too the police station with all its records was burnt down by the villagers. Similarly, the demolition of the Bulandshahr district headquarters was the combined work of the Gujars from the surrounding countryside and the inhabitants of that town: they burnt down the dak bungalow and other official residences, destroyed all government buildings and their records, carried off or consigned to fire whatever property fell into their hands and released all prisoners.

At Badaun, again, the pillage of the bungalows belonging to the Europeans, the attacks on administrative offices and the police station and the destruction of records were carried out by villagers from the immediate neighbourhood backed by the townspeople. In Bundelkhand the peasants from the surrounding villages poured into Jhansi, broke open the jail, liberated the detainees and set fire to all the bungalows. At Muzaffarnagar, too, some of the bungalows were burnt down, kacharis destroyed, the jail barracks demolished and all their doors, shutters and iron rails carried off by the raiders who lived within an easy distance of the town. The pattern was the same everywhere. It repeated itself so often that one could hardly disagree with the Officiating Magistrate of the last named district when he observed: 'The burning of the cutcherries at Moozuffurnugger is not a solitary instance, on the contrary we

graph are FSUP: V 222 for Badaun; V 38, 39—Bulandshahr; III 47—Bundelkhand; V 689–91—Mathura; and V 76, 79, 81—Muzaffarnagar.

see that throughout this rebellion the first thing the "*budmashes*" have done in getting a footing in a station has been to burn the Government offices.'

Not merely government offices, but all that represented the Raj either directly or by association in any particular area—railways and railway stations as in Ghazipur and Allahabad, indigo and opium factories owned by white planters in Jaunpur and Ghazipur, bungalows as a clearly distinguished form of European residence everywhere, dispensaries and colleges run by the government as at Badaun and even charitable asylums set up by Christian effort, in fact 'every building however large or however insignificant with which we are connected' was, as a District Magistrate wrote viewing the carnage around him in July 1857, 'burnt down and demolished with as much ill-will as our public offices'.[72] Clearly no local representation of the authority of the Raj was safe from insurgent attack.

The other relationship which helped to determine the territoriality of this particular violence was the antagonism between peasants and moneylenders. The latter are described in all contemporary accounts as those who, apart from the government, were hurt most by the rural insurrection. 'I need scarcely say that the great feature in the rebellion here has been the universal ousting of all bankers, Buniyas, Marwarees, etc. from landed property in the district, by whatever means they acquired it, whether at auction, by private sale or otherwise.' This observation by the Collector and Magistrate of Hamirpur could apply equally well to almost any other part of the North-Western Provinces. Indeed, Spankie, the officer in charge of Saharanpur, was so greatly impressed by this phenomenon that to him it appeared 'as if the disturbances in the commencement were less directed against Government than against particular people and castes', that is, against banias and marwaris.[73] His idea that the uprisings developed in two stages—first against the mahajans and then against the regime—might have been true of particular instances, but there were innumerable occasions when the peasants attacked both these adversaries simultaneously or in reverse order.

In most cases, however, the insurgents made no attempt to

[72] FSUP: IV 128, 479, 556–7; V 222.

[73] For Hamirpur see ibid.: III 121 and for Saharanpur—V 94–5.

distinguish between them, for in their own experience, the two were inseparably linked. The economic and social aspects of that linkage have already been discussed in Chapter 1. What needs to be emphasized here is its local dimension.[74] In the eyes of the common villager the mufassil towns symbolized the alliance between sarkar and sahukar. The coexistence there of administrative buildings and bania wards—the coexistence of kachari and *haveli*—was its topographical expression; the interplay between legal processes and usurious transactions—its function. By focusing his violence on a sadar station or a township endowed with a tahsildari office the peasant registered his response to the local character of this symbiosis. Robertson, Assistant Magistrate of Saharanpur, showed a clear grasp of this aspect of insurgent mentality when he explained: 'The creditors of the poorer class of cultivators invariably inhabit the larger towns, so that these towns naturally enough became a point of attack when the civil power was paralysed.' What he saw in that district fully confirmed this. For the raiders came in a large body from villages around Nakur, the headquarters of the pargana of that name, burnt down its police station and tahsil offices, and tore up and scattered all records including mahajans' bonds and accounts.

Again, the sack of Deoband where the bankers and banias had been living in constant fear of 'invasion from without and sedition from within', was the work of Pandar Rajputs and Gujars, all of whom belonged to the pargana of which that town was the principal administrative centre. As Stokes has noticed, all eight of the most offending villages selected by Robertson for his two punitive expeditions in this region 'stood close to the Kali Nadi or its tributaries north and east of Deoband and within a 4 to 5 miles radius'. The district headquarters of Muzaffarnagar too fell to the wrath of its surrounding countryside. 'Here as in other parts of the country', wrote its Officiating Magistrate, 'the Buneahs and Mahajans were in the majority of cases the victims and fearfully have many of them been made to suffer for their previous rapacity and avarice.' And here, as elsewhere, the villagers 'burnt the Government offices so that all the transactions of sale and mortgage of property of Maha-

[74] Sources for our evidence and citations in this and the next paragraph are Stokes: 165, 166, 172–4, and FSUP: V 82, 91, 96.

jans and other papers . . . might be destroyed', thus demonstrating yet again their understanding—and dislike—of the complicity between moneylenders and government at the local level.

The territoriality of these uprisings of 1857–8 derived also from their ethnic character. All contemporaries testify to this phenomenon. To some extent, of course, it is the very language of the current system of classification which made them do so. For in the nineteenth century it was customary with both native and foreign observers to conceptualize Indian society in ethnic—primarily caste—terms. Yet this taxonomic bias was itself an index of the social organization which inspired it—that is, the tendency of large populations belonging to the same caste to congregate in contiguous areas and perpetuate this territorial arrangement by ritual and kinship. It is common therefore for the Mutiny records to describe the peasant rebellions of the time as the revolt of particular ethnic masses—of the Rajputs, the Mewatis, the Gujars and so on.

To start off with the Rajputs and a fairly transparent case of territoriality relating to the most prominent of its ethnic constituents, the rebellion in Bundelkhand was reported as the work of the eponymous Rajput sept, regarded by Crooke as 'almost entirely' confined to that part of the country. A caste with a strong sense of attachment to their traditional habitat—their prohibitions against marriage included 'residence among foreign peoples'—they were active in vast numbers in the Jhansi area. A rebel camp of over 20,000 men at Mhow was, according to British army intelligence, made up entirely of Bundelas. Again, it was the 'fighting horsemen and kinsmen' of the Bundela gentry of Gohand in Hamirpur who were said to be responsible for the serious and prolonged disturbances in that district. In Azamgarh the uprising was led by the Palwars who were very numerous there and belonged to the same *gotra*. Their challenge to the Raj was serious enough to make its end appear imminent in the eyes of the common people of the area: 'When at Azamgarh the battle raged between the British troops and the Palwars, many illiterate persons gathered and awaited the result; if the Palwars became victorious they also would join the Palwars.'

In the adjoining district of Jaunpur it was yet another hostile concentration of Rajputs—those of the Rajkumar sept—who constituted a threat to British power on this highly sensitive border of Awadh. The rebellion in Bhadohi, noticed below, came to be identified with the Monas, the most numerous and powerful caste of that pargana in Mirzapur district. The revolt headed by Shazada Firoz Shah in September 1857 at Mandsore in Malwa was based largely on the support of the local Mewatis who constituted nearly half of the insurgent army. Lieutenant-Colonel Durand recognized this as an advantage of some significance in his enemy's favour. 'It must be remembered', he wrote surveying the military situation from his camp at Mhow, 'that this Shazada has selected his point Mundisore judiciously enough, for that neighbourhood abounds with turbulent Mewatees.'[75]

It was the Gujars who were the main force behind the series of jacqueries that convulsed the north-western districts of Uttar Pradesh.[76] In Saharanpur the 'hard-core areas' of the rebellion were the western part of Deoband pargana, eastern Rampur, a small sector of Nagal and all of the parganas of Nakur and Gangoh, forming what Stokes calls 'the Gujar heartland'. According to him, 'Here solid clan settlement provided a powerful framework of organisation for revolt. Of particular importance was the cluster of 52 villages in Gangoh and Laknauti held by the Batar subdivision (*gotra*) of Gujars.' In Meerut, too, they set the country afire. 'The Goojurs throughout this district are in open rebellion', reported the Magistrate on 28 June 1857. Some five thousand of them led by Shah Mal of Bijroul sacked the township of Baraut, looted a bazaar at Baghpat, and tried to wreck a strategic bridge on the Hindan river in order to cut off military access to that region. They elected Kadam Singh of Parichhatgarh as their raja 'in furtherance of the plan of establishing a Goojur Government'. And their raids on the prosperous and loyalist Jat villages who 'almost invariably

[75] On the identity and role of the various groups as discussed in this paragraph see for Bundelas—Crooke (1896): II 163 and FSUP: III 607, 612–13, 626–7; Mewatis—FSUP: III 154, 156, 196; Palwars—Crooke (1896): IV 113 and FSUP: IV 105; Rajkumars—FSUP: IV 174.

[76] On Gujar participation as discussed here see Stokes: 165, and FSUP: V 35, 40–51, 108–9.

behaved nobly in the support of law and order', helped to emphasize by contrast the specifically Gujar character of the uprising. In Bulandshahr again the principal area of the insurrection coincided with that of the compact Gujar settlements in Dadri and Sikandarabad parganas, described officially as 'the most turbulent part of the district inhabited principally by Goojurs'. The latter rose in arms as soon as they heard of the events in Delhi and Meerut and 'at once commenced plundering in all directions, burning Dak Bungalows and destroying the Telegraph'. The attack on the district headquarters of Bulandshahr and the pillage of the township of Sikandarabad were mainly the work of peasants of this particular caste from the surrounding villages—a classic case of country encircling the cities.

Most though by no means all of the villages from which the masses of armed peasantry issued from time to time to harry the nearest towns were single-caste settlements. In each of these nearly all the population, barring females acquired by marriage, claimed descent from a common patrilineage, consanguinal or mythical, and regarded themselves as members of the same clan or gotra. This belief in a shared ancestry made the village assert itself positively by acting as a solidarity unit and negatively by operating an elaborate code of discrimination against aliens. Habib cites a late seventeenth-century case to show that it was rare—and indeed risky, judging by the given instance—for a Rajput to take up residence in a Jat village. His remarks on the caste composition of the typical north Indian village during Aurangzeb's rule applied to conditions in the eighteen-fifties as well:

Although any number of castes existed among the peasants in general, peasants of a village probably belonged most often to the same caste. This is true of many villages today. In Central Doab, for example, villages are often distinguished according as they contain Thakurs, Jats, Ahirs, Gujars or other castes of peasants. One can conjecture that this was still more the case when the ties of castes were much stronger . . . The peasants of a village were most often members not only of the same caste, but also of the same division or subdivision of that caste. They claimed the same ancestry and so belonged to the same *bhaiya-chara*, brotherhood or fraternity. This fraternity by invoking ties of blood, bound the peasants in a unity far stronger than could have been expected among mere neighbours.[77]

These village-based primordial ties were the principal means of rebel mobilization, mauza by mauza, throughout northern and central India in 1857. Brought about by the peasants on their own initiative or by their landlord masters, its motivation in terms of caste or clan could vary according to idioms and occasions specific to particular localities. Often it was a case of mutineers returning home to inspire their relatives living in that area to take up arms emulating the sepoys.[78] This is how the soldier son of a Nadwasiya Gujar chief, 'who had mutinied and come from Meruth made resistance' in the Dadri region of Bulandshahr. Mutineers of local origin were the catalysts of the uprising in a part of Hamirpur too. 'The Zemindars of Romeree which forms part of Humeerpore are Thakoors', wrote the district officer in his narrative of the events of 1857, 'and many Sepoys, relatives of theirs, came in relating terrible tales of mutiny and bloodshed, which caused the Zemindars of the two *thokes*, Danda and Manjkhore, to band themselves together for plunder which they commenced early in June.' Further to the east, Ghazipur was the home of 'many Sepoys who had fled back to their hearths with halters round their necks', as a Jaunpur Magistrate put it. Since 'the sepoys themselves were residents of the district, wherever they went they found followers ready to their hand'. Indeed, more often than not, 'these men served as rallying points and leaders to their neighbours and clansmen'. There were about one hundred and fifty of them in Zamania where, it was said at the time, 'they formed nuclei round which large numbers of bad characters and disaffected zemindars rally whenever occasion offers'. Again in the Ballia and Rasra tahsildaris of Ghazipur where four to five hundred mutineers had returned to their villages, the local rebel force was recognized by the government as one 'consisting partly of sepoys of that neighbourhood and of their brotherhoods among the zemindars'. Altogether the uprising in that district was universally credited to the dual initiative of army deserters and their peasant kin, for, as it was put in an official narrative of

[77] Habib: 122–3.

[78] The instances cited in this paragraph are taken from FSUP: III 114; IV: 140, 142, 272, 486; V 44.

events in the summer of 1858: 'The mutineers have almost everywhere in this district the sympathy of the population with whom most of them are connected by ties of kindred.'

A local insurrection, whatever its immediate cause, tended invariably to adapt itself to the existing pattern of ethnic solidarity in a given area. Allahabad provided a classic example. Here the Mewati response to the outbreak of the Mutiny was so instantaneous that it looked as if 'the Mewatis were the real contrivers of the rebellion of the sepoys and the Risala'.[79] Known for their strong sense of communal identity, they used the customary authority of a panchayat to effect a massive mobilization of their close-knit exogamous villages—fifty-one of these were specified by name[80]—in the rural belt around that city. Indeed, they had made the insurrection their own so quickly and so completely that it was not easy to distinguish between its military and civilian moments. It was caste fellowship again which secured the support of the Thakurs of Serowlee Buzurg and Khurd for the rebel zamindars of Romeree mentioned above,[81] while in Badaun district the disturbances in tahsil Gunnaur was the work of 'the Aheer Zemindars of Neore Beora, Bheraothee and other adjacent villages of the same brotherhood'. In Bijnaur, too, the local uprising was considerably extended by ethnicity as 'the Gujars of [the] other side of the Ganges helped the Gujars of this side in the latter's activities'.

The sack of Sikandarabad was yet another demonstration of caste solidarity as a generalizing agent of the rebellion. The more militant of the Gujar villages prepared for this action by sending out their men to rally the others who were less forthcoming. 'The men of Khugooabas and Jhendoo, zemindar of Nugla Nyusookh, went to the Goojurs' villages, threw down their *pugries*, incited them all to disorder and assembled them in Punchayat at Tilbegumpoor.' The result was a spectacular and systematic act of pillage in which the entire community was involved. Primordial loyalty of this kind provided the in-

[79] FSUP: IV 548.

[80] This figure represents the total number of place-names plus the gaps indicating names which are not legible in the two lists published in FSUP: IV 549, 550.

[81] For this and all the other instances cited in this paragraph see FSUP: III 118–19 and V 38, 45, 224, 246.

surgents not merely with bases for attack on the towns but also with asylum in nearby peasant homes when pursued by the enemy. A British officer was to recall later on how he and his men repulsed a party of raiders just about to charge into the sadar station of Bulandshahr, but found that 'the main body spread over the country and concealed themselves in the neighbouring villages'. The raiders as well as the villagers who offered them refuge were Gujars.

Caste ambitions which motivated some of these jacqueries also helped to emphasize their regionality and ethnicity. Such ambitions directly related to a sense of loss on the part of a rebel community—loss of land, territory or prestige. It felt aggrieved because a substantial part of its lands had passed into the hands of moneylenders and auction purchasers; or because it had been ousted from what it considered its traditional homeland; or because a radical decline in the wealth or authority of its elite group had lowered its standing both in its own esteem and that of others. These were by no means mutually exclusive determinations, but coalesced to form the substance of almost any communal sense of deprivation. What brought them together was politics, for there was no loss, whatever its cause, that was not felt to be a loss of power. Even grievances arising from land alienations exceeded their purely economic character and were politicized. The ambiguity generated by such an overlap and its consequence for historiography may be seen in the difference between an administrator's interpretation of a local uprising and a scholar's. When the Rangars, a Muslim Rajput caste, broke out in revolt in Kunda Kalan, H. D. Robertson, the Assistant Magistrate of Saharanpur, could find no economic justification for it. 'Unlike the improvident Goojurs their villages are generally populous and wealthy', he wrote, 'so that plunder could hardly be their inducement to disaffection.' He ascribed the rebellion to sectarian enthusiasm, to 'their bigoted daring' as he put it. Eric Stokes has found this explanation far too narrowly political. Robertson, 'like most British officials', he says, 'believed the revolt to be political in origin'. He puts his own emphasis primarily on economic motivation: '. . . in the Gangoh khadir the loss of nearly half the land to the mahajans must have affected sharply the attitude of the Kundra Rangars, however much Robertson might form an impression of their comparative prosperity'.[82] Both interpretations contain a great deal of truth about this event but by trying to exclude each other demonstrate a failure to grasp its ambiguity. What apparently happened was that in an atmosphere charged with uncertainties about the very survival of the Raj an accumulation of economic discontent had caught fire and exploded as a formidable defiance of authority. The administrator on the spot registered his immediate response to its *éclat*; the historian, distanced by time, his reading of what triggered it. Neither came quite close to understanding its duplex character.

In some of the revolts involving these ethnic masses the political motivation could hardly be missed. They took up arms in order to recover what they believed to have been their ancestral domains. It was this which accounted for the power and extent of the Gujar uprising in Saharanpur for instance. Here the clan was so numerous that at one time the district was actually called Gujarat.[83] A leader like Futtuah, therefore, found it possible to set himself up as a raja here with the object of 'regaining the consequence tradition has assigned them in this part of the country, once the principality of their ancestors'.[84] Again, the Palwars, a Rajput sept, connected with Azamgarh by tradition and myth, muscled their way into the Mahul region of that district in June 1857 and 'claimed the villages of this pargana to be theirs'. In yet another eastern district, Mirzapur, the rebellion of both the Palwars and the Monas was said to have been inspired by their desire to make up for the decline in their former power. 'Both clans had, as they conceived, a long standing grievance and lost superiority to recover.'[85] Of the two it was the latter who were particularly

[82] Stokes: 166, 167, 170. [83] Crooke (1896): II 441.

[84] Stokes: 166, 167.

[85] For Palwar traditions see Crooke (1896): IV 111–12, and for their participation in the rebellion of 1857—FSUP: IV 102, 410. Judging by the documents published in FSUP: IV Palwar involvement in the Bhadohi disturbances appears to have been only marginal. Their leader, Sarnam Singh, was primarily responsible for the attack on the indigo factory at Palee. Apart from that they simply acted as auxiliaries and allies of the Monas who at one time were said to have been planning the rescue of some of the imprisoned Palwars like Dhowan Singh (FSUP: IV 80, 81). I suspect, however, that there is much more evidence yet to be recovered from the archives about Palwar involvement in Bhadohi.

active in the Bhadohi pargana of that district. The *émeute* they caused offers a clear example of the territorial and political ambitions of a caste as the motor of a local peasant rebellion.

If legend may be said even remotely to approximate history, the Monas must have wanted Bhadohi very badly indeed for themselves. A party of their ancestors who had set out from their rude homeland in Rajputana on a pilgrimage to Banaras, were so greatly impressed by this fertile region of what is now Mirzapur district and coveted it so fiercely that they won their way into it after a long and bloody contest with its former settlers, the Bhars. The precise date of this conquest is difficult to ascertain but it is known that the pargana was ruled by a succession of Monas chiefs for over two centuries until 1746–7 when it passed into the hands of the rajas of Banaras. However, 'although the Raj had passed from the Monus clan yet the old reigning family was by no means extinct and was much looked up to in the pergunnah'. Indeed its standing was still high enough to enable it to involve the local population in its own dynastic strife when on the outbreak of the Mutiny the head of the clan, Udwant Singh, assumed his ancestral title of Raja of Bhadohi, and 'on the strength of this newly regained nobility' raised a private army of nearly two thousand of his caste fellows, took 'benevolences', organized pillage and felt bold enough to close the Grand Trunk Road.

The Monas had a reputation for turbulence going back at least to the seventeenth century. Peter Mundy travelling from Agra to Patna in the late summer of 1632 was much harassed by the 'Buddoyns' who in their utter defiance of authority were almost a law unto themselves: 'They neither regard the kinge nor his lawes verie much.'[86] The same could be said of them with equal truth two hundred and twenty-five years later when in June 1857 they took up arms not only against the Raja of Banaras but also against the district administration regarded

[86] Mundy: 119. For some of his other observations on Bhadohi and the Monas, all to the same effect, see ibid.: 90, 115, 118, 120, 122, 148, 180–1. Habib, however, considers the editorial identification of Mundy's term 'Manasse' with the Mona Rajputs as 'a wild guess', and is certain that the author had 'meant to write, if he has not actually written, "Mavasse" ', which, according to him, means the same thing as *zor-talab*, that is, 'rebellious territory'.

by them 'as more or less a partisan of the Rajah'. The insurrection of the sepoys and the civilian population in Allahabad, Jaunpur and Banaras which enclosed Mirzapur on three sides had already alerted the British authorities about the possibility of an outbreak in the most lawless pargana of the latter district. Already on 3 June 1857 the police officers of Bhadohi had been 'ordered to intimate to the zemindars and other respectable men that they might keep armed men if they chose for the defence of their lives and their properties and to be able to assist each other in case of a general rising among the people'. On 7 June the thanadar of Bhadohi reported a dacoity in a village within his jurisdiction. Three days later a party of rebels crossed over from Jaunpur 'to plunder some wealthy zemindars of the Bhudohey pergunnah' but retreated before the combined forces of the police and the local gentry. The same day the *sazawal* of the Raja of Banaras was attacked and severely wounded by the villagers of Bhinda. The district authorities, to leave no doubt on which side they stood, allowed Munshi Darshan Lal, the Banaras Raja's estate manager, to raise a force of two thousand men in order to meet the Monas threat. 'Anarchy became universal. Oodwunt Singh and his people plundered and burnt the villages of those to whom they owed grudges, and the homes of Oodwunt Singh and his friends were in turn burnt and plundered by the adherents of the Rajah.' The crunch came when Munshi Darshan Lal lured the Monas chief and two of his 'dewans' to come unarmed to a rendezvous where they were seized and made over to W. R. Moore, Joint Magistrate and Deputy Collector of Mirzapur, who promptly sent them to the gallows. This exemplary punishment produced a backlash for which the authorities were by no means prepared. Far from taming the Monas, it converted what was essentially a dynastic feud among the elite into a popular rebellion against the colonial power itself—a classic instance of a vertical mobilization turned horizontal. For out of the ensuing turmoil there emerged a local leader of the insurgents, a Monas of no aristocratic pedigree—'his ancestors were only dependents of the old Monus Rajahs'—a man called Jhuri Singh who not only avenged Udwant Singh by killing Moore and presenting his head to the widow of the Monas chief, but involved the

Bhadohi peasantry in a protracted guerilla war against the Raj.[87]

The territoriality of a rebellion is not of course a matter of coincidence between its domain and a caste region in every case. A locality larger than a village, such as a pargana or a district, could also be the site of an uprising in which peasants of two or more castes joined forces.[88] In Badaun district, for instance, Muslims and Thakurs worked together in the jacqueries that broke out in Bisauli pargana, and these two groups plus Ahirs in pargana Sahaswan. In Bijnor district 'the Mardhas and the butchers of Akbarabad after forming a big gang first looted the Patwaris of Akbarabad, then plundered the Jats of Sikandarpur, and then invaded Hajipur [and] looted Rampur'. The attack on Chandpur tahsil on 26 May 1857 was a joint operation by Mewatis and Pachandey Jats. The district of Bijnor as a whole was, according to its Magistrate, the scene of a collective violence of Banjaras, Gujars, Mewatis and Balochis all of whom had simultaneously taken to arms. In Saharanpur, too, 'the Rajpoots in most parts of the District and the Goojurs throughout the whole District took advantage of the times to plunder and to commit all kinds of atrocities'. Spankie reported 'a large assemblage of Goojurs and Rangurs' to the south and south-west of Saharanpur pargana on 21 May 1857 and the subsequent pillage of Mullypore village close to the sadar station and treasury. Even in Bulandshahr district where the Gujars constituted the main force of the insurrection, they had the Girooas and the Gahlots as auxiliaries. All three groups were party to the sack of Sikandarabad and were represented at the panchayat at Tilbegampur which preceded and planned their combined onslaught. As one of the local

[87] Apart from the source mentioned in n. 86 above the information presented in this and the preceding paragraph is based on Crooke (1896): IV 1–2; FSUP: IV 30, 49–50, 51, 53, 78–84; and Drake-Brockman: 99–100, 124–8, 207–9, 221–2, 241–2. Following Crooke (1896) and our sources we have used the caste name in its anglicized form, 'Monas'.

[88] For the instances cited in this paragraph see FSUP: V 41, 43, 45, 66, 95, 225, 253–4, 254–5, 266 as well as Currie to Lowe quoted in Stokes: 150, and Spankie to Williams (26 Sept. 1857): 'The plundering tribe of Goojurs was the first affected and the Rangurs were not far behind them' (FSUP: V 94).

raises put it, 'there was no village of the Goojurs and Girooas in the neighbourhood which did not take part in this affair'. Indeed, Walidad Khan himself seems to have had such a plurality in mind when he wrote to Delhi about 'Gujars and other country-folk of this neighbourhood' having 'raised their heads'.

For an example of a local rebellion which had its territoriality articulated as an intercaste mobilization involving many villages in several contiguous parganas cutting across three districts one could turn to the uprising headed by Meghar Singh in Ghazipur.[89] In this the easternmost part of Uttar Pradesh bordering on Bihar the impact of the Mutiny did not register until about the middle of 1858. It took the incursion of Kunwar Singh's and Amar Singh's forces into this region to shatter its apparent calm. A police report of 30 May 1858 from the officer in charge of the thana at Dildarnagar in Zamania pargana is the first record we have of disturbances in eastern Ghazipur. It spoke of a raid on Rajpur in the Chausa pargana of Shahabad by a force of two platoons of Amar Singh's men—'250 or 300 armed persons who appeared to be absconders'—led by Meghar Singh, a Rajput zamindar of Gahmar in Zamania. The raiders killed a *barkandaz* and a *patwari* and were joined by a large number of sepoys who had returned home to their native villages in that pargana. They were said to have 'resolved to stay at Gahmar and Barah and to persuade the whole pargana to rebel against the Government'. For the next two days they camped in a grove at Dewal on the bank of the Karmanasa where the insurrection was publicly launched at an assembly of several thousand people from the neighbouring districts. Between 3 and 5 June they plundered and destroyed some factories and other buildings owned by an indigo planter at Gahmar and Bhadaura. The presence of Meghar Singh and four hundred 'rebel sipahis', that is, local peasants who had been in the army, was reported from the first of these two villages on 6 June. It was said that 'he went about from one village to the other to incite people to rebel', and apparently met with considerable success. For an informer's note dated 9 June mentioned 'sup-

[89] The primary source of our information for this entire section is FSUP: IV 117–22, 280–9, 482–3, 486–7, 491–3. For all data outside this source we have relied on Nevill (1907): *passim*, and Oldham: 43, 64, 68, 69.

plies and other assistance' sent him by the villagers of Naoli, Bara, Gahmar, Karepa and Bhorai.

On 11 June Brigadier Douglas arrived at Gahmar and burnt it down. But such exemplary punishment inflicted on what was regarded as the most wicked of all insurgent villages in the area had apparently little immediate effect, for according to an official telegram of 14 June the Magistrate of Ghazipur still found his district entirely disorganized. In fact the burning of Gahmar appears to have helped in spreading the revolt rather than containing it. The local police and revenue officials whose authority was the subject of universal defiance were sensitive to it. 'Although the residents of Gahmar have left the place', wrote a tahsildar on 18 June, 'their zamindars are staying in the neighbouring villages at the distances of three, four or five *kos* and harbour evil intentions.' For already two days before that Meghar Singh had been seen at the head of a force of one hundred at Diwathia, a village in Zamania pargana. 'They had got together the rebels residing in the different villages' and stopped over at Kashni. On 19 June they attacked Niwalwan in Chainpur pargana of Shahabad district and threatened a planter's warehouse there. Throughout the rest of that summer the guerilla army went on adding to its size. Contingents of armed peasantry, many of them forced out of their villages by the increasingly vigorous counter-insurgency operations, and bands of army deserters with local ties poured into its ranks from all over the region. In August, for instance, one hundred sepoys crossed over from the other side of the Ganges to join Meghar Singh at Gahmar. Subsequently he was to recall how at one time he had as many as twelve thousand men at his command—a genuinely popular army which, he emphasized, 'made no raids for plunder'. It was 'the people of the six parganas' ranged along the Ganges and the Karmanasa in the Ghazipur–Shahabad border area who, he claimed, 'met our expenses'.

In the event, Meghar Singh met the fate of all roving rebels. By December 1858 his army disintegrated under the impact of sustained military operations by the British. He retreated into Nepal with only about five hundred of his followers but was forced by the local raja to withdraw from there and re-enter Indian territory in the spring of 1860. He moved around for eight months as a pilgrim between various holy places—a motif which recurs in the careers of many of our defeated rebels—and surrendered himself to the authorities at Banaras on 7 November 1860. The statement that he made three weeks later before the court of the Special Commissioner there offers some of the most detailed information we have of a local rebel mobilization in nineteenth-century India.

It is clear from Meghar Singh's recollection of the beginnings of the revolt in eastern Ghazipur that the mobilization there followed the classic pattern of parley and assembly common to peasant insurgency everywhere. The crucial meeting which decided on the insurrection was a conference of thirty-eight persons representing four castes from eighteen villages in three parganas—one of Ghazipur and two of Shahabad—linked by a river (*vide* Table 2 below). Evidently, it was dominated by those who spoke for Zamania pargana which contributed as many as thirty, that is, nearly four-fifths of the total number of delegates. This was quite appropriate too. For it was the fear of a pre-emptive strike by the colonial army against some of its villages[90] which had triggered off that uprising in the first place. Besides, the two sites to figure most prominently in its preparation, namely, Biranji on the Karmanasa where it was planned and Dewal where it was inaugurated at a public gathering, were both located there. Above all it was Gahmar within that pargana which was clearly the epicentre of the revolt. The inhabitants of this village were largely responsible for its organization. They formed the party of scouts who were sent to Ghazipur to verify rumours concerning the imminence of British attacks and whose report hastened the decision in favour of the uprising. They also led the group of ten emissaries chosen by the insurgents to negotiate with Amar Singh for aid in arms and men. And it was this village which provided the rebellion with its leader Meghar Singh himself. The fact that fifteen out of thirty-eight delegates at the Biranji conference came from Gahmar and that the destruction of the latter was intended by the army to serve as an object lesson for all the unruly masses

[90] The six threatened villages mentioned by Meghar Singh were Gahmar, Reotipur, Sherpur, Bara, Usia and Khareba. I have been unable to identify the last of these. All others belonged to Zamania pargana.

Table 2 Distribution of Rebel Delegates at Biranji Conference by Locality and Caste.[91]

LOCALITY			CASTE				
District	*Pargana*	*Village*	*Pathan*	*Brahman*	*Rajput*	*Bhumihar*	*Total*
Ghazipur	Zamania	Bara	3	0	0	0	3
,,	,,	Baranpur	0	0	0	1	1
,,	,,	Basuka	0	0	0	1	1
,,	,,	Deoria	0	0	0	1	1
,,	,,	Gahmar	0	0	15	0	15
,,	,,	Hasanpara	0	0	0	1	1
,,	,,	Kahrna	0	0	1	0	1
,,	,,	Nauli	0	0	1	0	1
,,	,,	Reotipur	0	0	0	1	1
,,	,,	Sherpur	0	0	0	2	2
,,	,,	Sohwal	0	0	0	1	1
,,	,,	Utrawal	0	0	2	0	2
Shahabad	Chausa	Indore	0	0	1	0	1
,,	,,	Manikpur	0	1	0	0	1
,,	,,	Sopna	0	0	0	1	1
,,	,,	Sukran	0	0	0	1	1
,,	Chainpur	Gura Sarai	0	0	3	0	3
,,	,,	Newhar	0	0	1	0	1
Totals			3	1	24	10	38

of Ghazipur–Shahabad region is a measure of the importance attached to it both by the rebels and their enemies.

Insurgent mobilization in Zamania was a function of geographical as well as ethnic arrangements in that area—that is, of both those sets of factors which combine to make up territoriality as we have defined it. The pargana derived much of its

[91] *Source*: FSUP: IV 284–5. For Utranhi in Meghar Singh's statement I have read Utrawal since its location in Zamania pargana is clearly indicated in the source. Nevill (1907) mentions a market called Utraon (Appendix, p. *xxxv*), but I have not included it here as its pargana location is given as Dehma. Delegates described by Meghar Singh as Kshatriyas have been classified here as Rajputs—for as Oldham says in his *Memoir*, the latter are called 'Chuttrees' in Ghazipur. The single Bhobar from Reotipur has been classified as a Bhumihar. In those instances where a delegate's caste is not specified I have followed the convention of identifying Singh and Rai respectively as Rajput and Bhumihar surnames after the general pattern of correspondence between caste and surname as found in Meghar Singh's statement as well as Oldham's authority to the effect that 'the Rajpoots of this district are commonly called Singh and the Bhoinhars Rai'. (Oldham: 43).

character from its separation on three sides from the rest of Ghazipur district by a broad bend of the Ganges and from being cut off from Shahabad by the Karmanasa on the remaining, eastern side. Within this arc the rivers with their deep beds and high banks, their floods and shallow backwaters and the alluvium deposited by them influenced not only the livelihood of the people as agriculturists but also their patterns of residence and communal life. The alluvial tract of the pargana boasted some of the largest villages in the district—in 1853 Reotipur had a population of 10,055, Gahmar 9,629, Sherpur 6,885 and so on—with their locations 'determined solely by the configuration of the ground', according to the *District Gazetteer*, 'the houses being built on the most elevated spot so as to be beyond the reach of the floods'. A village under these conditions tended to develop as the focal point for a number of hamlets each of which was occupied by a distinctive caste while the site as a whole presided over dependent villages existing only in name but indistinguishable in fact from the surrounding fields excluded from residential use and given over entirely to agriculture.

Vicinage conditioned thus by river boundaries and village sites was emphasized further by the pattern of ethnicity in the pargana. It had been colonized like the greater part of the district by Rajputs and Bhumihars. The distinction between these two castes was often unclear. Some of their subdivisions bore identical names: Gautam, Kausik, Kinwar or Sikarwar could designate either a Rajput or a Bhumihar. Members of the two castes bearing the same clan name often referred to the same city or country as their original habitat, and at least in one case they claimed a common ancestry.[92] It was therefore quite in order that all but one of the twelve villages represented at the Biranji conference should have sent men of one or the other caste to speak for them. The exception, Bara, described by the commander of a British gunboat as 'full of Badmashes' and shelled by him preceding an assault on its 'armed Mussulmans',[93] delegated some Pathans. However, the plurality suggested by this fact is deceptive. For the Pathans of Zamania were mostly 'not Pathans at all, but the descendants of converted Rajputs and Bhumihars', as the *District Gazetteer* observes. To be more specific about it, the Musalmans of Bara

[92] Oldham: 43. [93] FSUP: IV 120–2.

were a branch of the Rajdhar Rai sept of Kinwar Bhumihars who had taken to Islam.[94]

Thus the local mobilization inaugurated at Biranji was determined by two different kinds of proximity—geographical and ethnic. The former was reinforced further by communication in the form of a network of unmetalled roads which crisscrossed the pargana and the latter by the networks of caste and sept. A look at some of the villages for which we have information on both counts may indicate how the location of particular communities and their linkages were arranged along these coordinates. Bara which constituted the eastern terminal point of the arc of the Ganges around the pargana was directly joined by road to Gahmar. Its village lands lay along the Karmanasa connecting the local community with the peasantry on the Shahabad side of the river. Within the district it had its historical ties with Birpur, a village on the other bank of the Ganges, an ancient seat of Kinwar Bhumihars who had turned to Islam and dominated the two eastern parganas of Dehma and Muhammadabad. As such its delegation of three Musalmans represented an element of mobilization with a pull reaching beyond its strictly local limits. Basuka adjoined Nauli on the east. Its owners were Bhumihar Sikarwars descended from Puran Mal whose progeny by several wives spread over a number of villages including Gahmar, Reotipur and Sherpur. Nauli itself was the headquarters of the Suklabansi Rajputs who had colonized a large tract of the country in this particular neighbourhood. They related in caste terms with Utrawal, a little to the north, which was the only other village on our list with a large Suklabansi settlement. Both, it should be noted, were represented by Rajputs. Both the villages lay on the road between Bhadaura and Reotipur. The latter was in 1853 one of the most populous of all the rural sites in Zamania pargana. Caste and proprietary interests tied it historically to Sherpur on the opposite bank. Together these two villages formed a great taluqa held for many generations by the Sikarwar Bhumihars whose estate extended here over thirty-five villages along a seven-mile front on both sides of the river. The first Sikarwar to acquire these lands had by his three marriages and their issue planted the clan in several parts of the pargana. Its connections

[94] Oldham: 68.

with Basuka have already been mentioned above. Yet other bonds with Gahmar and Usia added considerably to its ethnic range. At the former of these the Bhumihar Sikarwars shared some kind of a primordial affinity with the Rajput sept of the same name. The latter, Usia, was one of the six villages a threat to which was the immediate cause of the uprising. Here they related to Bhumihars who together with those of seven other settlements in the neighbourhood had abandoned the Hindu faith for Islam. An important link was forged in this way between the Sikarwars and the rest of the large mass of Muslim converts of Zamania. Thus the ethnic space of the twin villages of Reotipur and Sherpur, both represented appropriately enough by Bhumihars at the rebel conference, reached well beyond their geographical area into much of eastern and southern Zamania.

By caste as well as by the road that ran east towards the river from Ghazipur through Sohwal—a largely Bhumihar settlement represented by a member of that caste at Biranji—Reotipur was directly linked with Gahmar. And both its caste composition and its physical location appear to have made the latter ideally suited to generate the kind of initiative that it did in the insurrection led by Meghar Singh. Colonized by Rajputs of the Sikarwar clan who still owned most of the taluqa there it had its ties not merely with settlements of the same caste elsewhere in that pargana but also with the Bhumihar Sikarwars of Reotipur–Sherpur and the Rajputs turned Muslim such as those of Bara and many other Zamania villages. Its ethnic range was thus nearly as wide as that of Reotipur. What however made Gahmar a place of relatively greater importance were two arterial roads the first of which situated it at a point equidistant between Ghazipur and Zamania, while the second, an older highway that bifurcated at the village, connected it with Banaras in one direction and Buxar at the other.

Communications such as these and the rivers whose junction a few miles further to the east below Birpur conferred on Gahmar a measure of strategic advantage, served as the practical instruments of rebel mobilization. They helped Meghar Singh,[95] a Sikarwar Rajput zamindar and *lambardar*, to weld

[95] The three variations of this name as found in the sources (FSUP: IV 180, 277, 280, 281, 282, *et passim*) are Megh Rai, Meghar Rai and Mygur Rai. Oldham refers

the primordial loyalties within the pargana into a fighting solidarity of all its principal ethnic communities, and what is equally important, to forge alliances beyond it. The roads carried his appeal westward to the raises of Mhanj and Narwan. The latter, in Banaras, was linked by tradition to Zamania pargana in so far as the Donwar Bhumihars of both places claimed common descent from ancestors who had once colonized the eastern part of Azamgarh district.[96] The Karmanasa conveyed his message southwards to the principal men of Sassaram, and its ferries along the eastern border of Zamania helped him to negotiate for and secure the support of the two key parganas of Shahabad on the other bank, namely, Chausa and Chainpur, both of which were represented at Biranji, significantly enough, by seven Rajputs and Bhumihars out of a total of eight delegates from six villages. It was that river again which witnessed at Dewal, an ancient Bhumihar village and ferry ghat, the decisive meeting of the people of Zamania with ten to twelve thousand men who had assembled there from other parts of Ghazipur, Banaras and Shahabad districts to hail the proclamation of insurgency.

This description of events in eastern Ghazipur in 1858 provides us with yet another instance of territoriality as an intersection

---

to him as Meygur Rai. The use of this surname differs from other references to him as Meghar Singh in the sources (FSUP: IV 283, 284, 491, 492, 493) and would make him a Bhumihar, going by local usage as noticed above (n. 91). However, the rebel leader's own deposition of 27 November 1860 helps to clear up all confusion about his identity. 'My name is Meghar Singh', he said, 'I am a Kshatriya. My father's name is Bhajan Singh. I am resident of Mauza Gahmar, pargana Zamania, District Ghazipur. My age is about 40 years. My profession is Zamindari and Nambardari' (FSUP: IV 283–4). This information agrees with what we know of 'Mygur Rai' from an entry in a 'Descriptive Roll of Leading Rebels' signed on 29 July 1858 by J. Bax, Officiating Magistrate, Ghazipur (*National Archives of India: Foreign Department Proceedings*, 31 Dec. 1858, No. 791). Here his father's name is given as 'Bhunjun Rai' and his caste as 'Rajpoot-Hindoo'. He is described as a person of 'dark complexion flat forehead unconnected eyebrows sheep eyes tall stature thin body, flat nose but projected on the point aged about 40 years'. The document mentions 'Mouzah Gahmar, Pergh. Zummaneah, Ghazeepoor' as his 'former residence', and in keeping with the force of those two words, an index of his status as a roving rebel, the remarks noted against his name read: 'Leading rebels in Pergunnah Zumann[e]ah'.

[96] Oldham: 69.

of ethnic space and physical space. It also shows that the domain of peasant insurgency need not be limited to single administrative units: it could indeed be as large as a pargana or even a number of parganas comprising many villages in a contiguous area extended over two or three neighbouring districts. And that takes us back to the question with which we began: how far does territoriality help or hinder the spread of a rebellion?

The answer provided by the evidence presented above is positive. Territoriality, in the conditions of nineteenth-century India, helped. The reason clearly lay in a *décalage*, that is, in the fact that the two kinds of space mentioned above did not quite coincide even when they converged. There were territorial units which were home to more than one ethnic group and there were ethnic regions which extended over more than one territorial unit. A peasant uprising tended, in either case, to fill in the gap by its own content and simulate a coincidence between community and habitat. An overlap of these two elements supplemented by the appropriation of one or the other by the act of rebellion was what constituted the latter's domain. This is how the domain of the hool came to include such non-Santal elements as lower-class Hindus and the Paharia Mal in the predominantly Santal territory of Damin-i-Koh, and that of the Hindu and Muslim peasants' revolt in the indigo districts of Bengal the adivasi labourers employed by the factories.[97] Conversely, the domain of the Kol insurrection of 1832 exceeded the limits of its geographical site in Chota Nagpur and drew in the Larka Kols who crossed over from Singhbhum to fight for their tribal brethren, while, to mention some non-tribal instances, the domain of Kunwar Singh's rebellion extended its ethnic range beyond Bihar to include his fellow Rajputs in the Ghazipur district of Uttar Pradesh and that of the Gujar uprising at Bijnor the members of that caste resident on the other side of the Ganges.[98]

The role of territoriality in thus enlarging and defining the domain of insurgency is, of course, not a development unique to the colonial period of Indian history. Habib has identified this as a factor in the Jat revolt and 'the "lawless" activities' of Mewatis, Wattus and Dogars in the late Mughal empire. Caste, he says, 'brought [the peasant] into contact with his peers in

[97] Guha (1974): 29–30. [98] FSUP: IV 267, 269 & V 246.

the most distant villages, through a thousand ties of blood and rites. If they took to arms, he could not stand aloof.'[99] What, however, adds to the significance of territoriality in the peasant rebellions during the period under discussion is that it provided the anti-colonialist mass struggles of our people with some kind of an armature, however imperfect this might have been, at a time when organized nationalism (barring some small militant groups) was elitist and collaborationist, and the class organizations of the working people were either non-existent or ineffective.

Quite clearly the domain of rebellion still fell far short of the domain of the nation, and the two arms of territoriality, that is, co-residential solidarity and primordial loyalty, acted to no small extent in putting the brakes on resistance against the Raj.[100] Narrow localism raised its head and impeded the progress of the insurgents at critical moments. Villagers would not allow a party of mutineers from other parts to cross the Ghaghra at Azamgarh. Caste would fight against caste—Gujars against Rohs and Jats, for instance. The same caste could be at war with the British in one region and on their side in another, as witness the contradictory careers of Gujar leaders like Futtuah and Sahib Singh. Even when solidarity between ethnic groups triumphed over separateness for a time, it weakened soon under pressure from their common enemy: the Mals and the Kumars ceased to co-operate with the Santals as counter-insurgency operations intensified. And the use made by the government of some sections of the non-tribal peasantry in order to suppress the hool demonstrated how ethnicity was no substitute for class consciousness in uniting the people against colonialism. In the event all resistance splintered into 'the hundred local revolutions as well as the hundred local reactions following them'.[101] Yet all such limitations notwithstanding, where else except in this fragmented insurgent consciousness is one to situate the beginnings of those militant mass movements which surged across the subcontinent in 1919, 1942 and 1946? Territoriality was not indeed the stuff with which to build a revolutionary

[99] Habib: 332.

[100] See FSUP: IV 188 and V 108–9, 146, 246–7, 251, 261 for the instances cited below.

[101] Engels (1926): 152.

party, as Mao Tse-tung sadly observed at his base in the Chingkang mountains.[102] But not to recognize in it the elements of what made the broader and more generalized struggles of the Indian people possible in the twentieth century would be to foreshorten history.

[102] Mao: I 93.

CHAPTER 8

EPILOGUE

A distorted image—the logic of distortion—the generality of insurgency—its extension into more recent times and modern political movements—the paradigm of insurgency.

To go back to the point made at the very beginning of this work, the historical phenomenon of insurgency meets the eye for the first time as an image framed in the prose, hence the outlook, of counter-insurgency—an image caught in a distorting mirror. However, the distortion has a logic to it. That is the logic of opposition between the rebels and their enemies not only as parties engaged in active hostility on a particular occasion but as the mutually antagonistic elements of a semi-feudal society under colonial rule. The antagonism is rooted deeply enough in the material and spiritual conditions of their existence to reduce the difference between elite and subaltern perceptions of a radical peasant movement to a difference between the terms of a binary pair. A rural uprising turns thus into a site for two rival cognitions to meet and define each other negatively.

It is precisely this contradiction which we have used in the foregoing pages as a key to our understanding of peasant rebellion as a representation of the will of its subjects. For that will has been known to us only in its mirror image. Inscribed in elite discourse it had to be read as a writing in reverse. Since our access to rebel consciousness lay, so to say, through enemy country, we had to seize on the evidence of elite consciousness and force it to show us the way to its Other. In short, we have been led to conclude that the documentation on insurgency must itself be turned upside down in order to reconstitute the insurgent's project aimed at reversing his world.

We had set out to describe the figure of insurgency in its *common form* and in terms of its *general ideas*. These, the reader will have noticed, have been made to emerge out of a welter of individual instances not all of them of the same hue or arranged in quite the same way. Visualized as a pattern, that form may indeed be said to be made up not only of elements and tendencies which are in agreement but also of those which clash and contrast. Altogether, it stands for a generality in which ideas, mentalities, notions, beliefs, attitudes, etc. of many different kinds come together to constitute a whole. However, it is not a generality which is 'something external to, or something in addition to' other features or abstract qualities of insurgency discovered by reflection. On the contrary, 'it is what permeates and includes in it everything particular'[1]—a pervasive theoretical consciousness which gives insurgency its categorical unity and helps to sort out its specific and separate moments.

This figure was of course a child of its times. It was predicated on a set of historical relations of power, namely the relations of dominance and subordination, as these prevailed in village India under the Raj until 1900. As explained in Chapter 1, this particular date was chosen only for the convenience of demonstration, that is, in order to show how the 'general ideas' of insurgency behaved in a 'pure' state prior to the involvement of the peasantry in latter-day politics. However, the actual career of this consciousness extends well beyond the nineteenth century Many of the mass movements which have swept through our land since then bear at least some of its hallmarks. If one looks carefully at the popular mobilizations accredited to nationalist and communist leaderships—at Rowlatt Satyagraha and Quit India or at Tebhaga and Telengana, to take only a couple of instances respectively of each kind—one cannot help noticing the structural similarities between their articulation and some of the 'elementary aspects' discussed above.

The parallelism has been underscored by much new writing on the history and politics of the last thirty years of British rule.[2] Pandey has shown in his pioneering study how in Uttar Pradesh mobilization for the nationalist campaigns of the inter-war

[1] Hegel (1975*): 240.

[2] The recent work I have in mind in this and the next paragraph includes Pandey (1978, 1981), Henningham and T. Sarkar on nationalist politics; Chatterjee on communalism; and Chakrabarty on working-class history.

period relied considerably on local initiative at the grassroot levels so that an imprimatur of peasant struggle was often put on movements launched by the elite leadership of the Congress independently of the latter's directives and indeed in defiance of these on some occasions. Henningham's researches on Bihar and Sarkar's on Bengal have proved that the story was very much the same in those regions as well.

It is clear in the light of such findings that Indian nationalism of the colonial period was not what elite historiography had made it out to be. As a praxis involving the masses it did not always conform to the rule book of the Congress Party or the tenets of Gandhism. On the contrary, it derived much of its striking power from a subaltern tradition going a long way back before the Mahatma's intervention in Indian politics towards the end of the First World War or Nehru's discovery of the peasantry of his home province soon afterwards. However, it was not nationalism and the agrarian question alone which came under the influence of this tradition. Its presence was felt in many of the more extensive and vigorous struggles of the urban poor and the industrial workers too. And again as has been so clearly established in a number of recent studies on communal conflict, even when a corrupt sectarianism replaced class consciousness as the content of mass violence, the latter still continued to bear some of the distinctive traces of insurgency in its *form*—in the means and manner of mobilization, in signalling, in solidarity and so on—which is indeed why there was often such a confusing overlap between anti-landlord jacqueries and Hindu–Muslim riots.

The tendency of all these rather different types of mobilization to agree with the general form of insurgency derived essentially from the latter's role as a *paradigm*. This had its roots in the relationship of dominance and subordination characteristic of Indian society for a very long period both before and during colonial rule. However, the tradition of oppression and exploitation predicated on that relationship was only as pervasive as the counter-tradition of defiance and revolt. These were reciprocal terms which conditioned and reproduced each other cyclically over the centuries, and were helped by the inertia of an age-old pre-capitalist culture to congeal as a pair of mutually determining but antagonistic elements within it.

It was thus that the rival paradigms of landlord authority and peasant rebellion continued to inspire and sustain each other, generating many patterns of elitist thought and practice with regard to the weak and the underprivileged in one case and those of subaltern resistance in the other. Indeed, the latter was powerful enough to transfer, by *atideśa*, the formal attributes of insurgency to almost any militant activity of the masses even when that originated from a contradiction among the people themselves (as in communal strife) rather than from a contradiction between the people and their enemies. By contrast when content accorded more happily with form, at least some of the elementary aspects of peasant insurgency impressed themselves on even the most short-lived of popular movements aimed at effecting a mutual substitution of *adhara* and *uttara* in the power structure.

No jacquerie in the countryside, no street riot in our towns is an exception in that respect. And one has merely to refer to some of the anti-*nasbandi* disturbances in rural Haryana and urban UP in 1976–7 to realize how little the transfer of power has done to diminish the force of the paradigm illustrated above by eighteenth- and nineteenth-century events. So long as landlord authority continues to function as a significant element in the ruling culture—and continue it will for long even after the genuine (as against spurious) end of landlordism in the economy and in property relations—all mass struggles will tend inevitably to model themselves on the unfinished projects of Titu, Kanhu, Birsa and Meghar Singh.

It is in order to assist this tendency to recognize itself that we have defined the structure and related the moments of the paradigm on which it relies for so much of its drive and orientation. For if the task of historiography is to interpret the past in order to help in changing the world and such a change involves a radical transformation of consciousness, one can do no better than to be guided by the observation that 'the reform of consciousness consists *only* in making the world aware of its own consciousness . . . in *explaining* to it the meaning of its own actions'.[3] The purpose of this essay has been to try and explain

[3] Marx to Ruge (Sept. 1843) in MECW: III 144.

the logic of a consciousness which informed some historic actions aimed at turning the rural world upside down. This, one hopes, may be of relevance for all efforts meant to bring about a more abiding and comprehensive reversal.

GLOSSARY

abwab	Miscellaneous cesses, imposts and charges levied by landlords and officials.
adhara	Nether; inferior.
adivasi	Autochthonous tribal people.
andar-mahal	Part of a Bengali landlord's house meant for exclusive use by members of his family and strictly out of bounds for outsiders.
atap	Sun-dried rice considered particularly suitable for ritual offerings.
āṭavika	Forest people of ancient India.
attah	Flour.
bania	Merchant; moneylender.
barkandaz	Armed watchman.
bhabati bhikshām dehi	Beggar's cry, in Sanskrit, meaning 'O lady, please give alms'.
bhooth, bhut	Ghost; ogre.
bhumihar	Descendant of the original settlers in Chota Nagpur.
bidroha	Rebellion; uprising. Hence, *bidrohi*, rebel.
bil	Marsh.
bonga	Deity; god.
budmash	Hooligan; rascal.
chasha	Contemptuous way of referring to a *chashi*, Bengali for peasant, tenant-cultivator, etc.
chowkidar	Village watchman.
chowkut	Wooden frame of a door.
coss	A measure of distance.
cutcherry	*kachari* (q.v.).
dalan-badi	Building in which images of Hindu deities are set up for ceremonial worship within the residential compound of a big Bengali landlord's estate.
daṇḍa	Punishment.
daroga	Police officer with the rank of a superintendent.
deko	*diku* (q.v.).
desmukh	District revenue official.

dewan	Member of the supervisory staff of a landlord's estate or of an indigo factory.
dheora, dheori	Messenger bough.
dhing	Rebellion; uprising.
dhoti	Cotton dress worn by Indians.
digdigi	Small drum.
diku	Foreigner; alien; outsider.
disum	Territory.
doogdoogi	Small drum.
dour	Literally, a run, the word was used in the colonial army to denote a foray or march.
dvandvasamāsa	Compound of noun phrases formed according to some rules of Sanskrit grammar.
ekada	Patidar marriage circle.
fauj	Army; troops.
faujdari adalat	Criminal court.
fituri	Rebellion; uprising.
gadi	Moneylender's or merchant's office.
grāma	'Mobile kinship group, later mobile village' (Kosambi (1972): 223).
hool	Rebellion; uprising.
hukumnamah	Written order.
ijaradar	Lease-holder.
jajmani	Services rendered by certain members of a rural community in accordance to obligations determined by caste status.
jāti	'Later castes of tribal origin, retaining endogamy and commensality' (Kosambi (1972): 225).
jenmi	Landlord.
jug	Epoch.
kachari	Landlord's office.
kachari-badi	Building in which a Bengali landlord's estate office is located.
khadir	Low or alluvial lands.
khata	Account-book.
kos	*coss* (q.v.).

lambardar Village headman or landowner who collects revenue on behalf of a number of co-sharing small proprietors.
lopa Elision as prescribed by Sanskrit grammatical rules.
lungi Dress worn in rural Bengal.

mahajan Moneylender.
majhi Santal chief.
malguzari Revenue.
masjid Mosque.
mathot Extra or occasional cess or tax imposed upon the cultivators for some special purpose or under some incidental pretext either by the government or its officials or landlords.
mauza Village which figures in the official records as a revenue-paying unit.
moira Grocer-moneylender.

nād Coorg territorial division consisting of several villages.
nagra Large drum.
naib Manager of a landlord's estate.
nasbandi Campaign for birth control introduced by the present Government of India.
nazar, nazarana Tribute or fee paid to the state or its representative; present or offering from an inferior to a superior, especially to a prince or a holy man.
nazir Officer charged with the duty of serving of process, taking depositions, investigating breaches of law, etc.

okka Patrilineal joint family of the Coorg.

pagri Turban.
paik Footman.
paṇa Ancient Indian coin of silver or copper.
panchayat Traditional consultative body.
parab Religious festival.
pargana Subdivision of a *tahsil* (q.v.).
parwana Writ; order.
pathsala Village primary school.
patwari Village accountant.
peada, peadah Footman; peon.

polo Trap used for fishing in swamps and ponds.
pracharak Catechist.
proja Tenant-cultivator.
pucca Brick-built.
puja Hindu ritual worship.
Puranak Militant follower of Birsa—one of those 'who never swerved from their original purpose of open revolt'.

rahar Pulse crop.
rais Noble or rich man.
rāshṭra Tribal kingdom of ancient India.
roza Ritual fasting by devout Musalmans during the sacred month of Ramzan.
ryot Officially recognized tenant; peasant.
ryotwari System of land settlement, first introduced by Munro in southern India, according to which each peasant was assessed separately for revenue owing to the state.

sadar Headquarters of a district administration in colonial India.
sahukar Moneylender.
sahukari Whatever appertains to *sahukar* (q.v.).
sarkar Government; regime.
sarkari Whatever appertains to *sarkar* (q.v.).
sazawal Landlord's steward employed mainly to collect rents and levies.
sipahi Sepoy.
sowcar *sahukar* (q.v.).
Subah Title by which the Santal insurgents designated their leaders during the *hool* (q.v.) of 1855; an abbreviation of *subahdar* (q.v.).
subahdar Governor or viceroy of a province under the Mughals; Indian officer in the East India Company's army holding a rank equivalent to that of captain under the European officers.
sud Foreigner; alien; outsider.

tahsil Subdivision of a district.
tahsildari Administrative area under the jurisdiction of an officer in charge of a *tahsil* (q.v.)
taluqa Estate made up of a number of dependent villages from which the owner collects revenues payable to the state.

taravad	Lineage segment.
thana	Police station.
tulsi	A plant regarded as holy by some Hindu sects.
ulgulan	Rebellion; uprising.
uttara	Upper; superior.
vākpārushyam	Verbal aggression.
vrata	Hindu propitiatory ritual.

BIBLIOGRAPHY

I. UNPUBLISHED MATERIAL

A. Archival Material

(1) India Office Library (London)

Board's Collections: 1361 (54222); 1362 (54223, 54224, 54225); 1363 (54226, 54227); 1502 (58891, 58893); 2354 (146775). Numerals outside the round brackets indicate the location of volumes within the series and those within brackets the location of documents within a particular volume. (*Abbreviation*: BC; JC)

Bombay Judicial Department Proceedings: Vols 54 (890); 61 (4315, 4316). References have been given by the date of proceedings. (*Abbreviation*: BJD)

(2) West Bengal State Archives (Calcutta)

Judicial Proceedings: May–December 1855. References have been given by the date of proceedings. (*Abbreviation*: JP)

Judicial Proceedings (Police Department): File no. 448: 'Pubna Riots'. (*Abbreviation*: JP(P))

(3) National Archives of India (New Delhi)

Foreign Department Proceedings: December 1858.

B. Other Unpublished Material

Henningham, Stephen, 'Protest and Control in North Bihar, India, 1917–1941' (Ph.D. thesis, Australian National University, 1978).

Sarkar, Tanika, 'National Movement and Popular Protest in Bengal, 1928–1934' (Ph.D. thesis, University of Delhi, 1980).

II. PUBLISHED MATERIAL

Abū-l Fazl, *Ā'īn-i Akbarī*, vol. 1, trs. H. Blochmann, 2nd ed. (Calcutta, 1927).

Ahmad, Imtiaz (ed.), *Caste and Social Stratification among the Muslims* (Delhi, 1973).

Allport, Gordon W. and Leo Postman, *The Psychology of Rumor* (New York, 1965).

Anon., 'Bagan', *Sadhana*, Agrahayan 1298 (Calcutta, 1891).

Anon., 'Gentlemen Killers of Kilvenmani', *Economic and Political Weekly*, vol. 8 (21), 26 May 1973, pp. 926–8.

Anon., 'The Sonthal Rebellion', *Calcutta Review*, vol. 26, January/June 1856, pp. 223–64.

Apte, V. S., *The Practical Sanskrit–English Dictionary* (Delhi, 1975).

Archer, W. G., 'Santal Rebellion Songs', *Man in India*, vol. 25(4), December 1945, p. 207.

Arnold, David, 'Dacoity and Rural Crime in Madras, 1860–1940', *Journal of Peasant Studies*, vol. 7(2), January 1979, pp. 140–67.

Babcock, Barbara A. (ed.), *The Reversible World: a Symbolic Inversion in Art and Society* (Ithaca, 1977).

Bandyopadhyay, Bhabanicharan, *Kalikata Kamalalay* (Calcutta, 1951; Bengali Year 1358).

Barthes, Roland, *Elements of Semiology* (London, 1967).

——, *Image–Music–Text* (Glasgow, 1977).

——, *Système de la Mode* (Paris, 1967*).

Bartlett, F. C., *Remembering* (Cambridge, 1967).

Baskay, Dhirendranath, *Saontal Ganasamgramer Itihas* (Calcutta, 1976).

Bax, E. Belfort, *The Peasants War in Germany, 1525–1526* (New York, 1968).

Beals, Alan R., *Gopalpur* (New York, 1962).

Bengal, Government of, *Report of the Land Revenue Commission*, vol. 1 (Alipore, 1940).

Berliner Missionsberichte, 'Der Ostafrikanische Aufstand', *Berliner Missionsberichte*, 1905, pp. 406–13.

Bhartṛhari, *The Vākyapadīyam of Bhartṛhari, Kāṇḍa II*, trs. K. A. Subramania Iyer (Delhi, 1977).

Bhowmick, P. K., *The Lodhas of West Bengal* (Calcutta, 1963).

Birbhum, 1786–1797 and 1855, West Bengal District Records: New Series, ed. A. Mitra (Calcutta, 1954).

Blum, Jerome, *Lord and Peasant in Russia* (Princeton, 1961).

Bombay, Government of, *Khandesh: Gazetteer of the Bombay Presidency*, vol. 12 (Bombay, 1880).

——, *Source Material for a History of the Freedom Movement in India (Collected from Bombay Government Records)*, vol. 2, 1885–1920 (Bombay, 1958).

Bompas, Cecil Henry, *Folklore of the Santal Parganas* (London, 1909).

Bopegamage, A. and P. V. Veeraraghavan, *Status Images in Changing India* (Bombay, 1967).

Bourdieu, Pierre, *Outline of a Theory of Practice* (Cambridge, 1977).

Bright, W. and A. K. Ramanujan, 'Sociolinguistic Variation and Language Change', in J. B. Pride and J. Holmes (eds), *Sociolinguistics*, pp. 157–66.

Brown, R. and A. Gilman, 'The Pronouns of Power and Solidarity',

in P. P. Giglioli (ed.), *Language and Social Context*, pp. 252–82.
Buckland, C. E., *Bengal Under the Lieutenant-Governors*, vol. 1 (Calcutta, 1901).
Bühler, G., see *The Laws of Manu.*
Burke, Peter, *Popular Culture in Early Modern Europe* (London, 1978).
Burridge, Kenelm, *Mambu* (London, 1960).
Calame-Griaule, Geneviève, *Ethnologie et Langage: La Parole chez les Dogon* (Paris, 1965).
Carey, W. H., *The Mahommedan Rebellion* (Roorkee, 1857).
Chakrabarty, Dipesh, 'Communal Riots and Labour: Bengal's Jute Mill Hands in the 1890s', *Past and Present*, no. 91, May 1981, pp. 140–64.
——, 'On Deifying and Defying Authority: Managers and Workers in the Jute Mills of Calcutta, c. 1890–1940' (forthcoming).
Chakravarti, Chintaharan, *Hindur Achar Anushthan* (Calcutta, 1970).
Charbonnier, G. (ed.), *Conversations with Claude Lévi-Strauss* (London, 1969).
Chatterjee, Partha, 'Agrarian Relations and Communalism in Bengal, 1926–1935', in R. Guha (ed.), *Subaltern Studies*, vol. 1 (Delhi, 1982).
Chaturvedi, B. S., *Face to Face with Criminals* (Delhi, 1970).
Chaudhuri, Binay Bhushan, 'Agrarian Economy and Agrarian Relations in Bengal (1859–1885)', in N. K. Sinha (ed.), *The History of Bengal, 1757–1905* (Calcutta, 1967), pp. 237–336.
——, 'The Story of a Peasant Revolt in a Bengal District', *Bengal Past and Present*, July/December 1973, pp. 220–78.
Chaudhuri, S. B., *Civil Disturbances during the British Rule in India* (Calcutta, 1955).
Cherry, E. Colin, 'The Communication of Information', in A. G. Smith (ed.), *Communication and Culture*, pp. 35–40.
Chowdhury, Benoy Kumar, see Chaudhuri, Binay Bhushan.
Chowdhury, Someshwarprasad, *Neelkar-bidroha* (Calcutta, 1972).
Clarke, Roger T., 'The Drum Language of the Tumba Tribe', in T. A. Sebeok and D. J. Umiker-Sebeok (eds), *Speech Surrogates*, pp. 418–33.
Cohn, Bernard S., 'The Changing Status of a Depressed Caste', in M. Marriott (ed.), *Village India*, pp. 52–77.
Corbett, Jim, *My India* (Madras, 1952).
Crooke, W., *The Popular Religion and Folklore of Northern India* (2nd ed., 1896), 2 vols (Reprint; Delhi, 1968).
——, *The Tribes and Castes of the North-Western Provinces and Oudh*, 4 vols (Calcutta, 1896).
Culshaw, W. J. and W. G. Archer, 'The Santal Rebellion', *Man in India*, vol. 25(4), December 1945, pp. 208–17.

Dalton, Edward Tuite, *Descriptive Ethnology of Bengal* (Calcutta, 1972).

Das Gupta, Anil Chandra (ed.), *The Days of the John Company: Selections from Calcutta Gazette 1824–1832* (Calcutta, 1959).

Datta, Charuchandra, *Purano Katha*, 2 vols (Calcutta, 1962–6).

Datta, K. K., 'The Santal Insurrection of 1855–57', in K. K. Datta, *Anti-British Plots and Movements before 1857* (Meerut, 1970), pp. 43–152.

Davis, Natalie Zemon, 'Women on Top: Symbolic Sexual Inversion and Political Disorder in Early Modern Europe', in Barbara A. Babcock (ed.), *The Reversible World*, pp. 147–90.

Day, Lal Behari, *Bengal Peasant Life* (Reprint; Calcutta, 1970).

Desmanjhi, Chotrae, 'Chotrae Desmanjhi Reak Katha', trs. Stephen Hari Tudu, *Man in India*, vol. 25(4), December 1945, pp. 232–9.

Dhanagare, D. N., 'Agrarian Conflict, Religion and Politics: the Moplah Rebellions in Malabar in the Nineteenth and Early Twentieth Centuries', *Past and Present*, no. 74, February 1977, pp. 112–41.

Dīkshita, Bhaṭṭoji, *The Siddhānta Kaumudī of Bhaṭṭoji Dīkshita*, ed. Srisa Chandra Vasu, 2 vols (Allahabad, 1906. Reprint; Delhi, n.d.).

Drake-Brockman, D. L. (ed.), *Mirzapur District Gazetteer* (Allahabad, 1911).

Dube, S. C., *The Kamar* (Lucknow, 1951).

Dumont, Louis, *Homo Hierarchicus* (London, 1972).

Dunlop, Robert Henry Wallace, *Service and Adventure with the Khakee Ressallah* (London, 1858).

Durkheim, Emile, *The Elementary Forms of the Religious Life* (New York, 1965).

Edwards, William, *Personal Adventures during the Indian Rebellion in Rohilcund, Futteghur, and Oude*, 4th ed. (London, 1859).

Elwin, Verrier, 'Saora Fituris', *Man in India*, vol. 25(4), December 1945, pp. 254–7.

Engels, Friedrich, *The Origin of the Family, Private Property and the State*, in K. Marx and F. Engels, *Selected Works* (London, 1968), pp. 468–593.

——, *The Peasant War in Germany*, ed. D. Riazanov (London, 1926).

Ferguson, C. A., 'Diglossia', in P. P. Giglioli (ed.), *Language and Social Context*, pp. 232–51.

Field, Daniel, *Rebels in the Name of the Tsar* (Boston, 1976).

Franz, Günther (ed.), *Quellen zur Geschichte des Bauernkriegs* (München, 1963).

Freeman, James M., *Untouchable: An Indian Life History* (London, 1979).

Freud, Sigmund, *Jokes and Their Relation to the Unconscious*, trs. J. Strachey (London, 1960).

Froissart, John, *Chronicles*, trs. and ed. G. Brereton (Harmondsworth, 1968).

Fuchs, Stephen, *The Children of Hari: a Study of the Nimar Balahis of the Central Provinces of India* (Vienna, 1950).

Geertz, C., 'Linguistic Etiquette', in J. B. Pride and J. Holmes (eds), *Sociolinguistics*, pp. 167–79.

Ghose, Benoy, *Samayik Patre Banglar Samajchitra*, vol. 4 (Calcutta, 1966).

Giglioli, P. P. (ed.), *Language and Social Context* (Harmondsworth, 1972).

Gluckman, Max, *Custom and Conflict in Africa* (Oxford, 1966).

——, *Order and Rebellion in Tribal Africa* (London, 1963).

Goody, Jack (ed.), *Literacy in Traditional Societies* (Cambridge, 1968).

——, 'Restricted Literacy in Northern Ghana', in J. Goody (ed.), *Literacy in Traditional Societies*, pp. 198–264.

Gough, E. Kathleen, 'Cults of the Dead among the Nayars', *Journal of American Folklore*, no. 71, 1958, pp. 446–78.

Gramsci, A., *Selections from the Prison Notebooks* (London, 1971).

Grierson, G. A., *Linguistic Survey of India*, vol. 5, pt. 1 (Reprint; Delhi, 1968).

Guha, Ranajit, 'Neel-Darpan: the Image of a Peasant Revolt in a Liberal Mirror', *Journal of Peasant Studies*, vol. 2(1), October 1974, pp. 1–46.

——, 'The Prose of Counter-insurgency', in R. Guha (ed.), *Subaltern Studies*, vol. 2 (Delhi, 1983).

Gumperz, John J., *Language in Social Groups* (Stanford, California, 1971).

Gwassa, G. C. K. and J. Iliffe (eds), *Records of the Maji-Maji Rising*, pt. 1 (Nairobi, 1968).

Habib, Irfan, *The Agrarian System of Mughal India* (London, 1963).

Hamp, Eric P., Fred W. Householder, and Robert Austerlitz (eds), *Readings in Linguistics II* (Chicago, 1966).

Hay, Douglas, P. Linebaugh, and E. P. Thompson (eds), *Albion's Fatal Tree: Crime and Society in Eighteenth Century England* (London, 1975).

Hay, Douglas, 'Poaching and the Game Laws on Cannock Chase', in D. Hay *et al.*, *Albion's Fatal Tree*, pp. 189–253.

Hegel, G. W. F., *Aesthetics*, trs. T. M. Knox, 2 vols (Oxford, 1975).

——, *Logic*, trs. W. Wallace, 3rd ed. (Oxford, 1975*).

Henvey, Frederick, *A Narrative of the Drought and Famine which prevailed in the North-West Provinces during the years 1868, 1869 and beginning of 1870* (Allahabad, 1871).

Hill, Christopher, *Change and Continuity in Seventeenth-Century England* (London, 1974).

——, *The World Turned Upside Down* (London, 1972).

Hilton, Rodney H., *Bond Men Made Free* (London, 1973).

Hinton, William, *Fanshen* (New York, 1966).

Hiro, Dilip, *The Untouchables of India*, Minority Rights Group Report, no. 26 (London, 1975).

Hobsbawm, E. J. and G. Rudé, *Captain Swing* (London, 1969).

Hobsbawm, E. J., *Primitive Rebels* (Manchester, 1959).

Holmes, T. Rice, *A History of the Indian Mutiny and of the Disturbances which Accompanied it Among the Civilian Population*, 5th ed. (London, 1904).

Hosein, Mir Mosharraf, *Rachanasamgraha*, vol. 1 (Calcutta, 1978).

Huizinga, J., *The Waning of the Middle Ages* (Harmondsworth, 1976).

Hunter, W. W., *The Annals of Rural Bengal*, 7th ed. (London, 1897).

——, *Statistical Account of Bengal*, vol. 9 (London, 1875).

Inden, Ronald B. and Ralph W. Nicholas, *Kinship in Bengali Culture* (Chicago, 1977).

Innes, J. J. McLeod, *Lucknow and Oude in the Mutiny* (London, 1895).

The Institutes of Viṣṇu, trs. Julius Jolly (Oxford, 1880).

Isaacman, Allen F., *The Tradition of Resistance in Mozambique* (London, 1976).

Iyer, K. A. Subramania, *Bhartṛhari* (Poona, 1969).

Jaiminī, *The Mīmāṃsā Sūtras of Jaiminī*, trs. Mohan Lal Sandel (Allahabad, 1923).

Jakobson, Roman, *Questions de Poétique* (Paris, 1973).

——, *Selected Writings, 2: Word and Language* (The Hague, 1971).

Jha, Ganganatha, *Hindu Law and its Sources*, vol. 1 (Allahabad, 1930).

Jha, J. C., *Kol Insurrection in Chota-Nagpur* (Calcutta, 1964).

Jolly, Julius, see *The Institutes of Viṣṇu.*

Julião, Francisco, *Cambão, the Yoke* (Harmondsworth, 1972).

Kauṭilya, *Arthaśāstrā*, trs. R. Shamasastry, 8th ed. (Mysore, 1967).

Kaviraj, Narahari, *A Peasant Uprising in Bengal, 1783* (New Delhi, 1972).

Kaye, J. and G. B. Malleson, *History of the Indian Mutiny*, New Edition, 6 vols (London, 1897).

Khan, Muin-ud-din Ahmad, *History of the Fara'idi Movement in Bengal, 1818–1906* (Karachi, 1965).

——, *Selections from Bengal Government Records on Wahhabi Trials, 1863–1870* (Dacca, 1961).

King, Anthony D., *Colonial Urban Development* (London, 1976).

Kling, Blair B, *The Blue Mutiny: the Indigo Disturbances in Bengal 1859–1862* (Philadelphia, 1966).

Kosambi, Damodar Dharmanand, *The Culture and Civilisation of Ancient India in Historical Outline* (Delhi, 1972).

——, *An Introduction to the Study of Indian History*, 2nd ed. (Bombay, 1975).

——, *Myth and Reality* (Bombay, 1962).
Kripalani, J. B., *Gandhi, his Life and Thought* (New Delhi, 1970).
Kumar, Ravinder, *Western India in the Nineteenth Century* (London, 1968).
Lambrick, H. T., *The Terrorist* (London, 1972).
Lang, K. and G. E. Lang, *Collective Dynamics* (New York, 1963).
The Laws of Manu, ed. G. Bühler, Sacred Books of the East Series, vol. 25 (Oxford, 1886).
Lefebvre, Georges, *La Grande Peur de 1789* (Paris, 1970).
——, *The Great Fear* (London, 1973).
Lévi-Strauss, Claude, *Conversations with Claude Lévi-Strauss*, ed. G. Charbonnier (London, 1969).
——, *Structural Anthropology*, vol. 2 (Harmondsworth, 1978).
——, *Tristes Tropiques* (Harmondsworth, 1976).
Lewis, Oscar, *Village Life in Northern India* (New York, 1965).
Livy, *The Early History of Rome* (Harmondsworth, 1969).
Logan, William, *Malabar*, vol. 1 (Reprint; Madras, 1951).
Lotman, Ju. M., 'Problems in the Typology of Culture', in Daniel P. Lucid (ed.), *Soviet Semiotics*, pp. 213–21.
Lotman, Ju. M. and A. M. Pjatigorskij, 'Text and Function', in Daniel P. Lucid (ed.), *Soviet Semiotics*, pp. 125–35.
Lowie, Robert H., *The Origin of the State* (New York, 1962).
Lucid, Daniel P. (ed.), *Soviet Semiotics* (Baltimore, 1977).
Lush, Allan J., 'Kiganda Drums', in T. A. Sebeok and D. J. Umiker-Sebeok (eds), *Speech Surrogates*, pp. 458–73.
Lyons, John, *Semantics*, 2 vols (Cambridge, 1977).
Macy, J., Jr., L. S. Christie and R. D. Luce, 'Coding Noise in a Task-oriented Group', in A. G. Smith (ed.), *Communication and Culture*, pp. 285–94.
Maharaja Deby Sinha (Nashipur Raj Estate, 1914).
Maine, Henry, *Ancient Law* (Oxford, 1959).
Majumdar, R. C., *The Sepoy Mutiny and the Revolt of 1857* (Calcutta, 1957).
Manu, see *The Laws of Manu* and *Manusaṃhitā*.
Manusaṃhitā, ed. Bharatchandra Shiromani (Calcutta, 1866).
Mao Tse-tung, *Selected Works of Mao Tse-tung*, vols 1, 2 (Peking, 1967).
Mare Hapram Ko Reak Katha (*The Traditions and Institutions of the Saontals*), trs. Baidyanath Hansdah, in *Census 1951, West Bengal District Handbooks: Bankura*, Appendix V, 1953, pp. *lxxxvii-clxxi*.
Marriott, McKim, 'The Feast of Love', in M. Singer (ed.), *Krishna: Myths, Rites and Attitudes*, pp. 200–31.
——, (ed.) *Village India* (Chicago, 1969).
Marx, K. and F. Engels, *Collected Works*, vols 3, 6, 10, 11 (London, 1975–8).

——, *Selected Works* (London, 1968).

Mayer, Adrian C., *Caste and Kinship in Central India* (Berkeley, 1970).

Metcalfe, Charles Theophilus, *Two Native Narratives of the Mutiny in Delhi* (Westminster, 1898).

Miller, Eric J., 'Caste and Territory in Malabar', *American Anthropologist*, vol. 54(3), 1954, pp. 410–20.

Mitra, Dinabandhu, *Dinabandhu Rachanabali*, Sahitya Samsad ed. (Calcutta, 1967).

Mitra, Satis Chandra, *Jasohar-Khulnar Itihas*, vol. 1, 3rd ed. (Calcutta, 1963); vol. 2, 2nd ed. (Calcutta, 1965).

Mundy, Peter, *The Travels of Peter Mundy in Europe and Asia, 1608–1667*, vol. 2: *Travels in Asia 1628–1634* (London, 1914).

Mustowfi, Srijan Nath, *Ular Mustowfi Bangsha* (Ula, 1937).

Nadel, S. F., *A Black Byzantium* (London, 1942).

Nevill, H. R., *Ballia: a Gazetteer* (Allahabad, 1907*).

——, *Ghazipur: a Gazetteer* (Allahabad, 1907).

North Indian Notes and Queries, vol. 1(5), 1891.

Oldham, Wilton, *Historical and Statistical Memoir of the Ghazeepoor District*, pt. 1 (Allahabad, 1870).

O'Malley, L. S. S., *Bengal District Gazetteers: Faridpur* (Calcutta, 1925).

——, *Bengal District Gazetteers: Pabna* (Calcutta, 1923).

Oman, John Campbell, *Cults, Customs and Superstitions of India* (Reprint; Delhi, 1972).

Pandey, Gyanendra, *The Ascendancy of the Congress in Uttar Pradesh, 1926–1934* (Delhi, 1978).

——, 'Peasant Revolt and Indian Nationalism: The Peasant Movement in Awadh, 1919–22', in R. Guha (ed.), *Subaltern Studies*, vol. 1 (Delhi, 1982).

Pāṇini, *The Ashṭādhyāyī of Pāṇini*, ed. by Srisa Chandra Vasu, 2 vols (Delhi, 1977).

Pearse, Andrew, *The Latin American Peasant* (London, 1975).

Philips, C. H. (ed.), *Politics and Society in India* (London, 1963).

Pocock, David F., *Kanbi and Patidar* (Oxford, 1972).

Prasad, J. 'The Psychology of Rumour', *British Journal of Psychology*, vol. 26(1), July 1935, pp. 1–15.

Pride, J. B. and J. Holmes (eds), *Sociolinguistics* (Harmondsworth, 1972).

Propp, Vladimir, 'Les Transformations des Contes Fantastiques', in T. Todorov (ed.), *Théorie de la Littérature* (Paris, 1965), pp. 234–62.

Rāmāyaṇam, ed. Panchanan Tarkaratna, 4th ed. (Calcutta, 1908).

Ray, Suprakash, *Bharater Baiplabik Samgramer Itihas* (Calcutta, 1970).

——, *Bharater Krishak-bidroha O Ganatantrik Samgram*, vol. 1 (Calcutta, 1966).

Report of the Commission Appointed in India to Inquire into the Causes of the

Riots which took place in the year 1875 in the Poona and Ahmednagar Districts of the Bombay Presidency, Cmd. 2071 (London, 1878).
Ibid., vol. 2; Appendices B and C (Bombay, 1876).
Report of the Indigo Commission Appointed under Act XI of 1860 with the Minutes of Evidence taken before them; and Appendix (Calcutta, 1860).
Rizvi, S. A. A. (ed.), *Freedom Struggle in Uttar Pradesh*, 6 vols (Lucknow, 1960).
Roy, S. C., *Mundas and their Country* (Calcutta, 1912).
Russell, R. V. and H. Lal, *Tribes and Castes of the Central Provinces of India*, 4 vols (London, 1916).
Saha, Radharaman, *Pabna Jelar Itihas*, 3 vols (Pabna, 1923–6; Bengali Years: 1330–3).
Sarkar, Biharilal, *Titu Mir*, ed. Swapon Basu (Calcutta, 1981).
Sarkar, Jadunath (ed.), *The History of Bengal*, vol. 2 (Dacca, 1948).
Saussure, Ferdinand de, *Course in General Linguistics* (Glasgow, 1974).
Schachter, S. and H. Burdick, 'A Field Experiment on Rumor Transmission and Distortion', in A. G. Smith (ed.), *Communication and Culture*, pp. 294–308.
Schumann, Christian, 'Die Schreckenstage auf der Missionsstation Jakobi', *Berliner Missionsberichte*, 1906, pp. 62–76.
Sebeok, T. A. and D. J. Umiker-Sebeok (eds), *Speech Surrogates: Drum and Whistle Systems* (The Hague, 1976).
Sen, Dinesh Chandra (ed.), *Eastern Bengal Ballads*, vol. 2, pt. 1 (Calcutta, 1926).
——, *Vanga Sahitya Parichaya* (Calcutta, 1914).
Sen, Sunil, *Agrarian Struggle in Bengal 1946–47* (New Delhi, 1972).
Sen, Surendra Nath, *Eighteen Fifty-Seven* (Delhi, 1957).
Sen Gupta, Kalyan Kumar, *Pabna Disturbances and the Politics of Rent 1873–1885* (New Delhi, 1974).
Sherer, J. W., *Daily Life during the Indian Mutiny* (London, 1898).
Sherwill, Walter Stanhope, *Geographical and Statistical Report of the District of Bhaugulpoor* (Calcutta, 1854).
Shiromani, Bharatchandra, see *Manusaṃhitā*.
Showers, C. L., *A Missing Chapter of the Indian Mutiny* (London, 1888).
Singer, M. (ed.), *Krishna: Myths, Rites and Attitudes* (Honolulu, 1966).
Singh, Suresh, *Dust-storm and Hanging Mist* (Calcutta, 1966).
Sinha, S. C., J. Sen and S. Panchbhai, 'The Concept of Diku among the Tribes of Chotanagpur', *Man in India*, vol. 49(2), April/June 1969, pp. 121–38.
Smith, Alfred G. (ed.), *Communication and Culture* (New York, 1966).
Srinivas, M. N., *Caste in Modern India and other Essays* (Bombay, 1962).
——, *Religion and Society among the Coorgs of South India* (Oxford, 1952).
Steed, Gitel P., 'Notes on an Approach to a Study of Personality Formation in a Hindu Village in Gujarat', in M. Marriott (ed.),

Village India, pp. 102–44.
Stokes, Eric, *The Peasant and the Raj* (Cambridge, 1978).
Sundarayya, P., *Telengana People's Struggle and its Lessons* (Calcutta, 1972).
Syed Ahmed Khan, *An Essay on the Causes of the Indian Revolt*, trs. W. N. Lees (Calcutta, 1870).
Tarkaratna, Panchanan (ed.), *Rāmāyaṇam*, 4th ed. (Calcutta, 1908).
——, *Vāyupurāṇam* (Calcutta, 1910).
Thomas, Keith, *Religion and the Decline of Magic* (Harmondsworth, 1973).
Thompson, E. P., 'The Crime of Anonymity', in D. Hay *et al.* (eds), *Albion's Fatal Tree*, pp. 255–344.
——, *Whigs and Hunters* (London, 1975).
Thornhill, Mark, *The Personal Adventures and Experiences of a Magistrate during the Rise, Progress and Suppression of the Indian Mutiny* (London, 1884).
Toporov, V. N., 'The Semiotics of Prophecy in Suetonius', in Daniel P. Lucid (ed.), *Soviet Semiotics*, pp. 157–67.
Trotsky, Leon, *1905* (Harmondsworth, 1973).
Turner, George William, *Stylistics* (Harmondsworth, 1973).
Turner, Victor W., *The Ritual Process* (London, 1969).
Ullmann, Stephen, *Semantics: An Introduction to the Science of Meaning* (Oxford, 1972).
Vachek, Josef (ed.), *A Prague School Reader in Linguistics* (Bloomington, 1964).
Vachek, Josef, 'Some Remarks on Writing and Phonetic Transcription', in E. P. Hamp *et al.*, *Readings in Linguistics II*, pp. 152–7.
——, 'Written Language and Printed Language', in J. Vachek (ed.), *A Prague School Reader in Linguistics*, pp. 453–60.
Vansina, Jan, *Oral Tradition: a Study in Historical Methodology* (London, 1961).
Vasu, Srisa Chandra, see Dīkshita, Bhaṭṭoji and Pāṇini.
Vāyupurāṇam, ed. Panchanan Tarkaratna (Calcutta, 1910).
Viṣṇusmṛti, see *The Institutes of Viṣṇu.*
Vygotsky, Lev Semenovich, *Thought and Language* (Cambridge, Mass., 1967).
Wehrmeister, Cyrillus, 'Reisebilder aus Deutsch-Ostafrika vor und während des Aufstandes', *Missionsblätter von St. Ottilien*, 1906, pp. 70–3.
Whitehead, Henry, *The Village Gods of South India* (Calcutta, 1921).
Winslow, Cal, 'Sussex Smugglers', in D. Hay *et al.* (eds), *Albion's Fatal Tree*, pp. 119–66.
Zimmermann, Wilhelm, *Geschichte des grossen Bauernkrieges nach den Urkunden und Augenzeugen*, 2 vols (Leipzig, 1939).

INDEX

Ranajit Guha, formerly of the University of Sussex and the Australian National University, is the founder-editor of Subaltern Studies. His publications include *A Rule of Property for Bengal* (1963, 1982, 1996) and *Dominance without Hegemony: History and Power in Colonial India* (1997).

Library of Congress Cataloging-in-Publication Data
Guha, Ranajit.
Elementary aspects of peasant insurgency in colonial India /
Ranajit Guha; foreword by James Scott.
p. cm.
Originally published: New Delhi : Oxford University Press, 1983.
Includes bibliographical references and index.
ISBN 0-8223-2348-6 (alk. paper)
1. Peasant uprisings—India. 2. India—Politics and government—1765–1947. I. Title.
DS463.G84 1999
954.03—dc21 98-31625
CIP